PostModernPositions

A Monograph Series in Cultural Studies
General Editor, Robert Merrill

Unconscious

~~[struck through]~~

Symbolic Act

History or the Real

Unconscious attempts to express the Real (that which
is irrepresentible in itself figures the unconscious
(re Freud+Lacan) in that it is the accumulated
experience of the Real (filtered thru ideology)
that is engraved on the Unconscious; this repression
of the Real is what constitutes narrative as a
symbolic act

Institute for Advanced Cultural Studies
Washington, DC

PostModernPositions

Maisonneuve Press

P. O. Box 2980, Washington, DC 10023-2980, USA

The press invites manuscripts and proposals in critical cultural studies

POSTMODERNISM

JAMESON

CRITIQUE

Edited By
Douglas Kellner

PostModernPositions, Volume 4

MAISONNEUVE PRESS

Publications of the Institute for Advanced Cultural Studies

Douglas Kellner, ed., *Postmodernism/Jameson/Critique*

Copyright © 1989 by Maisonneuve Press
          P. O. Drawer 2980, Washington, DC 20013-2980

Maisonneuve Press is a subsidiary of the **Institute for Advanced Cultural Studies,** a non-profit collective of scholars concerned with the critical study of culture. Write to the Director for information about Institute programs.

Printed in the United States by BookCrafters, Chelsea, MI. This book has been manufactured to meet the durability guidlines set forth by the Committee on Production Guidelines for Book Longevitly of the Council on Library Resources.

Cover design by Lisa Kendall

Library of Congress Cataloging-in-Publication Data
main entry under title:

Kellner, Douglas, editor
      Postmodernism/Jameson/Critique.
         (PostModernPositions; v. 4)
         "Bibliography for Fredric Jameson" p. 389-395
         Bibliography: p. 396-408
         Includes index, p. 409-414
      1. Jameson, Fredric. 2. Marxist criticism. 3. Postmodernism. I.
Kellner, Douglas, 1943-   . II. Series.
PN98.C6P67 1989   801'.95'0924   89-2354

ISBN 0-944624-06-5 (cloth binding, alk paper)
ISBN 0-944624-07-3 (paper binding, alk paper)

And it is certain that there is a strange quasi-Sartrean irony— a 'winner loses' logic—which tends to surround any effort to describe a 'system', a totalizing dynamic, as these are detected in the movement of contemporary society. What happens is that the more powerful the vision of some increasingly total system or logic . . . the more powerless the reader comes to feel. Insofar as the theorist wins, therefore, by constructing an increasingly closed and terrifying machine, to that very degree he loses, since the critical capacity of his work is thereby paralyzed, and the impulses of negation and revolt, not to speak of those of social transformation, are increasingly perceived as vain and trivial in the face of the model itself.

—Fredric Jameson

Contents

Abbreviations for frequently cited works by Fredric Jameson

FA *Fables of Aggression: Wyndam Lewis, The Modernist as Fascist* (1979)
IT *The Ideologies of Theory* (1988)
MF *Marxism and Form: Twentieth Century Dialectical Theories of Literature* (1971)
PH *The Prison-House of Language* (1972)
PU *The Political Unconscious: Narrative as a Socially Symbolic Act* (1981)
SS *Sartre: The Origins of a Style* (1961)

"ACI" Architecture and the Critique of Ideology (1985)
"CMP" Cognitive Mapping (1988)
"FJF" Foreward to Jean-François Lyotard's *Postmodern Condition* (1984)
"FRP" Figural Relativism, or The Poetics of Historiography (1976)
"HCC" *History and Class Consciousness* as an Unfinished Project (1988)
"ITT" The Ideology of the Text (1975)
"MAH" Marxism and Historicism (1979)
"MTC" Metacommentary (1971)
"PAU" Postmodernism and Utopia (1988)
"PCL" Postmodernism, or The Cultural Logic of Late Capitalism (1984)
"PCS" Postmodernism and the Consumer Society (1983)
"PPI" Pleasure: A Political Issue (1983)
"PTI" The Politics of Theory: Ideological Positions in the Postmodernism Debate (1984)
"PTS" Periodizing the Sixties (1984)
"RIC" Reflections in Conclusion (1977)
"RMC" Reification and Utopia in Mass Culture (1984)
"RPM" Regarding Postmodernism—A Conversation with Fredric Jameson (1987)
"TWL" Third World Literature in the Era of Multinational Capitalism (1986)

Introduction:
Jameson, Marxism, and Postmodernism

Douglas Kellner
University of Texas

By the mid-1980s, debates about postmodern art, culture, and society became a topic of intense interest in the United States and in many of the countries of Western Europe. Focus centered at first on postmodernism in the arts and the alleged breaks with high modernism manifested in contemporary forms of architecture, literature, cinema, and other cultural domains which renounced the purity and elitism associated with modernism in favor of a populist eclecticism—a mix of forms and styles from different periods which cited, repeated, and pastiched previous styles, works, and authors. A postmodern turn in philosophy was also noted in the breaks with the tradition of modern philosophy in thinkers like Nietzsche, Heidegger, Derrida, and Rorty. Theorists like Baudrillard, Lyotard, Jameson, and Kroker/Cook developed more global social theories which described the society of simulacra, the "postmodern condition," "postmodernism as the cultural logic of late capitalism," and the "postmodern scene" which they claimed constituted a radically new social system and a mutation and rupture in history which required new theories, concepts, and responses.[1]

The postmodern moment had arrived and perplexed intellectuals, artists, and cultural entrepreneurs wondered whether they should get on the bandwagon and join the carnival, or sit on the side-lines until the new fad disappeared into the whirl of cultural fashion. Yet postmodernism refused to go away. Conference after conference, article after article, and now book after book are appearing to describe, dissect, denounce, celebrate, or participate in the hottest game in town. At first, there was no clear sense as to what constituted postmodernism, when it arrived, what it meant, and what effects it was having and would be likely to have in the future. Eventually, more systematic and sustained discussions took place and the essays in this collection are an effect and symptom of the current debates over the nature, meaning, and effects of postmodernism in a variety of disciplines and domains of contemporary culture and society.

Fredric Jameson's intervention in the postmodernism debates was at first—to some of us—surprising. A professor of French and comparative literature at the University of California, San Diego, (1967-1976) who moved to the Yale University French department from 1976-1983, Jameson's book *The Political Unconscious* (1981) had established him as one of the foremost Marxist literary critics of our era. Much of his work had focused on literary studies and contemporary theory, particularly Marxian theory which he applied to cultural analysis and used to criticize and contextualize other forms of criticism. Why, then, was a good Marxist like Jameson getting involved with the polemics and passions of the postmodern? What was really at stake in these debates? In this introduction, I shall argue that no less than the status of Marxism and the radical political project to which it is committed is at issue. From this perspective, Jameson's writings on postmodernism constitute both a defense of Marxism and an attempt to show that a reconstructed Marxian theory can provide the most comprehensive and penetrating theory of postmodernism itself.

Looking backward, it is now clear that Jameson's article "Postmodernism, or The Cultural Logic of Late Capitalism" presents one of the most illuminating analyses of postmodern culture and is probably the most quoted, discussed, and debated article of the past decade. The text provides the culmination of a series of historical and theoretical studies which provide part of the methodology, framework, and theoretical analyses requisite for a theory of contemporary society which Jameson conceptualizes as a product of a specific historical trajectory: the transition from a discrete national system of state/monopoly capitalism to an interlocking system multinational corporate capitalism.

I. Jameson and Marxism

So it is that in conceptualizing postmodernism Jameson pays homage to Marxism, culminating his efforts to introduce, defend, and develop the Marxian theory in a climate and situation often ignorant of or hostile to the radical tradition of which Marxism is a key component. In retrospect, Jameson's work over the last two decades can be seen, firstly, as an attempt to enlarge our conception of the literary text which involves efforts both to transcend aestheticizing approaches to high culture and to expand the focus of literary analysis from "literature" proper (as defined by hegemonic academic canons) to cultural production as such, including film, television, advertising, and the other "texts" of consumer capitalism. Yet Jameson's work can be seen, secondly, as an attempt to popularize and disseminate the Marxian theory by providing attractive Marxian analyses and by contributing to the revitalization and development of the theory itself.

In many ways, the postmodern debate challenges the classical Marxian theory through claims that postmodernism constitutes a fundamental rupture in history which requires new social theories, epistemologies, and politics. Certain postmodernist thinkers—most significantly, Lyotard in *The Postmodern Condition* (1984), Baudrillard in *The Mirror of Production* (1975), and Foucault in *The Order of Things* (1970) and *The Archaeology of Knowledge* (1972)—challenge Marxian presuppositions, theories, and politics by claiming that in addition to being obsolete, Marxist theories are reductive or even "totalitarian," aiding and abetting the allegedly oppressive Enlightenment project of the domination of nature and human beings while suppressing difference, particularity, and heterogeneity. Many of Jameson's critics and some of the contributors to this volume have criticized him from these positions.

Against these critiques, Jameson argues that it is Marxism which can best incorporate and mediate competing postmodern perspectives—a project similar to his attempt in *The Political Unconscious* to present Marxism as the all-encompassing horizon and master narrative for contemporary literary theory. Yet to grasp fully Jameson's complex defenses of Marxism and his responses to the postmodern challenge, one must read the totality of his work, the various texts which set forth in detail the Marxian dialectical methodology, its central categories and positions, and its political ramifications. Consequently, the articles in this reader frequently confront Jameson's positions in the post-modernism debate in terms of his own theoretical trajectory and his well-established and staked out positions. Indeed, there has been growing interest in Jameson's works during the 1980s and a proliferating critical literature which explicates, defends, and attacks his works—especially his texts of the last decade.[2]

Thus this volume is in part an effect of the growing Jameson controversy and of the debates surrounding it. The texts collected here provide both critical perspectives on Jameson's work and defenses of it while appraising his positions on postmodernism. Not surprisingly, given Jameson's own polemical animus, many of the articles in this reader are highly critical of him, yet it is not clear that all of the authors included exhibit his own character-istic dialectical generosity, his deep immersion in texts and positions opposed to his own, or his (Hegelian-hermeneutical) desire to extract insights and weapons even out of his opponent's work. Yet Jameson *is* highly controversial and he has positioned himself at the center of a series of contemporary theoretical and political battles. Consequently, a many-sided polemical reception is evident in this volume which replicates the conflicting responses Jameson's work has received in the past decade.

In interpreting Jameson's work as a whole, no early/late dichotomy in his publications presents itself as a viable hermeneutical device—other than the obvious distinction between his pre-Marxian text *Sartre: The Origins of a Style* (1961), written as his doctoral dissertation at Yale and published during an Instructorship at Harvard, and his subsequent writings. Rather, what is striking are the remarkable continuities in Jameson's works. One can pick up his articles or books from the early 1970s through the late 1980s and discover that they exhibit strong similarities with the concerns, styles, and politics of his *oeuvre* as a whole. Indeed, one gets the feeling in reading Jameson's two-volume collection of essays, *The Ideologies of Theory* (1988), that they all could have been written yesterday—or 10-15 years ago.

Yet, as Jameson notes, in the "Introduction" to the collection of his theoretical essays—and further volumes are being prepared for other presses which will collect his essays on literature, film and mass culture, and postmodernism—there is a fundamental shift of emphasis in his works which he describes as "a shift from the vertical to the horizontal: from an interest in the multiple dimensions and levels of a text to the multiple interweavings of an only fitfully readable (or writable) narrative; from problems of interpretation to problems of historiography; from the attempt to talk about the sentence to the (equally impossible) attempt to talk about modes of production" (*IT*, xxix).

In other words, Jameson's focus has shifted from vertical emphasis on the many dimensions of the text—its ideological, psychoanalytic, formal, mythic-symbolical levels—which require a sophisticated and multivalent practice of reading to horizontal emphasis on the ways that texts are inserted into historical sequences and thus on how history helps constitute texts. Yet this shift in emphasis also points to continuities in Jameson's work, for from the late 1960s to the present, he has privileged the historical dimension of texts and historical readings, bringing his critical practice into the slaughter-house of history, moving critical discourse from the ivory tower of academia and the prison house of language to the vicissitudes and contingencies of that field (difficult to theorize adequately) for which the term "history" serves as a marker.

One therefore reads Jameson as a (still open) totality, as a relatively unified theoretical project in which the various texts provide parts of a whole. Consequently, to understand any of Jameson's texts one needs to grasp their place in the history of the Jamesonian *oeuvre*, as articulations of a relatively stable and coherent theoretical project. In this introduction, I shall therefore provide an interpretive mapping of Jameson's work in order to produce a context within which one can read and interpret his various texts as parts of a discernible theoretical project. From this vantage point, we can situate his position within the postmodern controversy and see the continuity between his writings on postmodernism and his earlier work. The focus, guided by the concerns of this text, will be on the ways that his earlier works provide anticipations, theoretical articulations, and problems which clear the way and eventually demand an analysis of postmodernism as the cultural logic of late capitalism.

II. Toward Dialectical Criticism

Jameson's first three major books and most of his early articles are attempts to develop a literary criticism which cuts against the dominant formalist and conservative models of new criticism and the academic Anglo-American literary establishment. Although his first book, *Sartre*, is a pre-Marxian text, while the two texts which follow a decade later—*Marxism and Form* (1971) and *The Prison-House of Language* (1972)—are aggressively Marxian in methodology, commitment, and effect, these works nonetheless can be read as part of a sustained attempt to develop the prerequisites for a critical literary theory. *Sartre* could easily be "transcoded" into the Marxian vocabulary of his later works with its concepts of totality, "thingification," and dialectic while its emphasis on style and literary form, its hermeneutical problematics, and its attempts to relate Sartre's literary works with ethical concerns are congruent with Jameson's later concerns. Furthermore, *Sartre's* style, its dense sentence-construction, and the way it reads and feels are highly continuous with Jameson's later writings. Yet Sartre's own political concerns are conspicuously absent in the early text as is his concern with history and the present moment—topics which would define Jameson's own later work.

Jameson's method in his first book is also far more phenomenological than dialectical, and he uses Sartre's own categories to explicate his writings, showing a deep identification with Sartre which would remain fundamental to Jameson's work.

For Jameson has appropriated much of Sartre's ontology and his view of the world, and this Sartrean component would help shape his later writings. Yet history, which will eventually become the demiurge of the Jamesonian text, lies brooding and dormant in the background, but is rarely foregrounded and never reaches the dignity of a concept—as it will repeatedly in his later work which is constantly concerned to chart out the trajectories and vicissitudes of History itself. Furthermore, *Sartre* bears the marks of academic literary study as it contains primarily literary analyses of Sartre's literary texts—an approach which he would rectify in *Marxism and Form* where Sartre's theoretical production is the focus. Jameson's early *Sartre* book is generally innocent of Marxian categories and instead employs analyses— influenced by his teacher Erich Auerbach and by the stylistics associated with Leo Spitzer—of Sartre's style, narrative structures, values, and vision of the world.

In retrospect, the *Sartre* book can be read symptomatically as an indication that Jameson's "original choice" was to be an intellectual, involved in the activity of writing a certain sort of sentence or constructing a certain sort of text. Read in the context of the stifling conformism and banal business society of the 1950s, Jameson's choice of his subject matter (Sartre) and his choice of an intricate literary-theoretical writing style (already the infamous Jamesonian sentences appear full-blown) can be seen as an attempt to create himself as a critical intellectual against the conformist currents of the epoch. One also sees him already turning against the literary establishment, against the dominant modes of literary criticism. All of Jameson's works constitute critical interventions against the hegemonic forms of literary criticism and modes of thought regnant in the Anglo-American world. His first book shows Jameson turning to Jean-Paul Sartre, perhaps the most influential continental intellectual of the period as a theoretical (and eventually political) model and alternative to Anglo-American positivism, scientism, and the aestheticism embedded in the then hegemonic New Criticism (Fekete 1978; Lentricchia 1980). Jameson would henceforth use Sartrean categories and examples throughout his work and would return to write about and reflect upon Sartre many times.[3]

Later he revealed, "In my own case, however, it turns out that I came to Marxism *through* Sartre and not against him; and not even through the later, Marx-oriented works such as the *Critique*, but very precisely through the 'classical' existential texts of the immediate post-war period . . . for other Europeans . . . as well as for Americans like myself, Sartre represented *the* model of the political intellectual, one of the few role models we had, but a sufficient one . . . for myself, the moment of overt intellectual conversion [to Marxism] came on reading Henri Lefebvre's study of Pascal, but it had been prepared by the Sartrean texts I have mentioned" ("OAS," 122-123). And in the "Introduction" to *The Ideologies of Theory*, he notes: "my own intellectual formation was not merely aesthetic or aestheticizing ('style study' of the Romance philological kind, but also, let us say, the poetry of Ezra Pound)—but also existential, and very specifically Sartrean" (*IT*, xxviii).

Sartre was thus taken by Jameson as a paradigm of the non-conformist, critical intellectual, the writer who addresses the central moral and political concerns of the day, who uses his vocation as a writer to struggle against the evils of the present age. The early Sartre was received in the 1950s in the U.S. and elsewhere as a figure of the individualist radical intellectual, as the rebel against convention of all sorts. During the 1950s, Sartre turned toward Marxism, committed himself to socialism, and intensified his stance of political activism. One finds both dimensions of Sartre in Jameson's own work: to the present, his texts exhibit a strongly individual style and mode of expression, as well as a phenomenological impulse toward the concrete and lived experience, combined with intervention in a variety of literary, theoretical, and political debates. Indeed, one is tempted to see Sartre's conversion from existential theorist and non-conformist intellectual to para-Marxist political activist as an anticipation of, and perhaps influence on, Jameson's own trajectory.

Furthermore, the individualist posture in Jameson's first book is incarnated in the absence of citations or references to other critics (until the conclusion) and he eschews the standard translations of Sartre's literary works. Such an approach manifests, on one hand, the phenomenological lust for the thing itself, for approaching the object of study without preconceptions, standard interpretations, or conventional concepts. On the other hand, it points to an isolation of the radical intelligentsia in the McCarthyist era and its aftermath which lacked a tradition at hand which could be brought to bear on its cultural concerns, or which could politically mobilize it or offer models of radical self-identification.

Soon, Jameson would overcome such isolation with the luminaries of the Western Marxist tradition. Reading Jameson contextually, one thus encounters a young literary critic, radicalized by study in Europe during the 1950s and by the political movements of the 1960s, turning to Marxism as the solution to his own theoretical and political dilemmas. His 1960s and early 70s *Salmagundi* articles—"T. W. Adorno; or, Historical Tropes," "On Politics and Literature," "Walter Benjamin; or, Nostalgia," and "The Case for Georg Lukács"—show Jameson now concerned with Marxian themes and thinkers and his conversion to Marxism emerges full-blown in *Marxism and Form*—a remarkable text that can now be read as the matrix of Jameson's theoretical project. The turn to Marxism is clear in the very title of the text, as is the distinctive and original focus on *form*, on the conjunction between Marxism and form. The full title—and indeed the book as a whole—points to the need to develop a Marxian literary theory which can meet the requirements of the present age—a project signalled by the book's subtitle, *Twentieth Century Dialectical Theories of Literature*.

Situating this text in the totality of Jameson's work suggests that his fundamental project was developing a systematic Marxian literary theory (later expanded to cultural theory) which assimilated the most advanced currents of contemporary thought for the Marxian project. His conversion was part of a generational shift, the "generation of the 60s," whose members moved to the most radical alternatives within contemporary politics and theory. For Jameson and many of his cohorts this meant a turn to Marxism and in particular to the dialectical versions of Marxism associated with the tradition of European Hegelian Marxism. *Marxism and Form* opens with references to 1930s Marxian literary theory and calls for a "new Marxism," thus pointing to the sort of "vulgar Marxism" which Jameson and his contemporaries were hoping to overcome. He finds aspects of this more sophisticated theory in the "relatively Hegelian kind of Marxism" (*MF*, ix) found in the works of Sartre, Lukács, and the Frankfurt School. Thus, on one level his text can be read as an introduction to the new versions of Hegelian Marxism—still mostly untranslated and unknown in the English-speaking world—which began to appear in Europe and the U.S. in the late 1960s and early 1970s. Yet it can also be read as an introduction to Jameson's emerging theoretical position and as providing the groundwork for a neo-Marxian literary theory.

As Jameson presents some of the basic positions of Adorno, Benjamin, Marcuse, Bloch, Lukács, Sartre, and so on, one finds his own concepts and positions emerging from the analyses. In particular, he makes clear his attraction both to Lukács and to his version of Hegelian Marxism—an allegiance which would remain with Jameson to this day and which he would reaffirm in a recent essay, *"History and Class Consciousness* as an 'Unfinished Project,'"* which calls for the rethinking of the Lukácsian project in the light of contemporary conditions (see also the discussion of Lukács' influence on Jameson in Sprinker 1987). In a sense, Lukács was always Jameson's master of literary analysis, always the model and ideal of what literary criticism could do. In particular, Lukács' work on realism and on the historical novel strongly influenced Jameson's way of seeing and situating literature and while he never accepted Lukács' polemics against modernism, as I shall indicate later, he appropriated central Lukácsian categories such as reification to describe the fate of culture in contemporary capitalism.

Yet *Marxism and Form* also reveals how Jameson's appropriation of Lukács is tempered by attraction to the Marxian hermeneutical tradition—however diverse—of Adorno, Benjamin, Marcuse, and Bloch. Indeed, the varying perspectives of these often quarrelling comrades turn up in Jameson's own work and produce a fascinatingly complex mixture of heterogeneous strands of dialectical thought. In particular, Jameson emphasizes the importance of the utopian Marxism of Ernst Bloch who saw cultural texts as articulations of desire for a better world, of hope for a utopian future. Jameson—along with Marcuse and Raymond Williams—defends both a utopian mode of cultural interpretation and a utopian political alternative to contemporary capitalism and "actually existing socialism." These concepts are explicated in *Marxism and Form* and frequently appear in his later works—such as the controversial conclusion to *The Political Unconscious* where utopian categories emerge to play a starring role in Jameson's spectacular excursion into the history of literary form and subjectivity which I shall discuss below (see also "RMC").

Indeed, the two longest chapters of the book—"Versions of a Marxist Hermeneutic" and "Toward Dialectical Criticism"—contain rather systematic presentations of what would become two of Jameson's central concerns to the present. Jameson is one of the few Marxian critics who is unabashedly committed to hermeneutics (see Shumway and Best, in this volume), and in *Marxism and Form* he finds antecedents for this project in the neo-Marxian modes of interpretation found in Benjamin, Marcuse, and Bloch. In "Toward Dialectical Criticism," Jameson presents his own version of dialectical literary criticism, explicating important components of the method and positions which he would henceforth use. Such is the continuity of his writings—that this text remains the best introduction to his work as a whole and the tradition of which his work is an important part.

The essay "Metacommentary" (1971) provides a mediating link in Jameson's work between *Marxism and Form* and *The Prison-House of Language*. Its last several pages excerpt concluding portions of *Marxism and Form* and much of the essay provides a précis of *The Prison-House of Language* and defense of a critical hermeneutics against the sort of "anti-interpretation" popularized by Susan Sontag (1969) which would later become a distinguishing feature of poststructuralism (Deleuze-Guattari 1977 and Coward-Ellis 1977). The title "Metacommentary" provides another way of presenting Jameson's notion of a dialectical criticism which reflects on the categories and methods used in criticism while engaging in critical activity on its textual objects. Such multi-levelled critique, or "metacommentary" (a term that he would continue to use; see *PU*, 9-10, 208-209 and *IT*, viii), would characterize his own critical activity.

One also discovers in "Metacommentary" a dialectical attempt to synthesize competing positions and methods into a more comprehensive theory—a project amplified in *The Prison-House of Language*. This text provides his first systematic engagement with the new modes of French thought and with the new structuralisms, formalisms, and semiotic theories which were displacing in France and elsewhere the phenomenological, existential, and Marxian problematics in which the early Jameson was immersed. Despite his attachment to many of the objects of critique of the new French theories, and despite his growing commitment to Marxism, Jameson is characteristically generous and sympathetic to these new currents. Refusing the orthodox Marxian gesture of ideology critique as mere polemical negation, as a simple rejection of mystification and false consciousness, Jameson engages in a hermeneutical project which attempts to appropriate the useful aspects of competing critical theories while criticizing their limitations. He sympathetically presents the basic outlines of Saussure's semiological theories, of Russian formalism, and of a wide variety of French structuralist thought while critically evaluating these movements from the standpoint of his emerging Marxian theory.

During his surveys, as in *Marxism and Form*, one also encounters Jameson presenting his own views on a variety of literary and other topics, and one discovers that Jameson was immersing himself not only in Hegelian Marxism but in the theories of Barthes, Althusser, Derrida, and the other avatars of the newly emerging current of thought which would be named "poststructuralism." Henceforth, Jameson's project would be characterized by a unique synthesis of Hegelian Marxism and New French Theory. Yet Jameson's critical positions toward semiology, Russian formalism, and structuralism are also evident. In the introduction to the book, he calls attention to the new paradigm of *language* and claims that a structuring principle of the new modes of linguistic thought is the distinction between diachronic and synchronic thinking. Structuralism and its relatives are primarily synchronic modes which formalize and systematize various configurations of thought and social reality in terms of their rules of organization and of their dominant structures and functions within a systemic whole. Diachronic thinking by contrast is historical thinking which is comparative and which attempts to grasp change, movement, development, and rupture.

Jameson's own thought is relentlessly diachronic and "history" emerges as his master category. Yet he persistently calls for a synthesis of diachronic and synchronic thinking, as well as for combining structural analyses of a given historical moment with diachronic analysis of change, development, and ruptures. This position allows him to criticize such synchronic thinking as structuralism and various self-contained formalisms for being inadequately historical, for suppressing a crucial dimension of analysis.[4] His dialectical thinking is also resolutely utopian, seeking visions of utopian reconciliations of subject and object, individual and society, in literature and other cultural forms. Following the path of the utopian Marxists Ernst Bloch and Herbert Marcuse, Jameson claims that radical cultural theory should seek those utopian visions of another world in cultural texts and that this utopian dimension keeps alive revolutionary hopes and can provide an impetus to struggle for the better world that utopian literature projects.[5] Eventually, Jameson will argue that ideology itself must contain an utopian dimension to attract individuals to its resolutions of social conflicts while attempting to manage potentially disruptive hopes and fears ("RMC" and *PU*). Consequently, a "double hermeneutic" of ideological and utopian analysis should be part of a properly Marxian cultural theory.

Dialectical criticism thus involves for Jameson thinking which reflects on categories and methods while carrying out concrete analyses; thinking which contextualizes the object of study in its historical environment; utopian thinking which finds utopian hope in literature, philosophy, and other cultural texts and which draws attention to these hopes as a vital source of critique and struggle; and a theorizing of history within which dialectical criticism can operate. All of these aspects would continue to be operative in Jameson's later works with the total-izing element coming more prominently (and controversially) to the fore as his work evolved.

During the 1970s, Jameson published a wealth of theoretical

studies and many more diverse cultural studies. One begins to encounter the characteristic range of interests and depth of penetration in his studies of such genres as science fiction, film, magical narrative, painting, and both realist and modernist literature. One also finds articles concerning Marxian cultural politics, imperialism, Palestinian liberation, Marxian teaching methods, and the revitalization of the Left.[6] Jameson also undertook new studies and attempts to systematize his work. Many of the key essays have been collected in *The Ideologies of Theory* (1988, two volumes) which provide the laboratory for the theoretical project worked out in *The Political Unconscious* and *Fables of Aggression*. These texts should be read together—with the essays on postmodernism—as inseparable parts of a multi-levelled theory of the interconnections between the history of literary form, modes of subjectivity, and stages of capitalism.

Jameson's emerging syncretic and utopian Marxian histor-icism is evident in his "Criticism in History" (1976) which can be read in retrospect as a concise anticipation of the theoretical project realized in *The Political Unconscious*. Jameson provides an inventory of the dominant methods of criticism prevalent at the time—stylistic analysis, ethical and myth criticism, Freudian criticism, and structuralism—and claims that these methods either consciously and illicitly suppress history, or themselves lead to and find their completion in history, in a more compre-hensive historical theory. This emerging historicism helps illuminate the privileging of Marxism in Jameson's critical repertoire for he interprets Marxism as *the* theory of history, and thus as the most inclusive, comprehensive, and concrete theoretical framework and horizon for all interpretation—a position explicated in "Marxism and Historicism" (1979) that would also emerge as central in *The Political Unconscious* and would be affirmed once again in the "Introduction" to *The Ideologies of Theory* (xxvii). This "absolute presupposition" of Jameson's project would be severely attacked by his critics—including several in this reader—and would become a highly contested element of his project.

III. On the Way Toward Postmodernism

In *The Political Unconscious* (1981), Jameson's theoretical synthesis finds it most systematic development. The text contains an articulation of Jameson's literary method, a systematic inventory of the history of literary forms, and a history of the forms and modes of subjectivity itself, as he traverses the field of culture and experience. Jameson boldly attempts to establish Marxian literary criticism as the most all inclusive and comprehensive theoretical framework by incorporating a disparate set of competing approaches into his analysis. He provides an overview of the history of literary form, and concludes with an articulation of a "double hermeneutic" of ideology and utopia—which both critiques ideology while preserving utopian moments—as the properly Marxian method of interpretation.

Jameson employs a Lukácsian-inspired historical narrative to tell the story of how cultural texts contain a "political unconscious," buried narratives and social experience, which require sophisticated hermeneutics to decipher. One particular narrative of *The Political Unconscious* concerns, in Jameson's striking phrase, "the construction of the bourgeois subject in emergent capitalism and its schizophrenic disintegration in our own time" (*PU*, 9). Key stages in the odyssey of the disintegrating bourgeois subjectivity are articulated in Gissing, Conrad, and Wyndham Lewis, a story which will find its completion in Jameson's account of postmodernism.

After the long theoretical introduction, the journey begins with examination of "magical narratives," of those myths and fairy tales characteristic of precapitalist society. The literary studies continue with analysis of key episodes in the history of the novel, focusing on works which exhibit features of succeeding stages of capitalism and the complex relationships between modes of literary form, bourgeois subjectivity, and various stages of capitalism.[7] "Magical narratives" refer to those social products which embody the collective experience and consciousness of relatively unified, pre-capitalist modes of production. With the rise of capitalism, new modes of expression and experience emerge that find emblematic articulation in the novel which becomes the paradigmatic voice of bourgeois subjectivity. In the early novels of Balzac, which Jameson analyzes in detail, consciousness is for the most part unified, confident, and centered. This relatively coherent bourgeois subjectivity becomes in turn the structuring principle of the novel which finds articulation in the omniscient narrator without a specific point of view or epistemic failings. Later novels, in Jameson's reading, register changes in subjectivity in bourgeois society and are connected to fundamental developments within capitalism. In general, following Lukács' *The Theory of the Novel* (1971), Jameson interprets the novel as the privileged form for an individualist capitalist society which is its appropriate mode of expression. Yet, again following Lukács' *Realism in Our Time* (1964), Jameson claims that later developments in the novel, in style and form as well as content, register a process of disintegration within bourgeois society and subjectivity.

Jameson focuses on writers who disclose the accelerating fragmentation and reification of experience in capitalist society. He follows here the accounts of rationalization and "disenchantment" developed by Max Weber, *Economy and Society* (1968), and Lukács, *History and Class Consciousness* (1971), and discusses literary representations of this experience which he sees as revealing the growing crisis of bourgeois subjectivity in capitalism. Gissing represents the estrangement of middle-class (and declassé) intellectuals from both a rising proletariat and a powerful and wealthy bourgeoisie. The dominant figure of this consciousness is what Nietzsche described as *"ressentiment"* and Jameson uses this figure to describe the works of Gissing which he presents as a sign of bourgeois consciousness losing its confidence and direction by the end of the nineteenth century. Other writers like Dreiser, and the increasing centrality of point-of-view and the author's subjectivity in the novel, exhibit a growing subjectivism and growing alienation from bourgeois society as a whole.

The crisis intensifies in the twentieth century expansion of imperialism and Jameson takes the novels of Conrad as providing key articulations of intensifying fragmentation of individual consciousness in an age of growing commodification and brutal colonialization. Jameson claims that shifts in the form of the novel register these developments. He reads Gissing's quasi-modernist experimental style as an attempt to escape from resentment and to create a new realm of experience beyond market society and class antagonisms. The intensified subjectivity and point of view in Henry James, Dreiser, Joyce, Hemingway, and others is read as a utopian compensation for the very decline of subjectivity in bourgeois society. The divided style in Conrad's *Lord Jim* is read as a split between an attempt to provide a modernist realm of intense subjectivity (the complex modernist style of the first half) and an attempt to become popular in the age of commodification (the adventure story format in the second half).

Conrad is also read as a sign of the growing reification of mass culture and the revolt against reification in modernism. In Jameson's reading, bourgeois consciousness and culture were becoming increasingly divided and fragmented in response to capitalist development and Conrad's novels register these experiences. On another level, Conrad's novels are read as articulations of fears of *Otherness* in Third World cultures during the Age of Imperialism, and, more generally, his work is read as articulating a series of antinomies of bourgeois culture which bourgeois society itself is unable to resolve. For instance, the vivid perceptual and acoustic elements in lush aestheticizing modernism are read as compensatory responses to the reification and fragmentation of life under capitalism. Yet depersonalization and the erasing of the author, already evident in Flaubert, are also striking features of Conrad's modernism, attesting to the decline of subjectivity in late capitalism. And Conrad's novels testify as well to the meaninglessness of life under capitalism, while the religion of art, which they share to some extent, points to the decline of conventional religion.

The Political Unconscious can thus be read as an allegory of the history of subjectivity which could be compared with Horkheimer's and Adorno's analysis of this odyssey in *Dialectic of Enlightenment* (1972). Although Jameson himself does not systematically articulate this theme, the various stages of subjectivity are related to various stages of socio-economic development and cultural forms. Or rather, subjectivity and literary form itself are read as products of changing and evolving social conditions, concretizing Marx's dictum that consciousness is a product of social being. In relating cultural forms to their socio-historical environment and stages of economic development, however, Jameson wants to avoid the reductionistic features of so-called "vulgar Marxism." He explicitly rejects a certain orthodox interpretation of the "base/superstructure" thesis—which would present culture as an epiphenomenon of the economy—in favor of a more complex model that draws on Hegelian Marxism, Althusser, and Freud (*PU*, 23-58). In depicting relations between culture and the other superstructures and their socio-economic foundation, Jameson urges the use of categories like overdetermination, uneven development, semi-autonomy, and reciprocal interaction to describe the complex relationships between various spheres or levels of social existence. He defends "mediation" as a dialectical category that relates and connects various spheres of existence (the economy, state, culture, etc.) without reducing one to the other (*PU*, 39ff). In describing relations between cultural texts and their historical environment, he also proposes using Freudian categories like condensation, displacement, repression, etc. to describe the complex ways that texts articulate social experience (*PU*, 44, 64f, *passim*). In this way, Jameson is faithful to the Marxian dialectic which relates all cultural and superstructural phenomena to the socio-economic foundation and which interprets stages of cultural and superstructural development in culture as part of the trajectory of the history of capitalism.

Fables of Aggression: Wyndham Lewis, the Modernist as Fascist (published in 1979, two years before *The Political Unconscious* but part of the same theoretical project) takes the odyssey one stage higher moving to more fearful and virulent forms of the disintegration of subjectivity in various twentieth century modernisms and fascism. Jameson's test case here is Wyndham Lewis whose modernism is spiritually akin to—and implicated in—fascism via his aggressive satire, his polemical political attacks, and his desperate and intense aesthetic experiments. Lewis' sentences explode with "immense, mechanical energy" (*FA*, 25) and his will to style blasts away established forms in literature, painting, and cultural decorum. Fascist aggression is thus read as a result of developments within capitalism and bourgeois subjectivity while the internal connections between certain forms of modernism and varieties of fascism are probed.

Yet in *The Political Unconscious* and *Fables of Aggression* something important is missing in Jameson's philosophy of history and the missing component is precisely an analysis of our own historical moment, of our own contemporary scene. Both *The Political Unconscious* and *Fables of Aggression* knock on the door of the present but neither crosses the threshold to our own historical milieu. Such is the accomplishment and logical, indeed necessary, progression of Jameson's thought in the essay on postmodernism. In fact, there are several important anticipations of his later theory of postmodernism in his 1970s texts. While reading *Marxism and Form* one encounters two remarkable anticipations which point to the lacunae of Jameson's theoretical project that he would eventually fill. In the "Preface" one reads:

> for the most part, and particularly in the United States, the development of postindustrial monopoly capitalism has brought with it an increasing occultation of the class structure through techniques of mystification practiced by the media and particularly by advertising in its enormous expansion since the onset of the Cold War. In existential terms, what this means is that our experience is no longer whole: we are no longer able to make any felt connection between the concerns of private life, as it follows its own course within the walls and confines of the affluent society, and the structural projections of the system in the outside world, in the form of neocolonialism, oppression, and counterinsurgency warfare. In psychological terms, we may say that as a service economy we are henceforth so far removed from the realities of production and work in the world that we inhabit a dream world of artificial stimuli and televised experience: never in any previous civilization have the great metaphysical preoccupations, the fund-

amental questions of being and of the meaning of life,
seemed so utterly remote and pointless. (*MF*, xvii-xviii)

We read here the Jamesonian *Urtext*, the articulation of the
primal scene out of which his later writings emerge and which
they seek to diagnose and hopefully, eventually, to cure. The situation of immense fragmentation, reification, immiseration, and
sheer meaninglessness in "the overdeveloped countries" requires
what Jameson calls a "postindustrial Marxism" (*MF*, xix), a
rethinking of Marxism in the light of the new historical
conditions and experiences. Once again, history itself requires
historical thought—in this case, revitalized Marxian thought—to
rethink radical social theory in the light of the present and to
think through and beyond the present with the help of the most
advanced theoretical perspectives at our disposal.

In any case, we can see Jameson's intervention in the
postmodernism debate, not as an accident, nor as an opportunistic
attempt to exploit the *Zeitgeist's* latest source of cultural capital,
but as a theoretical exigency of his earlier work, as an attempt to
fill an empty theoretical space in his *oeuvre*. In particular, there
was a burning need to provide a theoretical account of the present
age, to provide a neo-Marxian theoretical mapping of the current
scene, to provide "a genuinely dialectical attempt to think our
present moment of time in History" ("PCL," 85). For Jameson
perceived that we are now standing in a new and extraordinary
historical moment with new configurations of cultural form and
experience which require new theoretical articulations. At the
end of *Marxism and Form*, Jameson presents a striking
anticipation of his later theory of postmodernism:

Nonetheless it seems to me that something more must be
said in the face of such articulate defenses of modernism as
Susan Sontag's 'new sensibility' or Ihab Hassan's *Literature
of Silence*. These theories reflect a coherent culture with
which we are all familiar: John Cage's music, Andy
Warhol's movies, novels by Burroughs, plays by Beckett,
Godard, camp, Norman O. Brown's psychedelic experiences; and no critique can have any binding force which

does not begin by submitting to the fascination of all these things as stylizations of reality. (*MF*, 413)

Jameson himself submits to "these things." Eventually, he comes to separate these signs of what he calls here "this new modernism" into what he would later call "high modernism" and what he and others would name "postmodernism." By 1975, in fact, he is ready to declare the end of modernity and a rupture in history that will eventually be filled with the category of "postmodernism":

All the straws in the wind seem to confirm the wide-spread feeling that, as Roman Guardini used to put it, 'modern times are now over,' and that some fundamental divide, some basic *coupure* or qualitative leap, now separates us decisively from what used to be the new world of the early mid-twentieth century, of triumphant modernism and the revolt against positivism and Victorian or Third Republic bourgeois culture. MacLuhanism [sic], theories of the *société de consummation* and of post-industrial society, post-modernism in literature and art, the shift from physics to biology as the prototype of the hard sciences, the influence of the computer and information theory, the end of the Cold War and the ratification of a Soviet-American world system of 'peaceful coexistence,' the New Left and the countercultural instinctual politics, the primacy of the linguistic model with its ideological expression in Structuralism as a new movement—all of these phenomena testify to some irrevocable distance from the immediate past. ("ITT," 204)

Jameson's confrontation with postmodernism thus implies a turn from "literary" theory and analysis proper to more "cultural" theory and interpretation that effected an expansion of cultural theory and politics beyond concern with a specialized artifact ("literature") which was being displaced in the new cultural field that he, following a growing trend, names "postmodernism." Jameson ends *Marxism and Form* with an oft-quoted and revealing passage: "Anglo-American philosophy has long since been shorn of its dangerous speculative capacities, and as for political science, it suffices only to think of its distance from the great political and Utopian theories of the past to realize to what degree thought asphyxiates in our culture, with its absolute inability to imagine anything other than what is. It therefore falls to literary criticism to continue to pass judgment on the abstract quality of life in the present, and to keep alive the idea of a concrete future. May it prove equal to the task!" (*MF*, 417).

It didn't. Literary criticism had become an increasingly specialized part of an academic division of labor which "theory" itself must overcome and surpass. Even the new critical methodologies—such as deconstruction—were becoming specialized tools of professional critics which provided some new excuses to avoid biographical, historical, and political study. Overcoming the new formalisms and isolationism of contemporary literary theory would thus involve overcoming disciplinary boundaries and attending to new objects of cultural analysis (such as mass culture or new social forms and experience). Developing a new cultural theory also involved paying attention to contemporary historical shifts and charting the development through history of the mutation and emergence of a new socio-historical situation.

IV. Postmodernism as the Cultural Logic of Late Capitalism

And so we come to Jameson's 1980s essays on postmodernism which are the focus of this anthology and the telos of the previous account of his theoretical trajectory. His writings on postmodernism can be read as an attempt to meet the challenges to radical social theory posed by poststructuralist and postmodernist theorists like Baudrillard and Lyotard by providing an alternative model to the postmodern social theory of his French predecessors while appropriating their insights and contributions. His first discussions of "postmodern" cultural artifacts are found in references to recent films of Godard ("From Criticism to History" 1981) and studies of the films *The Shining* ("The Shining" 1981) and *Diva* ("On Diva" 1982). He presented his first analysis of the defining features of postmodern culture in an essay "Postmodernism and Consumer Society" (which was a publication of a 1982 lecture).[8] Eventually, he synthesized and elaborated his emerging analysis in the article "Postmodernism, or The Cultural Logic of Late Capitalism" (1984) which more systematically interprets postmodernism in terms of the Marxian theory of capitalism and as a new "cultural dominant."

Just as his previous works corresponded in certain ways to a generational trajectory, so too did his essays on postmodernism. For the 1980s were a difficult time for the Left with the rise to and consolidation of power by conservative regimes in the United States, Britain, Germany, Canada, and elsewhere. Many former 1960s radicals turned during this period to theoretical work, directing their political energies toward new work in theory while engaging in passionate and turbulent debates over theory and politics. For many, this involved abandonment of the radical perspectives of the 60s. Against the trends toward post- and anti-Marxism, Jameson held onto Marxism and his intervention in the postmodernism debate can be read as a defense of the Marxian theory against postmodern and poststructuralist attacks which characterized it as an outmoded totalizing, productivist, and reductionist discourse which failed to conceptualize the new features of contemporary postindustrial society (Baudrillard 1975 and Lyotard 1984, discussed in Kellner, "Postmodernism as Social Theory" 1988). Jameson relativizes the postmodern rupture to the cultural sphere as a new "cultural logic" which corresponds to a new stage of capitalist development. Yet he also incorporates many features of the new postmodern and poststructuralist theories into his analysis, signaling his use of New French Theory to help conceptualize the new conditions and experiences in post-modernity:

> The exposition will take up in turn the following con-stitutive features of the postmodern: a new depthlessness, which finds its prolongation both in contemporary 'theory' and in a whole new culture of the image or the simulacrum; a consequent weakening of historicity, both in our

relationship to public History and in the new forms of our private temporality, whole 'schizophrenic' structures (following Lacan) will determine new types of syntax or syntagmatic relationships in the more temporal arts; a whole new type of emotional ground tone—what I will call 'intensities'—which can best be grasped by a return to older theories of the sublime; the deep constitutive relationships of all this to a whole new technology, which is itself a figure for a whole new economic world system; and, after a brief account of postmodernist mutations in the lived experience of built space itself, some reflections on the mission of political art in the bewildering new world space of late multinational capital. ("PCL," 58)

Note the frequent use of the pathos of the "new" in this passage and the incorporation of themes of New French Theory to fill in the new social environment. For while Jameson's framework provides a synthesis of Hegelian-Marxian notions of totality, Mandel's theory of the stages of capitalism, and Althusser's theory of "levels" of society, he utilizes familiar concepts of New French Theory such as "simulacrum" (Deleuze and Baudrillard), "schizophrenic" (Lacan and Deleuze/Guattari) "intensities" and "sublime" (Lyotard) to articulate the moments of the postmodern. Like Baudrillard and Lyotard, Jameson argues that there are radically new cultural and social forms and experiences, and thus something like a "postmodern condition," yet he believes that it can be theorized within the framework of a neo-Marxian social theory. Thus, Jameson attempts to incorporate the new features of the postmodern within Marxism, and unlike some postmodernists, he attempts as well to delineate the epistemological and political issues involved in providing such a theory.

His essay "Postmodernism" attempts to provide an account of the features, contours, genesis, and possibilities of contemporary culture and—congruent with his other major 1980s texts—of its new forms of experience and subjectivity. It is important to note that postmodernism for Jameson is not just a style or an aesthetic phenomenon, but it circumscribes an entire culture, figuring a new stage of history with new cultural forms and modes of experience and subjectivity. Jameson's studies expand the discussion concerning postmodernism to include a wide range of cultural, social, economic, and political phenomena, and thus move the postmodernism debate out of the arenas of cultural theory and metatheory into the field of social theory. After citing a list of contemporary claims that we have decisively broken with the past and are entering into a new stage of society and history, Jameson argues, first, that postmodern culture is distinguished by the effacement "of the older (essentially high-modernist) frontier between high culture and so-called mass or commercial culture, and the emergence of new kinds of texts infused with the forms, categories and contents of that very Culture Industry so passionately denounced by all the ideologues of the modern, from Leavis and the American New Criticism all the way to Adorno and the Frankfurt School" ("PCL," 54-55). Postmodernist culture—such things as the novels of Doctorow, the films of Kubrick, the architecture of Philip Johnson and Michael Graves, the music of Philip Glass—combines high culture's classical forms with forms and material traditionally associated with mass culture so as to obliterate the boundary between "high" and "low" culture which informed both the horizon of establishment literary theory and Critical Theory's view on art and emancipation.

Within his analysis, Jameson situates postmodern culture in the framework of a theory of stages of society—based on a neo-Marxian model of stages of capitalist development—and argues that postmodernism is part of a new stage of capitalism. Every theory of postmodernism, he claims, contains an implicit periodization of history, and "an implicitly or explicitly political stance on the nature of multinational capitalism today" ("PCL," 55; see also "PTI," 53). Following Ernest Mandel's periodization in his book *Late Capitalism* (1975), Jameson claims "that there have been three fundamental moments in capitalism, each one marking a dialectical expansion over the previous stage: these are market capitalism, the monopoly stage or the stage of imperialism, and our own—wrongly called postindustrial, but what might better be termed multinational capital" ("PCL," 78). To these forms of society, there corresponds the cultural forms of realism, modernism, and postmodernism.

In an argument similar to the Frankfurt School's notion of the end of the individual (Kellner, *Critical Theory* 1989), Jameson argues that postmodernist culture marks the end of the problematics of alienation, anxiety, and the bourgeois individual ("PCS," 114f and "PCL," 61ff). Moreover, it also points to, he suggests, the end of the era of the great *auteurs*, of individual style and expression in cultural production, and of the centered subject in art and life. Indeed, Jameson suggests that there are correspondences between postmodern texts and subjects in contemporary capitalist societies. In both, there are lacks of unity, coherence, and depth, and they are both dispersed, schizoid, and characterized by a network of relations which are shifting, unstable, fragmentary, and decentered.

This analysis of complex relationships between types of texts and modes of social experience fits, as I argued earlier, with the form of analysis in *The Political Unconscious* and *Fables of Aggression* and thus provides the completion of an historical problematics set forth in earlier texts. Consequently, I am proposing that Jameson's studies of postmodernism be read within the context of his earlier works and as their logical extension. Jameson continues to illustrate his contrast between modernist and postmodernist culture with a wealth of examples and arguments that will be taken up in the various contributions to this reader. He rejects both mindless celebrations of "this aesthetic new world" and moralizing critiques that simply reject so-called postmodernism *en masse* without seeing it as a crucial component of our contemporary stage of history ("PCL," 85ff). The proper standpoint for appraising postmodernism is, he suggests, that of Marx who in *The Communist Manifesto* conceived of capitalism both as an extremely progressive and utterly destructive historical development. Jameson proposes such a dialectical analysis which will "think the cultural evolution of late capitalism dialectically," positively and negatively at once, "as catastrophe and progress all together" ("PCL," 86). Such a dialectical position toward postmodernism would thus involve both criticism of its destructive and regressive features, analysis of its positive possibilities, and new political and cultural strategies which take account of the new social situation. I shall shortly discuss Jameson's cultural politics but first want to raise some criticisms concerning Jameson's analysis of postmodernism.

V. Postmodernism as Cultural Dominant?

One might question whether such an ambitious theory of the present age can be derived from a primarily cultural analysis and may want to raise questions about Jameson's periodization and totalizing mode of thought, as well as the details of analysis and the political conclusions drawn. Such questions are raised by several contributors to this reader and to provide a contextual framework for this debate, I want to suggest why Jameson might focus so intensely on culture in his 1980s studies—that is, why a Marxist theorist might take analysis of contemporary culture as a source of cognitive insight into the very trajectory of capitalism itself. Obviously, one determinant (and such fundamental choices are always overdetermined) concerns Jameson's own formation as a literary/cultural critic and his choice to write on theoretical and political topics in a complex style for an academic audience. Yet perhaps the strongest theoretical argument concerning the importance of analysis of culture for radical social theory today concerns the increased importance of culture in the reproduction of contemporary capitalist society.

Indeed, cultural phenomena like the media, advertising, political spectacle, and the aestheticization of everyday life in the consumer society play a fundamental role in the very organization and reproduction of contemporary capitalism. The realm of culture can be said to have imploded into the very base of the society so that the economy itself is increasingly constituted by cultural phenomena. In this original situation, analysis of culture plays an increasingly important role in radical social theory itself. However, it is also likely that the defeat of the Left contributed as well to Jameson's prioritizing culture, for the 1980s exhibit a marked decline of left-wing political activism in the capitalist countries. In the absence of radical political struggle, culture provides one of the more satisfying compensatory realms—as I noted in my study of Marcuse who turned to aesthetics for consolation after each cycle of political defeat suffered by the Left (*Marcuse and the Crisis of Marxism* 1984).

One might still question, however, whether a theory of the present historical moment is best derived from analysis of primarily cultural phenomena, as Jameson does in the essays so far examined. Here, one might compare his method in the postmodernism essay with his studies of the 1960s in the anthology *The 60s Without Apology* (1984). In his article "Periodizing the 60s," Jameson defends a totalizing and periodizing attempt to globally characterize an entire epoch, this time "the 60s, " against the attacks on such totalizing procedures. In this essay, however, Jameson begins with an analysis of salient political and historical origins and features of the epoch, moving from discussions of its "Third World Beginnings," its politics, the fate of philosophy, transformations in culture, and the connections of political, cultural, and social developments with economic developments. Here, Jameson privileges the political as he earlier privileged the cultural in his postmodernism studies.

Both essays attempt to ground their analyses in developments of the economy and both conceptualize changes in politics, society, and culture in terms of changes in the mode of production (utilizing Mandel's *Late Capitalism* (1975) to produce a theory of both the historical stages of capitalism and a theory of the present stage of multinational capitalism). The analysis of the relationship between the new configurations of the economy and culture, and the failure to say much about the supposed new stage of multinational capitalism is, arguably, the weakest part of Jameson's analysis—i.e., he does not provide adequate mediations between the economic and the cultural and political in these essays and does not adequately provide a foundation for his theory in a systematic analysis of the political economy of the present age. Jameson's studies, however, raise the question of whether theories of the present age should be developed as theories of postmodernism or as a new stage of capitalism to be characterized

by the term "multinational capitalism" or some other concept
such as "techno-capitalism" (Kellner, *Critical Theory*).

One might also question whether "postmodernism" actually
is a "cultural dominant" or whether it is arguably better con-
ceptualized as an "emergent" form of culture which appears
dominant in certain groups and social sectors but which is not yet
a dominant for any society as a whole (see Featherstone,
Shumway, and Best in this volume). Indeed, one could argue that
sometimes Jameson goes much too far in accepting key elements
of current postmodernist theories and that such positions
undermine his attempts to preserve Marxism. Has the individual
subject, for instance, been eclipsed in contemporary culture to the
extent to which Jameson claims? Do postmodern cultural texts
and experiences really manifest the lack of depth and flatness
which Jameson attributes to them? Are the problematics of
alienation, anxiety, and liberation really historically obsolete? If
this were really so, then the sort of Marxian hermeneutic which
Jameson had previously attempted to develop is severely
undermined for there would be neither a subject nor object of
interpretation if the alleged dispersal of the subject and its alleged
fragmentation and schizophrenic disorder actually prevailed. For
if the texts themselves were as flat, one-dimensional, and resistant
to interpretation as Jameson's analysis argues, then the grand era
of hermeneutics is over and all cultural criticism can do is to play
with the remnants—a position that Baudrillard embraces (see
Kellner, *Jean Baudrillard* 1989) but one which I would imagine a
Marxist cultural critic should find unacceptable.⁹

Furthermore, a Marxian political theory would seem to need a
subject of praxis, while dissolving the subject into schizophrenic
pieces hardly seems the most productive route for a new radical
politics. Jameson himself might insist that this is not a condition
which he is celebrating (as do Deleuze/Guattari and others) but is
rather a challenge to overcome and surmount (the discussion of
cognitive mapping in the next section advances this position). In
fact, Jameson's article on the 60s reveals the extent to which he
remains committed to a classical Marxian class politics which
most postmodernists reject. He concludes his study with a
political prognosis of the future:

With the end of the 60s, with the world economic crisis, all
the old infrastructural bills then slowly come due once
more; and the 80s will be characterized by an effort, on a
world scale, to proletarianize all those unbound social
forces which gave the 60s their energy, by an extension of
class struggle, in other words, into the farthest reaches of
the globe as well as the most minute configurations of local
institutions (such as the university system). The unifying
force here is the new vocation of a henceforth global
capitalism, which may also be expected to unify the
unequal, fragmented, or local resistances to the process.
And this is finally also the solution to the so-called 'crisis'
of Marxism and to the widely noted inapplicability of its
forms of class analysis to the new social realities with
which the 60s confronted us: 'traditional' Marxism, if
'untrue' during this period of a proliferation of new subjects
of history, must necessarily become true again when the
dreary realities of exploitation, extraction of surplus value,
proletarianization and the resistance to it in the form of
class struggle, all slowly reassert themselves on a new and
expanded world scale, as they seem currently in the process
of doing. ("PTS," 209)

It remains to be seen whether the oppressive realities of
contemporary capitalist societies are producing a new proletarianization of the underlying population, or whether the glitzy joys
of its culture and consumerism will continue to entrap the
majority of the underlying population in its massified and
commodified pleasures and its simulated politics. It is also not
clear that this situation will produce further fragmentation and
disintegration of the subject or a resurgence of both individual and
class consciousness, accompanied by an explosion of both
individual rebellion and class politics. In any case, there is tension
between Jameson's positions—adumbrated during the same
period—that a new proletarianization is on the horizon compared
with the postmodern position that the subject is increasingly
being fragmented and dissolved. In fact, both processes are

conceivably happening at once making it questionable to affirm unambiguously that postmodernism is a new cultural dominant.

Consequently, one could question whether *any* of the features which Jameson ascribes to postmodern culture can really be characterized as a cultural dominant rather than simply as emergent features of a new type of culture which is at most dominant in restricted circles. One might also question whether the specific features which he ascribes to postmodernism cohere into anything like a unified cultural logic or new type of social experience and order. Against postmodern scepticism as to whether such a project is even possible (Lyotard 1984), Jameson attempts to advance a multi-dimensional, dialectical narrative that is both diachronic and synchronic, that holds together the moments of the present while providing an optic that allows us to see the movement from the past to the present into the future. This project parallels the 1930s work of Critical Theory which attempted to develop a supradisciplinary theory of the new stage of capitalism which they saw emerging (see Kellner, *Critical Theory* 1989). Jameson's studies replicate Critical Theory's Hegelian-Marxian and Lukácsian attempt to provide a theory of the totality of contemporary capitalism which he contrasts with earlier forms of culture, society, and experience in capitalist societies. Yet Jameson also develops his theory in terms of an Althusserian totality of relatively autonomous levels which reciprocally interact within a decentered structural totality (see Best in this volume). In these ways, Jameson attempts to demonstrate the continued relevance of Marxian social theory to the present age and to develop Marxism itself in relation to new socio-historical conditions and experiences.

Despite occasional bouts of pessimism, Jameson never really surrenders, as do many postmodernists, to Leftist melancholy or defeatism. True to the revolutionary spirit of the 1960s—which helped energize him through the 1970s—Jameson continued the struggle for revolutionary theory and practice in the terrain of cultural theory. He also turned increasingly to focus on the Third World, visiting Cuba and China and reflecting on their and other Third World cultures.[10] In these essays, he increasingly generalized his cultural analyses as part of a more comprehensive theoretical project so that his analysis of postmodernism, Third World cultures, and so forth becomes part of what one might see as an emerging—but not yet developed—postmodern theory of the dynamics of the totality of contemporary world history. Jameson's interventions in all of these concerns suggest that critical social theory today must attempt to analyze new and emergent social conditions and to revise accordingly one's previous theories and politics in the light of these changes. Thus, one of the purposes of his analysis is to provide an inventory of these new conditions and a challenge to previous radical orthodoxies. Radical cultural politics is also an integral part of social theory and the next section will concern the implications for aesthetics and cultural politics of Jameson's analysis of postmodernism.

VI. Politics, Art, and Cognitive Mapping

One consequence of Jameson's analysis of postmodern cultural phenomena is to force theorists of political art to rethink their previous aesthetic theories and concepts of "authentic" or "emancipatory" art. Indeed, Jameson raises the question of whether high modernist art, which gained its power precisely in its distance from the consumer society and cultural industry, could even exist today—or find a properly receptive audience. Thus, if Jameson's diagnosis of postmodern culture is valid, then it is unlikely that new forms of the sort of highly complex, totally negative and oppositional, works of "autonomous" or "authentic" art beloved by Adorno and his followers will emerge today, or will have efficacious political effects. Jameson's argument is, first, that high modernist works are canonized, co-opted, and henceforth devoid of their power to shock or scandalize audiences ("PCS," 123f and "PCL," 53ff). In this view, the era of high modernism is over, its great individual authors have vanished, its styles are exhausted, and its monumental works are no longer possible. Yet Jameson also claims that culture itself no longer constitutes a separate dimension, another world, from the world of consumer capitalism. Instead, in an aestheticized consumer society, culture—and its images, spectacles, and allure—is part and parcel of everyday life, losing its critical and transcendent possibilities. Thus, he concludes that "critical distance" which characterized modernist art has

> been abolished in the new space of postmodernism. We are submerged in its henceforth filled and suffused volumes to the point where our now postmodernist bodies are . . . incapable of distantiation. . . . The short-hand language of 'cooptation' is for this reason omnipresent on the Left; but offers a most inadequate theoretical basis for understanding a situation in which we all, in one way or another, dimly feel that not only punctual and local countercultural forms of cultural resistance and guerilla warfare, but also even overtly political interventions like those of *The Clash*, are all somehow secretly disarmed and reabsorbed by a system of which they themselves might well be considered a part, since they can achieve no distance from it." ("PCL," 87)

In this situation, what, then, is the task for both critical social theory and emancipatory art today? Jameson points to what he considers "the need for maps," for new theoretical and aesthetic mappings of postmodern society and culture ("PCL," 89ff). He claims that spatial dislocation and confusion (i.e. not knowing where we are) are salient characteristics of the postmodern condition, illustrating the difficulties of representation and spatial visualization through discussion of postmodern architecture (the Bonaventure Hotel in Los Angeles is his privileged structure, Highland Mall in Austin, Texas, is mine), postmodern warfare (he reads Herr's *Dispatches* as pointing to the difficulties of representing contemporary war), the postmodern city, new technologies like computers, and multinational capitalism itself which Jameson presents as the economic base of postmodern culture and society.

Jameson claims that the seemingly fragmented, chaotic, and non-representable nature of the postmodern world presents new challenges to social theory, art, and radical politics. As a response, Jameson calls for a theoretics, aesthetics, and politics of what he calls *cognitive mapping*. Citing difficulties of orientation and mapping in postmodern cities and architecture, he suggests that: "Disalienation in the traditional city, then, involves the practical reconquest of a sense of place, and the construction or reconstruction of an articulated ensemble which can be retained in memory and which the individual subject can map and remap along the moments of mobile, alternative trajectories" ("PCL," 89). Such cognitive mapping is precisely one of the functions of theory and Jameson calls for new theories of "the larger national and global spaces" of the postmodern world which both theory and art could provide.

Then, presumably, once we've mapped and begun to understand the new cultural and socio-political field we can devise radical cultural politics and other political strategies. In the concluding discussion of "the need for maps," Jameson suggests in his "Postmodernism" article that progressive art in the postmodernist era would be pedagogical and didactic, and would presumably involve new representational and mapping strategies to provide critical perceptions in the postmodern world ("PCL," 89ff). While he does not provide any examples there, in an article published in *Social Text* from the same period ("TWL"), he presents some third world novels as illustrations of how novels might serve to provide cognitive maps for their nations. In particular, he reads Lu Xun's "Diary of a Madman" and Sembene Ousmane's *Xala* as allegories of national identity which combine the personal and the political, and the fates of the individual and the nation, in ways that illuminate the place of the individual in relation to her or his society and to the political demands posed in a particular society in a given era. In another article, "On Magical Realism in Film," he sketches out some of the ways that "magical realist" novels and films provide mapping functions.

In "Cognitive Mapping" (1988), Jameson spells out more of what is included in the postmodern aesthetic that he imagines. Here he reveals that the term "cognitive mapping" derives from Brecht scholar Darko Suvin's emphasis on the cognitive function of art and aesthetics, Kevin Lynch's attempt to discover how people map urban space, and Althusser's theory of ideology as "the Imaginary representation of the subject's relationship to his or her

Real conditions of existence." Just as Jameson argued in *The Political Unconscious* that constructing narratives was a fundamental activity of human beings, he now seems to argue that individuals need some sort of image or mapping of their society and the world as a whole. "Cognitive mapping" thus involves the task of individuals, artists, and theorists in providing orientation, a sense of time (history) and place through theoretical models of how society is structured combined with historical analyses of stages of development. Jameson claims that this sort of mapping is of crucial importance for both social theory and politics for "the incapacity to map socially is as crippling to political experience as the analogous incapacity to map spatially is for the urban experience. It follows that an aesthetic of cognitive mapping in this sense is an integral part of any socialist political project" ("CMP," 353).

Jameson is thus attempting to answer the poststructuralist/postmodernist critique of representation by stressing that we need representations of our society, however imperfect, to get about in the world. In a sense, "cognitive mapping" becomes the most inclusive category which covers certain totalizing and representational strategies which Jameson privileges. Lukács' narrative totalizing, Sartre's totalizations, Althusser's overdetermined structural totality, as well as Jameson's analysis of postmodernism, can all be read as strategies of cognitive mapping. As a theoretical model, Jameson's own sketches thus can be taken as cognitive maps of postmodern space, and from this perspective he poses the challenge to social theory to provide similar cognitive mapping of the allegedly new postmodern society. Yet cognitive mapping also covers individuals' attempts to map their own space and varying aesthetic strategies and projects as well. Realism, modernism, and now postmodernism can be read as differing strategies to cognitively map social space.

From this perspective, Jameson's earlier call for a "new realism" and his frequent attempts to undercut the distinction between realism and modernism which has plagued cultural theory for several decades can also be subsumed under the category of cognitive mapping. For on one hand, Jameson is calling, in effect, for a renewal of the realist project of mapping or representing social space *and* the modernist project of altering our modes of sense perception and theoretical cognition with new cultural forms and creation. This aesthetic project is combined with theoretical efforts to provide new cognitive mapping which, in a Hegelian-Marxian fashion, would provide a new type of totalizing social theory, ambitiously advanced against postmodern and poststructuralist attacks on the very concept of totality. In this sense, Jameson is offering his own totalizing theory of the present age—precisely the traditional function and important contribution of Hegelian Marxism. Jameson points to the debilitating effects of living in the fragments of a social space one cannot grasp and "just gaming" with the remnants, and he argues that new cognitive mapping is needed to contextualize and critique our contemporary moment.

Yet Jameson also advocates more properly "postmodern" strategies as well in order to critique postmodernism itself. In the interview on postmodernism included in this volume, Jameson proposes a strategy similar to what Baudrillard called "fatal strategies": pursing the logic of a phenomena to the end, beyond its boundaries, to explode or turn against established trends or elements of the existing society (Baudrillard, *Les strategies fatales* 1983, discussed in Kellner, *Jean Baudrillard* 1989). Jameson uses the metaphor of homeopathic medicine to delineate the strategy: "To undo postmodernism homeopathically by the methods of postmodernism: to work at dissolving the pastiche by using all the instruments of pastiche itself, to reconquer some genuine historical sense by using the instruments of what I have called substitutes for history" ("RPM," 59f). Jameson's example is the work of the novelist E. L. Doctorow who in novels like *Ragtime*, *Loon Lake*, or *Daniel* attempts to use postmodernist techniques of pastiche, historical nostalgia, and cliché to recover a genuine sense of history and to overcome the limits of postmodern fragmentation, loss of a sense of history, and so on. Thus Jameson now proposes using the strategies, techniques, and elements of postmodernism against postmodernism itself, though in the same interview he argues that the socialist world must create an attractive and appealing global style and culture which can compete with the postmodernism of the capitalist world ("RPM," 57ff).

Jameson has yet to work out a radical cultural politics and such a project is the next logical step in his itinerary. It is to be hoped that an increased level of struggle by new social movements and general upsurge in the fortunes of the Left as we move into the 1990s will make such projects an increasingly important part of the Left's theoretical and political agenda. For the Left Turn requires a radical cultural politics as the necessary supplement to its theoretical and political agendas in view of the increased importance of the role of culture and ideology in contemporary society. Thus if radical political change is to be possible, alternative cultural forms and practices, new ways of seeing and a new sensibility are indispensible parts of a resurgence of a new politics which is yet to be invented.

VII. Reading Jameson Critically

The papers collected in this reader intensify a process, already begun, of reading Jameson critically. The project originated in a workshop on Jameson held at a conference on postmodernism at the University of Kansas in May, 1987. The essays were revised to help produce a systematic examination of Jameson's 1980s work and some new essays were commissioned especially for the collection. The following studies attempt to understand and appraise Jameson's analyses of postmodernism in the context of his own theoretical development and contemporary theoretical and political debates. The opening selection is an interview with Jameson in which he clarifies and amplifies his earlier articles on postmodernism, and relates the debate over postmodernism to other key issues in literary and cultural theory, as well as to political and social theory. This interview is followed by a series of studies which attempt to contextualize Jameson's analysis of postmodernism. Martin Donougho situates Jameson's recent work in the context of his theoretical development and focuses on his analysis of the differences between modernism and post-modernism and the specific features of Jameson's analysis of postmodernism. David Gross follows by explicating the Marxian positions in Jameson's theory and describes Jameson's successive texts as attempts to defend and reconstruct Marxism against contemporary theoretical and political challenges of the last two decades. Mike Featherstone then interprets Jameson's work on postmodernism from a sociological analysis of the role of practitioners and commentators in promoting a culture of postmodernism. Featherstone grounds these endeavors in terms of a theory of the rise of a new middle class and, against Jameson, he proposes a more sociological and empirical approach to postmodernism based on the theories of Pierre Bourdieu.

John O'Neill describes what he considers the religious dimension in Jameson's work, and compares it with Durkheim and Daniel Bell. Christopher Sharrett shows how Jameson's theory of postmodernism can be used to distinguish modernist and postmodernist architecture via an analysis of two New York restaurants. Several articles then describe Jameson's work in the context of what Terry Eagleton once termed "Marxist aesthetic duels": the debates over aesthetics and politics in the work of Lukács, Brecht, Bloch, and the Frankfurt School. David Shumway explicates the hermeneutical position within Jameson's thought, and defends it against recent poststructuralist attacks on hermeneutics. Lambert Zuidervaart positions Jameson's work in relation to debates between Lukács and Adorno, and presents Jameson's work as an attempt to mediate opposed positions within contemporary Marxian literary theory. He also challenges Jameson to fill the "empty chair" of a new political art in the face of the postmodernist challenge. And then Thomas Huhn presents an Adornoesque critique of Jameson's theory, claiming that Jameson resurrects a "master subject" and subverts or ignores Adorno's concepts of "aesthetic experience" and "authentic art."

Several lively polemical interventions follow which criticize Jameson's positions from varying poststructuralist and postmodernist theories. Philip Goldstein carries out a poststructuralist critique of Jameson's literary theory, while Haynes Horne criticizes the presuppositions of Jameson's work from a neo-Lyotardian position, and R. Radhakrishnan criticizes Jameson from his own version of Derridean deconstruction. Steven Best defends Jameson's work against such poststructuralist critiques and attempts to demonstrate the misunderstandings and problems contained in these polemics. To conclude, Fredric Jameson replies to his commentators and critics and offers his most direct commentary so far on the articulation of postmodernism and Marxism as well as his own stance with regard to the problem of totalization and periodization.

It is interesting here and elsewhere to observe the ways that Jameson's effort to synthesize Marxism with poststructuralism and other competing modes of thought are criticized by both sides. Generally, poststructuralists and others claim that Jameson is guilty of excessively totalizing, subjectivizing, historicizing, and of utilizing humanist and reductive modes of thought (Horne, Huhn, Radhakrishnan, Goldstein) while Marxist and other critics claim that Jameson goes too far in the direction of dissolving and fragmenting subjectivity and in accepting postmodernism as (Featherstone, Shumway, and Best), or they criticize him for pessimistically reifying society into a massive systemic totality, invulnerable to political struggle (Goldstein). Jameson attempts to mediate between opposing positions but the question arises as to whether it is possible to synthesize Althusser with Lukács, structural with Hegelian Marxism, and Marxism with poststructuralism. The debates will continue and no doubt Jameson's own work and the contributions to this volume can be read as signs of a divided Left and critical intelligentsia attempting either to articulate differences or to forge consensus and unity, or, as with Jameson, to do both at once. For the Left—like everything else—is hopelessly fragmented and divided and only the overcoming of this condition will make possible the political and methodological move to a common and higher ground that will take us beyond the conservativism of the 1980s into a better future.

Notes

For helpful comments on earlier drafts, I would like to thank Bob Antonio, Dennis Crow, Gail Faurschou, Fred Jameson, and especially Steve Best who made many incisive comments on various versions of this introduction as well as on other articles included in this volume.

1. For discussion of the debates over postmodern theory and culture, see Foster 1983; Huyssen 1984; and Kellner 1988. On postmodernism in philosophy, see Rorty 1979; Bernstein 1985; and Baynes, et al. 1987.

2. The main signposts in the growing literature on Jameson include *Diacritics*, 12 (Fall, 1982), *Critical Exchange*, 14 (Fall, 1983), *New Orleans Review*, 11 (Spring, 1984), Dowling 1984, and the present reader.

3. His key texts on Sartre include: *Sartre: The Origins of a Style* (1961), *Marxism and Form* (1971), "Three Methods in Sartre's Literary Criticism" (1972), "On Aronson's Sartre" (1982).

4. The call for a synthesis of diachronic and synchronic thinking, and German hermeneutics and French structuralism, at the end of *The Prison House of Language* is a typical feature of Jameson's dialectics: "There is no immutable fatality at work in the history of philosophy to bring such a new methodological development to pass. Yet it is only, it seems to me, at the price of such a development, or of something like it, that the twin, apparently incommensurable, demands of a synchronic analysis and historical awareness, of structure and self-consciousness, language and history can be reconciled" (*PH*, 216). A similar call for synthesis is found in "Metacommentary" (pp. 15f.) and "The Ideology of the Text" (1975) where he writes that "the principle critical business of our time . . . is to forge a kind of methodological synthesis from the multiplicity of critical codes" (*IT*, 59).

5. See, "Change, Science Fiction, and Marxism: Open or Closed Universes? In Retrospect" (1974); "World Reduction in Le Guin: The Emergence of Utopian Narrative" (1975); "Introduction/Prospectus: To Reconsider the Relationship of Marxism to Utopian Thought" (1976); "Reification and Utopia in Mass Culture" (1979); Futuristic visions that tell us about right now" (1982); and "Progress versus Utopia, or, Can We Imagine the Future" (1982).

6. See, "Notes Towards a Marxist Cultural Politics" (1975); "Modernism and its Repressed: Robbe-Grillet as Anti-Colonialist" (1976); "But Their Cause Is Just: Israel and the Palestinians" 1979); and "Marxism and Teaching" (1979).

7. *The Political Unconscious* is a highly dialectical (in Jameson's sense) text which is equally concerned with method and with the categories of analysis as well as with the objects of textual analysis. Most discussion of the text has focused on the former, yet I am focusing on the latter in order to point to some lines of continuity between Jameson's work in *The Political Unconscious* and *Fables of Aggression* and his studies of postmodernism.

8. Jameson's first published study of postmodernism merely attempts to distinguish some traits of so-called postmodernist from modernist culture ("PCS" 1983) while by his *New Left Review* version ("PCL" 1984), he was interpreting postmodernism as a new cultural totality and cultural dominant corresponding to a new stage of contemporary capitalism.

9. For a critique of postmodern attempts to reject hermeneutics and a defense of a Marxian hermeneutics, even for so-called postmodern texts, see Best and Kellner 1987 and Best 1988.

10. See, "Third World Literature in the Era of Multinational Capitalism" (1986); "On Magical Realism in Film" (1986); "Regarding Postmodernism" (1987 and reprinted in this volume); and "Discussion: Contemporary Chinese Writing" (1988).

11. Refusing to side with either a realist or modernist aesthetics, Jameson tends to historicize both movements, interpreting them as aesthetic responses to determinate social conditions rather than as opposing normative models between which one must choose. See Jameson, *Ideologies of Theory*, Volume One: *Situations of Theory*, pp. 17ff. and the 1977 afterword to *Aesthetics and Politics* where he writes: "the function of a new realism would be clear: to resist the power of reification in consumer society and to reinvent that category of totality which, systematically undermined by existential fragmentation on all levels of life and social organization today, can alone project structural relations between classes as well as class struggles in other countries, in what has increasingly become a world system. Such a conception of realism would incorporate what was always most concrete in the dialectical counterconcept of modernism—its emphasis on violent renewal of perception in a world in which experience has solidified into a mass of habits and automatisms. . . . Other conceptions of realism, other kinds of political aesthetics,

obviously remain conceivable. The realism / modernism debate teaches us the need to judge them in terms of the historical and social conjuncture in which they are called to function" ("Reflections in Conclusion," 146-147).

Regarding Postmodernism:
A Conversation with Fredric Jameson

Anders Stephanson

Anders Stephanson: Your argument about postmodernism has two levels: on the one hand an inventory of constitutive features, and on the other an account of a vaster reality which these features are said to express.

Fredric Jameson: The idea is to create a mediatory concept, to construct a model which can be articulated in, and descriptive of, a whole series of different cultural phenomena. This unity or system is then placed in a relation to the infrastructural reality of late capitalism. The aim, in other words, is to provide something which can face in two directions: a principle for the analysis of cultural texts which is at the same time a working system that can show the general ideological function of all these features taken together. I'm not sure that my analysis has covered all the essentials, but I tried to range across a set of qualitatively different things, starting with the visual, passing through the temporal, and then returning to a new conception of space itself.

Since our first concepts of postmodernism have tended to be negative (i.e., it isn't this, it isn't that, it isn't a whole series of things that modernism was), I begin by comparing modernism and postmodernism. However, the object is ultimately a positive description, not in any sense of value (so that postmodernism would then be "better" than modernism) but in order to grasp postmodernism as a new cultural logic in its own right, as something more than a mere reaction. Historically, of course it *did* begin as a reaction against the institutionalization of modernism in universities, museums and concert halls, against the canonization of a certain kind of architecture. This entrenchment is felt to be oppressive by the generation that comes of age, roughly speaking, in the 60s; and, not surprisingly, it then tries systematically to make a breathing space for itself by repudiating modernist values. In the literary context, values thus repudiated include complexity and ambiguity of language, irony, the concrete universal, and the construction of elaborate symbolic systems. The specific features would of course have been different in other arts.

You begin the exploration with an analysis of depth and surface in painting.

I wanted to focus on a certain flatness, not to be confused with the way in which modernist painting famously reconquered the surface of the painting. I describe this in terms of the disappearance of a certain *depth*, a word I wanted to function in a deliberately ambiguous way. I meant not only visual depth—that was already happening in modern painting—but also interpretative depth, the idea that the object was fascinating because of the density of its secrets and that these were then to be uncovered by interpretation. All this vanishes. Similarly, because it is a subtheme of the relationship between postmodernism in the arts and contemporary theory, I tried to show how this goes along with a new kind of conceptualization which no longer involves *philosophic* notions of depth, that is, various hermeneutics in which one interprets an appearance in terms of some underlying reality which these philosophies then uncode. Finally, there is also the abolition of historicity and historical depth, what used to be called historical consciousness or the sense of the past. In short, objects fall into the world and become decoration again, visual depth and systems of interpretation fade away; and something peculiar happens to historical time.

This is then accompanied by a transformation of the depth of psychological *affect* in that a particular kind of phenomenological or emotional reaction to the world disappears. Symptomatic here is the changeover from anxiety—the dominant feeling or affect in modernism—to a different system of which schizophrenic or drug language gives the key notion. I am referring to what the French have started to call *intensities* of highs and lows. These have nothing to do with "feelings" that offer clues to meaning in the way anxiety did. Anxiety is a hermeneutic emotion, it expresses an underlying nightmare state of the world; whereas highs and lows really don't imply anything about the world, you can feel them on whatever occasion. They are no longer cognitive.

You speak here of "the hysterical sublime" and "the exhilaration of the gleaming surface." In the "dialectical intensification of the autoreferentiality of all modern culture," we face a complete lack of affect punctured by moments of extreme intensity.

Dialectically, in the conscious sublime it is the self that touches the limit; here it is the body that is touching its limits, "volatilized" in this experience of images to the point of being outside of itself, losing itself. It is a reduction of time to an instant in a most intense final punctual experience of all these things, but it is no longer *subjective* in the older sense that a personality is standing in front of the Alps and knowing the limits of the individual subject and the human ego. On the contrary, it is a kind of non-humanist experience of limits beyond which you get dissolved.

Whereupon we reach the temporal aspect?

Yes. The visual metaphoric depth gives way to a description of temporal disconnection and fragmentation, the kind of thing embodied for example in John Cage's music. Discontinuity in sound and time is then seen as emblematic of the disappearance of certain relationships to history and the past. Analogously, it is related to the way we describe a text today as the production of discontinuous sentences without any larger unifying forms. A rhetoric of texts replaces older notions of work organized according to this or that form. Indeed, the language of form disappears.

In the 60s, I was once told, the average camera movement—a change of view, a zoom, a pan—did not go below something like 1 per 7.5 seconds in an ordinary 30-second commercial, the reason being that this was considered the optimum of what the human perception could handle. It is now down to something like 3.5 or less. I have actually timed commercials where it is about 1 change per 2 seconds, 15 changes in a matter of 30 seconds.

We are approaching a logic of subliminality there and your example effectively illustrates this new logic of difference to which we are being programmed, these increasingly rapid and empty breaks in our time. Each training in an increased tempo is a training in feeling it natural to shift from one thing to another.

Paik's video art is, as you say, a valuable postmodernist place to explore this problem.

As a kind of training in a new logic of difference. An empty formal training or programming in a new way of perceiving difference.

What exactly is that new way of perceiving difference?

I tried to put this in the slogan "difference relates." The very perception of breaks and differences becomes a meaning in itself, not a meaning that has content but one that seems to be a meaningful yet new form of unity. This kind of view does not pose the problem "how do we relate those things, how do we turn those things back into continuities or similarities"; it simply says, "when you register difference, something positive is happening in your mind." It's a way of getting rid of content.

From this diagnosis of the temporal you proceed to the spatial.

I then link these two sets of features (surface, fragmentation) in terms of the spatialization of time. Time has become a perpetual present and thus spatial. Our relationship to the past is now a spatial one.

Why does it necessarily become spatial?

One privileged language in modernism, Proust or Thomas

Mann for example, always used temporal description. That notion of "deep time," Bergsonian time, seems radically irrelevant to our contemporary experience, which is one of a perpetual spatial present. Our *theoretical* categories also tend to become spatial: structural analyses with graphs of synchronic multiplicities of spatially related things (as opposed to, say, the dialectic and its temporal moments), and languages like Foucault's with its empty rhetoric of cutting, sorting and modifying, a kind of spatial language in which you organize data like a great bloc to be chopped up in various ways. This happens to be how I in particular "use" Foucault, with limitations that will probably infuriate his disciples. Much of Foucault, on the other hand, was already familiar: the binary opposition between center and margin was largely developed in Sartre/Saint Genet; the concepts of power had emerged in many places, but fundamentally in the anarchist tradition; the totalizing strategies of his various schemes also have many analogies from Weber on. I propose rather to consider Foucault in terms of the *cognitive mapping* of power, the construction of spatial figures. But then, of course, once one puts it that way, his own figures—the grid, for example—become starkly relativized and cease to be theories as such.

Where does "hyper-space" come into the spatial argument?

Normal space is made up of things, or organized by things. Here we are talking about the dissolution of things. In this final component of hyperspace, one cannot talk about components anymore. We used to talk about this in terms of subject-object dialectics; but in a situation where subjects and objects have been dissolved, hyperspace is the ultimate of the object-pole, intensity the ultimate of the subject-pole, though we no longer have subjects and objects.

At any rate, the notion of spatialization replacing temporalization leads back to architecture and new experiences of space which I think are very different from any previous moments of the space of the city, to name one example. What is striking about the new urban ensembles around Paris, for example, is that there is absolutely no *perspective at all*. Not only has the street disappeared (that was already the task of modernism) but all profiles have disappeared as well. This is bewildering and I use existential bewilderment in this new postmodern space to make a final diagnosis of the loss of our ability to *position ourselves within this space and cognitively map it.* This is then projected back on the emergence of a global multinational culture which is decentered and cannot be visualized, a culture in which one cannot position oneself. That is the conclusion.

To be more specific, you use, very elegantly, Portman's Bonaventure Hotel in Los Angeles as an example: a mirror façade, a self-enclosed structure in which it is impossible to orientate oneself. Yet the new commercial spaces around Rodeo Drive are the very opposite of what you describe: quaint squares, readily visible spaces where things can be purchased in quite obvious and conventional ways.

But that is the Disney version of postmodern architecture, the Disneyland pastiche of the older square or piazza or whatever. I picked emblematic things and by no means everything can be analyzed in that vein. These other examples are not exemplary of the hyperspace, but they certainly are exemplary of the production of simulacra. Disney's EPCOT is another excellent example.

His compressed version of the world in other words, little toy countries where you can orientate yourself in no time at all.

I suppose you can orient yourself because paths have been laid long for you to move along, but where you actually are is a real problem. For you may in fact be in the Florida Everglades and in this case you are not only in a swamp but also in a simulacrum of somewhere else. Disneyland is on the whole supremely prophetic and paradigmatic of a lot of stuff.

The emergence of postmodernism is materially tied in your analysis to the rise of American capital on a global scale, dated to the late 50s and early 60s. However, the United States was then actually beginning to experience a relative decline in its postwar dominance: other nations were coming back economically, there was an upsurge of third-world liberation movements and the return in the first world

of oppositional ideologies very much fashioned on the depth model
(Marxism for one).

Notions of the discontinuity of culture and economics can account for some of that. The setting in place of American power is one thing; the development of a culture which both reflects and perpetuates that power is a somewhat different matter. The old culture slate had to be wiped clean and the reason that could happen in the United States rather than in Europe was the persistence of *l'ancien regime* in European culture. Once modernism broke down, the absence of traditional forms of culture in the US opened up a field for a whole new cultural production across the board. Individual things could be pioneered in Europe, but a *system* of culture could only emerge from this American possibility. At the moment when American power then begins to be questioned, a new cultural apparatus becomes necessary to reinforce it. The system of postmodernism comes in as the vehicle for a new kind of ideological hegemony which might not have been required before.

Isn't this view close to straightforward functionalism or instrumentalism?

Yes and no. There is certainly a way in which this system—from the export of American television shows to so-called high cultural values, above all the very logic and practice of "American" consumption itself—is as effective a vehicle for depoliticization as religion may once have been. There had to be channels of transmission and those are laid in place with communications systems, television, computers and so forth. Worldwide, that's really only available in the 60s. Suffice it simply for a power elite to say: "Well, in this situation we need a cultural system which has to correspond to changes that are taking place in people's lives and offer a kind of content." The new life experience embodied in postmodernism is very powerful precisely because it has a great deal of *content* that seems to come as a solution to existential problems.

A lot of other discontinuous systems are going on here too. Some of the social effects of American hegemony are not felt until the 60s—the agricultural revolution for example—so it's wrong to see this merely in terms of political power. A lot of the social resistance of the 60s comes when people—peasants for instance—begin to realize what the neo-colonial systems are doing to ways of life that had been exploited before but left relatively intact. The emergence of resistance does not necessarily merely mean the rolling back of American influence; it can be a symptom of the disintegrating forces of that influence on deeper levels of social life than the political one.

When you depict the capitalist destruction of Van Gogh's world of peasant shoes and Heidegger's country pathway, you do so in terms of Tafuri's account of the modernist project in architecture: the aim of insuring that the future holds no surprises, the idea of "planification" and elimination of future risk. This seems a valid point. However, you skate rather easily over the modernizing features of Marxism itself, the results of which are clear and obvious in the unthinking destruction of the environment in Soviet-style societies. Planification with a vengeance, it actually prepares the grounds for future disaster. The obliteration of Heidegger's pathway can thus be seen as an integral feature of any modernizing ethic.

Plainly, in an advanced society our immediate oppositional tendency is to talk about restraining technological progress. I am not sure poor societies always have that option. Some of these features, what is happening to cities like Moscow, are part of what could be called *the cultural debt crisis*. Think of the 60s and 70s here, where they were sucked into the world system and began to feel they had to have tourists and build big hotels. One has to distinguish between the Promethean scenario—the struggle with nature—and other kinds of commodification that they really get from us in a lot of ways.

Yet Stalin was a great admirer of American technology and Taylorist efficiency. The fact that they engage in this sort of destruction is not only a question of wanting to catch up with the west or having to compete with the west; it is also embedded in a certain kind of Marxist theory. By delineating the problematic in an exclusively capitalist domain, you render yourself open to the objection that there is a strong element of conquering nature and older "logics" in Marxist as well as capitalist thought. Marcuse's analysis of Soviet theory is surely unequivocal on this point. If your argument, in short, is built on the idea of the relentless ordering of the world in terms of commodifying logic of capital, then it must also be clear that certain Marxisms are far from innocent.

I agree. But the emphasis on production and productivity and catching up with capitalism is at least part of the rivalry that capitalism has laid on these underdeveloped countries; they have to catch up. Therefore we have a very elaborate dialectical process where these societies have found it necessary to go beyond self-sufficiency or autarchy to generate modernization for a lot of reasons like armament.

Yes, but the conception of modernity is there from the outset.

That is indeed an ideological conception, and no doubt it needs to be rethought.

Your model goes from the microlevel, assorted things here and there, to the macrolevel represented by Mandel's concept of Late Capitalism. These "homologies" between the three moments of capital and the three moments in cultural development (realism, modernism and postmodernism) lend credence to descriptions of your position as unreconstructed Lukácsianism. It does seem a case of expressive causality, correspondences and all.

However, it is difficult to see how one can preserve a consistent political commitment if one adopts poststructuralist fantasies of pure contingency and non-relation. In a nutshell, a certain amount of reductionism is necessary. Hence, objections to the actual concept of three stages of capitalism aside, I think the idea of this kind of model perfectly proper. Problems arise, however, with the mediating instances, the way in which you jump from the minute to the staggeringly global.

But Lukács takes a moralizing position on modernism which is neither historical nor dialectical. He thinks it is something essentially morally wrong that can be eliminated by an effort of the will. That is something different from my presentation of something that seems *more* morally horrendous, namely post-modernism. As for expressive causality, I find it paradoxical that a discontinuous and dialectical model of something can be criticized for being an idealistic continuity which includes a telos. Each of these moments is dialectically different from each other and has different laws and modes of operation. I also make a place for overdetermination, that is, some things are enabled by developments in the cultural realm which tie into others at certain conjunctures. I don't think that's what one would do in a model of "the Spirit of the Age." For example, the notion of hegemony is not normally thought to be Hegelian. In talking about a certain kind of cultural hegemony, I have left a space for oppositional or enclaves of resistance, all kinds of things not integrated into the global model but necessarily defined against it. I can see how in some very loose and general sense one can make the sort of characterization you made, and in the same loose and general sense it wouldn't bother me. If we talk about the specifics of the thing, then I would want to see what reprehensible things it ended up doing before I accepted it. On the other hand, as you say, any attempt to be systematic potentially attracts those criticisms because one is trying to make a reduction.

What distinguishes your concept of postmodernism is in fact that it is conceived not as a stylistic mode but as a cultural dominant. In that way it bears little relation to the ideas of everyone from Tafuri to Lyotard.

Two things here. First, it's important to understand that this notion of a dominant does not exclude forms of resistance. In fact, the whole point for me in undertaking this analysis was the idea that one wouldn't be able to measure the effectiveness of resistance unless one knew what the dominant forces were. My conception of postmodernism is thus not meant to be a mono-lithic thing but to allow evaluations of other currents within this system—which cannot be measured unless one knows what the system is.

In the second place I want to propose a dialectical view in which we neither see postmodernism as immoral, frivolous or reprehensible because of its lack of high seriousness, nor as good in the McLuhanist, celebratory sense of the emergence of some wonderful new utopia. Features of both are going on at once. Certain aspects of postmodernism can be seen as relatively positive, such as the return of storytelling after the sort of poetic novels that modernism used to produce. Other features are obviously negative (the loss of a sense of history, for example). All in all, these developments have to be confronted as a historical situation rather than as something one morally deplores or simply celebrates.

Moralizing aside, is postmodernism not predominantly negative from a Marxist perspective?

Think of its popular character and the relative democratization involved in various postmodernist forms. This is an experience of culture accessible to far more people than the older modernist languages were. Certainly, that cannot be altogether bad. Culturalization of things on a very wide front might be deplored by people for whom modernism was a very sophisticated language to be conquered by dint of self-formation, of which postmodernism is then a bastardization and vulgarization. Why this should be condemned from a left standpoint is however not clear to me.

In that sense no, but as you yourself have emphasized, simple opposition to totality in the name of some celebrated fragmentation and heterogeneity renders the very idea of critique difficult.

Yet even heterogeneity is a positive thing; the social rhetoric of differences reflected in this and that is surely not in itself a bad thing. The point is that many of these seemingly negative features can be looked at positively if they are seen historically. If you see them as items in a defense of postmodern art, then they don't look the same. Postmodern architecture is demonstrably a symptom of democratization, of a new relationship of culture to people, but this does not mean that you can defend or glamorize the buildings of the postmodernist because they are populist buildings.

It is obvious, nevertheless, that postmodernist discourse makes it difficult to say things about the whole.

One of the ways of describing this is as a modification in the very nature of the cultural sphere: a loss of the autonomy of culture, a case of culture falling into the world. As you say, this makes it much more difficult to speak of cultural systems and so evaluate them in isolation. A whole new theoretical problem is posed. Thinking at once negatively and positively about it is a beginning, but what we need is a new vocabulary. The languages that have been useful in talking about culture and politics in the past don't really seem adequate to this historical moment.

So you retain the classical Marxist paradigm: the master narrative underneath this search for a new vocabulary is very traditional.

Traditional in a sense but it implies a third stage of capitalism which is not present in Marx. . . .

Nor indeed is the second one, "monopoly capitalism," which was an invention of the Second International bought wholesale and with very bad results by the Third.

The Marxist framework is still indispensable for understanding the new historical content, which demands, not a modification of the Marxist framework, but an expansion of it.

Why is that clear?

Contemporary Marxist economics and social science is not a rewriting of 19th century Marxism. One can dramatize this as Mandel does by saying that it is not that reality has evolved away from the model, it is not that this is no longer the capitalism analyzed by Marx, but that it is a much closer, *purer* version of capitalism. A feature of this third stage is that the precapitalist enclaves have systematically been penetrated, commodified and assimilated to the dynamics of the system. If the original instruments of Marxism are unserviceable it is not that Marxism is wrong now but that it is truer now than in Marx's time. Hence we need an expansion of these instruments rather than a replacement of them.

The old Lukácsian model of truth and false consciousness is, I suppose, one casualty in this regard.

In the more interesting parts of Lukács, that is not in fact the model. Let me put that in a more personal way. Obviously, there is false consciousness and there are moments when one wants to denounce certain things as sheer false consciousness. That is essentially a political decision and part of a struggle that has to be. In ideological analysis, on the other hand, the denunciation of works of art for embodying false consciousness was possible only in a more heterogeneous class situation, where the working classes were a nation within the nation and did not consume bourgeois culture. When one takes one's stand in such circumstances then one can see that certain kinds of objects—Proust for example—are decadent in the sense of not being the mode in which either experience or artistic form makes any sense to people who work. From that viewpoint one can denounce the decadence and false consciousness which Proust undoubtedly embodied. But now, when these class differences are no longer secured by social isolation and with a continuing process of massive democratic culturalization, there is no space which the left can be outside. My position on ideological analysis of works of art today is therefore that you don't denounce them from the outside. If you want to denounce them as false consciousness, you have to do it from the inside and it has to be a self-critique. It is not because false consciousness doesn't exist anymore—perhaps because it is everywhere—that we have to talk about it in a different way.

You propose, then, to preserve "the moment of truth" in postmodernism. What exactly is it?

I am using contemporary German post-Hegelian language here. Ideological analysis from that vantage point means talking about the moment of truth and the moment of untruth, and in this case I am trying to say that insofar as postmodernism really expresses multinational capitalism, there is some cognitive content to it. It is articulating something that is going on. If the subject is lost in it, and if in social life the psychic subject has been decentered by late capitalism, then this art faithfully and authentically registers that. That's its moment of truth.

Modernism, as you have argued, emerges at the same time as mass culture to which it is thus inextricably linked. Postmodernism can then be seen as the collapse of these two into one again. Terry Eagleton has reformulated this as a kind of sick joke on the historical avant-garde, where the avant-garde attempt to break down the boundaries between art and social life suddenly becomes a reactionary implosion.

It's not a matter of becoming that, but being revealed as that. The other version of that account which I find very persuasive is that of Tafuri in connection with architecture. He tries to show that the protopolitical aesthetic revolution first laid down in Schiller—i.e., we must change our existential experience and that will in itself be a revolution—is virtually taken over word for word by Le Corbusier: we change the space we live in and then we don't need political revolution. The protopolitical impulse of modernism, according to Tafuri, is necessarily always predicated on exclusion, for the radical new space of the modern thing must begin by a gesture of excluding the old fallen space that is to be revolutionized. Implicit here is the belief that this new space will fan out and transform the old space. Instead it simply remains an enclave space; and when the existential and cultural spatial revolution fails to take hold in this fallen outlying world, the building or work of art becomes an isolated monument, testifying to its own sterility or impotence. It ceases to be a revolutionary gesture. So what Eagleton is ironizing is in Tafuri's account already implicit in the first modernisms.

There is a misreading of your reading of Tafuri which seems to say that by calling for a "properly Gramscian architecture" you are simple calling from some cleared enclave of resistance, not quite what you are arguing.

In my appeal to a Gramscian architecture, I also mentioned Lefebvre. I was thinking not of an architectural practice as such but of an awareness that the locus of our new reality and the cultural politics by which it must be confronted is that of space. We must therefore begin to think of cultural politics in terms of space and the struggle for space. Then we are no longer thinking in old categories of critical distance but in some new way where the disinherited and essentially modernist language of subversion and negation is conceived differently. Tafuri's argument is couched in cultural terms, but what matters in any defeat or success of a plan to transform the city is political power, control over speculation and land values and so on. That's a very healthy infrastructural awareness.

How does this differ from traditional politics?

The difference is that the political is projected onto at least two levels: the practical matter of this place, this terrain, and these resistances; and then, above and beyond that, the cultural vision of utopian space of which this particular enclave is but a specific figure. All of which can be said in a more banal way in terms of the decay of the very concept of socialism which we can observe everywhere (in all three worlds): it is a matter of reinventing that concept as a powerful cultural and social vision, something one does not do simply by repeating a worn-out name or term. But it is a two-level strategy: the specific space or place *and* the global vision of which the first is only one particular manifestation or local fulfillment. Add to this the fact and problem of the new global systemic space and we have a demand made on the political imagination which is historically unparalleled.

Let me put it this way: there exists today a global capitalist, or late capitalist culture, which we call, as is now apparent, postmodernism. It is a tremendously powerful force which, in sheer gravitational attraction and capability of diffusion, is known, or used to be known, as cultural imperialism. Nothing like a global socialist culture exists as a distinct oppositional force and style to this. On the other hand, when one proposes such a political project to some of the interested parties, they rightly begin at once to worry about the dissolution of that national situation and culture which has generally played such a powerful role in socialist revolutions. What is wanted is therefore a new relationship between a global cultural style and the specificity and demands of a concrete local or national situation.

Is the spatial aspect not really what social democrats in Europe have been concerned with, sometimes successfully, for a long time?

The problem with the social democratic governments is that they've gained power in a nation-state whose economic realities are really controlled by the international market. They are therefore not in control of their own national space. Ultimately, I am talking about a global space which is not an abstract speculative thing. I am talking about the fact that the proletariat of the first world is now in the third world, that production is taking place around the Pacific basin or wherever. These are practical realities, and the control of national space may itself be an outmoded idea a situation of multinationals.

Indeed, one can take your macro-analysis to mean that the task of radical first-world intellectuals is a kind of "third-worldism." This, to my mind, recalls various "bribery theories" of the 60s—using the absence of movement among the western working class as a justification for fixation on the other and less quiescent continents. Eventually these positions were discarded and rightly so.

The attractiveness of "third-worldism" as an ideology rises and falls with the condition of the third world itself, but the political movement going on today—such as there is—is in places like Nicaragua and South Africa. Surely, then, the third world is still very much alive as a possibility. It is not a matter of cheering for third-world countries to make their revolutions; it is a dialectical matter of seeing that we here are involved in these areas and are busy trying to put them down, that they are part of our power relations.

But that tends to end up in moralism: "we shouldn't do this and we shouldn't do that in the third world." Once one has realized that, what is there to do? No particular politics follows as far as the first world itself is concerned. One tends to end up with Paul Sweezy's position where the only thing to do is to prevent interventions in the third world. This strikes me as a bit barren.

Well, what are the alternatives? We are talking about culture and culture is a matter of awareness; and it would not be a bad kind of awareness to generate that we in the superstate are at all times a presence in third-world realities, that our affluence and power are in the process of doing something to them. The form this awareness takes in American culture has to do not only with foreign policy but also with the notion that the US itself is a third-world country. In a way, we have become the biggest third-world country, in the production of unemployment, the production of non-production, the flight of factories and so on.

Why does that make us a third-world country? It seems like the definition of a first-world one.

If the third world is defined, as it sometimes has been, as the development of underdevelopment, then it does seem clear that we have begun to do this to ourselves as well. In any case, the apparent return to some finance capitalism with dizzying edifices of credit and paper no longer reposing on the infrastructure or "ground" of real production offers some peculiar analogies to current (poststructuralist) theory itself. Let's say that here the first world—if it does not revert back into third-world realities— unexpectedly and in a peculiar dialectical reversal begins to touch some features of third-world experience, perhaps another reason third-world culture has lately become one of our passionate interests.

In arguing against condemnation and celebration, you wish to encourage a critique which goes through postmodernism in a sort of "homeopathic" way.

To undo postmodernism homeopathically by the methods of postmodernism: to work at dissolving the pastiche by using all the instruments of pastiche itself, to reconquer some genuine historical sense by using the instruments of what I have called substitutes for history.

How is this "homeopathic" operation to be understood more specifically?

The figure of homeopathic medicine here does not imply that that is the only way culture functions, but it is often the case. Modernism, for example, was an experience of nascent commodification which fought reification by means of reification, in terms of reification. It was itself a gigantic process of reification internalized as a homeopathic way of seizing on this force, mastering it and opposing the result to reifications passively submitted to an external reality. I am wondering whether some positive features of postmodernism couldn't do that as well: an attempt somehow to master these things by choosing them and pushing them to their limits. There is a whole range of so-called oppositional arts, whether it's punk writing, or ethnic writing, which really try to use postmodern techniques—though for obvious reasons I dislike the term technique—to go through and beyond. It's certainly wrong to go down the list of contemporary trends and once again, in typical leftwing fashion, try and find out which is progressive. The only way through a crisis of space is to invent a new space.

Despite the disappearance of a sense of history, there is no lack of historical elements in postmodern culture.

When I talked about the loss of history, I didn't mean the disappearance of images of history, for instance in the cast of nostalgia film. The increasing number of films about the past are no longer historical but images, simulacra, pastiches of the past. It is effectively a way of satisfying a chemical craving for historicity with a product which is a substitute for it and which blocks it.

But historical images are always in a way substitutes.

That is not the way Lukács analyzed the historical novel in its emergent form. I would also argue that something like science fiction can occasionally be looked at as a way of breaking through to history in a new way, achieving a distinctive historical consciousness by way of the future rather than the past, becoming conscious of our present as the past of some unexpected future rather than as the future of a heroic national past (the traditional historic novel of Lukács). But nostalgia art gives us the image of various generations of the past as fashion-plate images, which entertain no determinable ideological relationship to other moments of time: they are not the outcome of anything, nor the antecedents of our present; they are simply images. This is the sense in which I describe them as substitutes for any genuine historical consciousness rather than specific new forms of the latter.

The cannibalizing of styles is part and parcel of this type of "historicity."

What the architects call historicism, the eclectic use of dead languages.

I first became aware of this a couple of years ago with regard to fashion, when the 50s was being mined along with its ideological orientation: the schlock of the Eisenhower epoch, the fascination with television series of that period and so forth. Now, when that seems exhausted, there is excavation of the 60s, not the politicized 60s but the 60s of the go-go girls. One can imagine that even the militant 60s can be used for stylistic innovation, rather in the manner in which Macy's department store instantly transforms East Village vogues into commercial values.

Perhaps one could write a history of these nostalgias. It would be plausible to say that in a moment of exhaustion with politics the images that are cannibalized and offered by nostalgia film are those of a great depoliticized era. Then, when unconsciously political drives begin to reawaken, they are contained by offering images of a politicized era. We are all happy to have a movie like *Reds*, but is that not also a nostalgia film?

Perhaps, but nostalgia is difficult to avoid in popular depictions of the past.

What is at stake is a historical situation and one can't wish this postmodern blockage of historicity out of existence by mere self-critical self-consciousness. If it's the case that we have a very real difficulty in imagining the radical difference with the past, then this difficulty cannot be overcome by an act of the will, by deciding that this is the wrong kind of history to have and that we ought to do it in some other way. This for me is the fascination with Doctorow's novels. Here we have a radical leftwing novelist who has seized the whole apparatus of nostalgia art, pastiche and postmodernism in order to work himself through them instead of attempting to resuscitate some older form of social realism, an alternative which would in itself become another pastiche. Doctorow's is not necessarily the only possible path, but I find it an intriguing attempt "homeopathically" to undo postmodernism by the methods of postmodernism: to work at dissolving the pastiche by using all instruments of what I have called substitutes for history.

In your terms this might be another version of third-worldism in the cultural sense. We come back to looking for some alternative place which is neither the past or the first world, the great moment of modernism, nor its present which is that of schizophrenic textuality.

But how is it possible, in a mode of cultural expression which, by definition, is superficial, to say anything about deep structures? After all, the essence of Marxism is to say something about what "really is."

There Doctorow is still my best example, for by turning the past into something which is obviously a black simulacrum he suddenly makes us realize that this is the only image of the past we have, in truth a projection on the walls of Plato's cave. This, if you like, is negative dialectics, or negative theology, an insistence of the very flatness and depthlessness of the thing which makes what isn't there very vivid. That is not negligible. It is not the reinvention of some sense of the past where one would fantasize about a healthier age of deeper historical sense: it is the use of these very limited instruments to show their limits. And it is not ironic.

But how does one use that perception of difference to get somewhere else? If you resort to homology, you've basically done the same thing that you criticize in Reds but not in Doctorow.

The problem of homologies (and the unsatisfactory nature of these parallels or analogies between levels) has been a constant theoretical concern for me. Something like homology does seem difficult to avoid when one attempts to correlate distinct semi-autonomous fields. I've played with alternative concepts: Sartre's notion of the *analagon* and Peirce's concept of the *interpretant*. Both of these stress the operation of reading analogies off the allegorical object, rather than discovering them ontologically, as "realities" in the world. And each seems in addition to contribute a little towards clarifying the process I've called cognitive mapping, the invention of ways of using one object and one reality to get a mental grasp of something else which one cannot represent or imagine. As an emblem of this process I might offer the picture of those hypersterilized laboratory chambers into which enormous gloves and instruments protrude, manipulated by the scientist from the outside. The normal body is doing one thing, but the results are taking place in another space altogether and according to other dimensions, other parameters. It must be a bewildering set of tasks to exercise, as far from our normal bodily operations as the deductive or abductive appropriation of the banana is for the laboratory monkey. But that, if it were possible, would give you an idea of the new kinds of representational process demanded here.

The personal "style" so typical of modernism has according to you become a mere code in postmodernism.

This is another feature developed primarily by post-structuralism, namely the eclipse of the old personal subject and ego. Modernism was predicated on the achievement of some unique personal style which could be parlayed out to the subject of genius, the charismatic subject, the supersubject if you like. If that subject has disappeared, the styles linked to it are no longer possible. A certain form of depersonalization thus seems implicit in all of this: even when modernism itself is pastiched, it is only an imitation of style, not style.

Still, I always insist on a third possibility beyond the old bourgeois ego and the schizophrenic subject of our organization society today: a *collective subject*, decentered but not schizophrenic. It emerges in certain forms of storytelling that can be found in third-world literature, in testimonial literature, in gossip and rumors and things of this kind. It is a storytelling which is neither personal in the modernist sense, nor depersonalized in the pathological sense of the schizophrenic text. It is decentered since the stories you tell there as an individual subject don't belong to you; you don't control them the way the master subject of modernism would. But you don't just suffer them in the schizophrenic isolation of the first-world subject of today. None of this is to reinvent style in the older sense.

Some years ago, in a wholly different context, you called the brush-stroke the very sign of the modern genius; pointing specifically to de Kooning's mega-brushstroke as the last gasp of some individualizing art. Yet the next morning neo-expressionism brought back this mega brushstroke with a vengeance. Would you then say that this was pastiche, not the surviving element of some older modernism?

Some of it is merely a pastiche of modernist subjectivity.

Certain of these painters, Immendorf for instance, were on the other hand quite explicitly political with interesting stories to tell.

A lot of it is European or from the semi-periphery of the American core (e.g. Canada). It would seem, for instance, that neo-expressionism flourished particularly in Italy and Germany, the two western countries which experienced the historical "break" of fascism. One could argue with Habermas here who sees the German version of neo-expressionism as reactionary. We, on the other hand, could perhaps use it in other ways, not classing it as a morbid attempt to reinvent a subjectivity which in the German tradition is tainted anyway.

And now we see the return of minimalism, blank surfaces and "neo-geo" forms looking rather like 60s and early 70s to me. The cannibalization of styles has apparently been "revved up," conceivably ending in some furious, vertiginous act of biting its own tail.

You suggest an interesting connection between Tafuri's rigorous anti-utopianism—his almost Adornian negative dialectics of architecture—and Venturi's celebration of Las Vegas: the system for both, is essentially a massively all-encompassing one which cannot be changed. The difference is that Tafuri stoically refuses it, while Venturi invents ways of "relaxing" within it.

For Tafuri, Venturi is himself part of an opposition which is rather that of Mies to Venturi. One solution is that of absolute Mallarmean purity and silence; the other is the abandonment of that final attempt at negative purity and the falling back into the world. The problem with Venturi's architecture or his "solution"—characteristic of a lot of poststructuralisms today—is the appeal to irony, which is a modernist solution. He wants to use the language of the vernacular of Las Vegas, but, being engaged in art and aesthetics, he also has to have some kind of minimal distance to it. All of this art, as Tafuri says, is predicated on distance and distance is always a failure: since it distances itself from what it wants to change, it can't change it.

This reminds me of your criticism of Lyotard's concept of postmodernism: he claims to have eliminated the master narratives but then smuggles them back in again.

His most famous statement on postmodernism is that it should prepare for the return of the great modernisms. Now does that mean the return of the great master narrative? Is there some nostalgia at work here? On the other hand, insofar as the refusal of narratives is viewed as the place of the perpetual present, of anarchist science to use Feyerabend's term (the random breaking of paradigms and so on), we're in full postmodernism.

So the master narratives in that sense are not dead.

All one has to do is to look at the reemergence of religious paradigms, whether it is Iran, or liberation theology, or American fundamentalism. There are all kinds of master narratives in this world which is presumably beyond narrative.

The appropriation of modernism in the United States, when it comes, is quite different from the European predecessors. Though in itself a depoliticized art, postwar modernism here is nevertheless employed in very instrumental ways.

The political elements of "original modernism" in its historical emergence were left out in this process of transplantation so that the various modernisms have been read as subjectivizing and inward-turning. Other features vanished too. The whole utopian and aesthetico-political element in modern architecture, Le Corbusier for example, is no longer visible when we are talking about great monuments and conventions imitated in the schools. At the same time one must say that this modernism was no longer being produced: there was not a living modernism that could have been encouraged in a different way.

You mention somewhere Habermas' defense of the idea of a possible high modernism again and point out that this seems to be a defense against a political reaction which in West Germany is still really anti-modernist. In this country the case is in fact the opposite, is it not! The Hilton Kramers here are obviously not defending radicalism. Defense of postmodernism—one thinks of Tom Wolfe— can on the other hand also be associated with rightwing politics.

The modernism Hilton Kramer wants to go back to is the subjectivizing modernism of the 50s, the American reading of modernism which has been sullied, lost its purity and so must be recovered. However, Habermas' modernism (I hesitate to call it the genuine article) is seen in the context of 1910 and is therefore something very different. Modernism elsewhere died a natural death and is thus no longer available, but modernism in Germany was of course cut short by Nazism and there is thus an unfulfilled character to that project which I presume someone like Habermas can attempt to take up again. But that option is not viable for us.

The coupure *in the "dominant" occurs, as you outline it, in the late 50s or early 60s. Art becomes completely enmeshed in the political economy of its own sphere, which in turn becomes part of a greater economic system. Emblematic among the pictorial artists here is Warhol, whom you contrast with van Gogh in the initial delineation of modernism/postmodernism. Warhol is perhaps almost too obvious a case. How does a contemporary of his like Rauschenberg fit in!*

Rauschenberg is transitional, coming in at the tail end of abstract expressionism but now in the most recent stuff developing a whole panoply of ways of doing postmodernism. His new works are all collage surfaces with the photographic images, of which there are, symptomatically, both modernist and postmodernist ones in the same work. The other thing about him is that he works a lot in third-world countries where a lot of these photographs are from.

In dealing with postmodernism, one can isolate people who made some pioneering contributions, but aesthetic questions about how great these are—questions that can legitimately be posed when you're dealing with modernism—make little sense. I don't know how great Rauschenberg is, but I saw a wonderful show of his in China, a glittering set of things which offered all kinds of postmodernist experiences. But when they're over, they're over. The textual object is not, in other words a work of art, a "masterwork" like the modernist monument was. The appreciation of it no longer requires the attachment of some permanent evaluation to the work as it would with the modernist painters or writers, and in that sense it is more of what I sometimes call a disposable text. You go into a Rauschenberg show and experience a process done in very expert and inventive ways; and when you leave, it's over.

What was the reaction of the Chinese audience?

Fascination, puzzlement. I tried to explain to my Chinese students about postmodernism, but for a general Chinese audience it would simply just be "western art." To understand it you have to understand it in our historical context: it isn't just modern art in general but a specific moment of it.

How are the traditional ways of apprehending art changing with all the great social transformations now going on in China? Is there an attempt to rejuvenate modernist notions of creativity, to replace tradition with western subjectivity?

It is not being replaced in that way. There is a lot of translation of western bestsellers but also of high culture; translations of *The Sound and the Fury*, Alice Walker's *The Color Purple*, but also lots of Arthur Haileys. Maybe I can explain it in terms of theory. The Chinese are now interested in two kinds of theory: western theory and traditional Chinese theory. It is felt that both of these are levers that can get them out of the kind of essentially Soviet cultural theory they were trained on in the 50s. As Deng You-mei, one of the most interesting Chinese writers, said to me: "We are not much interested in western modernism as such. We are bored by novels that don't tell stories." In other words, the elaborate symbolism you find in James Joyce or Virginia Woolf doesn't do anything for them. Right after the fall of the Gang of Four, it was important to recoup some of what had been forgotten, but when I got there and thought I was bringing some enlightenment about Kafka, they informed me that they had been interested in this at the end of the 70s but not anymore. Deng You-mei said: "What you have to realize is that for us realism is also western. Our realisms come out of the western traditions; certainly the dominant realism of the 50s was the Soviet one. We think there is something different from both modernism and realism and that is traditional Chinese storytelling."

This is the third world's input into the whole poststructuralist debate on representation which is loosely assimilated to realism over here: if it is representation and realism, it's bad, and you want to break it up with the decentered subject and so on. But these Chinese strings of episodic narratives fall outside this framework. They are an example of going back to the sort of storytelling which one finds both in the third world's discovery of its own way of telling stories and in a certain form of post-modernism. So one has to rethink this question of realism and representation in the Chinese context. I took a tour through some famous grottos with stalactites. Imagine the bourgeois public that hates modern art and here in the same way you have a guide with a little light projector who proclaims: "Look at these rocks. There is an old man, three children, there's the goddess, etc." And you think: this is the most rudimentary form of what we denounce as representation in the west, a public that thinks in these terms. But China developed, alongside this popular realistic or representational perception, a very different kind of spatial perception in the evolution of the written characters. It is possible, therefore, that an oppositional culture in China might take the form of a revival of certain kinds of popular ways of seeing things, ways which would not necessarily seem the same to us.

What about allegory here? You have referred to allegory in third-world novel as well as with regard to postmodernism.

That was one attempt to theorize a difference in third-world culture from our own. In non-hegemonic situations, in situations of economic or cultural subalternity, there tends to be a reference to the national situation that is always present and always felt in a way that it cannot be in the dominant culture of the superstate. But this type of analysis is not intended as a program for art to the effect that we should now begin to write allegories.

The Chinese cave mentioned before cannot be described as one of hyperspace.

Nor does it really betoken any radical cultural difference. This is exactly what the American tourist would do with the caves in Louisville, Kentucky. Whether it is a revolutionary peasantry looking at these or an American tourist is not relevant to that conception. If, as Bourdieu has explored, people have no institutional reason to justify the aesthetic operation to themselves, namely by seeing that it is somehow good and a sign of social distinction to have a little artistic training, then they have to have another reason for doing it, and that reason ends up in seeing likenesses. Seeing likenesses in this basically mimetic sense is not inherently a sign of the people or the popular either, but it is certainly an interesting index of the relationship of culture to people for whom culture is not a socially signifying property or attribute.

In postmodernism on the other hand, everyone has learned to consume culture through television and other mass media, so you no longer need a rationale. You look at advertising billboards, you look at collages of things because it is there in external reality. The whole matter of how you justify to yourself the time of consuming culture disappears: you are no longer even aware of consuming it. Everything is culture, the culture of the commodity. That's a very significant feature of postmodernism, which accounts for the disappearance from it of the traditional theories, justifications and rationalizations of what we used to call aesthetics (and of concepts of high culture).

Postmodern art may in some sense be disposable texts but its monetary value is of course anything but disposable and transient. Warhol, it should be underlined, does not appear in the model as, traditionally understood, an originator. Your object is the systemic, not the evaluation of contemporary artists.

In trying to theorize the systematic, I was using certain of these things as allegories. From this angle it makes no sense trying to look for individual trends, and individual artists are only interesting if one finds some moment where the system as a whole, or some limit of it, is being touched. Evaluation does come in since one can imagine a much less interesting postmodernist exhibition and one would then have to say that that painter is not as good as Rauschenberg. But this is not the same kind of use of aesthetic axiological evaluation that people felt themselves able to do when they were handling modernism, making relative assessments of Proust against Mann for example.

All great modernists invented modernism in their own fashion. It is likewise clear that no one single postmodernist can give us postmodernism since it is a system involving a whole range of things. Warhol is emblematic of one feature of post-modernism and the same goes for Paik. They allow you to analyze and specify something partial, and in that sense their activities are surely original: they have identified a whole range of things to do and then moved in to colonize this new space. However, this is not original in the world-historical sense of the great modernist creator. If a single artist actually embodied all of these things, Laurie Anderson for example, she would no doubt, be trans-cending postmodernism. But where Wagner, in the *Gesamtkunst-werk*, may have done something like that in a key moment of modernism, Laurie Anderson's *Gesamtkunstwerk* does not do that for a non-systematizable system, a non-totalizable system.

This leaves no great space for criticism of individual works. What is the task once one has related the part to the whole?

If they are no longer *works*, in other words. This is particularly true for video, which one usually sees in batches. You have put the finger on the fundamental methodological problem of the criticism of postmodernism. For to talk about any single one of these postmodernist texts is to reify it, to turn it into the work of art it no longer is, to endow it with a permanence and monument-ality that it is its vocation to dispel. A critic supposed to analyze individual texts is thus faced with almost insuperable problems: the moment you analyze a single piece of video art you do it violence, you remove some of its provisionality and anonymity and turn it into a masterpiece or at least a privileged text again. It's much easier to deal with it in terms of trends: here's a new trend (described as such and such) and here's another. But the whole language of trends is the dialectic of modernism.

We are returning here to the problem of evaluation.

The Cubans, who have a different system, point out that our sense of value, in a good as well as bad sense, is given to us by the art market. One possible opposite of this would be a situation— I'm expanding on their argument—where only a few styles would be permitted. But in a country like Cuba, devoid of an art market but exceedingly pluralistic culturally, where you will find everything from social realism to pop-art to abstract expressionism, there is no mechanism which can say that this is more advanced than that. One begins to sense then that the art market has an almost religious-ontological function for us. We don't have to face this radical plurality of style of "anything goes" because somebody is always around to tell us that this thing is a little newer than that one. Or more valuable, since I think now our value system depends on that transmission of the market mechanism.

So how do the Cubans evaluate?

It is a real problem: they don't know. They confront the death of value (in Nietzsche's version, the death of God) in a much more intense way than we do. We still have these marvelous theological mechanisms by which we pick things out and sort them. They have a more interesting problem of what the value of art would be in a situation of complete freedom, in the Nietzschean sense: freedom, that is, to do anything you want. Then value enters a crisis also of the Nietzschean type. This is not the case where there is still a market, or where only a few styles are permitted and anyone who pushes against the paradigm can be identified. Then, too, you certainly know where you stand in terms of value.

You say somewhere that the dialectical imagination to which

Marcuse refers has atrophied. Yet at the same time you say that a constitutive feature of mass culture is that it satisfies a deep utopian impulse in the consumer. If the imagination has been atrophied, the impulse has not?

Marcuse, ironically, was the great theorist of autonomy of culture. The problem is that he reverts in a much simpler manner to Adorno's modernism; to its autonomy. But Adorno's great aesthetics—the aesthetics you write when it is impossible to write aesthetics—involves time and death and history: experience is historical and condemned to death in a sense. Marcuse's concept finally simplified that complexity out of Adorno, taking up an older modernist model which is not now helpful. His notion of the utopian impulse is a different matter. The objection there is that he falls back on a position where the autonomy of art still permits a kind of full expression of the utopian impulse.

Adorno's negative dialectics is criticized in your account for allowing no resistance to the overall system. Nothing, seemingly, is to be done. You point to the similarities here with the poststructuralist tendency to see the system as complete and completely unchangeable in its systematicity; and I suppose one could indeed say that about Foucault et al. at certain times. The result is pessimism, and it matters less that the first model is dialectical while the latter is one of heterogeneity and contingency. Yet a quick reading of F. Jameson leaves one with a distinct residue of pessimism as well.

The whole point about the loss in postmodernism of the sense of the future is that it also involves a sense that nothing will change and there is no hope. Facile optimism is on the other hand not helpful either.

In "going through" poststructuralism and postmodernism and preserving its moment of truth, you are intermittently very hard and negative, quite rightly emphasizing the politically unsavory effects.

There one can make a distinction. There is a difference between the production of ideologies about this reality and the reality itself. They necessarily demand two different responses. I am not willing to engage this matter of pessimism and optimism about postmodernism since we are actually referring there to capitalism itself: one must know the worst and then see what can be done. I am much more polemical about postmodernist *theories*. Theories which either exalt this or deal with it in moral ways are not productive and that I think one can say something about.

The reconquest of a sense of place here, the attainment of a new cartography, is primarily a call directed to the left itself. We are not referring to any great political practice but about arguing with the 1500 people who happen to be deeply influenced by Deleuze and Guattari. For a large proportion of the intellectuals of self-professed radical persuasion would no doubt describe themselves as heavily influenced by poststructuralist ideologies.

That's why it's worthwhile to get a systemic sense where all these things come from so that we can see what our influences are and what to do about them. The proliferation of theoretical discourses was healthy because it led to some awareness of their political consequences. In moments of economic crisis or intervention abroad, people can determine more clearly what any given theory does or allows one to do. It is a matter of theoretical and historical self-knowledge, and what I am engaged in is in fact a struggle within theory as much as anything else. If I were making videos I would talk about this in a different way.

In that respect, yours is a systematic project of building "totalizing" models, something which, to understate the case, has been fairly unpopular among the western intelligentsia in the last decade. Are people now perhaps more receptive to "model-building"?

They are more receptive to the historical features of it, to the idea of thinking historically about it. They are not necessarily more receptive to the Marxist version of this historical inquiry but perhaps they willing to entertain it on some supermarket-pluralist basis.

The historical dimension counteracts the postmodernist immersion in the present, the dehistoricizing or nonhistorical project. In that sense it goes outside the postmodern paradigm.

That is essentially the rhetorical trick or solution that I was attempting: to see whether by systematizing something which is resolutely unhistorical, one couldn't force a historical way of thinking *at least about that*. And there are some signs that it is possible to go around it, to *outflank* it.

This interview took place on July 4, 1986 and was first published, in shorter form, in *Flash Art* (Milano), 131 (1986). This longer version is reprinted with permission from *Social Text*, 17 (1987).

Postmodern Jameson

Martin Donougho
University of South Carolina

The premise on which this anthology rests seems to be double. On the one hand it aims to examine and assess Fredric Jameson's writing in order to understand better that complex category/phenomenon that has come to be called "post-modernism" (for in his recent work he is as helpful as anyone in clarifying postmodernism as both theory and cultural practice).[1] And on the other, it asks how postmodernism fits (if it can properly fit) into the trajectory of Jameson's own critical project, that of a self-consciously Marxist theory and criticism, and whether his attending to it marks a change of motive, method, or presupposition. Both aims are critical as well as expository: it is possible either that his approach distorts what it describes, or that postmodernism represents a test case for his hermeneutic method.

But to begin with, a few general and preliminary remarks, written, if not on water, then on the sands of a postmodernist time. One problem in coming to terms with modernism is how to conceptualize at all adequately the mediating links (a) with modernity as a period, and (b) with modernization as a socio-economic process of rationalization, bureaucratization, etc. In his writings through the 70s and 80s, Jameson posits a linkage between semi-autonomous levels, one that is neither formal homology nor organic, totalizing ontology. Mediation is for him a kind of dialectical allegorizing, a transcoding operation that goes beyond the structuralist model he so sharply criticized in *The*

Prison-House of Language.[2] The problem of how to mediate (or describe the mediations) between distinct levels recurs and is exacerbated with postmodernism, as Jameson is aware. In his tentative diagnoses and prognoses, he has attempted to combine phenomenological description and socio-historical analysis.[3] The question remains how the combination of those different activities is to be theorized, and whether the allegorical mode Jameson had earlier favored is now formally adequate to present the relation (it may be that, to paraphrase Benjamin, there is allegory, but not for us).

At any rate, we should at the outset clearly distinguish, as many discussions do not, several different though connected realms or levels:

(i) Postmodernity as a *Lebenswelt*, a structure of experience or mode of sensibility with certain specific features.

(ii) Postmodernization, or some form of "late capitalism," "postindustrial" *social technology.* In this "post-age" (Ulmer) of communications and computers, we might facetiously speak of a data-base/superstructure model of explanation, as long as we remember that this classic model of explanation and ideological analysis has (after Althusser) been put in question.

(iii) Postmodernism as an *artistic practice*, i.e. the various contributions of literature (where—if we discount an earlier theological application and some references in the 40s and 50s— the term first entered common usage in the early 70s to refer to certain trends in American poetry and the novel), of theatre and dance ("performance" art, etc.), and of what an inspired misprint in one of Wellmer's articles calls "popstmodern" architecture. We have to bear in mind that there may be no unity within or between these arts, let alone across national frontiers, and that as the term acquires common currency it takes on new connotations, some of them ideological ("postmodernism" itself becoming part of the practice and its jargon of inauthenticity).

(iv) Lastly, postmodernism as *theoretical reflection* on the previous areas, or as a "discipline" that threatens to escape disciplinary confines into a realm of dissemination and conversation, a new kind of "scientific" knowledge, its mode variously thought of as pragmatist, anarchist, playful, paralogistic:

poststructuralism, deconstruction, post-Philosophical theory (philosophy as literature, Rorty would say)—but in any event, whether as sober analysis or as euphoric program, marking at long last an end to the illusion of self-transparency in thought.

In sum, in the postmodern we may hear announced the end of man, the end of ideology and the (industrial) capitalism it serves, the end of art, and the end of philosophy (of the project of modernity, of Enlightenment as dream of rationality).

Yet such an announcement is hardly without problems. For (as Wellmer rightly points out) we are here trying to characterize an historical transition as if it were a phenomenon to be dispassionately observed from afar or an image of a discrete entity; whereas really we can speak of it only provisionally and from some (theoretical, philosophical, moral) *perspective*—a view *of* the present and *in* the present (see Wellmer, "On the Dialectic of Modernism and Postmodernism").[4] I might add that modernism itself suffers from this same malady of self-awareness: it exists as the fact of (what we refer to as) modernism (Cavell[5]) or as the fact of (what we refer to as) art, in the era of its "de-definition." Indeed such historical awareness is part and parcel of the phenomenon itself, a feature that becomes paradoxical in the case of a postmodernism that is said to have elided history altogether.

In what follows I shall address three main questions which I think raise difficulties for Jameson (as he himself might disarmingly admit):

(1) What is postmodernism, such that it may in principle be distinguished from modernism? Is it an end or a beginning? How far is it tied up with the problematic legacy of modernism, as at once embodying the urge to innovate and laying down the "tradition" of the new? Is it anything more than an index of transition, when as Gramsci says, "The crisis consists precisely in the fact that the old is dying and the new cannot be born; in this interregnum a great variety of morbid symptoms appear" (*Prison Notebooks*). This is a question raised by many—e.g. Albrecht Wellmer, Jean-François Lyotard, Manfredo Tafuri, Paul de Man among others. Implicitly it is raised by Jameson himself when he notes that a genealogizing perspective such as the one he adopts avoids the illusion of continuity created by talk of source,

influence, declension, sedimentation (essentially a *modernist* vocabulary, and one that therefore begs the question as to whether we have said good-bye to the modern). Yet we might equally well ask whether it does not instead risk the illusion of *dis*continuity, thus begging the obverse question as to whether there really is something new here?[6]

(2) Is it possible—given the peculiar nature of the beast—to analyze and characterize it at all, to put it behind bars in some taxonomic or historical scheme? (Compare Wellmer's comment, already noted.) Futhermore, are there not formal problems in acquiring the necessary retrospective (?) distance and focus, or with telling (as Lyotard has it[7]) "le grand récit de la fin des grands récits?" To speak of particular works or artists, of specific styles or tendencies, is to reify our object of study, "to endow it with a permanence and monumentality that it is its vocation to dispel," as Jameson himself warns ("RPM," 70-71, above). Or again: "As for systematic accounts of postmodernism . . . (including my own), when they succeed they fail . . . " ("PAU," 16)—because in hypostatizing the phenomenon they suck it dry of all potential, especially any political meaning and effect it might contain. Given therefore that the analyst is necessarily implicated in the object analyzed, we are led to a further question:

(3) Where is Jameson himself to be located in our contemporary cultural zoo? This question has two aspects. First, whether we take him in his role as cultural critic or as political theorist, is his *own* position a postmodernist one, e.g. when he writes "like it or not, this aesthetic is a part of us"("ACI," 87)? For at the same time he takes his distance from postmodernism. While declaring that a moral judgment is not allowed, he nevertheless manages to criticize this new shift, seeking to go behind its back, as it were to "place" it ideologically, dialectically, and historically. Second, how does this new direction in his own work modify or throw new light on his overall project, a project we may label "critical" in both senses? Here I have in mind, for example, the utopian element that has always been present in his thinking: does that survive unscathed once we are seen as imprisoned in this new culture of superficiality, when even art and the artwork are thoroughly commodified? Or again—given

Althusser's problems in separating science and ideology—do Jameson's own figurations become merely regulative devices, in effect "metanarratives" of (il)legitimation?

These three sorts of questions can be summarized thus: What is postmodernism? How is it possible to get a fix on it? How can we get a fix on Jameson? In sketching out some answers I shall argue that Jameson is forced to abandon the narrative mode that had served him well as he traced a genealogical line of allegorical figuration from Romanticism through realism and down to (our own?) modernism. Jameson was never able to confront modernism directly, it must be noted, and could present it only via its genealogical preconditions; it was a kind of vanishing point in his historical perspective. But with postmodernism the paradox of unpresentability, especially via narrative, has now to be met on its own terms (or lack of them). Ultimately, I shall claim, Jameson has to ground his "position," whether theoretical or practical, in a kind of utopian optimism, polemically opposed to (say) Tafuri's and Adorno's pessimistic modernistic perspectives. In this he risks wanting to have his cake and eat it. He will treat postmodernism as a cultural period and phenomenon, yet allow that it escapes all such determinacy. He will seek to "decode" postmodernism while admitting that now there is nothing there to decode. He will note the spread of simulacra in culture, while remaining stubbornly attached to an aesthetics (and ethics) of work rather than textuality. He will call for the figuring of "enclaves" of resistance to the dominant hegemony of late capitalism and its commodification of the world, while admitting that the latter appears to be total; indeed, such a prefiguring of utopia is almost a defiance of the present. All this is done with the most honorable of motives; that of (in his own metaphor) keeping ajar the door to the future.

I. Beyond Modernism

Let me broach the first of my questions: what serves *radically* to mark off modernism from postmodernism? Or (to rephrase), what marks the break in Jameson's concerns from the late 70s on?

Until that point, postmodernism had not figured even peripherally in his scheme of things. Instead modernism had been what one might call the absent center of Jameson's work. This was so from his first book, on Sartre, through *Marxism and Form*, his analysis and critique of structuralism in *The Prison-House of Language*, to his most comprehensive and ambitious work, *The Political Unconscious*. Indeed, the unconscious thematized in the latter belongs to modernism and is the result of its repression of history.

Jameson understands modernity as (in terms of the *Lebenswelt*) the process of reification. Art both encodes and instantiates such a process. It foregrounds what proves problematic in reality, specifically: (a) temporality, here coded as *narrative* self-understanding, (b) the image or sensorium, (c) subjectivity, the self, resulting in a specifically modern (non)character subbing for the truant epic or romance "hero," and (d) the need to escape the marketplace by means of the compensating assertion of *style*, a thickening of the material texture of the work, a certain self-referentiality, etc. For both modernism and modernity, narrative paradigms are rendered untenable, thanks to the experience and articulation of a veritable *fabula rasa*. The structures of meaning in the everyday world collapse, lose their "aura," and the artist is forced back on the image as such, and on the medium of perception and the senses. The monadic, strenuous, bourgeois self typical of realism becomes decentered to be experienced as the diffused and serial effects of anonymous social structures and processes, a mere colligation of roles. The loss of such certainties—of narrative continuity, of immanent meaning, of selfhood—appears as at once painful and unavoidable.

Such is the pathos—the sickness, Nietzsche says—of the modern. But we should note (a point to come back to) that the problematic extends further, to modernism itself. For example, the modernist style itself becomes more and more illusory, a *fata morgana*. The symbolic image that was supposed to escape the commodification of the lifeworld risks being fetishized itself. Modernism thus tends towards reification; works of art produced under its aegis become almost from the start no more than wares to be purveyed in the market.

If modernism and its discontents are the result of recent history, let me go back to how Jameson tells of their emergence in *The Political Unconscious*, first recapping his story, then turning to his method. As Hayden White has perceived, Jameson's narrative is at the same time narrative analysis.[8] He analyzes the *combinatoire* of the nineteenth century literary imagination—its *pensée sauvage*—from the survival of romance in *Märchen*, through the forging of a properly realist narrative and agency, then via naturalism, up to the dawn of modernism proper in the twilight world of Conrad.

Two aspects of Jameson's procedure merit comment. He employs allegorical interpretations of his chosen texts, decoding them (i) as symbolic acts, a rewriting of a political, social, and legal subtext; (ii) as enacting a syntax of oppositional codes, usually drawn from class conflicts, for the sake of which the story is told (the formalist reversal); and (iii) as the attempt to resolve in artistic terms contradictions in the underlying reality, *viz.* those inhering in the modes of production. The latter—History, or the Real, in Jameson's terms—cannot be represented directly. "History is not a text," he writes (though, we might add, history is). It can only appear allegorically, as if in code. It can for example be glimpsed in the fissures *between* periods (feudal, high capitalist, etc), i.e. in the mixing of generic modes and narrative codings. Hence Jameson's interest in peripheral writers like Manzoni or Conrad; they manage to "mediate" *between* the combinatorial possibilities of these modes, e.g. between romance (feudalism, surfacing as the popular novel) and reification (surfacing as the modernist foregrounding of style), and even (in the diffused mechanics of Conrad's or Wyndham Lewis' sentences) looking ahead to postmodernism. Such mediations reveal the deep structure of History as manifest in the different generic and ideological codings.

The second aspect of Jameson's treatment I wish to point to is the paradox that he never treats modernism directly (Lewis is hardly the paradigmatic modernist). Modernism is the absent center of his project. And that paradox is rooted in the further paradox that modernity and the modern state have lost any intrinsic meaning or aura they might once have had. As phenomena they cannot be figured or represented, any more than History itself. Like Nostromo's Costaguana, the state has evolved to the point where it has no history and no heroes; it has no need of their legitimating function. All a realist story can do is tell of its formation, as of a black hole, which sucks in narrative and centered selfhood, or at least renders them epiphenomenal.

If realism can be seen (a) as comprising tales traced on the body politic and (b) as the forging of a strenuous selfhood, modernism amounts to the negation of realism in irony. It admits to the loss of "aura" and must problematize both narrative and character (or character-based action). But besides being the *expression* of reification—the disenchantment and commodification of the lifeworld—modernism is also *resistance* to it—a desperate attempt through sheer style to hold out against reality. It abstracts from history and reference, maintaining a precarious composure as a differential play of signifier-signified. That is to fight reification by means of reification, rationalization through a rationalizing of the aesthetic medium. Adorno was one of the first to identify the ironic logic of this move, and its attendant danger of fetishization. Aesthetic semblance (*Schein*) promises redemption from a reified world, but its very semblance (of formal self-sufficiency) is mere seeming, a blindness to the reality of which it is a part.[9]

The same resource and ideological danger may be seen in the intellectual or disciplinary analogue to modernism, namely formalism, whereby everything is reduced to relations without terms and without a history that has now become merely the "meaning effect" of structure. The irony here is that such an abstraction is precisely suited to a capitalist system reducing culture to such a nexus of commodities, a total system of signs. Hence Jameson's critique of structuralism: it lays itself open to the sheer contingency of history, but it also expresses the cultural logic of capitalism and so may be co-opted (as Jameson co-opts Lacanian-Greimasian syntactics) for ideological analysis. Hence too Jameson's attempt to go beyond Althusser's model of "structural" causality by going through it and out the other side.

What results is akin to the "expressive" model familiar from dialectical criticism and hermeneutics, though it claims to be non-totalizing, to use "totality" as no more than a critical category. Jameson never identifies his method as such. Perhaps I may dub it "figural realism," to bring out the affinity with and difference from Hayden White's tropological procedure, called by Jameson "figural relativism"("FRP"). White himself has recently applied the term to Jameson, with of course a different purpose: that of bringing out the parallel with Erich Auerbach's notion of *figura* (Auerbach was Jameson's teacher, by the way). If he is epistemologically a realist, it is no naive realism, then, but one thoroughly infused with Nietzschean ironies, aware that history is written (that is, lived) genealogically. A narrative—in this case Marxist, utopian, told by the collective subject—is taken as prefiguring History. In turn History (or the Real) is to be interpreted as the fulfillment of our collective narrative figuration. What is important for present purposes is the fact (if it is a fact) that modernism still harbors the utopian impulses that was explicit in romanticism and in the genre of romance. However reified it becomes, however "unpresentable," that hermeneutic and expressive promise is always there, for Jameson, and makes possible both his narrative and his narrative analysis.

Like Jameson, Lyotard is ironic at modernism's expense. But whereas Jameson sees modernism as harboring the traces of a collective future, Lyotard sees in it a guise for nostalgia.

> Modern aesthetics is an aesthetic of the sublime, though a nostalgic one. It allows the unpresentable to be put forward only as the missing contents; but the form . . . continues to offer to the reader or viewer matter for solace and pleasure." (*Postmodern Condition*, 81)

Which provides a convenient bridge to Jameson's encounter with postmodernism as the uncanny, the *"unheimlich,"* the desire to be at home nowhere. For where Lyotard places such features on the obverse side of modernism, Jameson wants to allegorize them, just as he had with modernism. In his view postmodernism amounts to nothing more than a new coding of material reality.

In his *New Left Review* article Jameson brings out the novelty of postmodernism by glancing at Heidegger's 1937 essay "The Origin of the Work of Art"—I'm tempted to add, ". . . in the Age of Mechanical Reproducibility"! Heidegger takes Van Gogh's painting of the old shoes (or is it the shoes themselves?) as opening up the rift between earth and world so as to allow us to sense the reliability of use objects, lodged in their narrow world—their pathways, we might say—between birth, labor, and death.[10] We may view this as a late example of a Romantic aesthetic of expression, with its emphasis on the sheer eruption of origin, the punctual creation of order out of the unnamable. But it is also an aesthetic of the *sublime*, and in its attack on the subject and its advocacy of repetition it resembles the modernist articulation. Nostalgia becomes ontalgia (to re-use Raymond Queneau's wonderful neologism).

Contrast this model with Andy Warhol's "Diamond Dust Shoes," which elides vernacular and elite modes, indulges and foregrounds the fetishistic element in the image, refuses the imputation of an inner essence expressing itself in some unique work of art, levels out emotion to a pallid and uninvolved succession of intensities. Here we have the *Erlebnis* and aesthetic of postmodernism proper, which Jameson analyzes into several parts:[11]

1. A new *depthlessness*, a lack of interiority—a notion that seems to me akin to Cavell's and Fried's term "theatricalization" to capture a rhetorical turn in modern art.[12] Interest and desire are directed solely at the sheer image or signifier, the simulacrum, the medium as such, the spectacle. Pastiche—"blank parody," without point, a diffused application of available styles—becomes its privileged vehicle.

2. The *historicist effacing of history*, through the diffused application of available styles, free-floating and jumbled together. This is most obvious in architecture, where the term was first applied by Charles Jencks to the "dual coding" of old and new. Note that this is more than the modernists' antihistorical concern with history, a concern Tafuri finds already in Brunelleschi and in sixteenth-century classicism (*Theories and History of Architecture*). Yet Jameson admits that Venturi's mixing of generic allusions is closer to irony (a modernist making of a point) than to pastiche; and if irony is hard to read, even more so is its lack.

3. A *waning of affect*, especially in connection with the

previous point[13]: a loss of mourning (as Lyotard puts it) along with any residual historicist pathos. At the same time, expression is replaced by new random *intensities*, as the body is plugged into the new electronic media (a mode Jameson nicely terms the "hysterical sublime"). Here Jameson seems to allude to the Deleuze-Lyotard schizophrenic model of a pure energetics.

4. The *decentering of self* announced by structuralist and post-structuralist writers like Foucault, Barthes, Althusser and Lacan (whose analysis of schizophrenia as a breakdown in the chain of signifiers is taken as emblematic of our new condition).

5. A sense of *placelessness*, a diffused experience of space, pre-eminently in the urban environment, and in our post- (or popst-) modern architecture, which conspires to shock the body in new ways, elides the distinction between individual building and urban structure, effaces any sense of place—there's no *there* there—and conditions not so much a new community as the sheer movement of communication (escalators, gondolas, etc., or an emphasis on the phatic—which is what Laurie Anderson is all about). The sheer "spacing" emphasized by certain poststructuralists has its analogue here; we cannot fix or totalize a "reading" of where we are, but we must defer, disseminate, or multiply meaning.[14]

6. A new social technology of *electronic media*, based on or rather expressing a new mode of production, one less of monopoly capitalism and imperialism than of a global economy or *multinational corporations*.[15]

7. The *infinite play of the signifier*—the bare, surface image—as opposed to a modernist celebration of the sign: now the primacy (and even relevance) of signified or determinate meaning is denied, not merely reference (History, the Real). This superabundance of the image or signifier is close to what Adorno calls "the crisis of semblance (*Schein*)," though Adorno takes a different path from postmodernism.

8. Where Adorno hopes to maintain a certain critical space for the aesthetic, via a modernist negation of the reified lifeworld, postmodernism accedes to what Jameson calls the *abolition of critical distance*. This last bastion of resistance—art and the work of art—is colonized too, while conversely the whole of culture has become aestheticized, no more than a nihilist "society of the

spectacle." In Jameson's project, accordingly, a certain tension is thus set up between the need for a "cognitive mapping" of cultural formations and the impossibility of taking one's distance so as to be able to accomplish this.

II. The Postmodern as Period (?)

Now let me belatedly turn (or return) to my initial question: What is so different about the postmodern? Isn't it just more of the same, but gaudier and unabashed? Differences there are, but are they sufficient to warrant a claim to novelty? Quickly to enumerate them:

First, literature is no longer the standard bearer of the new: with the hegemony of a general culture over literature, impure and popular "arts" such as film and architecture move to center-stage. And Jameson becomes much more the cultural rather than narrowly literary critic (though that side of his activities—attention to cinema, science-fiction, painting, etc.—was there all along). I would add (though Jameson himself makes little of this) that postmodernism and poststructuralism alike move away from *work* to *text*—in Barthes' useful phrase—and from production of an object to dissemination of a field (of force). And (to anticipate) this leads to unresolved tensions in Jameson's position, which still seems focused on an aesthetics and a politics of production and expression.

Such a shift brings with it a second. Whereas the modernist crisis was above all *temporal* and expressed itself in the impossibility of narrative paradigms, the postmodernist crisis is primarily *spatial*, as we have observed. We can no longer get a fix either on the environment or on the map. Moreover, whereas Jameson was able to co-opt Lacan and Althusser ironically to place the modernist ideology in history (via coding operations of sedimentation and anticipation) it is much more difficult as he concedes to place postmodernism in anything like the same way—a point I shall return to. The reason in brief is that whereas a formalist "meaning effect" could be interpreted as a "truth effect" (as Jameson has it), postmodernism eschews meaning (the signified) altogether, even as recovered in a recursive coding of language and metalanguage.

Third, this loss of center, interiority, place, meaning, and definition, is no longer taken as something to be mourned. Indeed this loss of loss, this invasion of the body-snatcher, is to be embraced, with your technological arms (as Laurie Anderson might say). Everything human is now alien to me.

Fourth, in place of formalist semiosis we have the dissemination of the signifier without a signified. Everything tends towards the condition of signifier. No distancing metalanguage, but only metaphor, language "beside itself" (which is why postmodernism and poststructuralism resist being placed and will not adopt "positions"). In lifeworld and artistic practice alike, the relation of signifier to meaning is one of sublimity: we can no longer figure it out. Discourse and figure become incommensurable (Lyotard). The very image becomes fetishized, on sale, on show.

Still, it is not obvious that these differences—so well described on the phenomenological level—amount to a difference of principle or period. Rather they serve merely to bring out the problematic already inherent in modernity and modernism. To quote Lyotard once more:

> The postmodern would be that which, in the modern, puts forward the unpresentable in presentation itself; that which denies itself the solace of the good forms, the consensus of a taste which would make it possible to share collectively the nostalgia for the unattainable. (*Postmodern Condition*, 81)

Or again more paradoxically:

> A work can become modern only if it is first postmodern. Postmodernism thus understood is not modernism at its end but in the nascent state, and this state is constant. (*Postmodern Condition*, 79)[16]

Thus challenged, Jameson has two further responses, it seems to me. For in the fifth place, Jameson would refer the change to a shift from monopoly capital (and its mechanical and electric technology) to the global logic of multi-nationals and a "post-industrial" society (the age of media, and nuclear-powered or electronic machinery). One must add that although he appeals, as noted, to Ernest Mandel's authority here, his point is not so much to make a factual claim as to offer a genealogical perspective; he wants to identify a "cultural dominant," not engage in rigid periodizing. Even so the stated *need* for such a shift of view may not convince. (Jameson uses postmodernism in architecture to show how high modernism is what we must go beyond; but the "need" here is local, and perverse.)

That seems less important, in any case, than the appeal to a sixth differential, which we may place on the side of praxis rather than theory, or rather, on the practical side of theory (the two are hardly to be separated after all). For what is most important to Jameson is that we avoid not just Lyotard's paralogistic quietism, but also a kind of closed historical narrative according to which we arrive as on a darkling plain at the end of history, our possibilities all played out. Such a polemical thrust emerges most clearly in his essay on Manfredo Tafuri (the Marxist theoretician and historian of architecture), in which Tafuri's pessimistic or at least stoic diagnosis of modernism is compared with the closed narratives of Barthes and Adorno (see "ACI," *passim*). In their stead Jameson enters a plea for what he calls the "Gramscian" alternative of a "long march through institutions"; a "counter-hegemony" that will work, not through the politics of enclaves, seeding the new society (something projected already and unsuccessfully by revolutionary modernism[17]), but through the holding open of imaginative possibilities (for architects, but equally for their customers, that is, us). Either we view ourselves as trapped within the now rather pointless rites of modernism, or else postmodernism may be seen as offering a new beginning—and who knows where the project may lead. To the objection that this makes it a matter of consciousness alone, Jameson replies that "We are talking about culture and culture is a matter of awareness" ("RPM," 58, above).[18] What we may glimpse here is a Sartrian attitude to history as project.

III. Mapping the Postmodern

Such an option sets the scene for some closing remarks on my second and third questions. For if the postmodern really is new, a complete elision of history (even the genealogy of modernism), then Jameson's allegorical method (renamed "cognitive mapping") is compromised. Let us suppose (as seems plausible) that critical distance is no longer possible, that even the aesthetic (*contra* Habermas) has been colonized, as culture reduces to a play of simulacra. Horkheimer and Adorno's "solution" to the ubiquity of commodifying reason—the gesture of mimesis of nature which nevertheless avoids nostalgia for some original, a gesture that cannot be "thought" in categories—is ruled out, because mimesis will always reduce to mere "simulation." And Althusser's gymnastic efforts to distinguish science and ideology demonstrate only that we cannot stand outside or "see through" the strategies of containment which constitute the lifeworld, art, and reflection alike.[19] The total system has become unnamable, unpresentable, unfigurable.

How then can we (or Jameson) escape? How can we "map" our individual experience on the total face of the universe, as Jameson urges ("PCL," 89f)? Or again, how can we historicize postmodernism, place its very placelessness, both in theory and in a practice that will perhaps develop a non-monadic self and a body able to absorb and yet resist the multiple inputs of the new urban environment? All that Jameson has done so far is offer a genealogy of legitimation—or rather, of "illegitimation"—with respect to specific economies of desire; as if to show how history has arrived at its current state of disenchantment and superficiality.

We are here in a double impasse: trapped in the ruses of ideological representation—reification—but further (and more specific to our own time), trapped in a now all-engulfing symbolic or figurative order which simply *becomes* reality. Jameson however detects some glimmers of a way out.

First off, the Third World might offer a kind of "peripheral vision" (somewhat like Manzoni's or Conrad's or Lewis') of the multinational system it is both outside and part of. Jameson has increasingly turned to its literature and cinema as a way of viewing capitalism whole, via "national allegories" which can still project a depth beneath the surface, a way that is no longer open to us hapless victims of consumer society (see "TWL").

Second, between the Lacanian orders of the Imaginary and the Real lies the Symbolic; and this "supreme fiction" of a Symbolic Order (I allude to Jameson's brilliant essay on Stevens) may serve not just to enthrall and "subject" us to its power but also to allow us a degree of self-liberation—it functions, so to say, as the cure for which it was meant to be the disease. Elsewhere Jameson expresses this as the practical need to forge a revolutionary ideology—"Historicize the future!" one might say—a utopian motivation that will preserve a certain space for criticism and optimism, though one quite different from Adorno's[20]; it is more akin to the "Gramscian" alternative mentioned above. Moreover, the subject that is "called forth" by this Symbolic Order is not the Cartesian or the bourgeois ego, nor yet a schizoid dispersion of selfhood (á la Deleuze or Lyotard), but—presumably—some plurality, a "nous" rather than a "je." Such a collective mapping has yet to be worked out, however, and I do not know how in Jameson's terms it would be.[21]

We should—or at least, one should—remember that Jameson's call is addressed both to practicing artists (or rather cultural activists) and to *theorists* of art and culture. The job of the latter would be to detect the genealogical anticipations beyond postmodernism, deep waves from the future which dislodge our current practices as if they were flakes of dead skin. Postmodernism no less its predecessor would be seen as laying itself open to the contingencies of history; it would tell its own allegorical story, even through its masks of death. Ultimately it would foretell its own death! Yet when all is said and done, this optative mood is no more warranted than Lyotard's quietism or Tafuri's stoicism.

Although Jameson wants to go "through and beyond" postmodernism, the fact remains that fundamentally he must refuse the entire option. For in the end he remains bound to the expressive model of the *work*. In that respect he is no different from Adorno, and false to the "performance" or disseminating orientation of a postmodernist aesthetic. Jameson's model is one not of reception but of production, of creation and expression; like Adorno, he is heir to the utopian dreams of a Romantic aesthetics. He looks for coding operations within a structured process and economy of desire; looks in short for the repressed narrative(s) of History. And for one who is tactically and tactually very alert to the observer's position in the field she enters, he remains curiously attached to *style*, both as practitioner and as analyst of this prototypical modernist effect; it is dialectics he practices after all, not pastiche. It is true that he calls for us (theorists and artists)

> [t]o undo postmodernism homeopathically by the methods of postmodernism: to work at dissolving the pastiche by using all the instruments of pastiche itself, to reconquer some genuine historical sense by using the instruments of what I have called substitutes for history. ("RPM," 59)[22]

But it is unclear how he himself could effect such a cure, given his preferred mode of allegorical interpretation, at once mathematically rigorous and micrologically suggestive (the model for the latter being Benjamin's or Adorno's "constellation" of details). Some may think that contingency enters also in Derridean or other guise, as the occasion that solicits a text, as a spacing, a dissemination that undoes the work. But ultimately Jameson will not abandon Van Gogh's (or rather Heidegger's) peasant shoes for Warhol's glitter, method for paralogism, subjectivity for surface. He would like (in some future perfect tense) to have identified the "Gestell" of postmodernism, and to have located the "Riss" between its dehumanized figures and the "earth"—History, the Real—which grounds it.

Notes

1. The main source is his magisterial essay "Postmodernism, or The Cultural Logic of Late Capitalism." Here Jameson displays to the full his prestidigitory skill—less sleight of hand than quickness of dialectical eye in keeping so many balls in the air at once. See also the following: "Pleasure: A Political Issue"; "Postmodernism and

Consumer Society"; "Wallace Stevens"; "The Politics of Theory: Ideological Positions in the Postmodernism Debate"; "Periodizing the Sixties"; "Architecture and the Critique of Ideology"; "On Magic Realism in Film,"; "Third-World Literature in the Era of Multi-national Capitalism."

2. His own method, best observed in *The Political Unconscious*, uses structuralist analysis as it were against itself, to decode not only the form of the content, but also the content of the form—the History which formalism both conceals and reveals.

3. See "Regarding Postmodernism—a Conversation with Fredric Jameson": "The idea is to create a mediatory concept, to construct a model which can be articulated in, and descriptive of, a whole series of different cultural phenomena. This unity or system is then placed in a relation to the infrastructural reality of late capitalism. The aim, in other words, is to provide something which can face in two directions . . ." (p. 43 in this volume).

4. The avowal of such a perspective need not amount to the Nietzschean perspectivism common to most poststructuralists. Wellmer adopts what he calls a dialectical (if non-totalizing) presentation. Adorno likewise concedes the historical contingency of the categories applied by theory (his own included).

5. See Cavell, *Must we Mean What We Say?* "The essential fact of (what I refer to as) the modern lies in the relation between the present practice of an enterprise and the history of that enterprise, in the fact that this relation has become problematic" (xix).

6. See e.g. Wellmer, "On the Dialectic . . . " and "Truth, Semblance, Reconciliation: Adorno's Aesthetic Redemption of Modernity"; Lyotard, *The Postmodern Condition*, especially the appendix, "Answering the Question: What is Postmodernism?" (the title parodies Kant, as does the answer). For Tafuri, see Jameson, "Architecture and the Critique of Ideology," *passim*; and on Jameson's genealogical approach, see his "Postmodernism, or The Cultural Logic of Late Capitalism."

7. J.-F. Lyotard, *Le différend*, p. 197. In fact Lyotard teases us by leaving it undecidable as to whether he favors such nostalgia or the incommensurable play of language games.

8. See Hayden White, *The Content of the Form: Narrative Discourse and Historical Representation*, pp. 142-168—"Getting Out of History: Jameson's Redemption of Narrative"—the best short treatment of Jameson's narratological method in *The Political*

Unconscious, first published as a review in *Diacritics* but now with important additions.

9. T. W. Adorno, *Aesthetic Theory*, p. 157. Adorno sees fetishization also as breaking the spell of the reality principle; see p. 468. Jameson's ironizing of modernism is similar.

10. I wonder whether we are not meant to understand here an implicit declension from the glorious days marked by the Greek temple that Heidegger goes on to discuss, a temple serving much more positively than the worn out shoes to situate the community in its world while also revealing the unimaginable limits represented by natural forces.

11. I draw mainly on "Postmodernism, or The Cultural Logic of Late Capitalism" Cf. Jameson's own summary:

> some properly postmodernist practice of pastiche, of a new free play of styles and historicist allusions now willing to 'learn from Las Vegas,' a moment of surface rather than of depth, of the 'death' of the old individual subject or bourgeois ego, and of the schizophrenic celebration of the commodity fetishism of the image, of a now 'delirious New York' and a countercultural California, a moment in which the logic of media capitalism penetrates the logic of advanced production itself and transforms the latter to the point where such distinctions as those between high and mass culture lose their significance . . . ("ACI," 75).

Allusions are to books by Rem Koolhaas (on New York) and Robert Venturi (on Las Vegas).

12. Fried had used the term initially to criticize certain tendencies of 1960s sculpture. More precisely, for him modernism is the attempt to integrate the polarity of "absorption" (a Heidegger-inspired notion) and "theatricality" present from the eighteenth century on, precisely through absorbing the latter. Postmodernism amounts to the refusal of the first pole altogether.

13. Note that the "blasé" was already part of nineteenth century experience of modernity: see T. J. Clark, *The Painting of Modern Life* pp. 238-239, 310; he is discussing Manet's "A Bar at the Folies-Bergère," and cites Simmel and Henry James' "In the Cage." Clark is influenced by Walter Benjamin, and we might note that Benjamin writes in "The Work of Art in an Age of Mechanical Reproducibility" of the tactile experience of architecture as emblematic of the new mode of experience of film—distracted, a matter of habit rather than

conscious attention, a collective phenomenon rather than individual and focused.

14. Jameson associates "spatialization" with the diffusion of meaning, and the art*work* with interpretive closure ("PAU," 15f). Derrida has recently written about Bernard Tschumi's designs for the Parc de La Villette outside Paris, and will himself design some parts of this exercise in "deconstructivism" or in what might be termed "differential" space.

15. Jameson relies on Ernest Mandel's periodizing in his *Late Capital*; but see Mike Davis, "Urban Renaisscance and the Spirit of Postmodernism," p. 107.

16. In fact Jameson's response to Lyotard (as to Tafuri) is subtle and dialectical; it undertakes to place the positions or hegemony within which they are able to assert their conclusions (and in this kind of ideological analysis Jameson has few peers). Such a maneuver is a kind of telling tales, of course. Lyotard is condemned for reducing the question of justice to "gaming" and paralogism; the only guarantee that such new science will not be used coercively would be political, not (as with the earlier Lyotard) because it rests on the enlightening protopolitical stance of a revolutionary aesthetic modernism.

17. Jameson sees the failure of Le Corbusier's proto-political revolution already in Schiller. Nor does he espouse "enclave" theory —the suggestion that small groups of resistance may "seed" the older hegemonic system—as is claimed by Margaret Soltan in her "Architectural Follies." Or rather, he endorses it not as a *practical* option but as anticipatory *consciousness*; he speaks for example of "the cultural vision of utopian space of which this particular enclave is but a specific figure" ("RPM," 57). Fulfillment is all.

18. The title—"Regarding Postmodernism"—now acquires added meaning.

19. In "Science versus Ideology," Jameson wonders whether the whole distinction is not itself outdated, no more than an ideological remnant—a felt need, that is, to map individual experience within the larger totalities of history and system; a need that will be frustrated now that even the aesthetic has been made the site of multiple simulacra. Jameson's answer is essentially to offer an activist epistemology: only a turn towards the future will allow us to cognize new possibilities.

20. Wellmer compares Jameson's allegorical strategy with Adorno's "non-violent unity of the multiple," but sees it as not

specifically postmodern. What is postmodern in Jameson would lie rather in his linking of aesthetics with a "micropolitics" of a decentered New Left (see Wellmer, "On the Dialectic of Modernism and Postmodernism," 339). Jameson himself would reject such a characterization as "protopolitical"—something to be found in an earlier phase of Lyotard's occasional existence, but not an option for him. His actual choices of alliances and their relation to his theoretical positions remain a problem. But perhaps—who knows—it is a problem for History to solve rather than Jameson himself.

21. Peter Dews' recent *Logics of Disintegration: Poststructuralist Thought and the Claims of Critical Theory*, pp. 234f. suggests that Lacan's attention to the "lie" in communication permits an intersubjective posing of the problem beyond the subject-object paradigm in which Jameson remains caught. But his book also shows very well how poststructuralism fails to see that the fragmentation of the subject, of "identity-thinking," etc. merely re-enacts the contemporary social process—precisely Adorno's point. It is Jameson's too—if only he could make it more precisely!

22. Cf. Adorno's famous call in *Negative Dialectics*, p. 15, "to transcend the concept by means of the concept," in turn an echo of Hegel's own homeopathic critique of reason.

Marxism and Resistance: Fredric Jameson and the Moment of Postmodernism

David S. Gross
University of Oklahoma

I. Jameson / Marxism / Postmodernism

Throughout his career, Fredric Jameson has developed his own positions by bringing his Marxist critique to bear on the major critical theorists of this century. In this he resembles Marx himself, whose early writings were critical engagements with Hegel and Feuerbach, and who presents *Capital* primarily as an argument against Adam Smith, David Ricardo, and bourgeois political economists in general. This "reactive" quality in Marx and Marxism anticipates the stress on inter-textuality in modern thought. As Jameson puts it in an early essay: "Marxism is a critical rather than a systematic philosophy." As such it presents "a correction of other positions . . . rather than a doctrine of a positivistic variety existing in its own right" (*MF*, 365).[1]

In his three essays on postmodernism—"The Politics of Theory: Ideological Positions in the Postmodernism Debate," "Periodizing the 60s," and "Postmodernism, or The Cultural Logic of Late Capitalism"—his most theoretically ambitious, fully developed and polemical critical essays in the mid-eighties, arguably in his career, Jameson engages both the artistic and mass cultural "stuff" of our time and the modes of thought and perception in poststructuralist and other postmodernist theory.

He foregrounds the conceptual operations of modern critical theory in order to model Marxist analysis and critique, and to assert the necessity to "periodize"—in the case of postmodernism, to see our own time historically—in the face of the various movements in contemporary theory which would deny both the validity of any totalizing, and thus of any historical view, and the value of any Marxist categories or theories.

The very title of Jameson's most important article on postmodernism—"Postmodernism, or The Cultural Logic of Late Capitalism"—asserts the validity and priority of the Marxist analysis, the ability of the Marxist mode of representing the social and the cultural "to grasp the design of history as such." The phrase is from Walter Benjamin's "Theoretics of Knowledge, Theory of Progress" describing his own project almost fifty years ago, and Jameson announces by his title his intention to do with regard to the texts of our recent past something very like what Benjamin does for Baudelaire, Paris, and early high capitalism— "to demonstrate through example that only Marxism can apply high philology to the texts of the past century"("Theoretics of Knowledge," 6, 25). The mode of thought Jameson defends and demonstrates insists that postmodernism must be seen as *the* cultural logic of late capitalism, which in turn implies that it is meaningful and correct to describe our era (period, moment) as "late capitalist," and that it is possible to understand late capitalism in such a way as to be able to deduce its "cultural logic." Both the definite article in the title and, especially, the appositional "or" challenge aggressively the anti-historicist tendencies in postmodern theory which Jameson is at pains to refute.[2]

Jameson is always fully aware that postmodernism is also many other things; his view gives full weight to deconstruction and other poststructuralist theories which insist on heterogeneity, uncertainty and indeterminacy in all meaning. Like the "post-Marxism" of Chantal Mouffe and Ernesto Laclau,[3] Jameson's version of Marxism recognizes and even stresses that the social, political and cultural phenomena we describe, discuss, and interpret as "postmodernist," like all historical products or "moments," are always overdetermined and have many causes.

But Jameson's title—like all his work on the subject—insists that postmodernism be seen and represented in the light of history, and that in our historicizing we engage the political and ethical issues of desire, power and control, production and consumption, injustice and privilege which have always been the concern of Marxism.

Later in "Postmodernism, or The Cultural Logic of Late Capitalism," Jameson expands and modifies the title phrase to make its totalizing claims even more explicit: "The conception of postmodernism outlined here is a historical rather than a merely stylistic one. I cannot stress too greatly the radical distinction between a view for which the postmodern is one (optional) style among many others available, and one which seeks to grasp it as the cultural dominant of the logic of late capitalism . . ." ("PCL," 85). He describes the later position (his own, of course, and one which he elaborates, demonstrates and defends in all three postmodernism articles) as "a genuinely dialectical attempt to think our present of time in History"; in "The Politics of Theory" the phrase is expanded to read "a present of time and of history in which we ourselves exist and struggle" ("PTI," 62).

Like Walter Benjamin, Jameson believes—and seeks to demonstrate—that the totalizing vision of Marxist historicism constitutes something like the enabling conditions of a possibility of a theoretics, conceptualizations of culture which lay bare its social function, its meaning in history. At a recent conference session devoted to his work on postmodernism,[4] Jameson insisted in discussion on a distinction between *totalizing* views of social and cultural practices and any view of society and culture as some fixed, essentialist *totality*—the straw man position attributed to Marxism by those who oppose all totalization as "totalitarian." The totalizing practice in Jameson's theory accommodates dialectically heterogeneity and *différance* (i.e., the rifts, gaps, and aporias disclosed by deconstruction), but not at the expense of the idea that "it's all connected," as he put it at the conference, criticizing theory which would "throw that out." The idea that "it's all connected" in ways which explain and indict the late capitalist present and carry a strong demand for social change has been a cornerstone of Jameson's theory from *Marxism and Form*.

In the preface to that book, in 1971, Jameson characterized the liberal pluralism and "humanism" hegemonic in academia at least since the 1950s as his "conceptual opponent": "that mixture of political liberalism, empiricism, and logical positivism which we know as Anglo-American philosophy and which is hostile at all points to the type of thinking outlined here" (*MF*, x). The attempt to defeat that position constitutes, he says, "the tendentious part of my book." He describes the "ideological potency" and negative effects of his opponent like this: "the anti-speculative bias of that tradition, its emphasis on the individual fact or item at the expense of the network of relationships in which that item may be embedded, continue to encourage submission to what is by pre-venting its followers from making connections, and in particular from drawing the otherwise unavoidable conclusions on the political level" (*MF*, x). Later in the book, Jameson develops more fully his picture of liberal humanism as cultural dominant:

> The dominant ideology of the Western countries is clearly that Anglo-American empirical realism for which all dialectical thinking represents a threat, and whose mission is essentially to serve as a check on social consciousness: allowing legal and ethical answers to be given to economic questions, substituting the language of political equality for that of economic inequality and considerations about freedom for doubts about capitalism itself. The method of such thinking, in its various forms and guises, consists in separating reality into airtight compartments, carefully distinguishing the political from the economic, the legal from the political, the sociological from the historical, so that the full implications of any given problem can never come into view; and in limiting all statements to the discrete and the immediately verifiable, in order to rule out any speculative and totalizing thought which might lead to a vision of social life as a whole. (*MF*, 367-368)

The contemporary poststructuralist thought Jameson seeks to correct in the postmodernism articles is no longer as confident about verifiable meaning as was the liberal pluralism Jameson described in 1971. Yet as "radical" as such thought may seem to itself and to those in the "anti-theory" camp (vestigial "humanists," defending the embattled Arnoldian shrine of what Marcuse called "affirmative culture"),[5] Jameson makes very clear how the insistence on absolute heterogeneity, the complete refusal of any totalizing thought, and the denial of all reliable signification, ends up—in terms of the social function of such thought—at one with the liberal pluralism which it attempts to displace as cultural dominant. The denial of meaning in history places poststructuralism in alliance with the more old-fashioned positions it supposedly opposes, especially in the refusal to make connections—the practice Jameson denounced in 1971, and again in Kansas in 1987.

In opposition to anti-historicist views, Jameson seeks to convince us that to analyze (to theorize successfully, to conceptualize) the world we live in—the personal, social, cultural reality we have to deal with in living, human existence—is to understand the effects of capitalism. In full awareness of the enormous changes since the time of Marx, and in no way taking specific *words* of Marx as dicta or dogma, Jameson argues as a Marxist that extremely diverse phenomena are "symptomatic" of life under capitalism, that architecture, movies, rock music, literature, cultural phenomena generally (including, especially, the history of thought, of critical theory) can best be understood as historically specific manifestations of late capitalism, that such an understanding is necessary if other modes of interpretation or understanding are to be effective, accurate, truthful.

The argument, as I see it in Jameson (and in Marx), is not that political-economic, social-cultural forces—some "totality" which exists "out there," completely prior to and pre-existing, separate from any thought or writing about it—constitute some sort of "master code" which has conceptual priority over all others. Rather Jameson implies that dialectical and historical materialism provides a necessary, if not in and of itself sufficient, perspective for understanding social reality, which requires the historical contextualization of all objects of understanding to properly explain or interpret them. Such a view does require totalizing perspectives; it does not imply the pre-existence of reified, hypostatized totalities.

I can only discuss briefly here "historical and dialectical materialism" as three important and controversial signifiers and cannot go into their changing implications when they are variously combined or used separately (at the Kansas conference Jameson mentioned that some of the disrepute which has gathered around the phrase has its source in Althusser, for whom "Hegel" is a code word for Stalin and "dialectical materialism" for Stalinism). What I mean by "historical" will be made clear as this essay proceeds. The historical is certainly crucial for Jameson's Marxism. *The Political Unconscious* begins with the words "Always historicize!"(PU, 9). And for him, as for Marx, the historical emphasis is on what humans have done, produced, in response to necessity and desire, the resulting relations among people, between people and the rest of "nature," and on how all that has changed in time. To foreground such matters in the time of capitalism and late capitalism (as to varying degrees, in different ways, in earlier eras) is to stand up against pain, suffering, exploitation, oppression, privilege, and deprivation—so that it seems indeed that "history is what hurts."

"Materialism" is the *easiest* of the three, even if the most misunderstood by non-initiates in this debate, who take it to mean an obsession with money and ownership. The key meaning of "materialist" lies in its contrast with idealist philosophies, which since Plato always postulate an ideal, essential realm outside time and history, "above" and somehow radically separate from material existence. Marx, Freud, and Nietzsche are all materialist thinkers; they insist on a view in which all human practice and the world of matter or "nature" are one, components in a material reality which includes all manifestations of the spiritual, the ideal, and the mental.

"Dialectical" is the hardest. It can seem either silly, unrigorous, Romantic/mystical—or as erring in the opposite direction, as mechanistic, rationalistic and shallow, in some simplistic version of the thesis-antithesis-synthesis triad. But it is an essential component in Jameson and in Marxism in at least two ways: the sense that "it's all connected," as Jameson put it at the conference, Hegel's "the truth is the whole" (which must include, as I understand it, the later Frankfurt school's stunning inversion, "the whole is the untrue"), and the insistence on contradiction, on interaction, conflict, and change in any interpretation of data or fact, in any meaning. Taken together my "two senses" exemplify the character of dialectical thought, with the necessary but flawed and vulnerable—in danger of congealing into dangerous rigidities or dissolving into the undifferentiated oneness of idealist mysticism—*totalizations* of the first part countered by the active, developing movement of the second. The Marxist dialectic involves the use of the imagination to make connections *and* to discern gaps, breaks, discontinuities, contradictions.

Marxism is linked to poststructuralism through a shared materialism, which in postmodernist thinkers mainly appears as a Nietzschean materialist sociology (and history) of culture. The dialectic makes the same link; among other things it is the component in Marxism which links it to the self-critical, self-scrutinizing thought about thought in modern theory, as Jameson pointed out (without mentioning Marxism, by the way) in his famous *PMLA* essay "Metacommentary," in 1971, the same year as *Marxism and Form*.[6] A genuinely historical and dialectical materialist perspective is necessary for understanding reality, and it is from that point of view that Jameson insists that we recognize the effects of late capitalism in the phenomena we experience in daily life, in the social and cultural forms and practices which are the objects of our theorizing, and in the assumptions and demands of those theories themselves.

The position remains controversial. That is why Jameson must engage in this battle. And if he and Marx are right, then resistance, repression, and denial comprise crucial elements in the refusal of his argument, in the power of Paul de Man's anti-historicism, in the anti-Marxist current in Foucault's thought. Almost in an aside, Jameson discusses the way in which the "currently fashionable rhetoric of power and domination" in Foucault and others with its "displacement from the economic to the political" is unsatisfactory, since "the various forms of power and domination . . . cannot be understood unless their functional relationships to economic exploitation are articulated—that is, until the political is once again subsumed beneath the economic" ("PTS," 184). The very title of Jameson's *The Political Uncon-*

scious suggests the role that resistance plays in fixing what Mikhail Bakhtin would call the conceptual horizons of the belief systems within which the validity of the Marxist argument is assessed, so that both awareness of the historical specificity of the negative effects of capitalism and hope for socialism are repressed or denied. In the postmodernism articles, Jameson shows a wide variety of phenomena and of shapes or patterns of movement in different areas or "levels" (economic, political, cultural) within the "moment" of postmodernism as linked effects of and responses to late capitalism. To the extent that his argument is convincing it breaks through repression and exposes the mystifications of hegemony.

II. Late Capitalism as Blinding Light: Postmodernism and Resistance

> Every present is determined by those images which are synchronic with it: every now is the moment of a specific recognition. In it truth is loaded to the bursting point with time. (This bursting point is nothing other than the death of the intention, which accordingly coincides with the birth of authentic historical time, the time of truth.) . . . The image that is read, I mean the image at the moment of recognition, bears to the highest degree the stamp of the critical, dangerous impulse that lies at the source of all reading.
>
> —Benjamin, "Theoretics of Knowledge"

The matter of our resistance—why we disagree, don't want to admit the value and validity of the Marxist view, why we bridle and claim that neither our intellectual approaches nor the "subject matter" we investigate has causal connections to economics generally or capitalism specifically—will be my focus here, as it is of central significance for Jameson. As a guiding metaphor for the discussion as a whole, I shall use a metaphorical passage from Benjamin. In the notebook containing reflections on Marxist critical methodology from which I chose the quotation to begin this section, Benjamin lays great stress on "the dialectical image" in which, he says, "the past and the now flash into a constellation. In other words: image is dialectic at a standstill" ("Theoretics of Knowledge," 7)[7] In his "On Some Motifs in Baudelaire" is a passage which contains just such a dialectical image which represents figurally the resistance I have been discussing. Benjamin is discussing the philosophies of Henri Bergson and others who sought around the turn of the century to understand better the nature of experience, to distinguish "'true' experience" from "the kind that manifests itself in the standardized, denatured life of the civilized masses." (The problematics of experience, its debasement or attenuation in modern life, its inevitably collective nature, is a constant concern for Benjamin in this essay and others from the mid-30's, and links his thought to Jameson's and Bakhtin's.) Benjamin says of Bergson that he rejects any historical determination of memory:

> He thus manages to stay clear of that experience from which his own philosophy evolved or, rather, in reaction to which it arose. It was the inhospitable, blinding age of big-scale industrialism. In shutting out this experience the eye perceives an experience of a complementary nature in the form of its spontaneous afterimage, as it were. Bergson's philosophy represents an attempt to give the detail of this afterimage and to fix it as a permanent record. ("On Some Motifs in Baudelaire," 157)

Along the same lines, Jameson argues in "The 60's" that the movement in thought from existentialism to "structuralism" should be seen as a response to the discovery "of the opacity of the Institution itself as the radically transindividual," of "a realm of impersonal logic in terms of which human consciousness is itself little more than an 'effect of structure.'"

> On this reading, then, the new philosophical turn will be interpreted less in the idealistic perspective of some discovery of a new scientific truth (the Symbolic) than as the symptom of an essentially protopolitical and social experience, the shock of some new, hard, unconcept-

ualized, resistant object which the older conceptuality cannot process and which thus gradually generates a whole new problematic. ("PTS," 190)

The shock Jameson speaks of there is Benjamin's blinding light—a reality from which we turn away, only to have it continue to dominate our perceptions, our ideological positions, our assumptions about the possibilities of human life, about "human nature," but always in the unacknowledged, denied, distorted forms which result when our thoughts and perceptions must follow the twisted paths through the political unconscious demanded by the forces of resistance, in a process which Freud called "the return of the repressed."[8] It is Jameson's task to restore this repressed material to conscious awareness, by showing us what we have learned to think of as "apolitical," non-ideological and, especially, unconnected phenomena such as developments in critical theory, the poems of John Ashberry in contrast to those of Wallace Stevens, the new Bonaventure Hotel in downtown Los Angeles, are manifestations of a postmodernism which constitutes the cultural logic of late capitalism.

In both major postmodernism essays, Jameson is trying to conceptualize the historically specific features of our own era, of a world we have experienced as adults from the 60s on. In so doing, he is constantly doing battle with anti-historicist views, by asserting and demonstrating the possibility (and, therefore the necessity) of reading meaning in history—of seeing the larger configurations, patterns, and dynamics of historical development. A key postulate he wishes to refute is that we are no longer living under capitalism, that the mode of analysis suggested by the use of such terminology is hopelessly dogmatic and entirely out of date. This is one of the most important positions in hegemonic anti-Marxism; it is a central tenet of liberal pluralism (of a writer like Daniel Bell) in North America at least since the 1950s, and it constitutes the most important link between such thought and "right" poststructuralism. Basing his historical analysis on that of Ernest Mandel in *Late Capitalism*, Jameson argues:

> that late or multinational or consumer capitalism, far from being inconsistent with Marx's great 19th-century analysis

constitues on the contrary the purest form of capital yet to
have emerged, a prodigious expansion of capital into
hitherto uncommodified areas. This purer capitalism of our
time thus eliminates the enclaves of precapitalist organization it had hitherto tolerated and exploited in a tributary
way. . . . ("PCL," 78)

Jameson describes such enclaves as "the last vestiges of
uncommodified or traditional space" which "are now ultimately
penetrated and colonized in their turn. Late capitalism can
therefore be described as the moment in which the last vestiges of
Nature which survived on into classical capitalism are at length
eliminated: namely the third world and the unconscious" ("PTS,"
207). (Another interesting instance of the process is the case of the
university, whose position as enclave has steadily eroded in this
era, as the penetration and colonization described by Jameson
takes place.)

What Jameson has in mind with regard to the third world is
the destruction of precapitalist patterns by the technological
industrialization of agriculture known as "the Green Revolution,"
by means of which "capitalism transforms its relationship to its
colonies from an old-fashioned imperialist control to market
penetration, destroying the older village communities and
creating a whole new wage-labor pool and lumpenproletariat"
("PTS," 207). The "colonization" or, perhaps better, the
"occupation" of the unconscious under late capitalism is
Jameson's central focus. He is referring to "the mechanization of
the superstructure, or in other words the penetration of culture
itself by what the Frankfurt school called the culture industry,"
the ascendency and proliferation everywhere of the media and the
advertising industry. The reference to the Frankfurt school is
another sign of the closeness of Jameson's argument to Benjamin,
who speaks so often of the attenuation of experience in modern
society, comparing newspapers unfavorably with oral tales and
stories, and arguing that the new "linguistic usages of newspapers
paralyzed the imagination of their readers" (*Illuminations*, 159).
Jameson's argument is that the technological and organizational
developments since, say, Benjamin's time are on such a scale as to

constitute the basis of a new era in culture which we are calling the postmodern. Thus what happened with regard to the relation between our experience and available forms of narrative discourse with the rise of the newspaper develops with unprecedented scope and depth (or lack of depth) in the hands of the television industry.

Jameson's view, in this regard, is close to the dystopian vision—associated with Adorno, Horkheimer and others of the more recent Frankfurt school—of the totally administered society, in which a behaviorist, "instrumental" view of "human relations" holds total sway, or the pessimistic visions of a Foucault whereby a "total system" of authority and power creates an interlocking set of institutions which "discipline and punish" in order to achieve complete obedience and control. Jameson is actually closer to Raymōnd Williams or Bakhtin, in recognizing the scope and power of hegemonic, monolithic authoritative discourse (Bakhtin's "the word of the fathers," *The Dialogic Imagination* 342), while at the same time insisting on the actual and potential strength of alternative and oppositional cultural formations.

As Jameson sees it, postmodernist cultural forms and practices tend to exhibit qualities like those Benjamin saw in Bergson's philosophy, symptoms of an experience which made him turn away, unable to face the historical truths about the "big-scale industrialism" in reaction to which, says Benjamin, his philosophy arose. Faced with the awesome power and seemingly universal penetration of the processes of late capitalism into all aspects of our existence—from the consumerist commodification of daily life, in which desire is so controlled and directed by television (not just advertising, marketing—teaching desire what to desire—but all the "programing," including the network news, whose definitions of reality prove so persuasive), and where even the unconscious can be said to have been penetrated and "colonized," with our plastic money cards, which seem to signify the apotheosis of the *interconnected* power of capitalism, the nightmarishly inter-woven global network which has been feared and represented by artists since Kafka, but now with a whole other level of penetration, of suffocating universality, with computerization, electronically fused banks and data banks (and the consequences, crushing personal debt, huge profits for finance capital), to the planetary level of this computerized inter-connectedness, as symbolized by the "multi-national corporation" and the relations among the superpowers, with the (again computerized) constant threat of nuclear war—faced with all that, we shut our eyes, we turn away. What we then do—in any area, but in my context, specifically, what we do culturally, the patterns of behavior, our discursive practices and formations—exhibits always traces of what we say we're not talking about, patterns and preoccupations which constitute what I am tempted to term "reaction formations," with their source in what Jameson allows us to see as the newly penetrated, colonized, politicized unconscious.

Jameson is concerned to show that the forces of repression, resistance, denial, and distortion which helped shape high modernism in reaction to the rise of monopoly capitalism, which Benjamin calls "big-scale industrialism," continue to constitute key features of postmodernism, in (non)reaction to late capitalism; a central concern of Jameson's in *The Political Unconscious* is to illustrate the actions of such forces in canonical modernism. Though given the vastly greater power, extent, and interconnect-edness of the present world system, the various effects symbolized in Benjamin's image of closing the eyes against a blinding light, with attempts to fix the details of the afterimage representing intellectual, cultural production, are so intensified as to constitute a new stage in cultural history, the moment of the postmodern.

As I have indicated, Jameson's two most important post-modernism articles are filled with illustrations—clearly drawn deliberately from the most disparate areas of human social activity, from third-world agriculture, to the world-political history of decolonization and anti-imperialism to the far, windy reaches of philosophical and theoretical debate—of the historical specificity of late capitalism. In a long section of "The 60's" called "The Adventures of the Sign" Jameson offers a definitive des-cription and extended discussion of postmodernism as a whole, from the "death" of the subject, through the eclipse of depth and historicity, and the now classic "freeing" of the sign from meaning and reference. He argues there that postmodernism differs from high modernism in terms of "the social functionality of culture," in that the earlier movement, "whatever its overt political content, was oppositional and marginal within a middle-class Victorian or philistine or gilded age culture," while postmodernism must be said to have achieved the position of "cultural dominant, with a precise socioeconomic functionality"—in the colonization of the unconscious by images from the spectacle, from Ronald Reagan to *Miami Vice* ("PTS," 195).[9]

Jameson presents here a brilliantly condensed and concentrated discussion of the source in resistance, in the denial of history, of the key (since Saussure) structuralist/poststructuralist radical separation of the sign from its referent (the insistence that the relation between them is entirely arbitrary) so that there are only texts and intertextuality and "freeplay" among signifiers, with the referent (history, reality) surviving only as "a ghostly residual aftereffect"—Benjamin's "afterimage" ("PTS," 196).[10] The next stage, as Jameson describes it, after ridding the sign as a whole from its connection to and dependence on a referent, is deconstruction within the sign, the radical separation of the signifier from the signified, as part of the "liberation" of words and all other signifiers from signification, from meaning proper. Jameson associates the results with Lacanian notions of schizophrenic discourse, with the breakdown of all syntactic order and meaningful relationships in time, and concludes with this bravura sentence:

> The break-up of the Sign in mid-air determines a fall back into a now absolutely fragmented and anarchic social reality; the broken pieces of language (the pure Signifiers) now falling again into the world, as so many more pieces of material junk among all the other rusting and superannuated apparatuses and buildings that litter the commodity landscape and strew the 'collage city,' the 'delirious New York' of a postmodernist late capitalism in full crisis. ("PTS," 201)

My argument is that this movement away from history, the problematizing of meaning and connection and privileging of heterogeneity and difference, is symptomatic of the blocking, repression, resistance symbolized by Benjamin's image of shutting the eyes against a blinding light. In terms of what I called above the social functionality of culture, that movement away (de Man's "swerve") is profoundly hegemonic. Born of reaction against, aversion to a monolithic, authoritative reality, it becomes dominant and hegemonic itself. Culture under late capitalism, has lost the "semi-autonomy" it enjoyed in previous periods:

> Culture itself falls into the world, and the result is not its disappearance but its prodigious expansion, to the point where culture becomes coterminous with social life in general: now all the levels become 'acculturated,' and in the society of the spectacle, the image, or the simulacrum, everything has at length become cultural, from the superstructures down into the mechanisms of the infrastructure itself. ("PTS," 201)

The acculturation of the mechanisms of the infrastructure is a major effect of what Mandel calls the "generalized universal industrialization" of late capitalism (cited in "PTS," 201), and is the main vehicle for a key task of any socio-economic order, what Henri Lefebvre terms "the reproduction of the relations of production" (see Aronowitz, *Crisis in Historical Materialism,* 97).

Throughout these essays Jameson takes great pains to demonstrate a dialectical "take" on postmodernism, which recognizes both its positive and negative, liberating and hegemonic aspects. The classic model for such thought is Marx's own analysis of the transformations which occur with the rise of capitalism. Jameson says that the famous analysis in the *Manifesto* demands:

> a type of thinking that would be capable of grasping the demonstrably baleful features of capitalism along with its extraordinary and liberating dynamism simultaneously, within a single thought, and without attenuating any of the force of either judgement. We are, somehow, to lift our minds to a point at which it is possible to understand that capitalism is at one and the same time the best thing that has ever happened to the human race, and the worst. ("PCL," 86)

In *The Political Unconscious* one of Jameson's chief concerns was to demonstrate a dialectical view of high modernism as, at once, a symptom of alienation and reification and utopian compensation for it. In these articles on postmodernism, he takes great pains to show both the positive and negative in, for example, the "liberation" of language from history, the liberation of the subject from connection to past and present. Since "personal identity is itself the effect of a certain temporal unification of past and future with the present before me," and "such active temporal unification is itself a function of language, or better still of the sentence, as it moves along its hermeneutic circle through time," the poststructuralist (or schizophrenic) break in the signifying chain can result in "an experience of pure material signifiers," (which certainly recalls art for art's sake, especially in the non-representational visual arts) "pure and unrelated presents in time" ("PCL," 72). Jameson then cites an account of actual schizophrenic experience and concludes:

> The breakdown of temporality suddenly releases its present of time from all the activities and intentionalities that might focus it and make it a space of praxis; thereby isolated, that present suddenly engulfs the subject with undescribable vividness, a materiality of perception properly overwhelming, which effectively dramatizes the power of the material—or better still, the literal—Signifier in isolation. This present of the world or material signifier comes before the subject with heightened intensity, bearing a mysterious charge of affect, here described in the negative terms of anxiety and loss of reality, but which one could just as well imagine in the positive terms of euphoria, the high, the intoxicatory or hallucinogenic intensity. ("PCL," 73)

At the end, Jameson recognizes the attraction of the "ludic" moment of free-play, postmodernism's moment of *jouissance*, what Jameson labels in the title of a major section, "The Hysterical Sublime." It is dependent upon, as a condition of possibility, freedom from anything resembling a Kantian ethical imperative, Sartrian or Dostoevskian responsibility in/for history. It is a great relief when we turn away from the blinding light, when we are able to "block" successfully, to deny the very reality of "the nightmare of history." But, as it has been the burden of this essay to show, the repressed, the referent, does not go away when we deny it, and its power and control may be greater if the effect of postmodernism as cultural dominant is to deny the reality of that power. Jameson says of the effects of the anti-historicist view:

> There cannot but be much that is deplorable in a cultural form of image addiction which, by transforming the past [into] visual mirages, stereotypes or texts, effectively abolishes any practical sense of the future and of the collective project, thereby abandoning the thinking of future change to fantasies of sheer catastrophe and inexplicable cataclysm—from visions of 'terrorism' on the social level to those of cancer on the personal. ("PCL," 85)

In an earlier article, Jameson describes this enabling retreat from meaning in history as "something like a defense mechanism, a repression, a neurotic denial, a preventive shutting off of affect, which itself finally reconfirms the vital threat of its object" ("MAH," 55). As symbolized by the movement within Benjamin's dialectical image, such resistance and repression is at the source of postmodernist cultural phenomena as a response to late capitalism. In the same discussion of the modern historical specificity of experience and consciousness under capitalism (with the work of Baudelaire in the foreground), Benjamin cites in a devastingly laconic, matter-of-fact way Freud's observation that the main function of consciousness is to protect the organism from perception (*Illuminations*, 161). Specific aspects of the distortions in perception and awareness which result from the protective gesture—in Benjamin's figure, the details of the afterimage—become key constitutive features of our culture, of our thought.

I shall close my discussion with an example of Jameson's analysis of postmodernism which is particularly close to Benjamin's image. Jameson is discussing our mixture of fascination and horror with computers and other powerful, sophisticated means of communication and reproduction—"high tech"—as instances of "the hysterical sublime." I will cite it at length without editing in order to illustrate the movement within the thought, to show the depth and relevance of the argument. He is separating his position from a view of technology itself as the "ultimately determining" social force:

> Rather, I want to suggest that our faulty representations of some immense communicational and computer network are themselves but a distorted figuration of something even deeper, namely the whole world system of present-day multinational capitalism. The technology of contemporary society is therefore mesmerizing and facinating, not so much in its own right, but because it seems to offer some privileged representational shorthand for grasping a network of power and control even more difficult for our minds and imaginations to grasp—namely the whole new decentered global network of the third stage of capital itself.

He cites as illustration of the popular culture manifestations of this vision the "high tech paranoia" of movie thrillers about high-level business and political conspiracies to gain wealth or cause disaster in ways in which large, complex computer networks loom large. He then concludes:

> Yet conspiracy theory (and its garish narrative manifestations) must be seen as a degraded attempt—through the figuration of advanced technology—to think the impossible totality of the contemporary world system. It is therefore in terms of that enormous and threatening, yet only dimly perceivable, other reality of economic and social institutions that in my opinion the postmodern sublime can alone be adequately theorized. ("PCL," 79-80)

Throughout that analysis Jameson is aware of our powerful desire to block or resist awareness of the extent and power of late capitalism, in Benjamin's words to ignore or deny the "historical determinations" of our thought and experience. The move away may even seem a progressive gesture, liberation from complete indoctrination and imbrication in the apparatus of hegemony.

Thus the *jouissance* or delight in the play of signifers: it feels like freedom. We feel relieved of the burden of intolerable awareness. But (to borrow, as does Jameson, Raymond Williams' distinctions among different social functions of culture) that "oppositional" impulse slides easily through the "alternative" to a position as cultural "dominant," as it allows the (only "dimly perceived") processes of penetration and colonization of experience and existence to take place unchecked.

It has been the project of Jameson's career to show that not a retreat from meaning, from material, historical reality, but a critical engagement with the forces of late capitalism offers the insight and understanding which might help lead to the successful realization of the collective project to wrest the realm of freedom from the realm of necessity. In this way, Jameson vindicates the relevance of Marxism for contemporary cultural theory against the now fashionable anti-Marxist, anti-historicist polemics. He forces us to see the "moment" of postmodernism as our own "time of the now," a cultural dominant against which we must struggle, not through denial and renunciation, but by means of the sorts of oppositional strategies which are so brilliantly modeled in his own analysis and interpretration of postmodernism.

Notes

1. In a note on this page (p. 365) Jameson cites Sidney Hook's observation that "Marx came to critical self-consciousness by settling accounts with the varied intellectual traditions and attitudes of his day. . . ."

2. Perhaps the best example of such "right" postmodern theory is Jean-François Lyotard's *The Postmodern Condition*. Jameson contributes a lengthy foreword to this slim volume, in which he outlines both the strengths of Lyotard's position and the ways in which such views contribute to the continuation of the very "condition" which they critique with such force and insight.

3. Ernesto Laclau and Chantal Mouffe, *Hegemony and Socialist Strategy*. This book, with its revision of Marxism through critique of the notions of the privileged place of the working class as historical subject and of any sort of historical inevitability, maintains the

strengths of the Marxist tradition while ridding it of those features most often the object of anti-Marxist attacks. While they are certainly more *post*-Marxist than Jameson, at many points their arguments are strikingly similar to his, with their incorporation into a new sort of Marxism insights from Althusser, Lacan, and deconstruction.

4. *Postmodernism: Texts, Politics, Instruction,* International Association for Philosophy and Literature conference, The University of Kansas, Lawrence, KS, April 30-May 2, 1987.

5. Herbert Marcuse, "The Affirmative Character of Culture," *Negations: Essays in Critical Theory,* pp. 88-133. On several occasions Jameson calls attention to this brilliant essay, originally written and published in German in 1937.

6. For more on the way I use Jameson to see the dialectic, see my "Infinite Indignation: Teaching, Dialectical Vision, and Blake's *Marriage of Heaven and Hell.*" Jameson is most specific on the subject in *Marxism and Form,* especially pp. 8, 53-54, 308, and in the long concluding chapter, "Towards Dialectical Criticism." All his subsequent work assumes the value, significance, and necessity of dialectical thought which are spelled out fully in that early work.

7. Benjamin, "Theoretics of Knowledge," p. 7. Much could be written on the significance of the image in Benjamin, as in dialectical thought generally. By its very nature the image stands as an alternative to the pseudo-transparency of the language and the scientistic practices of the dominant discourse, which recognizes as valid only rationalistic demonstration through logical argument— Marcuse's "one-dimensional thought," Blake's "single vision." Jameson argues in *Marxism and Form* that "insofar as dialectical thinking characteristically involves a conjunction of opposites or at least conceptually disparate phenomena, it may truly be said of the dialectical sentence what the Surrealists said about the image, namely, that its strength increases proportionally as the realities linked [in the quotation from Benjamin which follows here, Bergson's philosophy and "big-scale industrialism"] are distant and distinct from each other" (pp. 53-54). And I cannot refrain from citing Guy Debord's observation that "The spectacle is *capital* to such a degree of accumulation that it becomes an image." *Society of the Spectacle* (no pagination, paragraph 34).

8. Benjamin's image and Jameson's formulation strike very similar chords (or discords) as Arthur Kroker's "panic" positions in Kroker and Cook, *The Postmodern Scene.* Kroker tends to see the phenomena of postmodernism as responses of shock, pain, panic to

the degraded, brutalizing "mediascape" of late capitalism, with the turning away or denial—what Jameson calls "a preventive shutting off of affect" ("PCL," 85)—accomplished through his flip, sardonic, passionately dispassionate discourse, registering the murderous shocks of late capitalism, just for the hell of it. I see Kroker's lineage in Guy Debord (*Society of the Spectacle*) and the Situationists International counter-cultural politics of the late sixties in Europe (including their leadership role in May 1968 in Paris, which, for well or ill, had a significant effect on the way events unfolded) to surrealism and Dada, and even to Alfred Jarry at the beginning of the century. Deconstruction through disrespect, offenses against decorum—including the alternately lofty pieties and down to earth earnestness of the academic essay or address after Arnold, which seeks to elicit enlightened assent. Jameson remains closer to such rhetorical strategies; Kroker leaves such paths entirely.

9. When Jameson speaks of the "socioeconomic functionality" of culture here, and in his assumptions in that regard in his analysis as a whole, he is very close to Mouffe and Laclau in *Hegemony and Socialist Strategy*, with their post-Marxist, post-Althusserian, neo-Gramscian sense of hegemony as absent cause, present only in terms of specific articulations of discourse, as institutional practice producing subjects.

10. The sources and implications of that movement in thought form Jameson's central concerns in his *The Prison House of Language*.

Postmodernism, Cultural Change, and Social Practice

Mike Featherstone
Teesside Polytechnic

The coming into prominence of the term postmodernism has aroused a good deal of interest amongst academics and intellectuals. While some dismiss it as merely a transient and shallow intellectual fad, others regard it as signifying a deep-seated break not only with artistic modernism, but with the larger epoch of modernity. This entails a resultant rejection of all the cultural manifestations of modernity as passé, and here the term culture would be extended to include wider cultural production not just in the arts, but also in the spheres of science, law, and morality which Weber saw as originating as part of the differentiation process of modernity. The reversal of this differentiation process, or *de-differentiation* as some would refer to it, also suggests a far-reaching transformation of the nature of cultural production and regimes of signification (see Lash, "Discourse or Figure"). The implications of the alleged shift towards the postmodern are thus to highlight the significance of culture in a dual emphasis upon *a)* the emergence of new techniques of cultural production and reproduction which transform everyday experiences and practices and *b)* the questioning of the deep cultural coding of modernity in which knowledge was given foundational status in the sense that science, humanism, Marxism, or feminism claimed or aspired to offer humankind authoritative guidelines for both knowledge of the world and practical action within it. Postmodernism has therefore raised far-reaching questions about the nature of cultural change and the underlying metatheoretical nexus with which we seek to analyze it.

As many critics have pointed out, one of the problems faced by those such as Lyotard who formulate the postmodern as the end of master narratives is that they too require a metanarrative to explain the emergence of the postmodern which necessarily includes some theory of society and social development leading up to the alleged rupture (see for example, Kellner 1988). The fact that to date many of those theorizing the postmodern have done so from a philosophical, literary, or humanities background, along with the anti-substantivist and anti-evidential logic of their theories means that what were formerly regarded as facts and treated with a degree of caution within social science circles, can now be treated in a more cavalier fashion; in its worst excesses postmodernism can legitimate the writing of thin histories and "anything goes" or the idiosyncratic use of evidence to back up the claim of the eclipse of evidentiality. This is at times coupled with the tendency to generalize and read-off the transformation of social processes and social practices from evidence gleaned from the analysis of literary and artistic texts which are regarded as harbingers of the new "disordered" social order.

It is one of the merits of the work of Fredric Jameson that he seeks to walk this particular tightrope: to treat the postmodern seriously and understand it as a sign of a major cultural transformation and at the same time to attempt to explain it in terms of social processes, as well as to *evaluate* it to assess its practical significance. Jameson's work on postmodernism has been highly influential, as he has not only sought to detect and understand the particular quality of the cultural experiences designated postmodern, but also sought to locate them within a social framework (see esp. "PCL," "PCS," "PTI," and "RPM"). Jameson's theory of society and development is derived from Marxism and he locates postmodernism as the cultural dominant which is associated with the move to late capitalism in the post World War II era. In this paper I shall examine some aspects of Jameson's characterization of postmodernism, in particular his use of culture. It will be argued that Jameson directs us towards the social processes and structures within which postmodernism should be understood and explained. In this sense his endeavor to totalize—which is the target for much criticism from postmodernists and others—is laudable (see e.g. During, "Postmodernism or Post-Colonialism" and O'Neill, "Religion and Postmodernism"). Yet I shall also argue that there are problems with the way in which Jameson situates culture within late capitalism via his focus upon cultural experiences and not cultural practices.

I. Late Capitalism and Social Practice

Jameson persistently refers to postmodernism as the cultural logic of late capitalism and analyzes the ways in which cultural changes such as postmodernism "express the deeper logic" of the "late, consumer, or multinational" capitalist social system ("PCS," 125). His periodization of this third stage of capitalism as post-World War II multinational capitalism follows Mandel's scheme in *Late Capitalism* (1975). Apart from the reductionism in regarding historical changes as a consequence of the logic of capital accumulation and technological changes, his analysis is accompanied by a neat cultural periodization. Thus for Jameson, realism corresponds to market capitalism, modernism to monopoly capitalism, and postmodernism to late / multinational / consumer capitalism ("PCL," 78). From this perspective, culture seems to be regarded as taking place on "the superstructural levels" ("FJF," xv). While Jameson tries to shy away from the economistic implications of this position, it is clear that his view of culture largely works within the confines of a base-superstructure model which entails a whole series of problems I shall discuss here.

Apart from the fact that Mandel associates High Modernism and the International Style, not Postmodernism, with late capitalism (see Cooke, "Modernity, Postmodernity, and the City"), we do not find the assumed even-spread of modernism in monopoly capitalist societies. Indeed, it is noticeable how geographically uneven its distribution is, with England and the Scandinavian countries in the developed West scarcely generating sustained modernist movements whereas Germany, Italy, France, Russia, America, and the Netherlands did. It is therefore difficult to link artistic movements with specific stages of the development of capitalism.

In addition, approaches like those of Jameson tend to regard history as the outcome of a particular relentless developmental logic and play down the role played by classes, social movements and groups in creating the preconditions for such a logic in their various power balances, interdependencies and struggles for hegemony. In effect our focus of attention should not just be on the higher-level relatively abstract systems theorization of capital, but on the way capitalism has been practiced by specific groups, classes, and class fractions. Here we can refer to the debate between E. P. Thompson and Perry Anderson on the "peculiarities of the English" which took place in the 1960s, and Anderson's recent retrospective on the debate, "The Figures of Descent," in *New Left Review* (1987). Anderson defends his earlier position and emphasizes the role of the landed aristocracy in controlling English society in the nineteenth century. Effectively, feudalism did not just slip away and the bourgeoisie reign supreme; rather, contrary to the canons of the established theory, the landowners remained the hegemonic class in Victorian Britian (Wiener, *English Culture* 1981). Hence, it would seem important to acknowledge the different power balances and trajectories of domination in different capitalist societies, and to counter tendencies towards economistic readings with those which are more open to cultural differences, or what has been called by Richard Johnson "culturalism."

With regard to Jameson's general characterization of culture a number of points can be made. The first one relates to Jameson's designation of the role of culture in late capitalism as one of cultural profusion produced by the logic of the commodity form. Jameson, for example, has written that culture is "the very element of consumer society itself; no society has ever been saturated with signs and images like this one" ("RMC," 131). This statement has more recently been incorporated into Jameson's writings on postmodern culture when he refers to the destruction of "the semi-autonomy of the cultural sphere" to be replaced by "a prodigious expansion of culture throughout the social realm, to the point at which everything in our social life . . . can be said to have become 'cultural' . . . " ("PCL," 87).

The first point I'd like to raise about this statement is the implied contrast between late capitalist culturally-saturated societies and other societies. If it is based upon the assumption that nineteenth century capitalism was more purely economic, that transactions and social interactions were based on pure exchange value, with goods regarded as utilities, not commodity-signs, then some anthropologists and sociologists would take exception. It is possible to conceive of "the culture of the economy"; or the cultural underpinning of economic behavior as does Elwert (1984) who, following Durkheim refers to "the culturally embedded economy." Sahlins (1974, 1976), Douglas and Isherwood (1978) and Leiss (1983) have all pointed to the role goods play as "communicators," cultural signs, in both "primitive" and modern societies. We therefore need to take seriously notions of the culture of production and not just focus on the production of culture. Economic transactions themselves take place within a cultural matrix of taken-for-granted assumptions which should not be naturalized. Reddy, in *The Rise of Market Culture* (1984), has argued in his study of the rise of market culture in France that the notion that capitalist societies became transformed into a competitive market society is largely a mirage. Rather than an effective market in labor working in nineteenth century England and France, which was not the case, we have to reformulate this economic myth of the industrial revolution to consider the call for unregulated competition and the assumption that people are motivated by gain as elements of a new culture, a market culture, which progressively infiltrated discourse. In addition we need to ask the question how this discourse was transmitted and sustained which points to the need to examine the rise in the power potential of economic specialists and a change in their relation to other groups. Elias, in "On the Sociogenesis of Sociology" (1984), for example, has drawn attention to the way in which the growing autonomy of social phenomena such as markets must be related to the growth in the power potential of actual economic specialists in commerce, trade and industry, and the growth of autonomy of thinking about these phenomena (the emergence of a science of economics). Hence we need to inquire into the sociogenesis of economics and the economic sphere and the crucial role of culture in this process.

Furthermore if we look at other writers, such as Baudrillard, who have explored the logic of the commodity form and investigated the profusion of images and the growth of a simulational society which is similar to the postmodern culture Jameson talks of, we note some very different conclusions. In *The Mirror of Production* and the *Critique of the Political Economy of the Sign*, Baudrillard has theorized the logic of the commodity to point to the way in which under capitalism the commodity has become a sign in the Saussurean sense with its meaning arbitrarily determined by its position in a self-referential system of signifiers. We can therefore talk about commodity-signs, and the consumption of signs, and in an earlier piece—"Reification and Mass Culture" (1979)—Jameson followed Baudrillard thus far and would agree with his description that consumer culture and television have produced a surfeit of images and signs which have given rise to a simulational world which has effaced the distinction between the real and the imaginary: a depthless aestheticised hallucination of reality. For Baudrillard, however, this discovery of the nihilism at the heart of the logic of the capitalist commodity form—of Nietzsche as the completion of Marx (Kroker 1986)—is such to break all "referential illusions." To use one of Baudrillard's favorite metaphors: all the privileged domains of finalities—labor, use-value, sex, science, society, human emancipation and their theorizations (what Lyotard refers to as meta-narratives)—are sucked into a "black-hole" (*Simulations*). For Baudrillard, then, the logic of commodity production has produced a particular reversal in which culture once determined, now becomes free-floating and determining to the extent that today we can talk about the triumph of signifying culture, to the extent that we can no longer speak of class or normativity which belong to the prior stage of the system as people are reduced to a glutinous mass which refuses to stabilize in its absorption, reflection and cynical parody of media images. It is neither manipulated nor manipulable according to Baudrillard (see *In the Shadow of the Silent Majorities* 1983).

Jameson clearly follows Baudrillard in his depiction of the consumer society as saturated with signs, messages, and images and adds that "the priorities of the real become reversed, and everything is mediated by culture to the point where even the political and ideological 'levels' have initially to be disentangled from their primary mode of representation which is cultural" ("RMC," 139). From our above discussion, it is clear that the distinction between culturally saturated and non-culturally saturated societies needs a higher degree of specificity. As we will see below, it is a distinction which plays off the confusion of two meanings of culture: the anthropological or everyday meaning in the sense that all societies involve signifying practices, and culture in the sense of high culture, the product of specialists of symbolic production whose gain in power potential since the eighteenth century has given rise to the sense of an autonomous cultural sphere with pretensions to producing universal cultural guidelines for social practices. The assumption that this privileged cultural sphere has been eroded by the profusion of mass consumer cultural images and signs glosses over the long process of competition and interdependencies between the carriers of the market, consumer or mass culture and specialist high culture. We can discuss this by exploring two further aspects.

Many commentators would agree with Jameson's statement that the culture of postmodernism/late capitalism/post-industrial society is less unified than that of earlier capitalism (see Bell, Touraine, and Habermas). There is again, however, the danger we have discussed earlier that such a perspective is accompanied by a false dichotomy which implicitly regards the culture of traditional societies as integrated and unified. This viewpoint has been systematically criticized by Norbert Elias (1978, 1982), the Annales School (see Smith 1988) and Abercrombie, Hill and Turner (1980), much of whose research points to the way in which the popular culture of the fifteenth, sixteenth, and seventeenth centuries cannot be simply presented as a relatively unsophisticated forerunner of later developments. Many commentators unfortunately succumb to the writing of "thin histories" in which they attempt to think backwards from the upheavals of nineteenth century capitalism to some point of stability and pre-industrial organic unity, usually prior to 1750, and miss the complex, stratified nature of popular culture and its ritual inversions such as carnivals, festivals, and fairs (see Easton et al., *Disorder and Discipline*, 20). Hence it is dubious to claim that the parameters of order and disorder apply to modernity and postmodernity, respectively. Lyotard also argues that traces of this nostalgia can be found in Baudrillard's thesis that postmodernism has led to the end of the social, the disintegration of the social bond which turns society into an amorphous mass. For Lyotard this is a point of view "haunted by the paradisiac representation of a lost 'organic society'" (*Postmodern Condition*, 15)—a point which suggests that "the death of God" and the undermining of master narratives may be a bigger problem for intellectuals and their search for apodictic knowledge, that is to say, the centrality that cognitive beliefs play in their practices in contrast to those of ordinary men and women. Rather than succumb to the nostalgia of the intellectuals as Stauth and Turner point out (1988), we should acknowledge that particular versions of culture are carried and manipulated by various groups in a struggle to appropriate signs and use them in terms of their own particular interests.

It has often been noted that the distinction between high and mass culture has been used in this way by the intellectuals whose distaste for mass culture and preference for elitist high culture also betrays a nostalgia (Turner 1987). The conclusion of some commentators has been to regard the shift towards postmodern culture with the erosion of the distinction between mass culture and high culture as particularly threatening to the intellectuals. Jameson for example writes:

> This is perhaps the most distressing development of all from an academic standpoint, which has traditionally had a vested interest in preserving a realm of high or elite culture against the surrounding environment of philistinism, of schlock and kitsch, of TV series and *Reader Digest* culture, and in transmitting difficult and complex skills of reading, listening and seeing to its initiates. ("PCS," 112)

Academics do, of course, have an interest in reclaiming the investments they have made in accumulating their own cultural capital, and the bulwark against popular culture and non-privileged readings of consecrated "difficult" academic texts is to be seen throughout the academic institution with its pedagogy, examinations, refereeing procedures and "rigor." Yet Jameson is perhaps providing too homogenous a view of the intellectuals here. Not all intellectuals sit back and contemplate the erosion of high culture with horror. Rather, we can think of some groups, such as outsider intellectuals, who may contemplate the threat to the established order with less than concern, and indeed may themselves seek to hasten the process by proclaiming the virtues of popular, mass, and postmodern culture. This attack on the existing system of classification in the name of equality and democracy may then itself be followed by an attempted re-constitution of the symbolic hierarchy in favor of the outsider group. We are not of course yet in a situation of re-monopolization and it may very well be that this is no longer a realistic possibility today, yet it can be argued that the opening up of the cultural categories creates a space in which new interpretations, readings, and translations of the now acceptable mass/popular culture goods are in demand, and in the academy there is every sign that this will lead to the institutionalization of new pedagogies to guide initiates. We will return to the theme of the intellectuals and postmodernism at the end of the paper, suffice to say at this point that the current phase of cultural declassification both inside and outside the academy which has produced an interest in popular culture and postmodernism may undermine the power of some symbolic specialists while providing great opportunities for other symbolic specialists and cultural intermediaries.

II. Experience *vs* Practice

The next point about Jameson's approach I would like to raise relates to his focus on the experience of postmodernism to the neglect of the practices of postmodernism. It would seem important to distinguish between the commentator's experience of postmodernism and specific experiences of groups and class fractions who use postmodern cultural goods in particular practices. The latter may entail an analysis of how specialists in symbolic production (artists, intellectuals, academics) use post-modernism in their own practices as well as how members of specific groups (the audiences and publics) use specifically designated postmodern goods and experiences, as well as those experiences deemed to be postmodern by the critics (yet which may remain undesignated by the recipients) in particular everyday practices. To take an example with reference to Marshall Berman's work on modernity (*All That Is Solid Melts Into Air*), Janet Wolff in a paper titled "The Invisible *Flâneuse*" (1985) takes exception to Berman's restriction of the experience of modernity to public life. Berman, following Baudelaire sees the *flâneur*, the stroller, in the anonymous urban spaces of the modern city, as experiencing the shocks, jolts of the impersonal stimuli of the impressions gained in the crowd. Yet Berman has no place in his account for the *flâneuse*, and the absence of an account of women's experience of modernity is hardly justified by the limited capacity women had to appear in public life. Rather the experience of modernity of women in the private sphere constitutes an important yet missing relational element in any account of the experience of modernity.

If we turn to Jameson's account of the experience of modernity, he talks in detail about the imperative to expand our sensorium and our body when faced by the new hyperspace of postmodern architecture such as the Bonaventure Hotel in Los Angeles ("PCL," 80ff). We are given a fascinating interpretation of the meaning of the Bonaventure to Jameson, but little guidance as to how individuals from different groups incorporate the experience into their respective practices. Do individuals experience a new kind of shock, or are they unshockable? Or does the experience become a specifically postmodern one only after they have been told the building is postmodern? If so we need then to build into our analysis some account of the role of architects, intellectuals, and cultural intermediaries in seeking to educate and form the perceptions of publics.

The same argument could be presented with reference to two basic features of postmodernism Jameson identifies: the transformation of reality into images, and the fragmentation of time into a series of perpetual presents ("PCS," 115). With regard to the first, in a way similar to Baudrillard's discussion of postmodern imagistic culture, Jameson refers to pastiche and simulations, the stylistic diversity and heterogeneity which lead to the loss of the referent, "the death of the subject," and the end of individualism. Again we must raise the question who is experiencing this loss, and whether we are in danger of succumbing to nostalgia for a referent which may have been of little concern in the day-to-day practices of specific lower class groups in the *longue durée*. In addition, research into the practice of watching television has shown that a whole host of different activities in different groups takes place—eating, talking, working, sex, and so forth. Furthermore the actual reception and reading of programs is also filtered through a particular class habitus (Mullin and Taylor 1986; Leal and Oliven 1988). It is also important to note that television watching can be correlated to class and age. Those with the least capital, the old and the lower class, watch the most with viewing diminishing as one rises up the class scale and descends the age scale. Television for middle class groups provides a resource which is used in social encounters and is related to the important need to generate and sustain social contacts in the leisure time activities of these groups. Hence television watching is enclaved. TV is not the world and we need to inquire into the differential social uses of television (cf. DiMaggio 1987).

With regard to the second feature, the fragmentation of time into a series of perpetual presents, Jameson's paradigm here is schizophrenia. (Incidentally Baudrillard in *Silent Majorities* (1983) has also discussed the channel hopping TV viewer's fragmented perception of the world as inducing a schizophrenia which is an element of postmodernism.) Schizophrenia is regarded as the breakdown of the relationship between signifiers, the breakdown of temporality, memory, a sense of history. The schizophrenic's experience is of "isolated, disconnected, discontinuous material signifiers which fail to link up into a coherent sequence" ("PCS," 119). Although he/she therefore does not know personal identity, and has no projects, the immediate undifferentiated experience of the presentness of the world, leads to a sense of *intensities*: vivid, powerful experiences which bear "a mysterious and oppressive charge of affect" ("PCS," 120). This loss of a sense of narrative to the individual's life, and the disconnectedness of experience therefore links well with Jameson's first factor: the transformation of reality into images. It is difficult to comment adequately on postmodernism's alleged inducement of schizophrenic intensities, so I shall confine myself to making two brief points.

Firstly, how far have various religious and artistic subcultures down the ages celebrated the notion of such vivid intensities with the aid of group catharsis, drugs, and other means? Such liminal experiments are generally well circumscribed, and function as areas of excess demarcated from the seriality of everyday life. Here one thinks also of the discussions of the carnival of the Middle Ages by Bakhtin, Ladurie, and others (Stallybrass and White 1987; Featherstone, "Postmodernism and the Aestheticization of Everyday Life"). Whether or not individuals beyond these subcultures, or other groups outside certain well-defined occasions are experiencing greater intensities and loss of a sense of history, needs investigating. Jameson is guilty of over-generalization, therefore, and a lack of sensitivity to historical concreteness. His interest in totalizing and relating cultural changes to well-defined epochs means that he underestimates the differentiation of culture within pre-capitalist societies and hence the uniqueness of elements of the postmodern. Jameson provides very vivid and suggestive examples to illustrate his theory, yet they are only examples and only illustrative. One gets little sense of an interest in counter-tendencies and the openness and contingency of the lived structure of history as it is produced and reproduced, albeit blindly, by groups of individuals trapped together in competitive struggles and interdependencies in their everyday lives. This could be the stock objection of a social scientist against the more exploratory and openly imagistic modes of writing common in the humanities. But it is also central to the emergence and the problem of postmodernism which has brought together scholars from the humanities and social sciences on a common terrain. Jameson's totalizing interests and his attempts to outline a social theory of postmodernism do however put him firmly into the social science orbit and necessarily open him to their standards of judgment and rigor. This is especially so as Jameson is clearly unwilling to become an advocate of the new methods and practice postmodernism in his writings, which relates to his desire to stand outside postmodernism to explain and judge it.

Secondly, Norbert Elias' theory of *The Civilizing Process* (1978, 1982) which describes the internalization of external controls and increasing emotional constraint which accompanies the process of state formation has been recently modified by Cas Wouters (1986) who has worked closely with Elias to take into account tendencies which seem to run counter to this trend—e.g. the relaxation of emotional controls which took place in the 1960s. The resultant informalization process, a counter movement in the spiral development of the civilizing process, emphasizes that at certain points the balance may shift towards a "controlled de-control of the emotions" in which (and I would add especially for the new middle class) forms of behavior and modes of exploration of the emotions which were formerly forbidden and accompanied by strong interpersonal and psychic sanctions, now become permissible and even mandatory. In what follows, it should be possible to discover in more detail the increasing capacity of the new middle class to display a calculating hedonism, to engage in more varied (and often dangerous) aesthetic and emotional explorations which themselves do not amount to a rejection of controls, but a more carefully circumscribed and interpersonally responsible "controlled de-control" of the emotions which necessary entails some calculation and mutually expected respect for other persons. Hence we should go beyond the rational-emotional dichotomy and investigate those conditions and practices within the new middle class which create the possibility for a loosening of the controls on aesthetic and emotional experiences, which could lead to a greater receptivity to those symbolic goods and experiences which have been designated "postmodern."

To take some examples. One of the factors associated with postmodernism in the arts is an aesthetics of the body and sensation along with a movement from the discursive (language) to the figural (the direct experience of sensations and images), as Lash has shown in his "Discourse on Figure." A good example of this new sensibility is the body art of Dennis Oppenheim. One videotape of his work entitled "Disturbational Art" shows him eating ten gingerbread men and the microscopic color slides which are made of the excreta of the gingerbread men which are projected in art galleries alongside a running loop videotape of the whole ingestion and excremental process (Wall 1987). The point about this art, or anti-art like Dadaism, is that it is designed as a transgressive strategy, to shock and disgust audiences. Yet increasingly we have audiences who are educated in the tastes to appreciate such art and capable of the necessary controlled de-control of the emotions without feeling threatened by the transgression.

A second example is suggested by the work of Meyrowitz, *No Sense of Place* (1985), on the adult-like child and the child-like adult; he argues that adults today are given greater licence to explore emotions, act "spontaneously" and depart from former stricter controlled parental roles. Disneyworld and the proliferation of the theme parks clearly offer good examples of sites in which this emotional de-control and appreciation of sensations and adoption of behavior once restricted to children take place. Jameson cites Disneyland as paradigmatic of post-modern hyperspace and simulation ("RPM," 48). It has been argued that increasingly the contemporary tourist (or "post-tourist") approaches holiday locations such as resorts, theme parks, and increasingly museums in the knowledge that the spectacles offered are simulations and accepts the montaged world and hyper-reality for what it is (Urry, "Cultural Change and Contemporary Holiday-Making" 1988). That is, they do not quest after an authentic pre-simulational reality but have the necessary dispositions to engage in "the play of the real" and capacity to open up to surface sensations, spectacular imagery, liminoid experiences and intensities without the nostalgia for the real.

If one seeks to approach postmodern culture from this perspective, then it is possible to move away from some of the more abstract and hypostatized discussions of postmodernism and provide sociological evidence in terms of the classic evidential questions "who, when, why, and how many?" A study of the cultural practices and sites of postmodernism from this point of view could begin by examining what Zukin in "The Postmodern Debate over Urban Form" (1988) and Cooke in his "Modernity, Postmodernity, and the City" (1988) have dubbed "Postmodernization." With this term, they want to call our attention to the processes of restructuring socio-spatial relations by new patterns of investment which have led to the redevelopment of downtowns and waterfronts and the development of urban artistic and cultural centres and the gentrification which accompanies them. From this perspective, those particular groups which have the sensibilities and dispositions to attune themselves to postmodern cultural goods and experiences in the various roles of producers, transmitters, intermediaries, audiences, and consumers are in the first instance those whose habitus (taken-for-granted classificatory schemes and dispositions—Bourdieu 1984) predisposes them to be receptive to the kinds of experiences which have been designated as postmodern. The particular groups we have in mind here fall within the broad category of the new middle class. While there is a good deal of looseness in the usage of the term (see Burris 1986; Barbalet 1986), two points are of interest in respect to postmodernism. Firstly, this group has come into greater prominence in the postwar era, in particular the cohort known as the 60s generation which entered higher education in large numbers and which has many of the tastes and dispositions associated with postmodernism. Secondly, within it are large numbers of specialists in symbolic production and intermediaries who produce and disseminate information and culture and who are sensitized to the symbolic aspect of commodity production.

Bourdieu in *Distinction* (1984) has drawn attention to the emergence within what he calls the new *petite bourgeoisie* of new cultural intermediaries who provide symbolic goods and services; that is, marketing, advertising, public relations, radio and television producers and presenters, magazine journalists, fashion writers, the helping professions, social workers, marriage counsellors, sex therapists, dieticians, play leaders, etc. The new cultural intermediaries, like the intellectuals, typically invest in education and cultural capital. Bourdieu has referred to them as

"new intellectuals" who adopt a learning-mode towards life
(*Distinction*, 370). They quest for security and adventure, are
fascinated by identity, presentation, appearance, and lifestyle
(Featherstone 1987). Indeed their veneration of the artistic and
intellectual lifestyle is such that they consciously invent an art of
living in which their body, home, and car are regarded as an
extension of their *persona* which must be stylized to express the
individuality of the bearer. Bourdieu laconically tells us that this
quest for distinction via lifestyle cultivation "makes available to
almost everyone the distinctive poses, the distinctive games and
other external signs of inner riches previously reserved for
intellectuals" (*Distinction*, 371). The new cultural intermediaries
therefore help in transmitting both intellectual cultural goods and
the intellectual lifestyle to a wider audience. They also collude
with the intellectuals in seeking to legitimate the intellectual-
ization of new fields such as popular music, fashion, sport, and
popular culture which were previously excluded. Increasingly
these activities are subjected to serious analysis by intellectuals,
para-intellectuals, and the media cultural intermediaries.

It is therefore possible to point to the formation of audiences,
publics, and consumers of postmodern cultural goods, which is
part of a long-term process of the growth in the power potential of
symbol producers and the importance of the cultural sphere.
These changes have necessarily led to some de-classification and
de-monopolization of the power of the defenders of the long
established symbolic hierarchies in artistic, intellectual, and
academic institutions. The authority of the canon of the established, or of the aspirations of avant-gardes to become established,
thus becomes subject to challenge, critique, and attack. To take
the example of the arts. This is the result of a series of complex
changes in the interdependencies between business leaders, state,
and local politicians which has increased business and state
patronage for the arts and the power for the arts to become a major
market in its own right. Zukin in *Loft Living* (1988) has pointed to
the massive increase in artists working in New York since the
1970s and the growth of ancillary occupations, the gentrification
of SoHo and other districts which has made art a more acceptable,
profitable occupation and art itself appear more democratized.

Despite the cry for a return to Victorian values and the obliteration of the 60s culture by Thatcher and Reagan, it is interesting how difficult it is to remove symbol specialists and cultural centers and return to the old *petite bourgeois* mores.

There is not the space here to go into the changes within the various artistic and intellectual fields which have been associated with postmodernism save to make a few brief points (see also Featherstone, "In Pursuit of Postmodernism" and "Towards a Sociology of Postmodern Culture"). To understand postmodernism we need to focus upon the power balances and struggles within each particular field in the arts which opened up a space of cultural de-classification which made the emergence of the term and its advocacy by new outside groups against the established possible. Here the strategy of naming is important on the part of groups which seek to legitimate the closure and exhaustion of the old tradition and generate a new space ahead of the established. Hence "postmodern" became the term used in artistic and intellectual circles in the 1960s and 1970s to distance younger artists and critics from what they perceived as the exhausted and institutionalized modernism.

Likewise with the intellectuals, changes in the structures of their particular field may have worked on two levels to—a) open up pressures from below on the established by outsiders who seek to destabilize existing symbolic hierarchies and b) as a result of changes in the demand for intellectual goods in general by state agencies and the democratizing effect of being drawn into a wider cultural consumption market lead the intellectuals to engage in a searching reconsideration of the value, ends, and purpose of their endeavors. This latter position has been argued by Bauman in that he sees postmodernism as a direct articulation of the experience of the intellectuals who face a status and identity crisis as a result of the decline in demand for their goods which transforms them from the position of legislators with a universal project to the lesser role of interpreters, who must play with and translate for enlarged popular "transient" audiences the multiplicity of life-words and language games from the human cultural archive ("Is There a Postmodern Sociology"). Lyotard, in a 1988 "Interview," as well as others have pointed to the eclipse of the universal authority of the intellectuals. Some are happy to accept the move in which intellectuals have to more openly acknowledge their interests as a positive one and welcome the emergence of particular as opposed to universal intellectuals (see Bourdieu, "Interview"). For others such as Jacoby (1987), the destruction of the universal intellectual project of the "last intellectuals" who have no successors in the generation that follows them is a cause for concern.

III. Authority and Cultural Practice

From Jameson's perspective, there is a definite need on the part of intellectuals to resist the democratizing, populist spirit of postmodernism and retain the authority to speak for humankind. For example he argues from his Marxist perspective that the decay of the concept of socialism must be resisted and "it is a matter of re-inventing that concept as a powerful cultural and social vision" ("RPM," 57). It is a retention of the utopian aspect of Marxism which has laid Jameson open to accusations of a nostalgic neo-Durkheimian reaction to postmodernism such as that by O'Neill (139-161, in this volume). It could be that Jameson here has adopted an over-intellectualist approach to culture in which he over-estimates the power-potential of cultural images in producing social changes, and the necessity of integrative beliefs to sustain or produce social changes to the neglect of the ways in which culture is used and enacted on a "lower" taken-for-granted level in everyday practices. While many have welcomed the secularization of religion, perhaps the same should be said for the secularization of science (Douglas 1982). Indeed one way of understanding both forms of secularization, and that of intellectual knowledge in general, is to see it not in terms of the replacement of one set of beliefs or world-views by another, but a decline in the relative power potential of the symbol specialists in question—the clergy, scientists, and intellectuals—which is manifest in their inability to sustain the authority of their knowledge in the day-to-day power balances involving figurations of people. Of course there are clear differences in the nature and social effectivity of the types of knowledge involved. Bendix in "Culture, Social Structure, and Change" (1970) follows Weber in pointing out that religious specialists supplied beliefs which had a mundane meaning and practical usefulness for ordinary people. Yet the knowledge of artists and intellectuals does not offer similar practical benefits, despite the convictions of their advocates. Although artists and intellectuals possess formidable skills, these skills do not provide power in the religious sense, and arcane knowledge without apparent purpose makes cultural elites suspect to the populace.

It is therefore fitting that Jameson has referred to the democratization of culture as one aspect of postmodernism ("RPM," 53), yet he does so with a certain ambivalence, for he evaluates postmodernism negatively and wants to develop modes of analysis and artistic production which dissolve the postmodern pastiche and provide some renewed sense of social or global totality and history. In this sense, for Jameson, knowledge and art must retain some pedagogical function (see "PCL," 89-90). While this may be an understandable reaction to the acceptance of the disorder and playfulness of postmodernism as the paradigm for future social life and cultural production, it does leave him open to the postmodernist's riposte that he is nostalgically bemoaning the loss of authority of the intellectual aristocracy over the population (see Hutcheon, "Politics of Postmodernism" and During, "Postmodernism or Post-Colonialism").

To understand postmodernism then, we need to approach it on a number of levels. Firstly, it involves changes in the artistic intellectual and academic fields manifest in the competitive struggles in particular fields over the canon. Secondly, it involves changes in the broader cultural sphere in terms of the modes of production, circulation, and dissemination of symbolic goods which can be understood in terms of changes in the power-balances and interdependencies between groups and class fractions on inter- and intra- societal levels. Thirdly, it involves changes in the everyday practices and experiences of different groups who as a result of the first and second set of changes start to use regimes of signification in different ways and develop new means of orientation and identity structures. In many ways postmodernism stands as a sign for contemporary cultural change and should direct our attention to the interrelationship between the above areas or "levels" of culture and the necessary reflexivity which entails the inclusion of the academic intellectuals as socially interested parties in the process.

Like many other commentators, Jameson focuses on the experiential dimension of these changes, which is usually deciphered from texts and other modes of signification. Yet he has the merit of going beyond mere cultural analysis by attempting to locate postmodern cultural production in terms of the move to the third "purer" stage of late capitalism which has globalized the social. Here he rightly focuses on the eclipse of the state-society couplet with nation-states undermined by the expanded international market with its rapid capital and information flows. Yet while in this sense we could speak of the end of the social, for long the referent of sociology in the form of the identity of the state-society couplet, this does not mean the eclipse of social relations. Widening interdependencies and more complex balances of power between larger figurations of people can still be understood sociologically. The problem with Jameson's approach is that he moves from the economic to the cultural and misses out the mediating effect of the social, understood here as social relationships. That is, to understand postmodern culture, we need not just to read the signs but look at how the signs are used by figurations of people in their day-to-day practices. Of course a proliferation of signs, a flood of new cultural goods and commodities such as took place in eighteenth century England or mid-nineteenth century Paris has a culturally democratizing effect and makes it more difficult to "read the signs" to attribute a particular status and social position to the bearers of particular cultural goods and practices. Yet it can be argued that attempts will be continuously made to re-assign and read the attributes of cultural goods.

In short, the tendency is for social groups to seek to classify and order their social circumstances and use cultural goods as means of demarcation, as communicators which establish boundaries between some people and build bridges with others. Such a focus on the social usages of cultural goods firmly directs our attention to the practices of embodied persons who read-off and necessarily have to make judgments about others by decoding the cultural signs which others practice, display and consume. Postmodernism offers the prospect of the end of this social game, of a move beyond the social. Yet although we live in a phase of cultural de-classification, we must not discount the possibility of the re-establishment of a cultural order, nor fall for the temptation of treating liminoid enclaves of cultural disorder as co-extensive with culture as such.

In conclusion, then, postmodernism should be understood not only on the level of the unfolding of the logic of capitalism, but needs to be studied concretely in terms of the dynamic of the changing power balances, competitive struggles and interdependencies between various groups of specialists in symbolic production and economic specialists. That means we need to inquire into the role of the producers, transmitters, and disseminators of the alleged new forms of cultural production and consumption both inside and outside the academy. If postmodernism is a symptom of a societal or global shift towards cultural de-classification (DiMaggio 1987) which is manifest in a number of other areas such as the destabilization of long-established symbolic hierarchies which has opened up a space for the popularization and legitimation of the study of popular culture, then we need to locate it within the dynamic of changing intragroup struggles and interdependencies both on an inter- and intrasocietal level. To understand the postmodern, therefore, demands a good deal of reflexivity. We need to focus upon the carriers and transmitters of postmodernism who have an interest in the success of the term and all it implies within their struggles in the academy with the guardians of established symbolic hierarchies, and an interest in the creation and education of audiences and publics who can recognize and use postmodern cultural goods in practices.

Finally, we cannot ignore the role of academics, artists, and intellectuals in detecting traces of cultural change which they articulate and fashion as postmodernism. This is not to dismiss their interest in postmodernism as a cynical manipulation or moves within intellectual distinction games. Clearly, we are currently witnessing cultural changes which have raised the profile of culture within the culture-economy-society configuration and which demand careful research and theorization. Yet today the numerical force and power potential of the specialists in symbolic production has grown, particularly so if we compare the current debate over postmodernism with the earlier debate between the ancients and the moderns. If postmodernism points to a rise in the significance of culture—here one thinks of Baudrillard's assertion that today everything is cultural (*In the Shadow of the Silent Majorities*)—then we should not just understand this as an extension of the logic and technology of commodity production but also inquire into modes of transmission and consumption, the practices of symbolic specialists, cultural intermediaries and audiences which have dispositions which make them receptive to those sensibilities designated postmodern.

Religion and Postmodernism:
The Durkheimian Bond in Bell and Jameson
—With an Allegory of the Body Politic

John O'Neill
York University

In contemporary cultural criticism, whether the figures are neo-conservative or neo-marxist, it is generally agreed that our cultural malaise is at its height in postmodernism. But whereas Daniel Bell would argue that the collapse of the modern temper is to blame for the incivility of post-industrial society,[1] Fredric Jameson would consider late capitalism itself to be the source of the postmodern fragmentation of its cultural values ("PCL"). However, despite this analytic difference and their opposing political values, Bell and Jameson are inclined to call for a renewal of religious symbolism to restore the social bond against post-modern values which undermine equally the conservative and Marxist traditions (see *PU*). Postmodernism appears, therefore, to create a neo-modern opposition from both left and right. In turn it inspires a Durkheimian reflection on the sacred value of the social bond which is either backward looking, as in Bell's neo-conservatism, or else resolutely utopian, as in Benjamin, Bloch, Marcuse, and Jameson.

I think it is not unfair to Bell's argument to put it as follows: capitalism has successfully changed itself and the world without destroying itself through the class and ideological conflicts predicted by Marxists. Indeed, capitalism has successfully moved into a post-industrial phase in which its information sciences continuously revise its technological future, thereby solving the problem of crisis and again disappointing its Marxists critics. The post-industrial phase of the capitalist economy appears, however, to be threatened more by the contradictions which derive from its postmodern culture and policy than early capitalism was endangered by the cultural tensions of modernism. In short, late capitalism may prove unable to integrate its postmodern culture with its technological base. This is because the efficiency values of the latter are difficult to reconcile with a culture of narcissism and a politics of egalitarianism. While Bell insists that previous cultural critics were naive in supposing that modern society can collapse at any single point, his own articulation of the triplex of economy, policy, and culture nevertheless envisages the possibility of the post-industrial techno-culture being sapped by postmodern hedonism and self-gratification. For, despite the contempt which modernist artists expressed towards bourgeois scientism and materialism, they nevertheless shared the same "bounded" individualism exemplified in the Protestant ethic and its affinity for industrialism. That is to say, there existed a tension in modernism between its religious and its secular values as well as between its attitudes towards the self and towards society. But this tension has collapsed in postmodernism and its lack threatens to bring down post-industrialism. Bell, however, is quite unclear whether it is modernism or the collapse of modernism (and thus postmodernism), which undermines late (post-industrial) capitalism. How do we choose between the following observations?

> Today modernism is exhausted. There is no tension. The creative impulses have gone slack. It has become an empty vessel. The impulse to rebellion has become institutionalized by the 'culture mass' and its experimental forms have become the syntax and semiotics of advertising and *haute couture*. As a cultural style, it exists as radical chic, which allows the cultural mass the luxury of 'freer' lifestyles while holding comfortable jobs within an economic

system that has itself been transformed in its motivations.
(*Cultural Contradictions of Capitalism*, 20)

Here, then, modernity is damned if it does and damned if it does not underwrite capitalism. In the latter passage, however, we can hear more clearly Bell's neo-conservative lament for the moral values of a solidly bourgeois society in which the bond of religion is strong and resilient enough to bear the creative tensions of bounded Protestantism and spirited capitalism. At bottom, Bell attributes the crisis of capitalism to a crisis of religion, to a loss of ultimate meaning which undercuts its civic will (*Contradictions of Capitalism*, 21-22). By this he means that the obligations of collective life are reduced to subjective rights, the will to endure calamity is softened into the demand for instant gratification and religion is replaced by the utopiates of progress, rationality, and science:

> The real problem of *modernity* is the problem of belief. To use an unfashionable term, it is a spiritual crisis, since the new anchorages have proved illusory and the old ones have become submerged. . . . The effort to find excitement and meaning in literature and art as a substitute for religion led to modernism as a cultural mode. Yet modernism is exhausted and the various kinds of postmodernism (in the psychedelic efforts to expand consciousness without boundaries) are simply the decomposition of the self in an effort to erase individual ego. (*Contradictions*, 28-29)

Bell's conception of postmodernism seems to turn upon a rejection of everything in modernism except its puritanism as the matching ethic of bourgeois culture and mass industry. Everything else is thrown into a catch-all of hedonism, neurosis and death which exceeds the bounds of "traditional modernism" whose subversion, as he says, "still ranged itself on the side of order and, implicitly, of a rationality of form, if not of content." But, he continues, the vessels of art are smashed in postmodernism and religious restraint has vanished from the civil scene. Man himself disappears as a transcendental value. Worse still—for Bell is not worried so much by philosophical extravaganzas—postmodernism ushers in a crisis of middle-class values! Here bathos is the result of Bell's attempt to combine historical, philosophical, and sociological generalities to create a vision of cultural crisis which is universal and yet decidedly American.

What he gains in assigning a certain grandeur to the diagnosis of American problems, Bell loses when it comes to tackling them in any specific institutional setting. For example, he claims the road to post-industrialism involves three stages. In the first, we encounter a natural world; in the second, we deal with a fabricated world; whereas, in the third, our world is ourselves and our social interaction. Although one might have expected Bell to celebrate this last stage of sociability as a sociologist's (Simmel, Goffman) paradise, he finds instead that we have lost all sense of the social bond due to our progressive secularization:

> The primordial elements that provide men with common identification and effective reciprocity—family, synagogue, church and community—have become attenuated, and people have lost the capacity to maintain sustained relations with each other in both time and place. To say, then, that 'God is dead' is, in effect, to say that the social bonds have snapped and that society is dead. (*Contradictions of Capitalism*, 155)

Because he is at pains to avoid a Marxist (even a Critical Theory) analysis of the sources of "instability" in the American social order, Bell is obliged to leave things at the level of a neo-conservative lament over contemporary neo-liberalism, hedonism, and postmodernism. Thus America's final crisis is blamed upon a moral crisis whose sources are found in any number of situations (ignorance, poverty, and now AIDS) which seek to exceed the social compact and the proper arbitration of public and private goods. Without naming the excesses of the corporate culture and its willful barbarization of the masses, and by keeping silence with regard to the industrial military adventures that enraged American youth, Bell falls into dismissing the critical culture of the sixties in the same vein that Christopher Lasch trashes the culture of narcissism. Because they both suppress relevant distinctions regarding the systems of corporate power, whose production of the culture they despise determines its mass consumption,[2] Bell and Lasch cannot avoid the voice of a genteel modernism lamenting its own lost contexts of value with the fall into postmodernism.

Overall, Bell seems worried that the project of modernity will be overwhelmed by its own antinomianism. The latter may have served a positive good in its break with patriarchal and feudal authority, but without such authorities to kick against, antinomianism soon loses all sense of its own limitations and the result is that liberty turns to liberation against which we lack any overarching principle of legitimation. The death of God and now the death of man, rather than his expected resurrection, leaves society without value. This is the terrible price of the anti-bourgeois assault upon modernism. The curious thing, however, is that, despite Bell's vision of the erosion of authority, we have not seen any expansion of social revolutions other than in the name of the very bourgeois and Christian values discounted by postmodernism. The reason may be, as the Grand Inquisitor well knew, that the masses retain that coherence of meaning and value which Bell believes it is the task of his own exhausted elite to reimpose. Thus, whatever the changes in the institutions and rites of religion, its basic existential responses are perhaps less endangered because they are more necessary than ever.

Bell seriously underestimates the popular resistance (if not indifference) to the elite culture of unrestrained individualism, impulsive art, and moral nihilism which he defines as modernity's gift to postmodernism. Apart from remarking upon the resurgence of idolatry in the Chinese and Soviet Party, he does not make enough of the power of religious values to sustain resistance among intellectuals as well as old women. Of course, one is not appealing to the current prevalence of cults and sects of one sort and another which flourish whilst official religions appear to wane. Yet Bell is bold enough to forecast the appearance of three new religions or types of religious practice:[3]

(1) **Moralizing religion:** Fundamentalist, evangelical, rooted in the 'silent majority';

(2) Redemptive religion: Retreating from (post-) modernity, rooted in the intellectual and professional classes; and the growth of intellectual and professional classes; and the growth of 'mediating institutions' of care (family, church, neighborhood, voluntary associations) opposed to the state;

(3) Mystical religion: Anti-scientist, anti-self, past oriented, rooted in the eternal cycle of existential predicaments.

If Bell's prediction were to be borne out, then we might hope for (post-) modernism to erase the "beyond" of modernity, returning to the limits which the great civilizations have imposed upon themselves. To do so, however, (post-) modernism would need to revive sacred institutions while not sacrificing our commitment to cultural pluralism. So far, no theorist has appeared with any positive vision of such a society.

In the meantime, we may turn to Jameson's reflections on postmodernism and his attempt to restore Marxism to what Bell would call a redemptive religion since each of them is in fact aware of his respective appeal to Walter Benjamin's insistence upon the indestructibility of the aura of religion in human history. Ordinarily, social scientists, and Marxists in particular, are not kind to messianism. This has made the reception of Benjamin slower on this score than the adoption of his studies of culture and society. In short, Benjamin's analysis of commodity fetishism and his messianic response to modernism have been separated, either to be expropriated in the analysis of postmodernism or else left to those whose sympathies lie with the unhappy consciousness deprived of any hope of redemptive institutions. It is to Jameson's credit, therefore, that in a phrase reminiscent of Benjamin he entertains the possibility of a "two-way street" between religion and Marxism. And we shall look at this argument more closely in our conclusion. Meantime, as an unrepentant Marxist, Jameson draws some of the necessary distinctions we found lacking in Bell's account of the role of mass culture in late capitalism. Yet it can also be shown that, despite their opposing political values, Bell's neo-conservatism and Jameson's neo-Marxism derive equally from a Durkheimian lament upon the dissolution of the social bond. But whereas Bell's ancient liberalism separates him from the Marxist vision of community, Jameson can enthusiastically invoke this communal vision as the ultimate emancipatory drive in the political unconscious of our culture.

Postmodernism certainly reflects the sense of an ending. The question is—what has ended? Is it industrialism—in which case both capitalism and socialism are finished? Bell would probably take this view. Yet he can find nothing to celebrate in post-industrialism because in the end he remains a high priest of modernism. But then, Bell, Habermas, and Jameson, despite their differences, are all open to the taunts of Lyotard who finds everything to celebrate in the postmodern dissolution of right and left consensus (*Postmodern Condition*).[4] For Habermas, too, is unwilling to abandon the modernist project to which Marxism is committed. With quite different values from those of Bell, Habermas has also set about the destruction of the French branch of postmodernism which currently infects North America and Western Europe (see "Modernity—An Incomplete Project"). Between such figures, Jameson's position is a little difficult since certain aspects of postmodern cultural criticism continue to appeal to him inasmuch as it belongs to the received radicalism of literary studies, art, and architecture with which he identifies himself.[5] Overall, however, Jameson manages to extricate himself from the postmodern dissolution of grand narratives and to oppose it with an eloquent, even if surprisingly religious appeal on behalf of Marxism as the transcendental ground of all human culture and community.

It might well be argued that such sociologies as those of Bell's post-industrialism, Lasch's culture of narcissism, and Toffler's third wave are themselves prime examples of the postmodern exorcism of ideology and class struggle essential to the culture industry of late capitalism. Thus Jameson insists upon drawing a number of distinctions in order to avoid both cultural homogeneity and cultural heterogeneity as twin aspects of postmodern mass culture. He therefore argues that:

(i) Cultural analysis always involves a buried or repressed theory of historical periodization;

(ii) Global and American, postmodern culture is the super-structural expression of American domination;

(iii) Under late capitalism aesthetic production has been integrated into commodity production;

(iv) Postmodernism cannot be treated as part of modernism without ignoring the shift from early to late capitalism and the latter's redefinition of the culture industry.

These distinctions enable Jameson, like Habermas, to argue that Marxism must survive as the neo-modernist opposition to late capitalism, absolutely opposed to its superficiality, its imaginary culture, and its total collapse of public and private history.[6] Jameson and Habermas are therefore insistent that Marxist discourse cannot flirt with contemporary fragmentation and subjectlessness. Marxism is the transcendental story, a utopian gesture without which humanity is unthinkable.

However incapable it has become of shocking the bourgeoisie, postmodernism certainly seems to *épater les marxistes!* Consider how Jameson contrasts Andy Warhol's "Diamond Dust Shoes" with Van Gogh's "Peasant Shoes," or rather, Heidegger's reflections upon them ("PCL," 58-62). Warhol's shoes are colorless and flat; they glitter like Hollywood stars, consumed by a light that bathes them in superficiality, denying them all interiority, making them appear crazy for want of any gesture that is rooted in a world beyond artifice. By contrast, Heidegger claims that the peasant's shoes tell a story that involves ordinary people; they are continuous with institutions whose meaningful history is the broader framework in which they figure as human artifacts. According to Jameson, all this is lost in the world of video space-time, in the hyperspatiality of postmodern architecture, and in the self-consuming arts of postmodern literature and music.

Like Bell, Jameson refuses the postmodern celebration of the fragment, the paralogical and paratactical arts that dissolve the modernist narrative, dancing upon the grave of identity, rationality, and authority. Yet Jameson insists that postmodernism should not be considered solely as a phenomenon of style:

It [postmodernism] is also, at least in my use, a periodizing concept whose function is to correlate the emergence of new formal features in culture with the emergence of a new type of social life and a new economic order—what is euphemistically called modernization, post-industrial or consumer society, the society of the media or the spectacle, or multinational capitalism. ("PCS," 113)

Here, so often, Jameson's piling up of alternative epithets for the description of the socio-economic system leaves it unanalyzed in favor of its exploration in terms of two cultural phenomena—pastiche and schizophrenia—to which we now turn.[7] The fascination of these phenomena for postmodernist theorists is itself a sign of the inextricable sense and non-sense that characterizes the a-historical and an-ecological predicament of late capitalism.[8] *Pastiche* involves the intertextuality, inter-modishness of codes-without-context whose inappropriateness suggests they never had even a local value and hence always prefigured the contemporary value chaos. As I see it, such codes create the illusion that "Bogart" experienced himself and his social institutions with the same affectation exhibited by today's *Rocky Horror Show* for kids without a society and for whom character cannot mean anything else than caricature. The illusion of recycled popular culture is that bourgeois capitalism never created the institutional settings in which "Bogey" was taken by himself and others for real. This is appealing because in the bureaucratic contexts of late capitalism "Bogey" could only be a pastiche/parody of lost subjectivity or individualism. Postmodern sophisticates would, of course, claim that "Bogey" is all there was from the beginning, i.e., the essential myth of individualism. Hence all that remains is to democratize the myth—everyman his own "Bogey," everywoman as "Bacall." All we can aspire to is auto-affection through style, fashion, fad, to the moment, the scene, regrouped on the collective level through nostalgia, and everyday life as an open museum, a junk store, a replay.

While drawing upon the evaluative connotations of *schizophrenia* as a diagnostic concept, Jameson nevertheless disavows any intention to engage in cultural psychoanalysis beyond the confines of the literary community. Thus schizophrenia, as Jameson takes it from Lacan, is a linguistic pathology, the inability—due to faulty oedipalisation—to assign signifiers any temporal and spatial fixed points of identity and reference. Everything floats in an imploded present; action, project, and orientation collapse in the literal, nauseous, and real present in which teenagers are typically trapped. To keep them in this docile state is a task for our education system as a part of the larger system of mass culture to which it occasionally opposes itself, as I have argued elsewhere regarding the functions of the disciplinary society and its therapeutic apparatus.[9] What Jameson (like Bell and Habermas, but from a different interpretation of the same materials) finds at work in pastiche and literary schizophrenia is the collapse of the oppositional culture of modernism so that these two cultural elements of postmodernism now feed the cultural sytle of late capitalist consumerism:

> I believe that the emergence of postmodernism is closely related to the emergence of this new moment of late, consumer or multi-national capitalism. I believe also its formal features in many ways express the deeper logic of the particular social system. ("PCS," 125)

By foreshortening the production process to the management of consumerism, the more difficult analysis of the social relations of production, power, class and racism is reduced to the operations of an imaginary logic of the political economy of signifiers, where everything floats on the surface of communication. Here Jameson's reliance upon Baudrillard's *For a Critique of the Political Economy of the Sign* commits him to the company of Daniel Bell in a lament over the flood of narcissistic consumerism deprived of the mirrors that reflected the old order identities of societies which subordinated exchange value to the higher symbolisms of gift, sacrifice, and community. Rather, postmodern consumers find themselves as mere switching points at video screens which miniaturize their lives in order to speed them up. The result is that their everyday lives are left devastated by the contrast between the archaic symbolic orders that consumers nevertheless inhabit and the imaginary flux in which they drift.

Thus, inside those soft bodies which wander through our shopping malls and whose minds are operated upon from the outside world, desire is deprived of all intelligence:

> This is the time of miniaturization, telecommand and the microprocession of time, bodies, pleasures. There is no longer any ideal principle for these things at a higher level, on a human scale. What remains are only concentrated effects, miniaturized and immediately available. This change from human scale to a system of nuclear matrices is visible everywhere: this body, our body, often appears simply superfluous, basically useless in its extension, the multiplicity and complexity of its organs, its tissues and functions since today everything is concentrated in the brain and in genetic codes; which alone sum up the operational definition of being. ("The Ecstasy of Communication," 128)

Here, then, we have a curious effect. How can analysts as varied as Bell, Jameson, Lasch, Baudrillard, and Habermas join common chorus against late capitalism when their politics vary so widely from right to left? The answer seems to be that as cultural critics of late capitalist consumerism they are all *neo-modernists*. In turn, Marx's own modernism may well be the guiding influence. The centrality of Marxism to the project of modernity, as argued for by Habermas and Jameson, can also be claimed on the consideration of Marx's writing, his imagery, style, and narrative conventions. Thus Berman and O'Neill have drawn attention to the modernist reading required in order to grasp Marx's polyvalent writings without reducing them either to narrow science or to mere mythology.[10] O'Neill has argued that because Marx's text so obviously turns upon its modernist aesthetics, the Althusserian reading of it as a text of science must be rejected (O'Neill, *For Marx Against Althusser*, 1-17), but without surrendering to Lyotard's reading of it as a lunatic text, or a pure work of art (Lyotard, "Le désir nommé Marx," 117-188).

What unites Bell and Jameson, despite the different nuances in their response to the culture of postmodernism, is the will to order. In Bell the order is backward-looking; in Jameson it is forward-looking. Both are in search of a new social bond and both believe that it cannot be discovered by severing our links with the past as the most mindless forms of postmodernism imagine. In this regard, even Lasch and Habermas share the same modernist sentiment, despite different ideas about its historical sources. Although orthodox Marxism and neo-conservatism are as opposed to postmodernism as they are to one another, with respect to the value of the past each is shot through with the contradictory impulses of modernism. Each may blame the self-consuming arti-facts of postmodernism for their cultural malaise, but the fact is that it is industrialism which institutionalizes discontent and, so to speak, condemns us to modernity. Yet the neo-Marxists seem just as unwilling as the neo-conservatives to switch their gods. As Marcuse saw, both continue to cling to the old god Prometheus. Both fight to keep out the young gods Orpheus and Narcissus whose pre-modern and post-industrial figure still fails to seduce Habermas and Bell. This is so, even though the social forecast of post-industrialism calls for a more creative divinity:

> In the light of the idea of non-repressive sublimation, Freud's definition of Eros as striving to 'form living substance into ever greater unities, so that life may be prolonged and brought to higher development' takes on added significance. The biological drive becomes a cultural drive. The pleasure principle reveals its own dialectic . . . the abolition of toil, the amelioration of the environment, the conquest of disease and decay, the creation of luxury. All these activities flow directly from the pleasure principle, and, at the same time, they constitute *work* which associates individuals to 'greater unities'; no longer confined within the mutilating dominion of the perform-ance principle, they modify the impulse without deflecting it from its aim. There is sublimation and, consequently, culture; but this sublimation proceeds in a system of expanding and enduring libidinal relations, which are in themselves work relations. (Marcuse, *Eros and Civilization*, 193-194)

Given the neo-Marxist and neo-conservative refusal of the new god Eros, a void is created in which Jameson can work to refurbish the Marxist vision of a collective utopia. Thus he argues that the death of the subject, the end of man, the migration of reason into madness, the collapse of social and historical narratives into schizophrenic case histories, are only acceptable visions of postmodern critique if we work for a renewal of Marxist history and hermeneutics. Jameson, still apprenticed to Marcuse and Bloch, assumes the Promethean task of binding his own myth to the utopian future of industrialism. He thereby seeks to retain the historical identity of the original Promethean myth with its utopian science of action and community bound by hope and memory:

> Now the origin of Utopian thinking becomes clear, for it is memory which serves as the fundamental mediator between the inside and outside, between the psychological and the poetical. . . . The primary energy of revolutionary activity, derives from this memory of prehistoric happiness which the individual can regain only through its external-ization through its reestablishment for society as a whole. The loss or repression of the very sense of such concepts as freedom and desire takes, therefore, the form of a kind of amnesia . . . which the hermeneutic activity, the stimu-lation of memory as the negation of the here and now, as the projection of Utopia, has its function to dispel, restoring to us the original clarity and force of our own most vital drives and wishes. (*MF*, 113-114)

Whereas capitalism displaces its own myths with secular science, utopian Marxism keeps the bond between myth and science as a history-making institution. Utopianism, then, is not a roman-ticism or nostalgia that refuses to learn from history. Rather, what can be learned from history, which preserves rather than represses its own genealogy, is that romanticism and myth cannot be contained by secularism and that in the end they are to be joined to the sciences of action and collectivity that they prefigure:

> Thus, to insist upon this term of Breton which corresponds
> both to Freudian usage and to our own hermeneutic vocab-
> ulary . . . a genuine plot, a genuine narrative, is that which
> can stand as the very figure of Desire itself: and this not
> only because in the Freudian sense pure physiological
> desire is inaccessible as such to consciousness, but also
> because in the socio-economic context, genuine desire risks
> being dissolved and lost. . . . In that sense desire is the form
> taken by freedom in the new commercial environment.
> (*MF*, 100-101)

In short, Jameson argues that every genre of thought (myth,
literature, science) has to be grasped as a psycho-historical master-
narrative (the political unconscious) which when properly
interpreted, is Marxism. Postmodernism cannot be a stage in this
narrative because it abandons history as a human motive, i.e., as
the motive to make ourselves human individually and collectively.

Whereas Bell and Lasch lament the dissolution of the social
bond, Habermas and Jameson continue to affirm its ultimate
historical, normative, and analytic primacy. Jameson's particular
strength, it must be said, lies in his will to carry the burden of the
dialectical switching between the secularization and the re-
enchantment of the life-world and its modern vocation while
seeking to avoid Weberian pessimism as well as Nietzschean
cynicism. He does so fully conscious that the age of religion has
passed and that for this very reason we are tempted to produce an
"aestheticized" religion, an imaginary or hallucinated community, in an age that is neither religious nor social. How, then,
can Marxism exempt itself from such sentimentalism? Jameson's
reply is that Marxism and religion can be embraced as elements of
"marital square" in which history and collectivity join individual
and community action and understanding against inaction and
ignorance that dispossess the community and exploits it in favor
of its masters. Jameson's fundamental claim is that all forms of
social consciousness—both of oppressor and of oppressed—are
utopian, inasmuch as these groups are themselves figures for an
unalienated collective life. Jameson is at pains to deny that such
an affirmation merely represents a return to a Durkheimian

symbolics of social solidarity, or to a neo-Marxist marriage of aesthetics and social hygiene. Marxism needs both a positive as well as a negative hermeneutics of social solidarity if it is not to degenerate into postmodern fragmentation, or into an absurd negativity that would separate forever its scientific utopianism from its primitive myth of communism:

> Only Marxism can give us an adequate account of the essential mystery of the cultural past, which, like Tiresias drinking the blood, is momentarily returned to life and warmth and allowed once more to speak, and to deliver its long forgotten message in surroundings utterly alien to it. This mystery can be re-enacted only if the human adventure is one; only thus—and not through . . . antiquarianism or the projections of the modernists—can we glimpse the vital claims upon us of such long-dead issues as the seasonal alternation of the economy of a primitive tribe, the passionate disputes about the nature of the Trinity . . . only if they are retold within the unity of a single great collective story . . . Marxism, the collective struggle to arrest a realm of Freedom from a realm of Necessity. . . . It is in detecting traces of the uninterrupted narrative, in restoring to the surface of the text the repressed and buried reality of this fundamental history, that the doctrine of a political unconscious finds its function and its necessity. (*PU*, 19-20)

Such passages are among the best in literary Marxism. Yet Jameson's claims are clearly exorbitant. They are so because he cannot identify any specific social forces to carry his utopianism— his proletariat is everywhere and nowhere—and so he throws the holy water of Marxist utopianism over any group, whether oppressor or oppressed, insofar as they are "figures" of an ultimately classless society!

In effect, Jameson achieves a remarkable inversion of the position of both Althusser and Lyotard with respect to the allegorical cathexis of master narratives or ideologies. History, in the large sense, is taken by Jameson to move through four levels— from the collective to individual and from the individual to

collective story, thereby refurbishing Marxism as the master
narrative, albeit as the "absent cause" or the political unconscious
of our times. The shifts involved between the collective and
biographical figures and between the individual and communal
levels of the social are achieved through the ideological categories
of class discourse insofar as its antagonistic figures are always
framed in an ultimately utopian reversal that results in a
transcendental community (*PU*, 30-33). The stages along the way,
so to speak, require that nature never be outside the romance in
which it can respond to our desire in figures of good and evil, of
wildness and civilization through which we, in turn, educate our
imagination, as Frye would say. Vico and Marx, as I understand
them,[11] would have said something similar. That is, each would
have insisted upon the positive continuity in the hermeneutics of
the past and the present in recognition of the social debt which
capitalism represses (as the basis of its unconscious) and which
socialism recognizes as its humanist *point d'honneur*. From this
standpoint, the Marxist critique of reification and fragmentation
is not simply an exercise in dialectical epistemology. It represents
an ethical rejection of every possessive appropriation of values and
relationships which breaks off, interrupts, and represses the
recognition of exchange, inter-generationality, and collective debt.
It is from this point of view that we understand the affinity
between capitalism and secularism. This unholy alliance is
constituted precisely through its suppression of the sacred and its
rituals for the redemption of mankind's debt to the creation. The
shift from *gemeinschaft* to *gesellschaft* represents the reduction of
social debt to the social contract as a device for the individual
appropriation of the pre-contractual values of reciprocity and
communal indebtedness.

It is time now to look a little closer at Jameson's attempt to
open a "two way street" between religion and Marxism. In turn,
this will oblige us to formulate, an alternative allegory of the body
politic in response to Jameson's efforts on these lines:

> . . . I have throughout the present work implied what I have
> suggested explicitly elsewhere, that any comparison of
> Marxism with religion is a two-way street, in which the

former is not necessarily discredited by its association with the latter. On the contrary, such a comparison may also function to rewrite certain religious concepts—most notably Christian historicism and the 'concept' of providence, but also the pretheological systems of primitive magic—as anticipatory foreshadowing of historical materialism within precapitalist social formations in which scientific thinking is unavailable as such. (*PU*, 285)

One might charitably interpret such passages as Jameson's effort to maintain solidarity with past societies and to recognize a certain indebtedness to them. But his benchmark of science in fact breaks the bond between them because it is still necessary for Jameson to consider Marxism a science, however riddled with hermeneutics and psychoanalysis. This is all the more curious since he is also engaged in the restoration of the sacred values which underwrite the Marxist text to make it central to humanity. By the same token, it should be noticed that Jameson treats only a very generalized concept of Christian history, abstracting from the rituals and communities in which Christian doctrine is practiced—and the same can be said of his concept of Marxism and mass culture. In each case, Jameson holds to the utopian position that, however degraded these forms of human culture may be, they never quite erase the aspiration towards individual and collective transfiguration which constitute class consciousness:

> . . . all class consciousness of whatever type is Utopian insofar as it expresses the unity of a collectivity; yet it must be added that this proposition is an *allegorical* one. The achieved collectivity or organic group of whatever kind—oppressors fully as much as oppressed—is Utopian not in itself, but only insofar as all such collectivities are themselves figures for the ultimate concrete life of an achieved Utopian or classless society. (*PU*, 291)

In this extraordinary embrace of class consciousness, Jameson appears to have exceeded even his own understanding of Durkheim's inscription of religious solidarity as the sub-text of all culture. His Utopianism demands an absolutely sublimated culture entirely free of any functionalist or ideological usage. Ultimately, this is achievable only on behalf of a totally collective subject who would entirely escape the arrows of the post-structuralist critique of subjective subjectivism. The only figure of such a collective subject that Jameson can produce at this point is the "body of the despot" contributed by the Asiatic mode of production:

> In most of the *Asiatic* land forms, the *comprehensive unity* standing above all these little communities appears as the higher *proprietor* or as the *sole* proprietor. . . . Because the *unity* is the real proprietor and the real presupposition of communal property . . . the relation of the individual to the *natural* conditions of labor and of reproduction . . . appears mediated for him through a cession of the total unity—a unity realized in the form of the despot, the father of many communities—to the individual, through the mediation of the particular commune. (*PU*, 295)

Despite the potentially regressive features in this figuration of "Orientalism," Jameson contents himself with noting the attendant controversy but does not consider whether any other figure of the symbolic enactment of social reciprocity might be drawn from elsewhere in our cultural heritage. Here I think we need to rethink the allegory of the body politic, as I have done elsewhere,[12] and to show how Jameson lets slip a figure that might well have served his purposes better than that of the despotic body.

The body politic certainly emerges from a long allegorical history of the desire for the representation of unity and difference in a just society. It contains both a myth and a metaphysic which has been appended to throughout the history of social and political conflict both for revolutionary and restorational purposes. It is a transgressive figure when opposed to caste interpretations of social division of labor, as well as a figure of difference and charismatic justice when opposed to the forces of rationalization and homogenization. It is above all, a figure operative on both levels of synchrony and diachrony, demanding reciprocity on the social level and inter-generational indebtedness on the level of history. Thus it may be said that the political community thinks itself as a community of difference and exchange, avoiding both any extreme naturalization of its difference and rejecting any hardened organic or totalitarian conception of its species existence. The body politic is not a purely natural figure because it already figures the desire for political community whose infrastructures are already in place at the levels of work, family, and society. It is therefore an act of interpretative violence for any theorist to treat the body politic as anything less than a mode of collective knowledge. It is not a mode of unconscious or of natural desire. Yet it is a transgressive figure because of its power to integrate what has been separated and to differentiate what has been homogenized.[13] The body politic is a civilizational concept, to use the language of Frye, and it functions on the highest level of allegory to transfigure society in terms of the human body itself imaginatively conceived as the universe of human potentiality.

Here, however, Jameson loses nerve and objects that the figure of the body politic is reprivatized and can reflect only itself, losing its analogical power as a collective organism (*PU*, 74). But Marx never conceived of the natural body as the subject of history for the very reason that he considered nature part of human history: "History is the true natural history of man."[14] Thus the history of the human body belongs to a collective history in which the figures of the body politic and of the *sensus communis* sketch out strategies of community and difference in the articulation of social life, economy, and policy. Vico's two basic axioms provide an initial formulation of the hermeneutic principles of the allegory of the body politic:

(i) Common sense is judgment without reflection, shared by an entire class, and entire people, and entire nation, or the entire human race.

(ii) Uniform ideas originating among entire peoples unknown to each other must have common ground in truth.[15]

Viewed in this fashion, the body politic requires that we construct scenarios for the mutual accountability of the communities of natural and social science within the larger democratic community of common sense political and legal practice. The metaphor of body-politics, in keeping with Vico's own views, would therefore replace the scientistic metaphor in the dominant imagery of the polity. In this way, we might restore the public functions of rhetoric in the rational advocacy of knowledge and values that address the three basic domains of the body politic, which we differentiate as follows:

	Levels	Institutions	Discourse
	(i) the bio-body	family	well-being
Body			
	(ii) the productive body	work	expression
Politic			
	(iii) the libidinal body	personality	happiness

By differentiating these three levels of the body politic, we further separate ourselves from naturalistic accounts of the political legitimacy problem by introducing a logic of ethical development as the fundamental myth of political life. The three levels of family, economic, and personal life represent an historical-ethical development and also permit it to identify contradictions or constraints and regressions in the body politic. Thus, we can identify alienation as a complex phenomenon that affects not only the productive body but also the bio-body and libidinal body. Conversely, alienation is not solved merely by satisfying organic needs, nor by the smooth engineering of productive relations since these do not meet the demands of the libidinal body. By the same token, we cannot abstract the dreams of libidinal life from our commitments to familial and economic life. Thus a critical theory of the legitimacy problems of the body politic is simultaneously a constitutive theory of social development and of members' recognition of the places in their lives where this development is blocked and even deteriorating. Members' expression of their experience with the underlying logic of development that sustains political legitimacy will not be limited to official electoral conduct. It will include such subversive practices as strikes, family breakdown, crime, protest, lampoons, neighborhood and street gatherings, music, song, poster, and wall art. A critical theory of political legitimacy does not discount the rationality of members' ordinary accounts of their political experience in terms of the vocabularies of family, work, and, person. Moreover, it does not presume upon either the found rationality or irrationality of such accounts.

Each of the three levels of the body politic is represented in a characteristic institution which is in turn allocated its proper domain of discourse. Although the various institutional and discourse realms of the body politic are only analytically differentiated, they may be said to constitute an evolutionary process in which the congruency of the three discursive orders maximizes the commonwealth.[16] Every society needs to reproduce itself biologically and materially. These needs are articulated at the institutional levels of work and the family where discourse focuses upon the translation of notion of well-being, health, suffering estrangement, and self-expression. Here we cannot deal with the institutions that are generated at these two levels of the body politic. In the later evolutionary stages, the articulation of the libidinal body generates discourse demands that impinge differentially upon the institutions of family and work. To date, the institutionalization of these "revolutionary" demands represents a challenge to all modes of scientistic, social, and political knowledge. Meantime, we can envisage an extension of Habermas' program for the rational justification of the ideal speech community in terms of the specific discursive contexts of the tri-level body politic.[17] It would be necessary to generate a topology of knowledge and evaluation claims with regard to the bio-body, the productive body, and the libidinal body at each appropriate institutional level, with further criteria for urgency, democratic force, and the like.

The libidinal body politic represents a level of desire that fulfills the order of personality insofar as it transcends the goods of family and economy. So long as men continue to be birthed and familied of one another, then the bodily, social, and libidinal orders of living will not be separable pursuits. By the same token, the body politic cannot be reduced to purely economistic satisfactions any more than to the dream of love's body. A distinctive feature of the metaphor of the body politic is that it allows us to stand away from the system, i.e., machine, cybernetic, and organization metaphors that reduce the problem of political legitimacy to sheerly cognitivist sciences. This shift in turn recovers the plain rationalities of everyday living, family survival, health, self-respect, love, and communion. Members are aware of the necessary interrelationships between their family, economic, and personal commitments. They judge the benefits of their labor in the productive sector of the body politic in terms of the returns to their familial and personal lives. They are willing to make trade-offs between the demands of family life and the ambitions of their personal and libidinal life. In short, members have a fairly complex understanding of their corporate life which is not reducible to the single pattern of utilitarian or decisionistic reasoning that governs calculations in the productive sector.

On the right and on the left, we are still waiting for history to deliver itself. Whether politics or religion will be the midwife remains undecided. After a bitter lesson, the sociologist puts his money on religion. Jameson meantime perseveres with the alchemy of a hermeneutics that will deliver history, politics, and religion. And so the stage of history takes another turn. The Ghost of Marx returns; there is much talk about talk in which Jameson is apparently more agile than Habermas who waits for a chance to articulate a final economy of truth, sincerity, and justice. Bell is silenced, but offstage the laughter of Lyotard still reaches us. Marcuse, Bloch—and perhaps ourselves—remain saddened.

Notes

1. Daniel Bell, *The Cultural Contradictions of Capitalism* and restatements, "Liberalism in the Postindustrial Society," "Beyond Modernism Beyond Self," pp. 228-244 and 275-302 in his *The Winding Passage*; also "Modernism Mummified," which nuances the argument but not sufficiently to alter our estimate of Bell's position.

2. See O'Neill, "Televideo *Ergo Sum*: Some Hypotheses on the Specular Functions of the Media."

3. Daniel Bell, "The Return of the Sacred? The Argument on the Future of Religion" in *The Winding Passage*, pp. 334-335.

4. The "translation" of this minor document into the scene of postmodernism is astounding to anyone who saw it almost a decade ago when it appeared as a "report" on the context of modern science.

5. Jameson is well informed about events on the contemporary cultural scene. His observations on art, photography and architecture are as much part of the arts of bricolage as commentaries upon them. Hence it is a matter of (in)convenience as to what one does in trying to keep up with Jameson's essays. See, for example, his "Pleasure: A Political Issue"; "Postmodernism and Utopia"; and "Architecture and the Critique of Ideology."

6. See O'Neill, "Public and Private Space," *Sociology as a Skin Trade: Essays Towards a Reflexive Sociology.*

7. I choose these two because one may as well.

8. Hal Foster, "(Post) Modern Polemics," *Recodings: Art, Spectacle, Cultural Politics.*

9. O'Neill, "The Disciplinary Society: From Weber to Foucault."

10. Marshall Berman, *All That is Solid Melts Into Air*; John O'Neill, "Marxism and Mythology," *For Marx Against Althusser.*

11. O'Neill, "Naturalism in Vico and Marx: A Discourse Theory of the Body Politic," in *For Marx Against Althusser*; and "Marx's Humanist Theory of Alienation," *George Lukács and His World*, ed. Ernest Joós.

12. O'Neill, *Five Bodies: The Human Shape of Modern Society.*

13. Henri Lefebvre, *Le manifeste différentialiste.*

14. Karl Marx, "Economic and Philosophical Manuscripts," *Karl Marx Early Texts*, trans. and ed. David McLellan.

15. *The New Science of Grambattista Vico*, trans. Thomas G. Bergin and Max H. Fisch. Pp. 142-144.

16. Habermas, "What is Universal Pragmatics?" *Communication and the Evolution of Society*, trans. Thomas McCarthy. Pp. 1-68.

17. See O'Neill, "Language and the Legitimation Problem," pp. 351-358.

Defining the Postmodern: The Case of SoHo Kitchen and *El Internacional*

Christopher Sharrett
Seton Hall

Architecture studies became involved early on in the debate on postmodern culture, noting the inadequacies of theories offered by literary critics such as Ihab Hassan and Leslie Fiedler.[1] While literary criticism in the 70s tended to regard postmodernism as "ultra" modernism—that is, an extreme extension of modernist aspirations—Charles Jencks, in *The Language of Post-Modern Architecture*, using the changing cityscape as a model of explanation, saw postmodernism as a distinct break from all that had gone before, a tendency that suggested a schizophrenia in postmodernism's manifestation as "part modernism, part something else." The work of Jencks and other architecture critics such as Robert Venturi (although Venturi is more evangelist than theorist) made tentative steps in placing postmodern art within a changing political, economic, and social framework. By emphasizing the eclecticism of postmodern architecture, Jencks suggested graphically the "legitimation crisis" of late capitalism, outlined with different methods in Jürgen Habermas' *Legitimation Crisis* and Jean François Lyotard's *The Postmodern Condition*. The pastiche structures designed by Michael Graves, the Chippendale pediment and Roman colonnade to Philip Johnson's AT&T Building, represent capitalism in its multinational, imperial phase, as architecture appropriates styles from various countries and historical periods, emphasizing mediation over real history, destroying the ethnic and historical specificity of culture, making the alienating appear at once *outré* and familiar, the *Unheimlich* read as Warhol's "bored but hyper" cityscape.

Fredric Jameson has developed in detail some notions intuited by Jencks, beginning with the assumption that architecture, as the art form most heavily involved with high finance, is a good index of cultural change ("PCL"). Yet Jameson's oft-cited analysis of John Portman's Bonaventure Hotel, and Venturi's postmodern manifesto *Learning from Las Vegas* have not resolved some contradictions regarding architecture as an embodiment of the postmodern temperament. The neo-conservative retrogression of postmodernism may be seen in the "grand hotel" aspect of the Bonaventure, with its huge mirror-plated silos suggesting an impervious citadel, reflecting capitalist victories (the other downtown skyscrapers) while shutting out, with cool detachment, the blight of Los Angeles. But isn't this same imperviousness associated with the steel and glass boxes of late modernism? Isn't the dislocating layout of the Bonaventure with its utopian free play with space—recalling William Cameron Menzies' *Things to Come*—the Promethean assault on nature begun with Romanticism? It does seem apparent that the excesses of Portman and Johnson are associated with a strategy designed to recoup credibility for "official" corporate architecture (Jameson notes that the Bonaventure is as much a tourist stop, a "popular" building as much as hotel). The atrium at the center of Portman's Hyatt Regencies suggests an almost hyperbolic bourgeois complacence and ease tempered slightly by the incorporation of nature and the blurring of outside and inside; the first floor mini-malls—while ludicrously foregrounding the role of capital and consumerism in the existence of these buildings—offer a "casual" approach to space, breaking down barriers between work and play, relaxation and consumption. For the new urban bourgeoisie, this play with space coincides well with the changing nature of labor in post-industrial society, with increased leisure hours, "flex-time" work schedules. These new environments also approximate, as Jameson suggests, the disruption of time, space, and history represented in the media landscape.

I will argue, however, that official architecture does not evidence postmodernism's site of struggle as easily as smaller shops, restaurants, and public buildings which address discrete elements of postmodern ideology, particularly as we examine works situated within those parts of the city identified with fringe or counter-culture, but which also function in defining an artistic vanguard. Sectors of New York, for example, have been involved in a kind of internecine feud regarding definitions of dominant culture, progressive art, and the modern. It may be erroneous, however, to separate this situation from the "mapping" undertaken by Jameson.

As one reads Jameson's analysis of the Portman-style big city skyscraper, it is apparent that his principal concern is with the sense of disorientation basic to postmodern culture, manifest here in the cultural mainstream (if such terms still have any application) and in structures available to an upwardly-mobile urban bourgeoisie (the buildings I will discuss are of course associated with bourgeois society—their distinction is their "artistic vanguard" affectation). In comparing the Bonaventure to boutiques and bars of, for example, downtown New York, it is useful to recall Jameson's notion of postmodernism as cultural dominant and as site of the decentered subject. Postmodernism is even less a "movement" than modernism, but if modernism's chief feature is its tendency toward utopian totalizations, post-modernism's main gesture is toward incorporating within itself wildly contradictory ideologies, impulses, styles. As an aspect of capitalism's "purer" phase (following on another notion of Jameson and Ernest Mandel), this may be read as both conscious and unconscious co-optation and absorption of adversarial components of culture, and, more importantly, a rendering of cultural schizophrenia and the fall of the subject. At one level there is not a great deal of difference between the Bonaventure's deliberately mannered labyrinth and the "primitive-pop" mélange of SoHo; both evacuate linear reasoning, history, the "destiny" of the subject (now rendered as consumer/voyeur). In downtown New York, the subject is reminded of his/her erasure by an historical rather than strictly spatial disorientation.

The SoHo Kitchen and *El Internacional*, two restaurants in New York's SoHo and TriBeCa areas, respectively, are manifestations of the collision between the ahistorical, regressive features of the postmodern (with its disruption of signification) and the avant-garde, adversarial (in relation to dominant culture) aspect of late modernism. It is important to state at the outset my sense of the avant-garde's relationship to modernism, since the two are often used as synonyms. "Modernism" can obviously conceal a host of sins, since it did as much (as Adorno and Horkheimer remind us) to advance the interests of industrial capital as to challenge received notions of order. I am for the moment viewing modernism as a container of a number of provocative and progressive tendencies, the most important of which is the formation into schools of aesthetic and artistic practice—perceptions of reality which were as political (aggressively so) as cultural. There is little need at this point to reiterate the importance of Marx and Freud to the major movements of this century. Even as modernism became co-opted with its commodification, its ability to speak to the personal and political crises of the century (alienation, repression, the attempt of myth to defeat an historical-materialist view of reality) remained constant. With some qualification, then, we can say that modernism evidences some progressive impulses. It is also important to refer to Jameson's "spatialized" periodizing strategy to maintain a dialectical approach; postmodernism contains within it some adversarial activity, and our conceit for the moment will be to split progressive and regressive tendencies of downtown culture apart through the use of this model. SoHo Kitchen tends to remind us (as much as it protests to the contrary) that modernism's aspirations are outdated given the commodification of the art object and the absorption of progressive tendencies by the socio-economic milieu of late capital and postmodernism.

The restaurant recalls very spontaneously bohemia, its black façade suggesting not the cool distance of the two-way mirror skin wrapped around the Bonaventure, but the hands-off sense of hip enclave, the place of sanctuary found in beat taverns (the White Horse Tavern or Jimmy Day's) and also the calculated nihilism of

Supranational Kitsch: *El International*, West Broadway, New York City. The free-play of signifiers suggests *gaming*, *jouissance*, or playing with the pieces of modernism (i.e., Lyotard) rather than opposition to the dominant culture. The tendency is to dehistoricize.

Ad Reinhardt's canvases, Brando's cycle jacket, and the turtle-necked sweaters of the beats. While neon seems a concession to the neon vogue of the 70s-80s, the single red sign in the Kitchen's window is a shock effect—understated, rather naive in the context of postmodernism's dominance. The Kitchen has one door opening into one rectangular room, a converted gallery with a tile floor and brick walls. The stoicism of early New York bohemia immediately comes through. The bar is centered in the room, all activity circulating around it. The conventionality of this construct, emphasizing the community of the bar, makes secondary the role of other objects which are both privileged and decorative. The art objects, all of which are generally abstract expressionist, merely confirm the bar as "art scene" site; they are a focus of interest but don't intrude into the austerity of the setting. More important, these paintings are included as individual *works*, titled, framed, and positioned in such a way as to suggest the traditional modernist idea of genius, the attempt to express forms of anxiety and alienation, the experimentation with size, color, and form. The dated aspect of these conventions perhaps explains the unobtrusive, even bland aspect of the setting. Above all is the seriousness of the bohemian gesture: a mood of introspection and intimacy simultaneous with conviviality.

SoHo Kitchen is most explicitly modernist in its clear signification; all referents are apparent, and all of them are within the realm of the "art world." The paintings are references to Rauchensberg, Johns, Pollock, DeKooning, Reinhardt; the setting, while suggesting the art scene of the late 60s Village, most importantly asserts high culture: fairly humorless, purposeful in gesture, with the existentialist/humanist instincts one associates with New York bohemia of the late 1950s and 60s.

Seriousness is one component of modernism most obviously eschewed at *El Internacional* on West Broadway, a tapas bar/restaurant, already a SoHo/TriBeCa landmark (featured briefly in the opening credits of "Saturday Night Live"). The pinto seat cover façade and Statue of Liberty pediment assert two immediate aspects of the postmodern: the emphasis on tackiness (jarring bad taste) and the free play of signifiers suggesting *jouissance* or gaming[2] rather than opposition to dominant culture. Indeed, the restaurant provides an example of postmodernism's dissolution of binary opposition associated with adversarial tendencies of art dating to the *Lyrical Ballads*. Especially foregrounded is postmodernism's tendency to "dehistoricize": history is presented as pop mediation, although the strictly presentational attitude of, say, Brecht is absent since there is no attempt to draw attention to any master code—to how and why history is written. The notion of universal brotherhood within the utopian aspects of revolution and socialism is sent up as real history, and along with the nation-state, the reifications are dissolved into disjunctive fragments: the new "international" style is now read as *schlock*. The overarching period which provides the dominant tone to *El Internacional's* decor is the 1950s; the "retro mode" aspect of postmodernism draws rather self-consciously on the 50s to suggest hyperbolically the blissful consumerism of the postwar era now reaching an apotheosis (in Jameson's term) in the late 80s, but also the impossibility of the mythic consciousness which the 50s tried desperately to reassert. This is not to say, however, that much in *El Internacional* points to an attempt in postmodernism to make a transition from a mythic to an historical view of reality.

On the contrary, the familiarity of *El Internacional's* pastiche and retro mode is strangely unsettling, recalling again Freud's notion of the *Unheimlich*. The divorced signifiers of *El Internacional* are unnerving, chintzy, but not decadent in the sense of any *fin-de-siéclè* malaise which again would be a purposive gesture. Pastiche is not, as Jameson notes, associated with parody's critical enterprise. Batista's Cuba, fascist Italy, Hollywood Babylon (a Jane Fonda/Capucine photo), Jules Verne via Walt Disney, and shards of surrealism (especially Dali) and pop become the restaurant's historical/cultural bouillabaisse. The graffiti covering the walls of a side dining room represents the only "style" or movement dominating the restaurant, fitting since graffiti has been assimilated and granted credibility as "populist discourse," the myth of the last independent form fighting the institutionalization of the art academy. Yet the graffiti, along with the plastic shiskabobs, the Roman emperor decanters, the F. W. Woolworth fish tank, has little to do with a cry of anguish or even an attempt to shock the bourgeoisie by defilement of property.

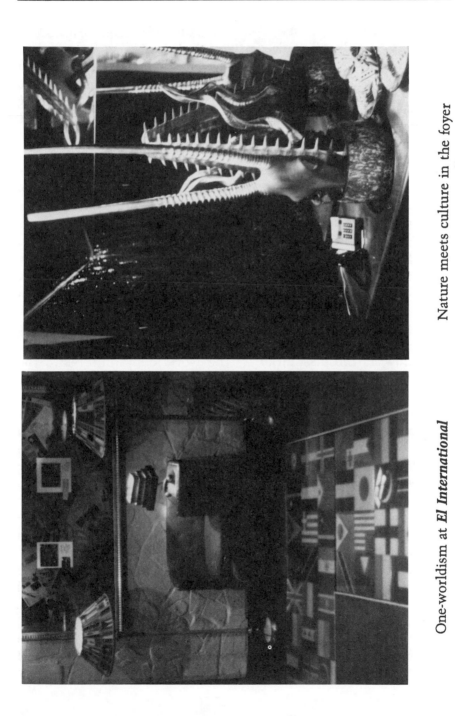

Nature meets culture in the foyer

One-worldism at *El International*

This form of discourse, like all signifiers in these postmodern buildings, is reduced to decorative banality. It may be useful to comment on the relationship of the particular notion of *kitch* associated with *El Internactional* to that of *Pee-Wee's Playhouse*, about which there has been much recent discussion regarding Pee-Wee Herman as a site of struggle. The "polymorphous perverse" send-up of 50s suburbia in *Pee-Wee's Playhouse*, like that of *El Internacional*, suggests an assault on the naiveté of a particular phase of image production and bourgeois consciousness even as this assault is absorbed into another (very similar) form of reaction.

The cheapness of the decor separates it, along with its playfulness, from the objective of modernism evident in SoHo Kitchen. Underneath the purple tablecloths we find vinyl-covered kitchen sets available at any discount retailer. Some tables are discarded "found" objects of the 50s-60s. The attempt to conceal commodification is only half-hearted, pointing perhaps to a progressive tendency. Yet *El Internacional's* attention to the commodification of history and experience—and "international-ism" now as the dissolution of the world community into the *kitsch* of multinational corporatism—does not diminish the consumerist ritual itself, nor the status of the restaurant decor as commodity.

Some postmodern discourse claims that its progressiveness is in its portrayal of the last phases of alienation associated with late capital, in the loss of the historical referent and the collapse of the signifying chain. Critics underscore a sense of the inevitable in postmodern's foregrounding of cultural bankruptcy, particularly in the failure of the whole notion of consensus implied in the symbolic values carried by language systems. Neo-Nietzschean apocalyptists such as Baudrillard find joy and possibility in the collapse they see in the current destruction of meaning and historicity. Postmodernism as site of struggle is indeed compelling, and it would be naive and pointless to recoup in some sense (in the manner of Habermas) the projects of Joyce and Eliot, Dada, Futurism, Abstract Expressionism, even the radical experimentation of Epic Theatre and Brecht. But in its lack of programmatic response (unless we read disavowal of all totalizing theory as response) and its dismissal of the progressive sentiments of certain aspects of modernism, postmodernism's most important feature may be a classic superstructural function as symptom rather than diagnosis of late capitalism's crisis.

Notes

1. Most important is Ihab Hassan, *Paracriticism* and *The Dismemberment of Orpheus: Toward a Postmodern Literature.*
2. Associated with Lyotard's use of Nietzsche's approach to language and meaning.

Retro Androgyny: Lavatory door insignia at *El Internacional.*

Jameson / Hermeneutics / Postmodernism

David R. Shumway
Carnegie Mellon University

This paper begins with an attempt to understand Fredric Jameson's project as more than a *Marxist* hermeneutic or method of interpretation—a Marxist *hermeneutics* or account of interpretation in general. Both variants of the term have long been important in Jameson's work. He concluded *The Prison House of Language* by noting in the work of A. J. Greimas the possibility of a "description of the Structuralist procedure as a genuine *hermeneutics*" (*PH*, 216, italics in original). He had already read structuralism as an interpretive project whose master code was language itself. In *Marxism and Form*, Jameson devoted his longest chapter to "Versions of a Marxist Hermeneutic," where the utopian, or positive, half of the double hermeneutic of *The Political Unconscious* is prefigured in discussions of Benjamin, Schiller, Marcuse, and Bloch. Finally, *The Political Unconscious* begins with a long chapter whose title, "On Interpretation," echoes that perhaps first self-conscious hermeneutic treatise of Aristotle. The book as a whole consists of hermeneutics (theory) or of hermeneutic (practice). There as earlier Jameson acknowledges Ricoeur and Gadamer as influences whose work remains limited by its religious orientation. What I want to do here is to try to unpack the connections between Jameson and philosophical hermeneutics. In the first section I will read *The Political Unconscious* in terms of this hermeneutic tradition. The second part will take up Jameson's claim that poststructuralist theories should be understood as alternative hermeneutics, not as anti-hermeneutic. Finally, in light of this discussion, I will evaluate Jameson's theory of postmodernism.

I. The Hermeneutic Tradition

Hermeneutics in *The Political Unconscious* is the other half of the horizon, which remains behind as one stands gazing facing the Marxist half. To put it another way, hermeneutics and Marxism are the dialectical poles of Jameson's theory which cannot finally be subsumed one to the other. Jameson's book aims at more than a Marxist method of interpretation, but to some extent it also fails to distinguish "methods of interpretation" or acts of interpretation from the larger problem of a Marxist hermeneutics. Clearly *The Political Unconscious* is not just the illustration of a Marxist exegetical system which borrows from Christian exegesis of the Middle Ages the four levels of interpretation and reads them through Frye as its own topography. By the title, the range, and the focus of "On Interpretation," Jameson signals his intent to give a general account of interpretation that belongs to the philosophical project of hermeneutics which began with Dilthey, developed in Heidegger, and finds its current expression in Betti, Hirsch, Ricoeur, and Gadamer. Such a project taken in historical perspective is an attempt to give an account of interpretation in general, or to deal with what Richard Palmer calls "the business of interpretation itself" ("Transcendability of Hermeneutics," 95). This conception is possible in spite of the fact that each philosopher conceived of hermeneutics as pertaining to specific interpretive tasks. Thus neither Jameson's Marxism nor his focus on literary interpretation would disqualify his work from this project. But one may ask, where on the current map of hermeneutics does Jameson's theory fit? Does Jameson, like Betti and Hirsch, promise universally valid meanings for literary works, or does he, like Ricoeur and Gadamer, explain the conditions of possibility for textual understanding? It seems to me that one can read Jameson both ways, and each has its consequences. If Jameson is taken to be offering a Marxist method for arriving at the one valid meaning of a text, it will severely limit the impact of his theorizing as a force for transforming Marxist cultural analysis. On the other hand, if we take him to have attempted to set out the conditions for the possibility of interpretation given Marxist assumptions, then *The Political Unconscious* may contribute to the current reformulation of cultural studies by demonstrating Marxism's significance for that project.

The issue needs to be addressed in terms of the specific totalizing claims that Jameson makes. Perhaps the most sweeping of these is that Marxist insights are "something like the ultimate *semantic* precondition for the intelligibility of literary and cultural texts" (*PU*, 75, italics in original). In articulating this claim, Jameson explicitly borrows the notion of horizon from phenomenology via Gadamer when he asserts that Marxism is the "'untranscendable horizon' that subsumes apparently antagonistic or incommensurable critical operations . . ." (*PU*, 10). He makes clear later that the notion of horizon does not mean merely the limits of interpretive possibility, that it is not merely a synonym for "all encompassing theory" when he goes on to describe interpretation as taking "place within three concentric frameworks which mark a widening out of the sense of the social ground of a text" (*PU*, 75). Jameson's concentric frameworks extend the notion of horizon to give it a specific structure: the first ring is "political history in the narrow sense of punctual event or chronological sequence"; the next ring is "society, in the now already less diachronic and less time bound sense of a constitutive tension and struggle between social classes"; the third ring is "history now conceived in its vastest sense of the sequence of modes of production and the succession and destiny of the various human social formations, from prehistoric life to whatever the future has in store for us" (*PU*, 75). Neither the priority of Marxism, nor its subsumption of other discourses, nor the unification of human history is necessarily an illegitimate claim, and all of them together do not make Jameson a Stalinist. But if one were to add to the others the claim that this combination can yield a single valid and highly certain reading of the culture and its texts, then totalizing becomes absolute.

Such an absolutism would violate the spirit of the notion of the horizon which is meant to describe the limitations of any interpreter's position relative to the world as whole. At the center of Jameson's rings, however, we find not the interpreter, but the text itself. The text, of course, does have a horizon since it also has a limited field of vision, but Jameson's exclusion of the interpreter is an unfortunate omission. Gadamer, by contrast, defines the process of understanding as the fusion of the horizons of the text and the interpreter. Jameson, however, claims that "fusion of horizons" does not allow for the radical alterity of earlier cultures that Marxism demands (*PU*, 75, n. 56). But it could be argued that Jameson disregards the fact that Marxism itself can be seen as a way of thinking which compromises the alterity of the past. To think an earlier period as a mode of production is not to think it as altogether other but in terms of the interpreter's categories.

Furthermore, Jameson reads Gadamer as if he were utterly undialectical, as if "the human adventure [were] one" and only one (*PU*, 19). Both Gadamer and Jameson in fact treat history as a dialectic of the same and the different, of the one and the many. For Gadamer this view of history is apparent in his notions of prejudice and tradition. Each of us belongs to history not only in its oneness but also in its fragmentation. History works in the act of interpretation not only as the social ground of text but also as the limitation of the interpreter's understanding. Thus in Gadamer, the notions of prejudice and tradition are hardly meant as synonyms for history as a whole. They are the pieces of history which each of us lives. Marxism uses the word "ideology" to describe this state of affairs, and Jameson—unlike vulgar Marxists—recognizes that Marxism is also affected by ideology. Thus at the center of Jameson's rings ought to be not merely the text, but also the interpreter whose horizon has become fused with the text's. The fusion of horizons is not the denial of difference as Jameson claims (*PU*, 75), but the background against which difference may be perceived.

As a consequence of his not having explicitly put the interpreter in the center, it may seem as though Jameson ignores the problem of pre-understanding, or fore-structure (Heidegger), or prejudice (Gadamer), or hypothesis (Hirsch) which has been a major issue of modern hermeneutics. Jameson need not deal explicitly in the description of pre-understanding because Marxism provides him with what is perhaps the most powerful account of it in the notion of ideology. "Ideology" in *The Political Unconscious* is an appropriately polysemous term: it can refer to both the "false consciousness" of ruling class cultural production and to genuinely oppositional cultural productions (*PU*, 84). But if we should not seek to fix the concept of ideology, there nevertheless remains in Jameson a contradiction in its use that he does not satisfactorily resolve. On the one hand, Jameson asserts that "a collective unity—whether that of a particular class, the proletariat, or of its 'organ of consciousness,' the revolutionary party—can achieve . . . transparency" (*PU*, 283). Because it is unsupported by any theory Jameson presents elsewhere in the text, this claim seems like an atavism of a Marxism he has largely discarded. Furthermore, how a collective may come to see through ideology is entirely occult, since Jameson also argues that an individual is never capable of such transparency because: "the individual subject is always positioned within the social totality (and this is Althusser's insistence on the *permanence* of ideology)" (*PU*, 283). This latter notion of ideology has more in common with Gadamer's concept of prejudice than with Habermas' (1968) conception of ideology as the object of pure rational critique. Jameson does not claim that one is able to stand apart from ideology to find a place to conduct a systematic critique of it as Habermas proposes. Rather, we are able to operate only in the terms that different ideologies provide us. This follows from an important innovation Jameson borrows from Nicos Poulantzas in arguing that we are always working, not within the seamless web of a single ideological system, but among several systems that reflect the persistence of modes of production after they have lost their dominance and modes which may be emerging (*PU*, 95-97).

But Jameson's treatment of the opposition between Gadamer's historicist relativism and Hirsch's absolute validity of interpretation seems to forget the ideological constraints he elsewhere suggested applied to all individual subjects. In calling Marxism an "absolute historicism" (*PU*, 75, n. 56), Jameson announces that this opposition may be reconciled. But Marxism can only be an absolute historicism in the last analysis, the one at the end of time. Meanwhile, Marxist historicism is relative to the ideological limitations Jameson so carefully describes. Furthermore, Jameson has described Gadamer from Hirsch's perspective. Gadamer would not describe himself as a relativist. Rather he would argue for the persistence of truth through history, just as Jameson must to provide a ground for "history in its vastest sense." It is the locus of such truth that is at issue between Hirsch and Gadamer. Hirsch claims that it resides in meanings which exist apart from particular linguistic expressions. This idealism seems to me to be one which Marxism cannot tolerate. Gadamer, on the other hand, locates the persistence of truth in language itself. Hirsch's meaning/significance opposition is accepted by Jameson as an "operational distinction" that parallels the Marxist one between science and ideology, yet Jameson himself calls into question the validity of these distinctions by noting current revisions in the idea of science (*PU*, 75, n. 56). Joel Weinsheimer makes a similar point about Gadamer assuming that science depends more on method than much current philosophy of science would claim (*Gadamer's Hermeneutics*, 4).

These revisions all emphasize the theoretical, linguistic, social, and cultural conditions of the production of scientific knowledge and thus call into question any talk of "absolute validity." More significantly, Hirsch's distinction, as Jameson also notes, is specifically between intrinsic "meaning" and our "'*ethical*' evaluation of its 'significance' for us" (*PU*, 75 n. 56; italics mine). For intrinsic, we should not read "immanent" here, for Hirsch locates meaning in the author's intention as an historically and linguistically grounded object of research. But such "meaning" could not serve as the object of Marxist interpretation because Marxism must largely disregard the author's intention, if not as a fiction of bourgeois individualism, then as irrelevant to the text's meaning as a social and historical product. This meaning would be consigned by Hirsch to the realm of ethical significance, where it would lose any validity that the association with science was perhaps supposed to lend it. The fact that Hirsch regards significance as ethical ought to have warned Jameson away from a distinction that is rooted in the positivist notion of value freedom, a necessarily anti-Marxist position.

Gadamer's notion of tradition is implied not only in Jameson's treatment of history, but also in his understanding of Marxism itself. In this connection, we need to turn to Jameson's appropriation of Ricoeur's notion of the two poles of modern hermeneutics, faith and suspicion. Ricoeur argues that "there is no general hermeneutics, no universal canon for exegesis, but only disparate and opposed theories concerning rules of interpretation. The hermeneutic field . . . is internally at variance with itself" (*Freud and Philosophy*, 26-27). Ricoeur's double hermeneutic is meant as a naming of two hermeneutic extremes, rather than as the dialectic of an interpretive process itself. Jameson's dialectical reading of the double hermeneutic is certainly a useful extension of Ricoeur, but it is also a misreading. Jameson's version of the two hermeneutics is his dialectic of hope and ideology. Although there are superficial connections between faith and hope on the one hand, and between suspicion and ideology on the other, in fact both hope and ideology are discovered via a hermeneutics of suspicion. The problem has nothing to do with Jameson's expressed objection to Ricoeur, i.e., that "his conception of 'positive' meaning as a kerygma . . . is modeled on the act of communication between individual subjects" (*PU*, 285). Rather, hope is discovered by the same process and by the same attitude toward the text as yields the discovery of ideology. While it is true that hope is regarded as a positive feature of the text while ideology is a mask for some other meaning, hope is also masked by ideology. Hope is a part of what is discovered when the text is subjected to the demystifying process of Marxist interpretation.

But Marxist interpretation is not exhausted by the hermeneutics of suspicion. There remains another body of texts which is not read in terms of the dialectic of hope and ideology, but in terms of an older dialectic of truth and error: these are the texts of the Marxist tradition itself. These texts—which are read by Jameson throughout *The Political Unconscious*—are not read as kerygma exactly, but they are read precisely as part of a tradition. In reading these texts as providing support for his own theory of interpretation, Jameson assumes the "truth" to which they point. This is not a question of recovering the intentions of the theorist, but of attempting to understand something beyond the text by means of the text. Thus there is another double hermeneutic in *The Political Unconscious*, this one between the hermeneutics applied to texts at large and the hermeneutics applied to texts of the Marxist tradition. The latter category is assumed to be at least partially free of ideological deception, while the former is not. Jameson's use of the Marxist tradition fits Gadamer's conception of tradition and the interpreter's relation to it precisely. These texts show that for Jameson as for Gadamer, authority is not always wrong (Gadamer, *Hermeneutics*, 33). Jameson's placing of the authority of Marxism in the narrative it tells rather than in its "scientific" laws and facts indicates his awareness that methodological reason alone cannot guarantee Marxism.

A better way to read Ricoeur's double hermeneutic dialectically is to recognize that a hermeneutics of suspicion cannot remain in that state forever. The interpreter must eventually point to a discourse in which he or she has faith. In this context it is worth noting that Jameson makes a point of Marxism's religious connections: "any comparison of Marxism with religion is a two way street, in which the former is not necessarily discredited by its association with the latter. On the contrary, such a comparison may also function to rewrite certain religious concepts—most notably Christian historicism and the 'concept' of providence, but also the pretheological systems of primitive magic—as anticipatory foreshadowings of historical materialism within precapitalist social formations in which scientific thinking is unavailable as such" (*PU*, 285). But Jameson does more than simply acknowledge the connections between Marxism and religion. The interpretive method he proposes is modeled on Christian hermeneutics, not merely as an empty structure, but also in that both share as ultimate horizons history in its vastest sense, "in which the text undergoes its ultimate rewriting in terms of the destiny of the human race as a whole" (*PU*, 31).

Dowling has convincingly described the parallel between the Marxist and Christian versions of human history and destiny: "it is clear that [Jameson's] notion of ideologies as strategies of containment extends to classical Marxism, to that salvational 'story' about the plot of History that is embodied in Marx's writing. . . . Marx's unwitting strategy of containment . . . was thus to tell a providential fable in which the various modes of production generate one another in neat succession until revolution and the withering away of the state are imminently at hand" (Jameson, *Althusser, Marx*, 54-55). Dowling believes that Jameson's negative dialectics "eschews the false comfort or any salvational view of history," (Jameson, *Althusser, Marx*, 56) but this is only half true. As Jameson's remarks about appropriating "providence" suggest, history is salvational, has to be salvational. The notion of the purely negative character of the totality suggests only that history is not the seamless web that Jameson supposes Foucault, Weber, and others to make it (*PU*, 53, 90). Jameson's insight is that Marxism needs this salvational story all the while noting that it is a story. That Marxism is a story differentiates it not one whit from any other version of history, and knowing that it is a narrative reminds us that any version of history (including especially those which claim to do without history) will be ideologically motivated.

Jameson's references to Christian hermeneutics, however, also belie what I would call a nostalgia for the hegemony of a single interpretive system. Jameson lapses into an uncharacteristic essentialism when, in arguing against the "infinity of possible meanings and methods and their ultimate equivalence," he asserts that "the mind is not content until it puts some order in these findings and invents a hierarchical relationship among its various interpretations" (*PU*, 31). Jameson is undoubtedly correct in his belief that the program of this "pluralism" is to forestall questions of social and historical grounds for texts and interpretations. But it does not follow that interpretive possibilities are as radically limited as Jameson suggests: "it was clear to the medieval theorists that their four levels constituted a methodological upper limit and a virtual exhaustion of interpretive possibilities" (*PU*, 32). Gadamer's hermeneutics does not hold all interpretations equal nor does it claim all are correct, but it does deny that any method can guarantee truth, even when the method is performed correctly. Were we merely to substitute Jameson's four levels for the medieval we would create an interpretive straight jacket that would ill serve both Marxism as a whole and Marxist criticism in particular.

Jameson's nostalgia for medieval order suggests one of the principle attractions of academic Marxism in the humanities or cultural studies today: precisely the coherence of its narrative and the orderliness of the structure of culture it implies. I do not mean to assert here, as a Derridian would, that such coherence and order are in themselves signs of Marxism's failure to avoid the mistakes of Western metaphysics. In fact, I would claim that Marxism's ability to make of history and culture a narrative and a system where seemingly disparate events and processes are related to one another is what gives us grounds to accept Jameson's claim for "the priority of a Marxian interpretive framework in terms of semantic richness" (*PU*, 10). I do think, however, that such orderliness, such coherence, such semantic richness can be seductive in ways that lead us away from the dialectical and conflicting multi-dimensional realities of history and culture. The vulgar Marxist "pigeon holing" which Jameson laments is only the most extreme example of this tendency. Understanding hermeneutics as a non-methodological but purely formal and apolitical reverse of Marxism as the horizon of cultural studies is a powerful corrective to such a tendency because it locates the dialectic within interpretation itself and forecloses the possibility of *methodological* hegemony or interpretive absolutism.

II. Poststructuralism as Alternative Hermeneutic

If understanding the implied hermeneutics of *The Political Unconscious* can make its claims for Marxism's priority more compelling, the book conversely may be understood to strengthen hermeneutics' claims to account for whole range of textual practices including those which claim to be anti-interpretive. Jameson makes what is perhaps the most explicit statement of this claim when he notes that "Deleuze and Guattari's proposal for an *anti*-interpretive method . . . can equally be grasped as a new hermeneutic in its own right" and that "most of the anti-interpretive positions . . . have felt the need to project new 'methods' of this kind: thus, the archaeology of knowledge, but also, more recently, the 'political technology of the body'

(Foucault), 'grammatology' and deconstruction (Derrida), 'symbolic exchange' (Baudrillard), libidinal economy (Lyotard), and 'semanalyse' (Julia Kristeva)" (*PU*, 23, n. 7). This suggestion comes in a footnote, but I would argue that Jameson stands or falls on this foot, and thus reject Geoff Bennington's claim that we can "ignore Jameson's attempt to neutralize" the Nietzschean anti-interpretive current "through the suggestion that these writers, in their attack on hermeneutics, are in fact projecting new hermeneutic 'methods' of their own. It is clear that to describe deconstruction . . . or Lyotard's 'libidinal economy' as hermeneutic methods is not to respect the strong sense of hermeneutics that Jameson is concerned to defend in *The Political Unconscious*" ("Not Yet," 29). Bennington may be right if what he means by "the strong sense of hermeneutics" is the absolutist position. But as I have argued above in connection with Hirsch, such a position is inconsistent with both Jameson's historicism and his rejection of ethics. I will assume, then, that Jameson does not mean by "anti-interpretive" merely the rejection of the possibility of determinate meaning.

The notion of a Nietzschean anti-interpretive current contains an ambiguity at its very center. Susan Sontag in the essay which was the first articulation of the anti-interpretive position in the American context, "Against Interpretation" (1966), provides a useful illustration of the problem: "Of course, I don't mean interpretation in the broadest sense, the sense in which Nietzsche (rightly) says, 'There are no facts, only interpretations.' By interpretation, I mean . . . a conscious act of the mind which illustrates a certain code, certain 'rules' of interpretation" ("Against Interpretation," 5). It would perhaps be fashionable but certainly utterly nihilistic to hold that there are only interpretations, but oppose interpretation. Such a formulation may well be worthy of Derrida or other poststructuralists, but I do not think they would be likely to state it as a final and unqualified position, since they are often at pains to protest against accusations of nihilism. In any event, Sontag clearly does not intend to advance nihilism as her position, yet her attempt to avoid it is not persuasive today given precisely our broader experience of poststructuralism. As Foucault has convincingly demonstrated, no acts of the mind, conscious or otherwise, fail to obey certain rules or codes. Sontag's essay displays a sort of pre-lapsarian innocence that not only finds "transparence" possible, but of the highest value, and which opposes hermeneutics and erotics as if the latter were some realm of experience that could be free of interpretation ("Against Interpretation," 13-14).

But if Sontag's is at best a proto-poststructuralism, you might argue, why should she be relevant to its anti-interpretation? The answer is that no anti-interpretive project can escape the dilemma that comes from interpretation being the inescapable ground of discursive practice—unless it is anti-interpretive from a positivist perspective: we should demand facts and not settle for interpretations. Poststructuralism then cannot eliminate the opposition, present since its Nietzschean origin, between truth and interpretation while maintaining Nietzsche's rejection of the foundations of current beliefs in fact and morality. To put it another way, once logic, morality, authority, perception, etc. and etc. are gotten rid of, what do you call your discourse but an interpretation? One could perhaps call poststructural activities simply discourse, but this depicts these activities as far more isolated and self-contained than they actually are. One characteristic poststructuralist activity is reading, as in *Reading Capital* or as in Derrida's elaborate readings of Husserl, Rousseau, and others. And what is intertextuality except the embedded interpretation of a text within another text? The fact is that by any of a number of definitions of the word, these self-proclaimed anti-interpretive projects are shot through with interpretations.

This cannot be the place to go through each poststructuralist project and show in detail how it turns out to be interpretation in the end. Not only is there a lack of time and space, but it would be boring. You can imagine the outlines of it already. We would start by recalling Heidegger's definition of interpretation as employing an "as-structure" because interpretation takes *something as something* (*Being and Time*, 189). Then we would show how this structure defines, say, what Derrida does when he discovers supplementarity in Rousseau, or what Althusser does when he reads terms Marx uses to describe capitalism such as "machinery" or "a construction" as signs of *Darstellung* in Marx

(Arac, *Postmodernism and Politics*, xxiii). But if this interpretation of the interpretation of anti-interpreters is obvious, one
point does need to be added. These readings always imply a
hierarchical relationship between the text being read and what it
is being read as. In spite of whatever claims for textuality these
theorists might make, their readings valorize the "as something"
over the text. Thus, supplementarity has priority over Rousseau's
Confessions in *Of Grammatology*. Derrida is not reading
Rousseau merely for the pleasure of generating another text, but
to demonstrate supplementarity, to show us how presence eludes
us. But in demonstrating this, Derrida involves himself in an
inevitable relationship of representation and reference. The text is
but a representation of supplementarity to which Derrida makes it
refer. It is irrelevant that we may consider supplementarity just
another text, because in this reading of Derrida's it is not just
another text, but the valorized text.

There is another variant of the anti-interpretive position that
is left to be discussed, the claim which Dreyfus and Rabinow
make on behalf of Foucault that his work goes beyond
hermeneutics. I take this to be a more subtle position than
straight-forward anti-interpretation since it assumes that Foucault
in some way incorporates interpretation as he moves on to
something better. In *Beyond Structuralism and Hermeneutics*,
Dreyfus and Rabinow characterize Foucault as displaying something like a hermeneutic position in *Madness and Civilization*, of
utilizing structuralist techniques in the work between then and
the *The Archaeology of Knowledge*, and in the later works to have
achieved a break-through to a new position which the authors call
"interpretive analytics." This designation is revealing in that it
implies that Dreyfus and Rabinow distinguish hermeneutics from
interpretation. In fact, by "hermeneutics" they mean the search
for "deep meaning," whether embedded in everyday practices or
ideologically masked. Interpretation is used synonymously with
exegesis as something Foucault opposes and gets beyond, but it is
also used to describe Foucault's post-hermeneutic work.

Dreyfus expands the treatment of these issues in his essay,
"Beyond Hermeneutics: Interpretation in Late Heidegger and
Recent Foucault." According to Dreyfus, Foucault uses the term

"commentary" for hermeneutics, which he defines as an operation that seeks "the re-apprehension through the manifest meaning of discourse of another meaning at once secondary and primary, that is, more hidden but also more fundamental" (*Order of Things*, 373). Thus Foucault equates commentary with what Ricoeur calls the hermeneutics of suspicion. Dreyfus compares Foucault's rejection of hermeneutics to what he sees as a similar position arrived at by the later Heidegger. This comparison is telling because it will determine the definitions of hermeneutics which Dreyfus will admit, all three of which have their origin in Heidegger. Most importantly, Dreyfus will identify hermeneutics with the attempt to understand the meaning of being. This peculiarly Heideggerian project makes it easy for Dreyfus to define Foucault's work as non-hermeneutic. Dreyfus' characterization of the hermeneutics of suspicion as the search for deep truth is also guaranteed to exclude Foucault since Foucault has already rejected that approach. My argument with Dreyfus is that he too readily accepts Foucault's dismissal of Freud and Marx as naive seekers after deep truth and therefore fails to see Foucault's kinship with a hermeneutics of suspicion that includes, as Ricoeur correctly asserts, Nietzsche.

Foucault, in *The Birth of the Clinic*, claims to be doing something other than commentary because of his anxiety about living in an age which produces only "discourses about discourses" (xvi). We need to understand part of this anxiety as stemming from Foucault's break with philosophy as a profession in dealing with the archive rather than the philosophical canon. If as Dreyfus asserts, Foucault is uninterested in the meanings that social practices have for their practitioners because the issue is not the meaning of these practices but their effects ("Beyond Hermeneutics," 79), then Foucault is calling precisely for a hermeneutics of suspicion. But Dreyfus distinguishes what Foucault does from hermeneutics of suspicion on two counts. The first is that this hermeneutics assumes that people do not know the real meaning of their actions and discourses because of a "motivated cover up" ("Beyond Hermeneutics," 79). Marxist hermeneutics, however, does not assume that ideology is always "motivated." It may be a "structural limitation" (*PU*, 285) which tends to support the hegemony of the mode of production that gave birth to it but is not designed to do so. The second distinction Dreyfus claims for Foucault is that his analysis does not rely on a conception of what Dreyfus calls "the true and deepest meaning of the surface behavior" ("Beyond Hermeneutics," 80). Thus Dreyfus thinks Foucault has avoided what I have called the other half of the dialectic, the return to faith in the reliability of some discourse. But Dreyfus' own description of Foucault's method shows this judgment is wrong: "Foucault seeks to demonstrate that the deeper meaning that authority directs the participant to uncover in his practices itself *hides another, more important meaning*, which is not directly available to the participant" ("Beyond Hermeneutics," 80, italics mine). All that Foucault adds here is another layer of suspicion. The strategies and technologies which Foucault calls the regime of discipline are as much an uncovered truth as are the structures and strategies of domination discovered in the analysis of a mode of production. And Foucault certainly is open to the often repeated charge that domination itself is the "big truth" to which all of his work points.

Even if we accept the claim that Foucault has avoided transcendental truth, however, this would not necessarily distinguish Foucault from all Marxist and Freudian interpreters. Dreyfus caricatures Marxism and psychoanalysis by asserting that each does little more than reduce all texts to the same things, such as the class struggle or the libido ("Beyond Hermeneutics," 72). It is true that Jameson's theory includes just such a transcendental element in its conception of the unity of history and humanity. But such transcendent categories are not what interpretation or exegesis seeks to reveal, since they are assumed in advance. Furthermore, in Jameson's view totality is purely negative: it is the ground against which difference becomes visible, but "totality is not available for representation" (*PU*, 55). Totality cannot be invoked therefore in the service of a particular reading, but only to establish the boundaries of all reading.

What I think I have shown about Foucault is that what he does is far more like other activities that have traditionally fallen under the domain of hermeneutics than it is unlike those activities. Having demonstrated that Foucault is not anti-interpretive, we can correct a misreading of him in *The Political Unconscious*. This misreading is curious because Jameson himself asserts that anti-interpretive projects should in fact be understood as new hermeneutic methods and much of the book is devoted to showing how these methods are accommodated within the Marxist horizon. Yet he still reads Foucault and other post-structuralists as creating seamless webs of the synchronic structures they analyze (*PU*, 90-92). But if we recognize that what these theorists are doing is nothing other than interpretation, then the seamless web cannot in fact be seamless. No genuinely totalized system can be imagined under Nietzsche's dictum that interpretation is all there is, since the system itself is a product of interpretation. Interpretation, as Heidegger shows, implies a relational structure of something as something or, to use the term Jameson borrows from Greimas, a process of transcoding.

In *The Prison House of Language*, Jameson quotes Greimas' assertion that "signification is . . . nothing but . . . transposition from one level of language to another, from one language to a different language, and meaning is nothing but the possibility of such *transcoding*" (*PH*, 215-216). Thus truth or "the truth-effect" involves or results from "the translation from one code to another" and such an understanding, by freeing structuralism from its conception of structure as object, permits us to comprehend structuralism as a hermeneutics which "by disclosing the presence of preexisting codes and models and by reemphasizing the place of analyst himself, reopen[s] the text and analytic process alike to the winds of history" (*PH*, 216). But if we are to take truth as transcoding seriously, there cannot be a uni-directional hierarchy of codes. We must assume a multi-directional relationship among different codes or levels. In this context, we would not read Foucault's description of the etiology of discipline as anti-Marxist because it does not trace this development to its ultimate economic base. Rather, Foucault's analysis is useful precisely because it shows how a particular set of social practices has a history that is properly its own. Reading Foucault's history of discipline in a Marxist context, we recognize that disciplinary technologies are integral to the development of capitalism, just as technologies such as steam power and the assembly line have always been recognized as such. But we can also recognize that such technologies are not a mere product of this economic formation, and that they can be quite easily adopted by socialist states.

This reading explains Stalinism not as a function of the totalizing character of Marxist theory, but of the disciplinary character of the social practices of the capitalist mode of production, which mode itself was the inadvertent but necessary goal of Soviet economic development. The transcoding metaphor for truth would permit not only our placing poststructuralist hermeneutics within a Marxist horizon, but would also lead inevitably to a poststructural Marxism. In such a Marxism, nineteenth-century mechanics is replaced by the poststructuralist problematic of representation, i.e., the simultaneous critique of claims to pure reference and the recognition of the inescapability of signification. This renders Marxism more self-reflexive and aware of its own historicity, and it makes impossible any conception of history represented as an extra-discursive ground. Such a new Marxism seems to be where Jameson wants to take us in *The Political Unconscious*, even if he does not always get us there. But in his more recent work, Jameson seems to move away from poststructuralism by treating it as a symptom of post-modernist depthlessness.

III. Interpretation and Postmodernism

In turning to Jameson's interpretation of contemporary culture as postmodern, the foregoing analysis will enable two points to be made. First, Jameson's own theory and practice of interpretation enables him to make a more convincing case for the concept of the "postmodern" than non-Marxist theorists have made, but it also leads him to an overly unified conception of contemporary culture, in spite of his protests that he has made "a place for overdetermination" and "left a space for . . . things not integrated into the global model" ("RPM," 52). Secondly, Jameson's treatment of postmodernism ignores his own insight that anti-hermeneutics are in fact best considered alternative hermeneutics. This leads us to question what is perhaps the major feature of postmodernism as Jameson describes it, the disappearance of depth: "not only visual depth . . . but also interpretive depth . . . philosophic notions of depth, that is, various hermeneutics in which one interprets an appearance in terms of some underlying reality . . . [and] historical depth, what used to be called historical consciousness or the sense of the past" ("RPM," 44). This questioning is reinforced by an examination of particular claims Jameson makes to support his notion of the postmodern. It is my argument that postmodernism in the broad sense, i.e., as a description of an entire period in Western cultural history, is not theoretically or empirically well supported, and that Jameson, like others, has failed to distinguish it adequately from modernism. Although we may be able to identify stylistic changes within particular art forms—as Brian McHale has done for fiction—which would justify the naming of a new era in their histories, such changes do not have enough in common to constitute support for the broader definition of postmodernism.

In literal terms, Jameson's analysis of postmodernism is not a systematic and comprehensive working out of the interpretive method articulated in *The Political Unconscious*. We don't find a discussion of the four levels of meaning of the paintings, buildings, and other artifacts he takes to be characteristic of postmodernism. But we do get a description of contemporary culture as a "unity or system . . . placed in relation to the infrastructural reality of late capitalism" ("RPM," 43). Hence the interpretive method applied in the work on postmodernism is similar, albeit less complex. Jameson in the traditional Marxist way limits the meaning of "culture" so that the term refers to "texts" of various kinds but not to broader field of human life to which it refers in anthropology (*PU*, 32, 36). Culture remains the most ephemeral layer of social life, even further removed from the base than ideology. The specific claim that Jameson makes for postmodernism is its dominance within this circumscribed realm. This claim is then considerably less sweeping than those of Jean Baudrillard and Arthur Kroker who do not limit postmodernism to culture or relegate culture to ephemeral status. While Jameson's theory may tend toward totalization, it is not nearly so totalizing as these other theories of postmodernism. For Jameson, postmodernism is a system which is related to, but has relative autonomy from, the economic system. Thus Jameson's work on postmodernism explores "homologies" between the cultural and the economic. Whatever the theoretical weaknesses of this limited conception of the cultural, its very circumscription enables "Postmodernism, or The Cultural Logic of Late Capitalism" to be one of the more compelling treatments of the subject.

Interestingly, however, the very strategy of homology represents one of the weaknesses of Jameson's argument. The problem here is not the theoretical one of, as Stephanson phrased it, "jumping from the minute to the staggeringly global," but the practical one of not describing the relevant characteristics of the economic ("RPM," 51). If Jameson could convincingly show that postmodern cultural productions represented a shift in the mode of production to what Ernest Mandel (1975) has called "late capitalism," then we would need to take postmodernism very seriously indeed. But it is precisely in this attempt that Jameson fails. His argument relies upon what remains an empty signifier, rather than on systematic reference to specific aspects of late capitalism. Ironically, it may be Jameson's desire to give the cultural its relative autonomy that leads him away from drawing clearer connections to the economic.

Jameson defines postmodernism not as a style or mere collection of features but as a cultural dominant, but this opposition of style and the dominance presents a difficulty. The Russian Formalist discussion of these issues ought to have alerted Jameson to the fact that to call something a dominant is to define it as a controlling style. Roman Jakobson defined the dominant as "the focusing component of a work of art: it rules, determines, and transforms the remaining components. . . . A poetic work [is] a structured system, a regularly ordered hierarchical set of artistic devices. Poetic evolution is a shift in this hierarchy" (McHale, *Postmodernist Fiction*, 6). McHale uses the Formalist notion of dominance to distinguish modernist fiction with its dominant of epistemology from postmodernist fiction with its dominant of ontology. Jameson seems to want to regard postmodernism as dominant in the entire culture in the same way as McHale claims that ontology is dominant in postmodern fiction. But notice that Jameson's use conflates what in Jakobson's terms are "device" and historical period. Dominance for Jakobson means the hierarchy of stylistic features. For Jameson dominance means hegemony, and the result is the tautology that the postmodern is dominant in the postmodern era. Of course, Jameson's argument cannot be reduced to this tautology because it masks the real assertion that postmodern culture reflects the hegemony of late capitalism. At this point, however, we are thrown back on the weak case Jameson makes for links between postmodernism and late capitalism.

Nevertheless Jameson's argument about postmodernism has powerful appeal because it brings to bear the orderliness, coherence, and semantic richness of Marxist interpretation we noted earlier. Unfortunately, it also falls prey to the seduction of these very qualities. Jameson's reification of dominance—his collapsing of the categories of stylistic dominance, cultural dominance, and mode of production—leads him away from recognizing conflicts within and among the discourses and practices he discusses. It is true that Jameson asserts that he does not regard all contemporary production as postmodern, but residual, emergent, and oppositional phenomena are absent almost entirely from his discussions, and they certainly play no role in shaping the conception of culture that emerges from them. What is that conception, if the term "postmodernism" allows Jameson to get away without telling us explicitly what the dominant element of contemporary culture is. The remarks quoted earlier from "Regarding Postmodernism" suggest that the absence of depth in this culture serves this function in practice. Jameson also asserts that postmodern culture is generally a culture of surfaces.

The most important cultural form for the discussion of postmodernism has been architecture, an enabling condition for several aspects of Jameson's argument. One is his focus on the transformation of space, which in architecture can be quite literal. The second is that it allows one of the few explicit connections to the economic. According to Jameson, "It is in the realm of architecture . . . that modifications in aesthetic production are most dramatically visible, and that their theoretical problems have been most centrally raised and articulated" ("PCL," 54). Architecture is one cultural sphere in which the concept of postmodernism clearly makes sense. But I will dispute Jameson on two points, one regarding the meaning and character of postmodernism in architecture, and the other concerning the extent to which problems raised and articulated in architecture are relevant to other cultural spheres. Jameson argues that "architecture is . . . of all the arts that closest constitutively to the economic . . . : it will therefore not be surprising to find the extraordinary flowering of the new postmodern architecture grounded in the patronage of multinational business, whose expansion and development is strictly contemporaneous with it" ("PCL," 56-57). This point must also be conceded and it would strongly support Jameson's larger argument if common features between postmodern architecture and other art forms could be discovered. But on this point Jameson is least convincing, in part because he seems to ignore the interpretations that leading architects and architectural critics—such as Venturi and Jencks— have given to postmodernism.

Jameson's principle example of postmodern architecture in the published materials so far is John Portman's Bonaventure Hotel. This is a poor choice because the Bonaventure would not be considered a postmodern building by most critics. Rather, it is an almost perfect example of what Charles Jencks calls late modernism. Jameson himself notes historical pastiche as characteristic of postmodern architecture, yet the Bonaventure displays nothing of this architectural historicism. Jameson admits that this building is uncharacteristic of postmodernist architecture, but he focuses on it because of what it demonstrates about postmodernist space. Jameson asserts that "I am proposing the motion [sic] that we are here in the presence of something like the mutation of built space itself" and he goes on to claim that we have not yet developed the "organs" to comprehend this new "hyperspace" ("PCL," 80). This discussion of the new space of the postmodern corresponds to Jameson's assertion of a postmodern preoccupation with space as opposed to the modernist concern with time. But it must be said that Jameson fails to deliver on his promise to show us a radically new space. What we get instead is space that seems quite modernist, albeit not in the International Style:

> The descent [in a glass elevator running outside along the four symmetrical towers] is dramatic enough, plummeting back down through the roof to splash down in the lake [which surrounds the central column]; what happens when you get there is something else, which I can only try to characterize as milling confusion, something like the vengeance this space takes on those who still seek to walk through it. Given the absolute symmetry of the four towers, it is quite impossible to get your bearings in this lobby; recently, color coding and directional signals have been added in a pitiful and revealing, rather desperate attempt to restore the coordinates of an older space. ("PCL," 83)

Jameson reads the lobby as a metaphor of a new sense of space characterized by surface without depth and by disorientation caused by the lack of traditional divisions. He compares one's immersion in the "hyperspace" of the lobby, "without any of that distance that formerly enabled the perception of perspective or volume," to "that suppression of depth I spoke of in postmodern painting or literature" ("PCL," 83). Secondly, the spatial confusion described above is likened to the inability of postmodern people to cognitively map "the great global multinational and decentered communicational network in which we find ourselves caught as individual subjects" ("PCL," 84). Both of these points seem to be exaggerations designed to make Jameson's homologies appear in every object he examines, but they work in different ways. The first is simply wrong. What the lobby of the Bonaventure contains is enormous depth; what it lacks are precisely the surfaces which are normally significant in hotel lobbies: walls which divide eating spaces from waiting spaces, which advertise services, or which display merchandise. Because the central column is only six levels high, we experience this space as depth rather than as height as we do in various other atrium hotels. The isolation of the lobby from both the city outside and from the guest rooms in the towers further gives the sense of being deep in bowels of some underground city, a sense which the difficulty of navigation only increases. The second homology, between spatial confusion and the failure of cognitive mapping, may not be false, but it surely is unintended. That of course does not negate Jameson's point, but it does complicate it since it has to be a spontaneous reflection of our disorientation, and not an architectural attempt to think that disorientation. More importantly, the dizzying experience of this space is accommodated perfectly well in terms of the futurist aspect of modernist culture which is also invoked by the phrase "in plummeting to splashdown" where Jameson takes up one of the oldest modernist tropes, the exhilaration of speed—in this case it is literal—associated with transportation machines. That we have achieved actual space travel does not change this experience fundamentally. Such a possibility has been imagined in modernist documents since at least the late nineteenth century. According to Jencks, the machine aesthetic is an important aspect of late modernism. While modern architecture emphasized "straight-forward" logic, mechanics, technology, and structure, the late modern takes these emphases to extremes.

Why has Jameson collapsed the categories of late modern and postmodern, which Venturi, Jencks, and others have carefully and persuasively articulated? The ideology articulated by postmodern architects and their apologists is at odds with the point Jameson wants to make. Rather than being the overt expression of multinational capital, postmodernism claims to be populist, environmentalist, and democratic. Jameson wants to call the Bonaventure populist because it is popular—tourists and locals both like it—but his own description of the hotel's alienation from its environment—the lack of a marquee, of street level windows, or even noticeable entrances suggests that the Bonaventure is elitist and exclusive, designed "to keep out the local population, predominantly poor and hispanic" (Jacoby, *The Last Intellectual*, 171). Jencks' claims for the populism of postmodern architecture are questionable for precisely the reasons Jameson has specified when he notes the connections between that art form and the economic dominant. Nevertheless, we do need to acknowledge an emergent cultural form in this architecture which runs counter to almost everything the Bonaventure represents. In his treatment of the Bonaventure, Jameson has failed to establish the postmodern as distinct from the modern, or to show convincingly that the building has the qualities he attributes to the postmodern.

Postmodern architecture as defined by Jencks and Venturi does not fit any of Jameson's claims for postmodernism, except one: its historical reference, or historicism in the sense of "complacent eclecticism . . . which randomly and without principle but with gusto cannibalizes all the architectural styles of the past" ("PCL," 66). So, however, as both Venturi and Jencks point out, does most every suburban dwelling above the economic level of Levitt's first developments of the 50s. What I want to challenge here is the claim that this attitude toward history itself represents some sort of rupture. Jameson would have us believe that earlier generations had a deep sense of the historical past, and this in spite of his relying on the absence of history in modernist architecture to distinguish the postmodern. When describing the postmodern effacement of history, Jameson conveniently forgets this modernist effacement and takes as his point of comparison the nineteenth century. The reverential attitude toward history here is represented in literature by the historical novel of Lukács' definition, in architecture by period revivals, and culturally by history as the genealogy of the bourgeois collective project. Jameson assumes that this nineteenth century history is somehow less a distortion of the past than postmodernist simulacral history—about which more in a moment. I think Jameson takes nineteenth century bourgeois history as the norm because Marxism itself is a product of the same mode of production. As Dowling puts it, Marxism is a "strategy of containment" produced in response to its historical situation (*Jameson, Althusser, Marx,* 55). Thus Marxist history may be understood as a version—albeit, a subversive version—of the genealogy of the bourgeois collective project. And even if we agree that such history is less distorting, this would still fail to establish the grounds for a change in the cultural dominant. The great historians of the nineteenth century are no more a reflection of the popular consciousness than are today's academic historians, whom we must credit with far greater literal accuracy to past than their nineteenth century predecessors. The popular history of the nineteenth century was mythic history as conveyed, for example, in dime novels or the hagiographies of George Washington.

To return to historical reference in architecture, Jameson apparently would have us believe that earlier architectural periods took history more seriously. Nineteenth-century architecture was punctuated by a series of revivals which Jameson's narrative would lead us to believe treated the past as depth rather than surface or image or simulacrum. But as Witold Rybczynski has shown, history was quite superficial here also (*Home*, 66). Although Rybczynski is speaking mainly of interior design, his points hold for architecture as well and they show that the primacy of the "neo" which Jameson takes over from Lefebvre is itself quite neo:

> It was taken for granted that interiors of houses—as indeed their exteriors—should be decorated in a period style . . . [which did not] necessarily demonstrate any particular interest in history. Eighteenth century classicism (which had been motivated by an authentic curiosity about the past) had been replaced by several period styles, and after 1820, rooms could be decorated and furnished in neo-Rococo, neo-Greek, neo-Gothic, neo-anything-you-fancied. Inevitably, this lead to eclecticism. (*Home*, 174)

William Seale has distinguished two kinds of revivals during the nineteenth and early twentieth centuries: creative and historical. "Creative revivals were not concerned with historical accuracy, but merely used traditional motifs and forms, often in a highly original way" (Rybczynski, 175). Rybczynski argues that most nineteenth century revivals were creative, which allowed the mixing of innovations such as the modern bathroom without any perceived contradiction with traditional design. The Queen Ann style—important in both architecture and interior design of the late nineteenth and early twentieth century—is treated by Jencks almost as precursor of postmodernism. It is both eclectic and historically inaccurate. The major design styles which followed the Queen Ann—Art Moderne, Art Nouveau, and Art Deco—were all ahistorical even though they were referential and metaphorical. In architectural history, then, genuine historical revival is quite rare, and cannot be regarded as dominant during the nineteenth century.

This discussion of the role of history in architecture and design I think challenges not only Jameson, but Baudrillard and other prophets of the apocalypse of images. The claims for the simulacral society are themselves based on a nostalgia for origins and the assumption that there was a time when most people had a deep understanding of their own place in history. While it might be argued that the mythic time of earlier periods has been replaced by some sense of time as radical present, this sense of time is precisely modern. It was in the face of this pervasive experience of time that modernist writers tried to recreate mythic time. But mythic time is no help to Marxists, because it is always ideological. Marx himself is a major prophet of the break with this sort of time, as Marshall Berman in *All That Is Solid Melts Into Air* has shown. That the entire notion of the simulacrum is Platonic should have warned poststructuralists away from it. To call something a simulacrum makes sense only in an essentialist context. It has taken on its present interest because one of the last widely valorized essences—the original work of art—is threatened by mechanical reproduction. But Marxists should recognize this valorization as a fetish, an early form of commodification and not its antithesis. Poststructuralists should be suspicious of anything claiming originality. Because of its particular history, the temptation for Marxism—and for Jameson—is nostalgia for primitive communism and for folk culture, both working class and peasant. Perhaps the one genuinely democratic aspect of mass culture is the production of art in such forms as sound recordings which precisely are simulacra. Recordings lack an elitist original that can valorized, live performance being another thing altogether given current recording technology. That Jameson also recognizes and values this increased cultural democracy distinguishes him from Baudrillard ("RPM," 53), but it does not cancel out his own nostalgia expressed in his treatment of history discussed above and in his readings of particular works, such as Van Gogh's *Peasant Shoes*.

This defense of the simulacrum might meet with the objection from Jameson that it is itself postmodernist. But that objection would seem to reflect a failure to distinguish theory or interpretive method from cultural products. Such a distinction is not an ultimate one since theories and methods may be considered products. But in order for there to be critique one must admit the possibility of this distinction which Jameson seems at times to obliterate. For example, he suggests that modernist works, such as Van Gogh's *Peasant Shoes*, call for "hermeneutical" readings, but postmodernist ones, such as Warhol's *Diamond Dust Shoes*, do not ("PCL," 59-60). It would seem that he wants us to think of his own interpretation of the Warhol painting as "postmodern." Taken to its logical conclusion, this conflation of the depthlessness of the painting with the cultural understanding of it that Jameson provides would make this understanding itself superficial. But Jameson's reading of the Warhol painting is not superficial precisely because it is as fully "hermeneutical" as the readings of Van Gogh. Jameson's claim of an identity between his reading and painting reflects the Hirschian essentialism we discovered in *The Political Unconscious*, but also the failure to acknowledge conflict and difference within the cultural system.

In another place, Jameson makes an explicit argument for a connection between contemporary theory and postmodernism. Theory is held to be a new form of thought which "conceives of its vocation, not as the discovery of truth and the repudiation of error, but rather as a struggle about purely linguistic formulations, as the attempt to formulate verbal propositions (material language) in such a way that they are unable to imply unwanted or ideological consequences . . . 'theory' will come to be grasped as a specific (or semi-autonomous) form of what must be called postmodernism generally" ("PTS," 194). In spite of his assertion of its semi-autonomy, Jameson in fact tends to collapse the distinction between "theory" (which I will call poststructuralism) and postmodernism. While I would not quibble with Jameson's definition of "theory," I will add that I identify poststructuralism with the work of Althusser, Lacan, Derrida, Foucault, and Barthes in France, and Rorty and Fish in the United States. Thus I would not consider Baudrillard or Lyotard poststructuralists, but postmodernists. There are, of course, important connections between the poststructuralists and these postmodern theorists, but the latter are distinguished precisely by their claims about special character of the contemporary era.

Jameson doesn't recognize this distinction, but more importantly, he treats the poststructuralists as symptoms of postmodernism. Unfortunately, this relationship is simplistically depicted in terms of themes common to poststructuralist theory and postmodernist works of art. The major thematic connection which Jameson makes between poststructuralism and post-modernism is their similar preference for surface rather than depth. He argues that "the poststructuralist critique of the hermeneutic, of what I . . . call the depth model, is useful for us as a very significant symptom of . . . postmodernist culture" ("PCL," 61). In this instance, as in the reference to the Van Gogh painting, Jameson seems to be using the word "hermeneutic" as a synonym for Foucault's word "commentary," and thus forgets his own point in *The Political Unconscious* that poststructuralism is best described as an alternative group of hermeneutics rather than as anti-hermeneutics. Four kinds of depth relationships are indicated by Jameson as being overturned by poststructuralist theory: essence and appearance, latent and manifest, authenticity and inauthenticity, signifier and signified. This theoretical rejection of depth is then related to the expression of depthlessness in postmodern culture such as the freestanding wall of the Crocker Bank Center in Los Angeles. Similarly, the self is regarded as surface so that the modernist alienation of the subject is replaced by the fragmentation of the subject in Warhol "figures—Marilyn [Monroe] and Edie Sedgewick" ("PCL," 63). Jameson believes that the same cultural change is responsible for an actual frag-mentation of a once-existing bourgeois subject of classical capitalism and for the theorizing of that fragmentation as the decentering of the subject.

Jameson's thematic association of poststructuralism and postmodernism ignores the specific ways in which metaphors of depth and surface have functioned in different theories and works. Earlier in this essay, I discussed this issue with regard to Foucault. There I claimed that Foucault does not deal in surfaces so much as even greater depth, and I would argue the same of the other poststructuralists as well. It is true that poststructuralism has called into question the oppositions which have characterized modernist thought, and this questioning may signal a rupture of sorts. But poststructuralism has not abandoned us to life on a thin sheet of Mylar as has the postmodernism of Baurillard and Kroker. Rather poststructuralism has reconceived of the depth of thought and of culture as radically unstable. Thus in the case of each opposition, the depth term is not erased, but is cut off from the surface. Poststructuralism does not deny the latent or the signified, it just argues that the manifest and the signifier will invariably mislead us. But this is another form of the hermeneutics of suspicion which Freud and Nietzsche would well recognize. The anti-foundationalism which Rorty and Fish proclaim is not the same as superficiality.

Merely noting changes in the valorization of highly abstract terms such as surface over depth or space over time seems particularly suspect as an indicator of major cultural change, although it is one which Foucault might approve. The presence of these themes in poststructuralism does not necessarily indicate their dominance in it, and thus would not account for its most interesting, distinctive, or useful features. "Surface" and "depth" in theoretical writing are metaphors which may or may not be governing tropes of a particular discourse. They may be dominant, for example, in Oscar Wilde, but not in Foucault or Derrida.

Jameson does not explicitly connect poststructuralism to his theme of the postmodern effacement of history, but this claim is so often made elsewhere that it ought to be addressed. While postmodernists such as Baudrillard and Kroker do efface history, most poststructuralists do not. What philosopher takes greater account of the history of philosophy than Derrida? What theorist of any sort is more historical than Foucault, who places his own studies of the asylum, the clinic, etc. in context of other twentieth century works such as Husserl's *The Crisis of European Sciences*? What poststructuralists do is not deny history, but, like Faulkner, problematize it. The fact that we cannot distinguish history from the discourse of historians does not efface history, but merely states the condition of its existence. Some people, maybe even some poststructuralists, may assume that problems of reference equal the unreality of history, but this position cannot be attributed to Foucault or Althusser, nor do I think to Lacan or to Derrida.

Postmodernism is such a nebulous concept in part because the modern is so polysemous. As Jonathan Arac has noted, major players in the postmodernism debate define the modern quite differently: Jameson identifies it with the period of modernist literature, i.e., through the first half of this century; Habermas associates the modern with the unfinished project of the enlightenment; Rorty locates the modern with Descartes and finds the postmodern already in Hegel (*Postmodernism and Politics*, xii-xiii). There is in Jameson a tendency to read out of modernism its more radical reversals of convention. And because Jameson treats modernism also as both a "cultural dominant," and an historical period, all manner of objects produced during the first half of the twentieth century are described as modernist, despite their widely differing styles. Thus the great *auteur* film directors, such as Hitchcock, are called modernist even though their narratives have far more in common with fiction that we would be inclined to call realist, and the Beatles and the Rolling Stones are regarded as the high modernist moment of rock ("PCL," 53; "PTI," 54). Here I think we can criticize Jameson for insufficient attention to capitalist economics. The notion of "modernism" itself conveys its own connection to capitalism which, as Marx pointed out, needs to have the perpetually modern:

> The bourgeoisie cannot exist without constantly revolutionizing the instruments of production, and with them the relations of production, and with them the whole relations of society. . . . Constant revolutionizing of production, uninterrupted disturbance of all social relations, everlasting uncertainty and agitation distinguish the bourgeois epoch from all earlier ones. All fixed, fast-frozen relations, with their train of ancient and venerable prejudices and opinions are swept away, all new-formed ones become antiquated before they can ossify. All that is solid melts into air, all that is holy is profaned, and man is at last compelled to face . . . his real conditions of life and his relations with his kind. (*Communist Manifesto*, 12)

Although he over-estimates the changes he discusses, especially in the optimistic, final words of the passage, Marx was right about much that he asserts here. Modernism is the doctrine of the perpetually new. As such, postmodernism is as inevitable—and as trivial—as the latest "new, improved" laundry detergent. Modernism has become too strongly identified with the past—I am here thinking mainly of modernism in aesthetic forms—to continue to seem revolutionary. But capitalism must have the new, so we invent the newer than new, the postnew, the post-modern. Thus the political significance of postmodernism is mainly that capitalism remains a cultural dominant and that it retains most of the traits Marx first found in it. To put the issue another way, is late capitalism more capitalist or late? Paradoxically, Jameson (and certainly Mandel) seems to say more capitalist, but he nevertheless falls victim to capitalism's own hype. A longer historical view of the phenomena Jameson calls postmodern will surely not see them as terribly distinct from other twentieth century productions. And there are some good reasons for taking such a view now. For example, it is useful and correct to understand Freud and Marx, not as prehistoric to post-structuralist theory, but as its fathers subject to attack by their Oedipally minded sons. This perspective would lend support to Arac's more positive sense of "postmodern" political possibilities by focusing our attention as Arac does on the resurgence of Marxist intellectual activity in England and North America (*Postmodernism and Politics*, xxxiv-xxxv). And here the differences between poststructuralism and postmodernism become significant for politics. The effect of poststructuralist theory in these contexts has not been the trivialization of politics, but rather the rebirth of politicized theory and practice within what were once simply the humanities, but which are increasingly today cultural studies. This development may not lead anywhere politically, but it seems to me to have a better chance than the explicitly humanist conceptions it is replacing.

Realism, Modernism, and the Empty Chair

Lambert Zuidervaart
Calvin College

> The Echternach dancing procession is not the march of
> the World Spirit; limitation and reservation are no way to
> represent the dialectic. Rather, the dialectic advances by
> way of extremes . . . . The prudence that restrains us from
> venturing too far ahead . . . is usually only an agent of social
> control, and so of stupefaction.
> —Adorno, *Minima Moralia*

Were it not for the dance of Fredric Jameson, Marxism and
postmodernism might well seem incompatible. Both as storytelling and as the story being told, postmodernism subverts the
central claims of Marxism. This is particularly so of Western
Marxism, whose critique of capitalism relies on claims about
totality, truth, and history. Such claims are of little use to a
movement that celebrates the particularity of the present moment.

Jameson is not about to join the celebration, but he is not
ready to condemn it either. His project is to enact a good story
about the postmodernist feast. A good story will be a Marxist
story, but it will give a new choreography to Marxist story-telling.
The notion of literary import or meaning (*Gehalt*) is a case in
point. By observing this notion at work among earlier Western
Marxists such as Lukács and Adorno, one gains perspective on
Jameson's attempt to update Marxist categories for a postmodern
culture.

This discussion will show that reinterpretative dances are not always fluid. More specifically, Jameson's attempt to update Western Marxist aesthetics for a postmodernist audience threatens to render his project incoherent. Contrary to Adorno's advice, the argument for this conclusion will mimic the dance of Echternach, in form at least, if not in content. Taking three steps forward, the essay will situate "import" in the Lukács-Adorno debate about realism, present Jameson's view of this debate, and examine his attempt to reconstruct "import" into "symbolic act." Stepping backwards, it will next discuss Jameson's attitude toward postmodernism and then read the notion of "reification" as a code shared by all three authors. The final section will suggest that Jameson must revise this code if his story about post-modernism is to become coherent.

I. Import and the Privileged Subject

"Postmodernism" indicates our context for reading Jameson. A partial sign of current academic fashion, the concept styles itself after "modernism," itself a multivalent concept. Rather than review recent debates about how the two concepts connect, let me pick out an aspect that helps one read Jameson's project. This aspect is the dialectic between subject and object in Western culture since the seventeenth century. "Subject" refers to the human knower or actor, whether individual or collective. "Object" refers to whatever the human knower or actor is thought to constitute or generate. The relevance of this subject-object dialectic is suggested by a comment on the "hyperspace" of post-modernism in Jameson's conversation with Anders Stephanson:

> We used to talk about this in terms of subject-object dialectics; but in a situation where subjects and objects have been dissolved, hyperspace is the ultimate of the object-pole, intensity the ultimate of the subject-pole, though we no longer have subjects and objects. ("RPM," 47)

"Postmodernism" can be regarded as a movement toward abandoning the subject-object dialectic.

Deep in this movement is the impulse to deprive the subject of its privileged position. In philosophy, this impulse toward deprivation opposes the constitutive knower first clearly articulated in Descartes' *cogito ergo sum*. In the arts, this impulse either destroys the privileged position of the artist or highlights a destruction that has already occurred. In literary criticism, the deprivation of the subject undermines both the authority of the author and the criteria of the critic.

The tendency to deprive the human subject of its privileged position is neither sudden nor arbitrary. It emerges gradually from modern Western culture, which is itself tied to the history of capitalism and industrialization. Astute historians such as Perry Anderson in his *In the Tracks of Historical Materialism* and Martin Jay in *Marxism and Totality* have found a similar tendency growing within Western Marxism. If they are correct, then a struggle over the subject's position may well be central to Western Marxism—central not as the center, but as an unavoidable struggle upon which depends much of its credibility and strength. Given the emphasis on subjective agency in traditional Marxist politics, the question of the subject's position has implications far beyond the fields of philosophy, art, and literary criticism. The implications become clearest at an intersection that one can label "cultural politics."

The transition from middle Lukács to late Adorno is particularly instructive in this regard. According to Martin Jay, Western Marxism begins by emphasizing a sociohistorical totality and by privileging a collective subject that can transform this totality. Lukács' *History and Class Consciousness* (1923) gives the classic presentation of this approach. Although spawned in part by Lukács' book, Adorno's *Negative Dialectics* (1966) appears to have demolished both the emphasis on totality and the privileging of a collective subject:

> No longer could a Western Marxist defend an expressive view of the whole in which a meta-subject was both the subject and the object of history. No longer could history itself be seen as a coherent whole with a positive conclusion as its telos. No longer could totality ignore the

non-identity of the historical and the natural and
subordinate the latter to human domination. (*Marxism and
Totality*, 274)

Yet one cannot ignore Adorno's expectation of a human transformation of society and his hope for a new relationship with
nature. His abandonment of Lukács' meta-subject does not entail
a complete anti-subjectivism. In paradoxical fashion, Adorno tries
to give an immanent critique of the privileged subject. His
philosophy tries "to use the strength of the subject to break
through the fallacy of constitutive subjectivity" (*Negative
Dialectics*, xx). The subject is to be deprivileged, but a privileged
subject must carry this out.

The paradox here lets one characterize Adorno's cultural
politics as one of paradoxical modernism. A good example of his
cultural politics, and a relevant one for understanding Jameson,
occurs in Adorno's debate with Lukács over realism and
modernism. In a well-known polemical review, Adorno once
accused Lukács of re-enacting Hegel's "reconciliation under
duress"[1] A few years later, Lukács charged Adorno with moving
into the "Grand Hotel Abyss."[2] The occasion for these
pleasantries was Lukács' *Realism in Our Time*,[3] published less
then ten years before Adorno's *Negative Dialectics*. Ostensibly
the Adorno-Lukács debate concerns the political merits of realism
and modernism in twentieth-century literature. Read from the
vantage point of Jameson's recent writings, however, the debate
also enacts a struggle over the position of the epistemic subject
relative to the import of the literary work. A brief reading from
this angle will help introduce the dance of Fredric Jameson.[4]

Lukács distinguishes three main streams in twentieth-
century literature: modernism, critical realism, and socialist
realism—represented by Franz Kafka, Thomas Mann, and Maxim
Gorky, respectively. One can simplify Lukács' descriptions as
follows. Modernist literature is bourgeois literature that is characterized by ahistorical angst in the face of monopoly capitalism.
Critical realism, although ideologically bourgeois, displays sober
optimism and does not reject socialism. Socialist realism is
similarly historical and optimistic. Unlike critical realism,

however, it uses a socialist perspective "to describe the forces working towards socialism *from the inside*" (*Realism in Our Time*, 93). Whereas critical and socialist realism can form a common front against the cold war, modernism inadvertently supports the forces of destruction.

Adorno rejects this system of classification and tries to subvert it case by case. He touts "modernist" works as genuinely realistic, in the sense that they provide "negative knowledge" of sociohistorical reality ("Reconciliation," 158-161). So-called "critical realist" works are claimed to be less "realist" and more "modernist" than Lukács thinks. So called "socialist realist" works are said by Adorno to be historically out of date and technically regressive. Their regressiveness originates in backward social forces of production and serves to hide oppressive features of Soviet society. In effect, Adorno declares socialist realist works to be both less modern and less realistic than the "modernist" works that Lukács condemns.

Behind these dramatically opposed interpretations lie different understandings and evaluations of the import of twentieth-century literature. For Lukács, the import of modernist works has at its heart an incorrect view of humanity. This literary worldview has profound formal and ideological ramifications. For Adorno, by contrast, the import of modernist works does not have any worldview at its heart. Nor does he consider import to be "form-determinative" (*Realism in Our Time*, 16). Although seeming to share the category of import, Lukács and Adorno construe it differently. Both construals concern the manner in which a work presents social reality; both provide overarching standards of literary criticism; yet the two are incompatible, with Adorno's construal being much less subject-centered than that of Lukács.

As others have noted, Lukács' approach to literary import is problematic; Adorno registers some of the problems without pinpointing their source. These problems do not result from Lukácsian blindness to form or technique; instead, they stem from what Adorno vaguely identifies as inadvertent subjectivism ("Reconciliation," 153). More precisely put, the main difficulties arise from a double expectation that literary import originates in the knowing subject and that this epistemic subject provides the key to interpreting literary import.

One can label this expectation a version of epistemic subjectivism. "Epistemic subjectivism" refers to a tendency to privilege the human knower as the ultimate source of "meaning," literary or otherwise. This privileged epistemic subject may be either individual or collective. The epistemic subject in literature may be the author, the reader, or the critic. It is not entirely clear which of these Lukács considers most important. It does seem clear, however, that he locates the ultimate source of literary import in the human knower. For Lukács, literary import originates in subjective worldviews, mediated by literary works; subjective worldviews provide the key to interpreting literary import.

Lukács' emphasis on worldview embodies a nineteenth-century expectation that meaning can ultimately be found in the subject's global outlook on life and society. His assessments of twentieth-century literature continually assume that authentic works will express such a global outlook. Adorno does not share this expectation. His emphasis on technique embodies a typically twentieth-century concern, and he rejects any attempt to locate the ultimate source of meaning in the epistemic subject. Adorno does not privilege the epistemic subject as a constituter of meaning, nor does he think of literary import as deriving from a subject's worldview.

Thus the realism-modernism debate turns out to enact a struggle over the position of the epistemic subject relative to the import of a literary work. This struggle reaches a new stage in Fredric Jameson's *The Political Unconscious*. The new stage becomes clear from his stance on the realism/modernism debate as well as from the category of "symbolic act" that informs his stance.

Jameson's work as a literary theorist and cultural critic owes much to both Lukács and Adorno, as well as to other prominent Western Marxists such as Bloch, Benjamin, Marcuse, and Sartre.[5] In recent years, Jameson has also been in conversation with structuralist Marxists such as Louis Althusser and various French poststructuralists such as Jacques Derrida, Michel Foucault,

Jacques Lacan, Jean Baudrillard, Gilles Deleuze, and Jean-François Lyotard. Along with this conversation has come a turn toward mass mediated art and the culture of postmodernism.[6] Like Lukács and Adorno, Jameson is concerned with the political implications of twentieth-century art and literature. Unlike Lukács and Adorno, however, Jameson does not privilege either realist or modernist works. Instead, Jameson seems opposed to assigning unusual political merit to any past or present cultural phenomena. Later his opposition will be described as an attitude of ambiguous postmodernism. First, however, we should consider his criticisms of his predecessors.

II. The Empty Chair

Jameson's criticisms take their cues from an orientation toward the future. Jameson concludes *The Political Unconscious* by trying to set the stage for "conceiving those new forms of collective thinking and collective culture which lie beyond the boundaries of our own world." Jameson's staging reserves "an empty chair . . . for some as yet unrealized, collective, and decentered cultural production of the future, beyond realism and modernism alike" (*PU*, 11). These general stage directions prompt three observations. First, Jameson is announcing a political task that remains unfulfilled in *The Political Unconscious*. While acknowledging the urgency of projecting a vital political culture, Jameson steps back to explore preconditions for doing so. Second, it seems no actual body of works can count as elements of a vital political culture. "An empty chair" is reserved for some future cultural production. Third, the vital political culture that Jameson awaits will be "beyond realism and modernism."

Recalling earlier Western Marxist debates, one surmises that Jameson is attempting to go beyond Lukács and Adorno. Lukács had tried to reinstate realism and dethrone modernism; Adorno had tried to install certain modernist works; Jameson wishes to unseat both realism and modernism in favor of some future culture. Whereas Lukács and Adorno see realism and modernism respectively as the best political culture for the present, Jameson wishes to hold the position open for some future culture. His book does not say how this culture would be connected with past and present cultural phenomena. Nor does it say what kind of culture would be politically preferable under current conditions.

Jameson's hesitation on the last score contrasts strongly with the militant tone of Adorno's essay on "Commitment."[7] The contrast is not surprising, however, since Jameson questions Adorno's militancy. Indeed, he calls Adorno's essay an "anti-political revival of the ideology of modernism" ("RIC," 209). Jameson credits Adorno with noting how consumer capitalism can turn even the most dangerous didactic works into mere commodities. This fact cuts more than one way, however. It also speaks against seeing modernist works as prototypically political. According to Jameson, consumer capitalism has rendered modernism innocuous.

Having thus begun to dethrone literary modernism, Jameson decodes it in *The Political Unconscious*. He does so by employing the concept of reification to "transcode" literary modernism and social life within monopoly capitalism (see *PU*, 40-42, 62-63, 225-237). Jameson applies the concept of reification to all modernist literature. Not only has consumer capitalism rendered modernism innocuous, but also modernism has always had reification as its precondition. In principle, then, no modernist work will be more capable than any other work of penetrating the reified façades of contemporary society. One cannot assign special political merit to authentic modernist works.

At the same time, however, Jameson questions Lukács' use of "reification" to repudiate various modernist styles. According to *The Political Unconscious*, no literary work, no matter how "reactionary" in intent, is "mere ideology" in the sense of being false consciousness pure and simple. The Marxist critic needs to examine the "strategies of containment" whereby all sorts of works repress deeply political impulses. When it comes to such strategies, modernism and realism are more intricately interwoven than Lukács thinks. Indeed, Jameson insists that realism has its own strategies of containment (*PU*, 193).

While acknowledging an affinity with Lukács' emphasis on reification, Jameson distances himself from *Realism in Our Time*:

> We must . . . place some distance between our use of the
> concept [of reification] and that to be found in Lukács'
> various later accounts of modernism, in which the term
> reification is simple shorthand for value judgment and for
> the repudiation by association of the various modern styles.
> Yet Lukács was not wrong to make the connection between
> modernism and the reification of daily life: his mistake was
> to have done so ahistorically and to have made his analysis
> the occasion for an ethical judgment rather than a
> historical perception. (*PU*, 226-227)

According to Jameson, Lukács' failure to historicize leads him to
ignore the "Utopian vocation" of modernist phenomena. The
increasing abstraction of visual art, for example, does more than
express the reification of daily life; such abstraction "also
constitutes a Utopian compensation for everything lost in . . . the
development of capitalism" such as the place of quality, feeling,
and sheer color and intensity (*PU*, 63, 236-237). Here Jameson
comes close to Adorno's notion of art as "the promise of
happiness, a promise that is constantly being broken," even while
he refuses to privilege those modernist works whose colorlessness
Adorno regards as a "negative apotheosis" of color.[8] The fact that
there is a utopian impulse is not peculiar to modernism nor to any
specific works of modern art. One may expect to find a utopian
impulse in every literary work: "all ideology in the strongest sense
. . . is in its very nature Utopian" (*PU*, 289).

Jameson's concern in *The Political Unconscious* is not to
promote those recent works which seem to have greatest political
merit, but to hold open a chair for some future culture beyond
realism and modernism alike. This culture will be "collective and
decentered" in ways that realism and modernism, with their links
to capitalism, never could have been. Having come earlier in the
development of capitalism, realism may not have had such
elaborate strategies for containing the utopian impulse as
modernism displays. Realism may also not have had reification as
its precondition. Yet realism is no less ideological than
modernism, just as modernism is no less utopian than realism.
Furthermore, both realism and modernism are dated literary

movements. Their political implications were conditioned by earlier stages of class struggle and cultural revolution. To ask which of these movements has greater merit today would be to misunderstand the present from which the questioner asks. It is the present of postmodernism and consumer capitalism.

Jameson's criticisms of Adorno's modernism and Lukács' antimodernism involve a clear departure from their emphases on literary import and indicate a new phase in the struggle over the epistemic subject. One way to illustrate this shift is to consider the category of "the symbolic act" in Jameson's literary theory.

III. The Symbolic Act

Jameson's notion of the symbolic act upstages the category of import in Lukács and Adorno. Despite their disagreements about the political merits of realism and modernism, both Lukács and Adorno promote comprehensive evaluations of the import of specific works. For Lukács, who favors realism, the key to such evaluations is the work's literary worldview. For Adorno, who favors modernism, the key to evaluating import is the work's literary technique.

Rather than coming down on either side, Jameson proposes a different, three-horizon model for literary criticism. Each horizon of interpretation is nested within the next. On Jameson's model, any literary text can be read as a symbolic act within a class discourse. The class discourse occurs within a more or less revolutionary social formation. The relationship between the symbolic act and its referent is one of text and subtext. There is a social reality from which the text emerges. When emerging, however, the text not only draws social reality into its own texture but also transforms that reality into a subtext and thereby hides the independent existence of its own social situation. The literary critic must rewrite the literary text "in such a way that the latter may itself be seen as the rewriting . . . of a prior . . . *subtext* [which] must itself always be (re)constructed after the fact" (*PU*, 81).

Jameson affirms with Kenneth Burke that the symbolic act is both a genuine *act*, albeit symbolic, and a genuine *symbol*, albeit active. "Symbolic" has the force of "projective," in the manner of dreams when subjected to psychoanalysis. The projection is of the political history of a specific time and place. Within the first horizon of interpretation, a Balzac novel, for example, would be read as a projective resolution of social contradictions in France after the failure of the Napoleonic revolution, during the demise of the country aristocracy. Formal or aesthetic contradictions in the text itself would be taken as imaginary and unavoidably incomplete resolutions of social contradictions in nineteenth-century France. Like the dream that hides the unconscious, the text hides its subtext until successfully analyzed (Dowling, 123). As a symbolic act, the text is a projection that tends to deny what it projects.

If one now asks whether there is an actor for this act, a projector for this projection, the best answer seems to be that the only actor is the act itself. Or perhaps one should say with Mohanty that "like the text, the author is seen as a node of interaction, as the criss-crossings of ideology, desire and the intransigence of history" ("History at the Edge of Discourse," 45). Jameson shares with structuralist Marxism the tendency to disregard questions of subjective agency. This tendency continues in his account of the other two horizons of interpretation. Jameson links the text to the structure of class discourse and proposes to read the text as the intersection of impulses from contradictory modes of cultural production. In spite of his talk of class conflict and cultural revolution, Jameson makes little attempt to address the traditional problems of human agency for these processes.

Texts are like dreams that occur and await interpretation. What counts for Jameson's interpretations is not the comprehensive evaluation of some import that is linked to an author's worldview (Lukács) or to an author's social experience and expertise (Adorno). What counts is a self-activating act, which is to be reactivated through interpretation. The author seems to have vanished along with the task of political evaluation. The text and its interpretation remain. On a larger scale, the epistemic subject not only seems to have lost its privileged position but also appears to have faded from the scene.

Jameson's reasons for upstaging the category of import and downplaying the role of the author are linked to his understanding of current historical imperatives. Two imperatives are especially high on his agenda. One is "the need to transcend individualistic categories and modes of interpretation" (*PU*, 68).[9] Jameson argues that "only the dialectic provides a way for 'decentering' the subject concretely, and for transcending the 'ethical' in the direction of the political and the collective" (*PU*, 60). The notion of a symbolic act is one way to transcend the apparently individualistic category of import and to move beyond the "ethical" judgments traditionally attached to this category. The second imperative, closely related to the first, is to maintain a sense of collective agency without reviving Lukács' meta-subject. The notion of import, with its implication of representative expression or effort, seems either outdated or premature ("RMC," 140).

Lukács and Adorno disagree over the political merits of modernist works, but they agree that these merits must be evaluated and that such evaluations hinge on literary import. The notion of a symbolic act lets Jameson change the rules of their game. He uses the debate about modernism to show how he would historicize individualistic, ethical categories such as good/bad and progressive/regressive by looking for the "ideological" and "Utopian" features of any given phenomenon (*PU*, 234-237). A similar procedure governs his interpretations of postmodernist phenomena. He points out their ideological and utopian features, but does not assess their relative political merits.

Given the need to transcend individualistic categories and ethical judgments, and given the need to maintain a sense of collective agency, one might wonder why Jameson does not give up the project of interpretation, which seems to emphasize the interpreter as an individual center of judgment. Must not the decentering dialectic itself be decentered?

It is clear from Jameson's criticism of postmodernist "ideologies of the text" that he wishes to retain the project of interpretation (*PU*, 17-23). He tries to retain the project of interpretation by decoupling his historiographic analysis of ideological and Utopian features from comprehensive evaluations concerning the political merits of cultural phenomena. Nevertheless, these decoupled judgments tend to coalesce in claims about his own project of interpretation. Jameson's claims about his own project are of a sort that he refuses to make about other cultural phenomena. Even though he assigns priority to the political perspective in interpretation, for example (*PU*, 17), he hesitates to do something similar with respect to literary production. So too, whereas Jameson expects that his own interpretations will prove to be "stronger" than others (*PU*, 13), he seems not to expect something similar with respect to specific texts. He ends up reserving an empty chair for some future culture, even though he is not willing to give up the task of making this reservation in the present.

The result seems to be a cultural politics within which lurks a strong potential for incoherence. This potential concerns three problems, all of them related to the apparent evaporation of the epistemic subject. To pose these problems and to examine Jameson's cultural politics more closely, it will be useful to return to his reasons for rejecting Adorno's "anti-political revival of the ideology of modernism."

IV. Ambiguous Postmodernism

Jameson has three reasons for rejecting Adorno's militant modernism. The first is that consumer capitalism has rendered modern art innocuous. The second is that modern art employs reifying strategies of containment. The third reason is that the presence of a utopian impulse is not peculiar to modern art. At first these reasons may seem convincing. Upon further reflection, however, one wonders whether any of these facts is peculiar to modern art. If none of them is, then some problems may arise for Jameson's own project.

Jameson's writings on postmodernism suggest a negative answer. His path-breaking article on this topic—"Postmodernism, or The Cultural Logic of Late Capitalism"—identifies postmodernism as the cultural dominant of consumer capitalism.

Jameson follows Ernest Mandel in positing three dialectical stages of capitalism: market capitalism, monopoly capitalism, and late, multinational, or consumer capitalism. Parallel to these stages are the cultural stages of realism, modernism, and postmodernism. Just as consumer capitalism is the purest stage of capitalism, so postmodernism is the virtual apotheosis of reification in culture. The clear implication of this periodization seems to be that under current conditions virtually every oppositional form of culture has been rendered innocuous and must employ reifying strategies of containment simply to survive. Furthermore, even if one can identify utopian impulses within an oppositional form, their existence will not be peculiar to such a form. Thus it seems that Jameson's reasons for rejecting Adorno's modernism are also reasons for expecting little genuine and effective opposition within postmodern culture. This would be an undesirable consequence for Marxist cultural politics. The question is whether Jameson has found ways to avoid it.

To show that genuine and effective opposition can be expected, Jameson would have to solve three problems tied to his reasons for rejecting Adorno's modernism. The first concerns the relationship of his interpretation to the postmodern culture in which it takes place. This is the problem of the precondition for a critique of postmodern culture. The second problem concerns the relationship of Jameson's interpretation to whatever oppositional forces exist within postmodern culture. This is the problem of the relation of theory to praxis within cultural politics. The third problem, which encompasses the other two, pertains to the possibility of a new political culture within the space of postmodernism. This is the problem of the empty chair.

An illustration of the first problem occurs in Jameson's discussion of recent debates about postmodernism in architecture. In "The Politics of Theory: Ideological Positions in the Postmodernism Debate," Jameson distinguishes four different positions. There are those like Charles Jencks and Tom Wolfe who are anti-modernist but pro-postmodernist, in contrast to Manfredo Tafuri, who opposes both modernism and postmodernism. There are others like Jean-François Lyotard who are both pro-modernist and pro-postmodernist, in contrast to Jürgen Habermas and Hilton

Kramer, who oppose postmodernism for pro-modernist reasons. Jameson regards all such positions as ethical judgments rather than historical perceptions. Since "we are *within* the culture of postmodernism," the point is neither to condemn nor to celebrate postmodernism but to give it "a genuinely historical and dialectical analysis" ("PTI," 62-63). Thus Jameson insists on his own location within postmodern culture but takes distance from postmodernist affirmations of postmodern culture. His approach is one of ambiguous postmodernism—postmodernist in the sense that it locates itself within postmodern culture, but ambiguous in the sense that it refuses to condemn or celebrate that culture.

The problem here is that Jameson's location within postmodern culture is ill-defined. His desire to give "a genuinely historical and dialectical analysis" is not a postmodern impulse. According to his own analysis, postmodern culture displays sheer discontinuity and the loss of historical depth. If Jameson's analysis is correct, then one may wonder whether there exist sources or tendencies within postmodern culture that make such an analysis possible. Perhaps the analysis is living on borrowed time, so to speak, drawing upon a Marxist tradition amidst the death of all traditions. If so, then the political prospects for such an analysis seem bleak. Or perhaps the analysis is made possible by certain oppositional forces alive within postmodern culture. If this were so, however, one would expect Jameson to show more sympathy for the traditional Marxist project of evaluating the political merits of existing cultural phenomena. The inappropriateness of condemning or celebrating postmodernism as whole need not mean that the Marxist interpreter should refrain from a political critique of specific phenomena.

Here one begins to see a second problem tied to Jameson's critique of Adorno. It is a problem not unlike one facing Adorno's paradoxical modernism, namely the problem of relating theory to praxis within cultural politics. What exactly is the relationship between Jameson's interpretation and whatever oppositional forces exist within postmodern culture? Jameson posits a certain homology between his theoretical project and the aesthetic task of "cognitive mapping." He also suggests that his empathetic critique of postmodernist "theories" is analogous to a homeopathic critique which, like Doctorow's work, would "undo postmodernism by the methods of postmodernism" ("RPM," 59). Nevertheless, homologies do not establish that there is an interaction between the two homologous fields, nor do analogies establish exactly how such interactions would proceed.

The first two problems are both manifestations of the problem of the empty chair. Given the space of postmodernism, which Jameson has analyzed in such an instructive fashion, what are the possibilities of a new political culture? This question encompasses both the preconditions for a critique of postmodern culture and the preconditions for oppositional forms of post-modern culture. To the question of oppositional forms, Jameson's article on postmodernism gives an excruciatingly tentative answer:

> the new political art—if it is indeed possible at all—will have to hold to the truth of postmodernism, that is, to say, to its fundamental object—the world space of multi-national capital—at the same time at which it achieves a breakthrough to some as yet unimaginable new mode of representing this last, in which we may again begin to grasp our positioning as individual and collective subjects and regain a capacity to act and struggle which is at present neutralized by our spatial as well as our social confusion. The political form of postmodernism, if there ever is any, will have as its vocation the invention and projection of a global cognitive mapping, on a social as well as a spatial scale. ("PCL," 92)

Jameson's answer is a delicate dance, calling for a new political culture while declaring it all but impossible under current conditions. The answer revives the theme of subjectivity while pointing out what militates against subjective initiative. The problem of the empty chair remains.

Obviously, Jameson is not unaware of this problem. A good deal of his energy in recent years has gone into addressing it. Absent to date, however, is a systematic re-examination of certain tendencies that make this problem a potential source of incoherence for his project. The move to reserve an empty chair at the end of The Political Unconscious may be more than a promise to project a vital political culture in subsequent writings. Reserving an empty chair might also be the inevitable outcome of troublesome tendencies noted by various commentators on Jameson's book.[10]

One tendency is of particular importance in the present context. It is the tendency to absolutize the concept of reification. After observing this tendency at work in *The Political Unconscious*, one can see Jameson's ambiguous postmodernism as the setting of a new stage for Western Marxism's struggle over the position of the epistemic subject. One can also suggest ways in which this staging must be modified if Jameson's project is not to become incoherent.

V. The Code of Reification

Jameson's book describes the concept of reification as a mediation. By "mediation" he means the analyst's inventing of a code that is applicable to two distinct objects or structural levels (*PU*, 40, 225). Jameson considers "reification" to be a most useful device for transcoding literary modernism and social life. Reification is not "a mere methodological fiction," however; society is assumed to be "a seamless web" despite its fragmented and multidimensional appearance. At the same time, this assumption about society has a "merely formal" appeal, except insofar as it provides "the philosophical justification" for the analyst's "local practice of mediation" (*PU*, 40).

There are some troubling aspects to Jameson's account of reification. One is the weakness of his rationale for using this specific mediation rather than others. The assumption of totality, which justifies the practice of mediations, needs some justification beyond the fact that mediations require this assumption. Furthermore, even if Jameson is successful in his attempt to give additional justification, the assumption of totality does not in itself justify the specific mediation of "reification." It is not clear that Jameson ever does argue convincingly for using "reification." Since this concept yields insightful results in specific interpretations, however, the apparent lack of a convincing argument may not be a serious problem. One thinks in this connection of Jameson's highly illuminating discussion of Joseph Conrad.

A more troublesome aspect of Jameson's account of reification is its circularity. When Jameson explains the need for mediations, of which reification is one, he does so in ways that already employ reification as a mediation. Consider the following passage:

> Mediations are thus a device of the analyst, whereby the fragmentation and autonomization, the compartmentalization and specialization of the various regions of social life . . . is at least locally overcome, on the occasion of a particular analysis. (*PU*, 40)

In positing that social life has undergone fragmentation, autonomization, and so on, Jameson is already invoking a global theory of reification. Although he never clearly presents this theory, Jameson continually aligns such phenomena as the "privatization of contemporary life" and the dehistoricizing of contemporary consciousness with reification. He also subsumes psychic fragmentation and the "autonomization of sexuality" under the dynamic of reification. Similar alignments or subsumptions occur with respect to professionalization, Taylorization, scientific specialization, the autonomizing of art works, the rationalizing of social institutions, and the instrumentalizing of "values" (see *PU*, 20, 62-64, 160-161, 190, 220-222, 225-227, 249-253, 260-261).[11] From a purely methodological perspective, it seems disingenuous to explain the need for mediations in terms that already assume the legitimacy of an assumed theory of reification. In addition, because the theory is assumed rather than elaborated, there is a strong possibility that the concept will become a master code for twentieth-century culture in the West, even though reification is supposed to be just one mediation among many. The tendency of such a master code is to become more suggestive than precise.

The most troublesome aspect of Jameson's use of "reification," however, is that it tends to make irrelevant all attempts to decide which phenomena are more or less resistant to reification. The long-range effect is to render problematic any attempt to give a political critique of contemporary culture. In this respect, Jameson's ambiguous postmodernism shares a code with Adorno's modernism and Lukács' anti-modernism but takes it one step further. The code is "reification."

Both Lukács and Adorno see reification as the central mechanism whereby the commodity form permeates the entire culture of capitalism. Both authors also treat certain works of art as privileged opponents of reification. For Lukács, realism provides the requisite works. The literary worldview in realist works ensures that these maintain a grasp on the sociohistorical totality and penetrate reified social life under capitalist conditions. For Adorno, certain modernist works have sufficient experiential depth and technical progressiveness to resist the commodification of consciousness and to expose the hidden contradictions of capitalism.

Jameson also sees reification as a central mechanism in the culture of capitalism. Under the conditions of consumer capitalism, however, reification seems to have reached the point where no works and no authors provide a strategic challenge to reification. For Jameson, one structural peculiarity of consumer capitalism is the nearly total colonization of consciousness by the process of commodification. His book assumes that we live in a society where reification has become nearly total both on the side of the subject and on the side of the object. In the hyperspace of postmodernism, "subjects and objects have been dissolved" ("RPM," 47). Thus it is understandable why the evaluation of relative political merits has become irrelevant. The difficulty for Jameson is to explain the possibility of any political consciousness today, whether in the producer, the consumer, or the text itself. The attempt to balance "ideology" and "Utopia" in all cultural phenomena seems to indicate precisely this difficulty. In consumer capitalism no specific "strategy of containment" has greater political liabilities than any other. So, too, no specific "perspective on the future" ("RPM," 52) has greater political prospects than any other. The reservation for something beyond realism and modernism is made from a highly reified present.

Here the question of the subject's position returns with a vengeance. If the present is as highly reified as Jameson suggests, one must wonder about the viability and legitimacy of any attempt to give a political interpretation of contemporary phenomena, including Jameson's own attempt. If the interpreter is indeed located squarely within the highly reified culture of postmodernism, how can the interpreter maintain political consciousness and make defensible claims about the legitimacy of the interpreter's own construal of culture? The same reasons for reserving an empty chair for some future culture seem to argue for vacating the present chair of political interpretation. Jameson's project threatens to become self-referentially incoherent.

Rather than accept this conclusion, one could just as easily argue against assuming that reification has become as pervasive as Lukács, Adorno, and Jameson seem to think. This argument need not claim that "reification" is a bogus concept. The concept can function as an illuminating theoretical construct with a basis in empirical research. Problems arise when this construct is made the key to a totalizing theory of sociohistorical reality. When this occurs, the specificity of Marx's economic critique evaporates, and the critique of culture gradually loses its point, whether through dogmatism, irrelevance, or indifference.

Dogmatism is clearly visible in Lukács' *a priori* rejection of modernist literature because of the supposedly reified and reifying character of its worldview. Dogmatism is also evident in his inattention to the socio-economic basis of realist literature, whose worldview supposedly penetrates reified social life. Adorno's approach is less dogmatic but no less problematic. The irrepressible question raised by his defenses of modernist works is "So what?" Why is it important, for example, that Beckett's *Endgame* powerfully presents the final history of subjectivity? What real contribution can such a work make to the liberation of consciousness, if capitalist culture is as monolithic as Adorno assumes?

Jameson avoids the dogmatism of Lukács and the irrelevance of Adorno, but he does so at the price of indifference. Jameson employs the concept of reification in such a way that it seems no longer useful to discriminate among phenomena that are more or less resistant to reification. Given the three problems noted earlier, however, it is hard to see how Jameson's project of political interpretation can avoid incoherence unless the concept of reification is relativized. The presumed pervasiveness of reification throughout postmodernism would eliminate the preconditions for a critique of postmodern culture, interrupt the relationship of Jameson's interpretation to any oppositional forces, and prevent the growth of a new political culture within the space of postmodernism.

Obviously the concept of reification cannot be relativized by fiat. One would have to rely on an empirically based structural and historical analysis of consumer capitalism and its culture. In theory, however, one can think of two ways in which to relativize the concept of reification. The first way would be to restrict its scope to a primarily economic meaning and to adopt a more refined vocabulary for analogues or extensions of the commodity form outside the strictly economic arena. Another way would be to suggest that reification either has not become as pervasive as Jameson thinks or has reversed itself in important respects during recent years. Either way would require a rethinking of the role of the subject in cultural politics.

VI. An Unfinished Project

Jameson himself has begun to move in this direction. Perhaps the best indication is his recent article on Georg Lukács, "*History and Class Consciousness* as an 'Unfinished Project.'" Jameson argues that the theory of reification provides the philosophical basis for Lukácsian aesthetics, just as "the consciousness of the proletariat" did in *History and Class Consciousness*. Jameson finds particularly significant the way in which Lukács' theory connects the logic of capitalism with the possibility and necessity of a counter-logic: "This allows us to imagine a collective project not merely capable of breaking the multiple systemic webs of reification, but which *must* do so in order to realize itself" ("HCC," 52). Equally significant is the fact that Lukács does not pursue this connection in the direction of a conventional subject-object synthesis but in the direction of a collective subject's de-reifying "aspiration to totality."

While one could quibble with aspects of Jameson's interpretation, it is more important to see what he makes of Lukács'
theory. Jameson highlights two implications for the postmodern
context. One is that the aspiration to totality points toward "a
collective project" ("HCC," 60). The second implication is that
particular social groups, classes, or class fragments have an
epistemological priority in capitalist society. Both implications
point toward the re-privileging of a collective subject, albeit not
the proletarian consciousness on which Lukács pinned his hopes
for a systemic transformation of society.

Jameson suggests that distinctive "moments of truth" can be
found in feminist theorizing as well as in the group experiences of
women, Blacks, and Central European Jews. To grasp a group's
"moment of truth" is not only to see how the group's social
constraints make possible an otherwise unavailable experience of
society but also to translate such experience "into new
possibilities of thought and knowledge" ("HCC," 70). Under
current conditions, then, Lukács' theory turns into a "principled
relativism" with a specific presupposition:

> The presupposition is that, owing to its structural situation
> in the social order and to the specific forms of oppression
> and exploitation unique to that situation, each group lives
> the world in a phenomenologically specific way that allows
> it to see, or better still, that makes it unavoidable for that
> group to see and to know, features of the world that remain
> obscure, invisible, or merely occasional and secondary for
> other groups. ("HCC," 65)

Does Jameson's "principled relativism" sufficiently relativize
the concept of reification to keep his project of political
interpretation from becoming self-referentially incoherent?
Certainly he has begun to relativize the concept. Lukács'
"reification" and "proletarian consciousness" give way to "the
variable structures of 'constraint' lived by . . . various marginal,
oppressed or dominated groups." The de-reifying aspiration to
totality makes room for an acknowledgement that each group's
experience produces its own view and its own "distinctive truth
claim" ("HCC," 71). The task now is to make an inventory of the

variable structures of constraint, always acknowledging, however, distinctive truth claims.

Translated into cultural politics, such language suggests that various cultural phenomena arising from various group experiences can provide strategic challenges to what was once called reification. Also suggested is the fact that a political interpretation of postmodern culture will receive instruction from such groups, even while it tries to provide a cohesive framework for understanding their experience.

At the same time, however, Jameson refers to "late capitalism" as the "absent common object of such 'theorization' from multiple 'standpoints'" ("HCC," 71), thereby once again indirectly invoking a non-relativized concept of reification. He also fails to address the question of how the truth of various claims will be determined and how the relative merits of conflicting truth claims will be adjudicated. An answer to either question would have to appeal to a systematic theory of the culture of capitalism. Inevitably the question would then arise as to the experiential base for such a theory. More pointedly, from what group standpoint will the distinctive truth claims of various groups be grasped? Does the systematic theory itself arise from the experience of a genuine collective subject—genuine in the sense of living common constraints in a way that produces shared illumination?

It seems that a non-relativized concept of reification continues to operate at the level of this last question. Jameson seems to hold that reification permeates postmodern culture, but that it releases various types of de-reifying consciousness in various groups occupying marginal or oppressed positions within late capitalist society. A dialectic occurs between the reifying structure of capitalism and various subsidiary structures. These subsidiary structures exist by virtue of the structure of capitalism, but they render transparent its reifying tendencies. It is to such groups or subsidiary structures that one must look for the vision and initiative to accomplish systemic transformation. One no longer sees an empty chair, but rather several that are occupied. But the position from which one sees these occupants is not yet transparent.

Jameson's appeal to a collective subject alleviates the threat of incoherence but does not eliminate it altogether. Much work must still be done to illuminate the preconditions for a critique of postmodern culture and to specify the relationship between such a critique and various oppositional forces within postmodern culture. Even if many chairs replace the chair of modernism, the positioning of these chairs remains a crucial question. Their place relative to each other, their contributions within postmodern culture, and their references to a postcapitalist culture must still be decided. This is an unfinished project and a collective project, one for which Jameson's reinterpretative dance is emblematic.

Notes

I wish to thank Lisa De Boer and Christopher Eberle for their research assistance on this article.

1. Theodor W. Adorno, "Reconciliation under Duress," in *Aesthetics and Politics*, ed. Ronald Taylor, pp. 151-176. Originally published as "Erpresste Versohnung. Zu Georg Lukács: 'Wider den missverstandenen Realismus,'" *Der Monat* 11 (November, 1958), pp. 37-49. Re-published in Adorno's *Noten zur Literatur* 2 (Frankfurt: Suhrkamp, 1961) and in his *Gesammelte Schriften*, Vol. 11 (Frankfurt: Suhrkamp, 1974), pp. 251-280. Citations are from the translation.

2. Georg Lukács, "Preface" (1962), *The Theory of the Novel*, p. 22.

3. Georg Lukács, *Realism in Our Time: Literature and the Class Struggle*, trans. John and Necke Mander. First published under the title *The Meaning of Contemporary Realism* (London: Merlin Press, 1962). The book originated in lectures at the Deutsche Akademie der Künste in January 1956 and repeated several times in Poland, Italy, and Austria. The book's German title—*Wider den missverstandenen Realismus* (Hamburg: Claassen Verlag, 1958)—has been replaced with the original title, "Die Gegenwartsbedeutung des kritischen Realismus" in Georg Lukács, *Essay über Realismus, Probleme des Realismus*, I, *Werke*, Vol. 4 (Neuwied: Luchterhand, 1971), pp. 457-603. Citations are from *Realism in Our Time*.

4. The author has discussed the Adorno-Lukács debate at greater length in "'Reconciliation Under Duress'? *Realism in Our Time*

Revisited" in *Georg Lukács and His World: A Reassessment*, ed. Ernest Joós, pp. 117-148.

5. Fredric Jameson's first major attempt to derive a methodology of "dialectical criticism" from these sources is in *Marxism and Form: Twentieth-Century Dialectical Theories of Literature*, 1971.

6. See in particular Jameson's "Reification and Utopia in Mass Culture"; "The Politics of Theory: Ideological Positions in the Postmodernism Debate"; and "Postmodernism, or The Cultural Logic of Late Capitalism." The latter article incorporates most of a talk given in the Fall of 1982 and published as "Postmodernism and Consumer Society." See also "On Magic Realism in Film" and "Cognitive Mapping."

7. Adorno, "Commitment," in *Aesthetics and Politics*, pp. 177-95; also in *The Essential Frankfurt School Reader*, ed. Andrew Arato and Eike Gebhardt, pp. 300-318. The German version, "Engagement," is in Adorno's *Gesammelte Schriften*, Vol. 11, pp. 409-430.

8. Adorno, *Aesthetic Theory*, trans. C. Lenhardt, p. 196; *Asthetische Theorie* (1970), 2d ed., *Gesammelte Schriften*, Vol. 7, pp. 204-205.

9. On the same page Jameson says this need is "in many ways the fundamental issue for my doctrine of the political unconscious."

10. In *Diacritics*, 12 (Fall, 1982) see Terry Eagleton, "Fredric Jameson: The Politics of Style," pp. 14-22, and Michael Sprinker, "The Part and the Whole," pp. 57-71. See also Dominick LaCapra's review essay in *History and Theory*, 21 (1982), pp. 83-106.

11. Cf. Jameson's "Reification and Utopia in Mass Culture," and the "Interview: Fredric Jameson" in *Diacritics*, 12 (Fall, 1982), pp. 72-91, especially pp. 86-89.

The Postmodern Return, With a Vengeance, of Subjectivity

Thomas Huhn
Getty Center for the History of
Art and the Humanities

Jameson is postmodern in his retreat from an aesthetics of modernism and in his throttling of what might be Other to make it speak with meaning. The central concern of this essay is to show that the form in which this retreat occurs reveals it as a further regression to dominating, masterful, and reified subjectivity. Jameson is thus postmodern in his regression behind an aesthetics of modernism that at least paid homage to the ideal of the non-subjective. This is not to imply, however, that modernism is the final form of aesthetic production but only that an aesthetic theory that refuses any potential opposition to reigning social relations destroys what has been, at least since Kant, the peculiar character of aesthetic artifacts, experience, and theory.

Jameson is an unwitting theoretical sponsor of a complacency with those aesthetic objects and articulations that are but the echo of subjectivity. He propounds an aesthetic theory that shrinks back from the dialectic in Adorno's conception of modern artworks (which reveals modernist works as simultaneously autonomous and social) and enters into a position from which a frightened subjectivity can once again assert that it is master—because everything turns out to be comprehensible, including aesthetic objects. But despite their social character, aesthetic objects retain an autonomy and exist as ciphers for an alterity that is never subsumed by a logic of comprehension. This is the fundamental insight of Kant's *Critique of Judgment*: subjectivity constitutes itself (and this is pleasurable) via an aesthetic judgment which cannot (yet nonetheless does) subsume a particular under a universal concept. Aesthetic judgment is thus the originary transformation of reason into cunning. The impossibility of articulating the content of the beautiful or the sublime is the subjective recognition of the alterity at the heart of subjectivity itself.

Jameson subsumes the entire category of aesthetic experience under a valorized subjectivity, which thereby serves to efface the very possibility of any opposition to reified subjectivity. Subjectivity can now rest, before its next onslaught against nature and itself, assured that everything artifactual does possess meaning, even those modernist works that refused their birthright to meaning. Jameson facilitates a return of a master subject—a subjectivity that doubles its mastery over self and nature by extending its reifying sway over that which opposes it—through an aesthetics of content. In his diligent pursuit of an aesthetics of meaningfulness that colonizes the space in which some sign of what might stand beyond subjectivity could come to appearance, Jameson functions as the avant-garde of dominating subjectivity. An alternative aesthetics would be one that cuts against the grain of subjectivity—an aesthetics that sought to restore the primacy of the object within subjective production, and not the primacy of a desiring subjectivity, whatever the content of its desire.

I. The Destruction of Form by Ideology

In *The Political Unconscious: Narrative as a Socially Symbolic Act*, Jameson writes, "The assertion of a political unconscious proposes that we . . . explore the multiple paths that lead to the unmasking of cultural artifacts as socially symbolic acts" (*PU*, 20). History, as both past experience and the presentation of past experience, becomes a cultural artifact and exists within each artifact. The political unconscious is the locale where history comes into being as narrative. The political unconscious, in other words, is the first and primary cultural artificer; it is the maker of both cultural artifacts and of culture *per se*. The generation of the appearance of history by the political unconscious and History as transcendent *noumenon* is described in Jameson's discussion of Althusser and Lacan:

> history is *not* a text, not a narrative, master or otherwise, but that, as an absent cause, it is inaccessible to us except in textual form, and . . . our approach to it and to the Real itself necessarily passes through its prior textualization, its narrativization in the political unconscious. (*PU*, 35)

Since History and the Real cannot be approached, let alone apprehended, except in the narratives produced by the political unconscious, the focus shifts to the symbolic act of narrative. The limitation here is to see narrative as solely symbolic in order to discern the content of both its symbolic function and the symbols themselves. Yet once any artifact is construed as symbolic, i.e., as a carrier of meaning, there is no further impediment to disclosing its meaning.

Narratives are social mediations which, as such, are at least in principle accessible to the constituting subject. The problem of the status of meaning arises not just when the constituting subject is alienated—at which time meaning becomes no longer accessible because it *seems* to be other—but rather in the subjective supposition that some originary meaning within any and all aesthetic objects exhausts the content *and form* of those objects. This supposition is the "unconscious" recognition of the loss of meaning and a reactionary attempt to posit and entrench meaning. This supposition is thus the reflex of a self-preservation that regresses behind the concept of culture: "culture—as that which goes beyond the system of self-preservation of the species— involves an irrevocably critical impulse toward the *status quo* and all institutions thereof" (Adorno, "Culture and Administration," 99-100). The "critical impulse" directed against the social and subjective *status quo* is precisely what falls by the wayside in Jameson's ideal of the transparency of aesthetic production and objects. Adorno remarks on such an ideal that, "The materialistic transparency of culture has not made it more honest, only more vulgar" (*Prisms*, 34).

Jameson tries to extend this tautology within meaning a step further: there should be no impediment to disclosing the meaning, the source of the production of meaning itself. He moves from the content of a particular narrative (meaning) to form (narrative) to content (meaning) of aesthetic form. It is this third and final move that is unwarranted by the nature of form and by the peculiar character of form in modernism. The social meaning of aesthetic form cannot be fully articulated—form itself cannot be exhausted by meaning.

Adorno's premise of aesthetic form as both autonomous and a *fait social* is the specification of the non-subjective and social aspects of those objects which Kant found underlying the possibility of aesthetic judgment. The autonomy of aesthetic form is what separates its products from every other form of social production. This autonomy is the recognition of Kant's insight that aesthetic objects resist and oppose the progress of subjectivity's instrumental rationality via concepts and meaning. Jameson forgets, despite his apparent recognition of the inarticulable nature of form as "unconscious," that form is necessarily opaque: it is the organization and positing of meaning which nonetheless implicitly opposes it. Although History and the Real may be approached via narrative, they are not genuinely symbolic since they cannot be apprehended in and of themselves. Instead of representing them, symbols are ciphers of their displacement. Although symbols stand in place of History and the Real, they do not stand *for* them: they point toward or away from them, not, as Jameson suggests, toward a precise referent.

What is specifically regressive for aesthetic theory, in Jameson's program of a political unconscious, is that he proposes to supply the referent for that which Kant and Adorno theorized as exceeding subjectivity. By locating subjectivity as the ultimate referent and source of an affirmative meaning, Jameson seems to grant to subjectivity a lost and longed for legitimacy. That this seeming restoration of the "meaning" of subjectivity (through Jameson's discovery of the "meaning" of its products) is but a further reification and defrauding of subjectivity is captured in a passage from *Negative Dialectics*: "The concept of meaning involves an objectivity beyond all 'making': as a made thing meaning is already fiction. Meaning duplicates the subject, however collective, and defrauds it of that which it appears to grant" (Adorno, 376, translation amended).

Jameson's enterprise should be judged in terms of whether he respects the autonomy of cultural artifacts or, alternatively, imposes a direction on them from above. Adorno writes, "The artifact is a monad, yet it is not; its elements, as such of a conceptual kind, point beyond the specific object in which they gather themselves" ("The Essay as Form," 162). Unfortunately, Jameson has broken off the dialectic of cultural artifacts in the "ideology" of their form. Adorno's statement should not be construed as describing a one-step move in which artifacts point beyond a specific object and then take up a static residence in some second object, i.e., meaning. This interpretation regresses to a time at least before Horkheimer and Adorno's transformation of ideology critique in *Dialectic of Enlightenment* and perhaps to a time before Nietzsche revealed the source and inadequacy of the appearance/essence dichotomy.

Where is the Jameson who warned in 1969, "The mind tends inevitably towards illusions of its own autonomy, if only because it is impossible to be self-conscious all the time, if only because thought inevitably tends to forget itself and to sink itself in its object" ("Introduction to T. W. Adorno," 142). Isn't the political unconscious just such an example of thought having forgotten itself in an illusion of autonomy, the usurpation of an autonomy that once belonged precisely to those things that opposed the ubiquity of thought? The political unconscious is not just thought sunk into its object but, more dangerously, subjectivity sunk into itself. It should come as no surprise when, with subjectivity collapsed into itself, one or another impulse of subjectivity is judged genuine, for there is no longer the possibility of some sign which might point away from subjectivity. Jameson continued his warning: "Then there comes into being an illusion of transparency, in which the mind looks like the world, and we stare at concepts as though they were things." Jameson has succumbed to precisely this illusion by transforming cultural artifacts, via the political unconscious, into pure transparency. Subjectivity, however, has a history—it cannot be reduced to an essentialism which posits one or another utopian desire as genuine, a desire that in turn serves as the *a priori* source of all its artifacts and forms of production.

To place these questions in the context of Adorno's aesthetics would be to ask whether narrative, as *the* (although artificial) form of expression, nonetheless does justice to silent, absent History and the Real.

Jameson offers an analysis limited to the symbolic structure of aesthetic artifacts, which depends upon a conflation of symbol and ideology that reduces the former to the latter. He reduces symbol to ideology by presuming Lévi-Strauss as an anthropological authority to make judgments concerning aesthetic phenomena. This analysis, however, is founded on a category mistake: that aesthetic artifacts may have a symbolic component (or even, following Jameson, be wholly symbolic) does not warrant the inference that any symbolic artifact is therefore aesthetic. Indeed, a minimal requirement for judging something aesthetic may just be that an artifact exist as something more than a symbol, if we take for example Nelson Goodman's argument that anything can be made to symbolize anything else without, I might add, making everything that symbolizes aesthetic. (This is, again, the premise of Kant's 3rd *Critique*.) But for Jameson it is the symbolic character of any mode of production that qualifies it as both aesthetic and ideological.

Consider Jameson's conclusion following a discussion of Lévi-Strauss' interpretation of face painting among the Caduveo Indians as the symbolic resolution of social contradictions:

> We may suggest that from this perspective, ideology is not something which informs or invests symbolic production; rather the aesthetic act is itself ideological, and the production of aesthetic or narrative form is to be seen as an ideological act in its own right, with the function of inventing imaginary or formal "solutions" to unresolvable social contradictions. (*PU*, 79)

A nagging question here is why Jameson chose Caduveo face painting as an example of aesthetic production. One is tempted to suppose that Caduveo face painting was a ripe candidate for aesthetic analysis because it is a kind of painting and, as everyone should know, painting is an aesthetic activity. And house painting? Perhaps house painters are after all agents "with the function of inventing imaginary or formal 'solutions' to unresolvable social contradictions." What if Caduveo face painting is more like house painting than fine arts painting; that is, what if it is not symbolic as Jameson and Lévi-Strauss assume? I want to leave unanswered this formulation of the question concerning the character of cultural production and grant willingly that all cultural production is to some degree symbolic, which is to grant no more to cultural production than that it may have meaning, without however granting that meaning exhausts or is equivalent to aesthetic form.

The referent of symbolic Caduveo face painting, as a socially meaningful action, is no more inaccessible to the Caduveo than is Lévi-Strauss' interpretation. Although the referent may not be transparent to the Caduveo, there is in principle nothing that bars them from it. Indeed, as Peter Winch has shown in his book, *The Idea of a Social Science*, in order for Lévi-Strauss to see Caduveo face painting as symbolic, that is, meaningful activity, the Caduveo must, in principle, be capable of seeing their own activity as symbolic.

The analogy here for Jameson would be not just to our symbolic production but also, since they are one and the same for him, to aesthetic form. All aesthetic artifacts, and the form in which they issue, are interpretable and transparent based on the warrant of the interpretability of Caduveo symbolic production as aesthetic production. If we understand the social function of symbolic activity, we have captured aesthetic form. But this collapse of aesthetic form into symbolic production is hardly justified by Jameson's use of the Caduveo example. Jameson claims that "the aesthetic act is itself ideological" and "aesthetic . . . form is to be seen . . . with the function of inventing imaginary or formal 'solutions' to unresolvable social contradictions." Yet it does not follow that this ideology or function is aesthetic. Can we not readily grant that Caduveo activity is symbolic (and ideological), even that its symbolic character has the function of inventing solutions, without being compelled to add that this activity and this function are aesthetic?

Consider an example a little closer, unfortunately, to home. Within an analysis of the social function of capital, one can readily admit that auto workers in Detroit are engaged in two realms of symbolic production, i.e., the production of commodities and, when not selling their labor power, the use of "leisure time" as the symbolic production of a solution to the unresolvable social contradictions in which they find themselves caught. Yet auto workers are not evidently engaged in aesthetic production in either of these two forms of symbolic production. If one were inclined to entertain the possibility of either of these forms being aesthetic, that of leisure time would appear the more likely candidate. Leisure time might be construed as having one of the features of the aesthetic: an imaginary solution to contradictory social relations. But leisure time does not stand opposed to the social relations it intends, imaginary or not, to resolve. The contemporary industrialization of leisure time and the ease of its susceptibility to colonization by industry reveal the character of leisure time as being no more nor less than that of the symbolic and ideological production that delivers commodities. Hence leisure time is not only populated by commodities but is itself one.

The genuine criterion for judging the aesthetic potential of leisure time in Detroit or of Caduveo face painting is whether the solution, imaginary or not, stands in opposition to unresolvable social relations. But this is precisely what Jameson's conception of aesthetic form as thoroughly ideological cannot allow. In effect Jameson argues that symbolic production is ideological production and we should call them both aesthetic in order to disallow any possibility of some sort of production that might oppose the production of meaning and ideology. This leads to the heart of Jameson's use of "unconscious," and the profound contradiction within any attempt to locate aesthetic production there. If the unconscious is, as Freud asserted, incapable of any negation, it cannot be argued that solutions—which by definition stand opposed to the *status quo*—issue from the unconscious. The negativity (read autonomy) of aesthetic form must have another source.

When Jameson writes that "the production of aesthetic or narrative form is to be seen as an ideological act in its own right," he presents the political unconscious as the basis of an ideology production that cannot help but taint all of its products, i.e., narratives, with ideology. Or, to put it more strongly, the political unconscious is the source of ideology. Insofar as all symbolic activity is founded within this unconscious, all meaningful activity is thoroughly ideological, and aesthetic form constitutes the most ideological cultural artifact. At first glance nothing would be lost by granting this point to Jameson, since it might amount to nothing more than the recognition of what Marcuse called the affirmative character of culture, except that Jameson insists that it is form itself which constitutes the ideological character of aesthetic artifacts. It is precisely this characterization of form that marks Jameson's break with Adorno's aesthetics and underpins his refusal to distinguish legitimate art (i.e., successful according to its own terms, living up to its own concept, aiding the non-identical, etc.) from illegitimate art. If Jameson instead argued that the *content* of symbolic artifacts (i.e., meaning) is necessarily ideological, he would be in agreement with Adorno's analysis of the illusory character of meaning. But Jameson's position here leaves unexplained the historical transformations not only of narrative but also within aesthetic form. If aesthetic form is always an ideological expression of a legitimate utopian impulse— and this impulse is timeless within the boundaries of culture— what account can explain the changes of form within any culture?

The ideological character of aesthetic form is easiest to discern, according to Jameson, in a particularly reified example such as the genre novel. "Genres are essentially literary *institutions*, or social contracts between a writer and a specific public, whose function is to specify the proper use of a particular cultural artifact" (*PU*, 106). In the case of genre then, it is not the political unconscious which gives rise to the genre form, at least not in contemporary society. The genre novel is not subject to an unconscious form-giving mechanism but is instead the object of the most explicit social "contract." How then is this particular aesthetic form to be regarded? Since genre narratives are no longer products of unconscious political machinations, what becomes of the genre form? To press further, since narrative is generated by the unconscious, can genre novels be construed as narratives at all?

The answers to these questions depend on a willingness to make distinctions between various kinds of aesthetic form. Jameson is unwilling to distinguish reified from non-reified aesthetic form. This is why he cannot, in turn, substantively distinguish modernism from mass culture.

One is tempted to speculate that the source of this unwillingness lies in a misplaced populism, a desire to legitimate what once was called folk culture by finding utopian impulses within its contemporary, transformed products. But this is truly audacious; can Jameson really suppose that the reading public, i.e., the marketplace, determines which genre novels it shall read? Is there a contract, then, between the reading public and publishers?

Jameson claims that "genre is essentially a socio-symbolic message, or in other terms . . . form is immanently and intrinsically an ideology in its own right" (*PU*, 141). Adorno's essay, "Lyric Poetry and Society," is directed at the same object of inquiry as Jameson's book, that is, at an understanding of the sociological content of aesthetic artifacts secured through an investigation of a single reified aesthetic form. Instead of the genre novel, Adorno examines lyric poetry, just as in *Dialectic of Enlightenment* he and Horkheimer examine the epic. In both cases, Adorno's analysis discloses a particular aesthetic form—not as a static and explicit contract but as an embodiment of cultural contradictions and, more importantly, as containing within it the transition to a new aesthetic form and a new subjectivity. The *Odyssey* is at once a recapitulation of the birth of subjectivity through domination, and a critique of bourgeois subjectivity that presages the transition to the novel form. That the artwork achieves this transcendence of itself and its conditions can be asserted only if its form is distinct from its ideological aspect and from its content. Adorno writes:

> It [ideology] manifests itself in the failure of art works, in their own intrinsic falsehood, and can be uncovered by

criticism. To say, however, of great works of art, which fix real existence in determinate forms and thus lend its contradictions a purpose-carrying reconciliation—to say of such works that they are ideological not only belies the truth which they contain: it falsifies the idea of ideology as well. . . . The concept of ideology seeks rather to unmask false thought and at the same time to grasp its historical necessity. The greatness of works of art lies solely in their power to let those things be heard which ideology conceals. Whether intended or not, their success transcends false consciousness. ("Lyric Poetry and Society," 58)

For Jameson, ideology is simply concealment and delusion reified as form. Jameson penetrates behind this concealment and delusion, behind aesthetic form, and posits there a legitimate utopian impulse as its originating impetus. There are two objections to this penetration. The first is that the inaccessibility of the Real as agent of history, and History as thing-in-itself proscribe any speculation of an originating cause that lies behind historical and aesthetic phenomena. The second and (for aesthetic theory) crucial objection is the destruction of aesthetic form as the place where "those things [could] be heard which ideology conceals." Form, as pure ideology, is transparent; but it is this transparency which conceals the very things that form allows to be heard. It is not the sounds of subjectivity, no matter how utopian or legitimate its impulses, which are to be heard in form but precisely the opposite: the objective sounds of opposition to the contradictions subjectivity has imposed upon itself and nature. For Jameson ideology is instead just the obfuscation of some contradiction and its imaginary solution, to which we have no other means of access—it is a closed totality of the subject.

The philosophic-historical context of Jameson's account of ideology and form becomes apparent in a dispute with Northrop Frye's conception of the romance genre. Frye understands romance not as the substitution of an ideal for mundane reality, but as the transformation of ordinary reality. Jameson is committed to the conception of any aesthetic form, but especially genre, as wholly artificial. Jameson writes:

Frye is therefore not wrong to evoke the intimate connection between romance as a mode and the 'natural' imagery of the earthly paradise or the waste land, of the bower of bliss or the enchanted wood. What is misleading is the implication that this 'nature' is in any sense itself a 'natural' rather than a very peculiar and specialized social and historical phenomenon. (*PU*, 112)

In other words, what Jameson cannot conceive is the possibility that aesthetic form is itself the constitution of a second nature, or at least the means for such a constitution. He cannot accede to the implication of Frye's statement that "the quest-romance is the search of the libido or desiring self for a fulfillment that will deliver it from the anxieties of reality *but will still contain that reality*" (*PU*, 110). Jameson cannot accept the possibility of a second nature, since it would mean that within aesthetic artifacts, and by extension within aesthetic form, the very reality they reject will be both contained and opposed. If aesthetic form were to contain some aspect of the reality it negates, aesthetic form would no longer be mere artifice or wholly ideological. For Jameson, the unacceptable corollary of Frye's statement is the implication that ordinary life "must already have been conceived, not as some humdrum place of secular contingency and 'normal' existence, but rather as the end product of curse and enchantment, black magic, baleful spells, and ritual desolation" (*PU*, 110-111). Since Jameson posits normal existence as the given, he cannot help but see the dichotomy of good and evil, inscribed in one fashion or another in romance, as having no basis nor counterpart in experience.

The central fault of Jameson's book lies in his account of experience and the form of subjectivity. The positing of mundane experience as a given precludes Jameson from seeing what Adorno has called the entwinement of myth and enlightenment. The misunderstanding of the form and history of experience leads Jameson to assert that the twin poles of every aesthetic artifact, ideology and utopia, are in fact simultaneous and profoundly interdependent. This might be put more strongly even while staying wholly within Jameson's conception: ideology and utopia are inseparable, interchangeable, and indistinguishable components of every artwork. They are, in effect, one and the same. The solution to the problem of form lies in the aporia of art prescribed by the very polarity of utopia and ideology: the utopian can only be expressed within a form that is necessarily ideological while all ideology contains a genuine utopian impulse.

The coexistence, within the artwork, of a utopian impulse and ideology, is the solution Jameson offers to the traditional Marxist formulation of the problem of the identity of the artwork:

> How is it possible for a cultural text which fulfills a demonstrably ideological function, as a hegemonic work whose formal categories as well as its content secure the legitimation of this or that form of class domination—how is it possible for such a text to embody a properly Utopian impulse, or to resonate a universal value inconsistent with the narrower limits of class privilege which inform its more immediate ideological vocation? (*PU*, 288)

The traditional formulation asks, in other words, how it is possible for a text to be both utopian and ideological. The traditional response solves this dilemma, but inadequately, by depending on the presupposition of liberalism that construes politics (i.e., the utopian impulse) and ideology as secondary and artificial aspects of authentic and primary "private" life. The problem with this solution is that it relegates both politics and ideology to artificiality. Jameson reverses this schema by placing the artificial as primary and then asserting that this artificiality is somehow connected to the Real and History.

He does so by first showing the ubiquity of ideology and utopia: "all ideology in the strongest sense, including the most exclusive forms of ruling-class consciousness just as much as that of oppositional or oppressed classes—is in its very nature Utopian" (*PU*, 289). He next argues for the authenticity of ideology despite its basis in strategic domination:

> even hegemonic or ruling-class culture and ideology are Utopian, not in spite of their instrumental function to secure and perpetuate class privilege and power, but rather

> precisely because that function is also in and of itself the affirmation of collective solidarity. (*PU*, 291)

In other words, ideology is authentic because it is the expression of an authentic utopian affirmation of collective solidarity (even though it does require some use of the imagination to view class identity as the product of an impulse toward the collective, rather than the selective; indeed, the necessity of "imagination" here captures just that function of the political unconscious). Ideology is inauthentic, however, because it finds expression, takes form, only through the political unconscious that transforms it into a symbol. Our contention has been that Jameson mistakenly supposes that aesthetic artifacts can be nothing but symbols.

If all ideology contains a moment of utopia, then there is nothing distinct about the artwork's utopian ideology. The conclusion here is that the artwork is just another artifact of ideology or class consciousness. Although artworks, as Adorno shows, have an ideological component, they cannot be reduced to ideology, even with the proviso that their ideology is utopian. If artworks are to be distinguished from every other human artifact, what may make them distinct is their unwillingness to be symbolic, to have and be exhausted by meaning.

Jameson's only hesitation in collapsing the distinction between ideology and utopia, and thus between class identity and collective solidarity (finally the distinction between aesthetic form and every other social artifact), is contained in his warning that the utopian impulse is to be read "allegorically" and as a "figure" of a potential future, "concrete" and utopian, collective. But to construe narrative and hence aesthetic form as exhausted by meaning (especially an originary, collective and utopian one) is to treat all aesthetic artifacts as symptoms rather than critical diagnoses of, and potential interventions in, the *status quo*. If all cultural production becomes the symptomatic reproduction of the "progress" of civilization—founded on self-preservation and domination—the concept of culture loses its specificity as that which, minimally, holds in check the barbarism immanent to the movement of civilization. It thus is no accident that Jameson *affirms* the "allegory" of a collective ideology at the heart of all social production and reproduction of the social. His affirmation is recognition of the loss of the critical function of culture in a false social totality. The purpose of the notion of a political unconscious is to place a socially affirming motor at the source of the generation of all social and cultural production. The immanent critique of the project of *The Political Unconscious* can be made by judging the social products and forms that issue from a collectivity-desiring subjectivity. The falsity of this desire is revealed in the necessity of Jameson's use of the term allegory: the "allegorical" character of all manifestations of subjective (especially genuine and utopian) desire is the implicit recognition of a disjunction between desire and its products. That social and aesthetic forms are only a "figure" of the genuine collective desire of subjectivity, implies a necessary mis-identity, and hence falsehood, within subjectivity itself. This mis-identity results not from the clash of something external to subjectivity (e.g., capital, exchange relations, a supposed economy of scarcity, etc.) and subjectivity's utopian impulse, but proceeds rather from the immanent falsehood of a desiring subjectivity as originary source of all production.

The "autonomy" of the aesthetic, as nonetheless a category of social and ideological production, is the nagging reminder of an alterity within any desiring subjectivity—regardless how genuine, collective, and utopian. Kant's figure of the sublime, and that of natural beauty, is the cipher for what exceeds the grasp of subjectivity. Jameson's aesthetics of a political unconscious locates the subject as *the* source of that which potentially exceeds it, and thereby collapses all production and potential objectivity into the bad infinity of a self-affirming and regressive subjectivism. This effacement of the critical character of aesthetic objects—and thus the denial of the oppositional function of culture *per se*—is effected by Jameson through a recapitulation of the same move that Hegel makes in trying to overcome Kant's aesthetic theory. Hegel's dismissal of any notion of natural beauty is the model, within the history of aesthetic theory, for Jameson's dismissal of all aesthetic artifacts as the fallen expressions of an originary collective subjectivity.

Jameson has succeeded in effecting a collapse and a reversal within two key elements of Adorno's aesthetic theory. He has managed to collapse the dialectic of myth and enlightenment and to reverse the position where genuine experience may take place. Myth and enlightenment are entwined, but they cannot be reduced to one another; their successive overcoming of each other in aesthetic artifacts is not a mere circularity—something more (*das Mehr*) is produced. This does not mean however that this *more*, which aesthetic artifacts point toward and infer, can be expropriated from the aesthetic realm and placed within social relations or history, nor does it mean that the dialectic of myth and enlightenment outside the aesthetic produces progress. Finally, the *more* that issues from successful artworks does not have its source in subjectivity. The production of the *more* leads Adorno to write that art has an internal history and thus there may be progress in art even when there is none in social relations or anywhere else. The collapse of the distinction between myth and enlightenment within artworks would presuppose that myth and enlightenment, along with utopia and ideology, are one and the same, when they are not.

The further problem here is the location of ideology. Although Adorno would agree with Jameson as to an ideological component within all artworks, he would not locate that component within the form of the artwork but rather in the content which proclaims that it contains meaning. To Adorno it is precisely the form of the artwork which allows the possibility of transcending its ideological content.

Because Jameson allows that form itself is ideological, he cannot allow any possibility of transcending the ideology or utopia that artworks embody. And because he cannot allow this transcendence he must find something recoverable and authentic within the ideology of the artwork. This he attempts by defining the utopian impulse as authentic and then equating it with ideology. What is to be recovered is not nature or subjectivity but the authenticity which led to ideology, i.e., domination. For Jameson, nature cannot be recovered except as a prior form of subjective experience. Within this prior form of experience we are to recover the authentic utopian impulse toward collectivity. The collective impulse, excused without argument from being an expression of domination, is judged authentic and utopian. Jameson writes in the concluding paragraph to the book that "within the symbolic power of art and culture the will to domination perseveres intact" (PU, 299). This would concur with Adorno's aesthetic theory except that by reducing all aesthetic production to the symbolic it relegates aesthetic appearance to the realm of the symptomatic. For Adorno the dynamic within aesthetic appearance is precisely the movement that attempts— through domination—to exceed the totality of domination, that is, it is a movement against the symptomatic and symbolic. Adorno's interpretation of modernism does not leave domination "intact" but instead explodes it in the shudder of subjectivity, which, we should add, would also be the shudder of the collective impulse.

For Jameson, the will to domination perseveres within the artwork because the symbolic dynamic continues to obscure and deform the authentic collective impulse and make it appear only as ideology. The implication here is that without the symbolic apparatus, i.e., without form, experience would be transparent and thereby render domination impossible. Authentic non-dominating experience is possible only outside the form imposed by the political unconscious as artwork. Jameson has reversed Adorno's contention that aesthetic experience today holds the only possibility for genuine experience. Aesthetic experience is thus not the recapitulation of subjectivity and experience but its deformation. The return to authentic non-dominating experience can be effected, for Jameson, not through or by means of aesthetic experience but only by the refusal of it.

Jameson's reduction of aesthetic experience to ideology is best revealed in his comments on the alleged failure of the *Dialectic of Enlightenment*. Jameson claims that in this book the utopian hermeneutic is

> obscured by an embattled commitment to high culture; yet it has not sufficiently been noticed that it has been displaced to the succeeding chapter of that work . . . in which . . . anti-semitism is shown to be profoundly Utopian in character, as a form of cultural envy which is at the same time a repressed recognition of the Utopian impulse. (PU, 288)

The two presuppositions which allow Jameson to reduce art to ideology are: 1) that a utopian impulse within any cultural artifact, aesthetic or not, is evidence of ideology; 2) that an artifact is ideological because it is false in the same way and about the same things as any other artifact. Both these presuppositions rely on the initial equation of utopia and ideology which depends, in turn, on a mistaken notion of ideology and the contradiction within Jameson's conception of form—hence the impossibility of locating the source of aesthetic form in an unconscious. Ideology (but especially aesthetic ideology) is not just falsehood; it contains within itself the possibility of recovering something true. While Jameson allows for something recoverable in his concept of ideology, it is precisely that which is recoverable, the collective impulse, which is false. Paradoxically enough, it is precisely Jameson's insertion of a political unconscious at the source of all ideology that serves to eviscerate just that form of subjectivity that he wishes to preserve. As Adorno writes: "The more abundantly a universal is equipped with the insignia of the collective subject, the more tracelessly do the subjects disappear within it" (*Negative Dialectics*, 338, translation amended). Jameson's implicit recognition of the loss of cultural meaning is not only *not* compensated for by the re-assertion of a subjective source of meaning, but this very attempt at compensation serves to further ideologize and reify whatever traces of opposition remain within a subjectively constituted culture. The paradox of Kant's aesthetics—of a subjectivity that constitutes itself on the basis of that which it cannot attain—is not resolved by Jameson's assertion of a subjectivity that fills the lack upon which it constitutes itself.

Social life will not be redeemed through a recovery of a form of social life that is still based on domination, even though that domination is made transparent by disclosing its impulse toward collectivity. What needs to be recovered is not a pre-ideological social life but rather a subjectivity whose relationship to nature is non-dominating. Genuine social life depends not on a subject whose motives toward other subjects are transparent, i.e., non-ideological and non-symbolic, but on a subjectivity whose mimetic relationship to nature is not dominated by fear, which is the more likely candidate for the source of ideology. Jameson comes surprisingly close to realizing the centrality of fear in ideology-production when he writes in the "Conclusion" of *The Political Unconscious* that

> Colin Turnbull's description of pygmy society suggests that the culture of pre-political society organizes itself around the external threat of the non-human or of nature, in the form of the rain forest, conceived as the over-arching spirit of the world. (*PU*, 290)

This "pre-political" social organization points not to a *political* unconscious as the origin of the desire for the collective, but instead to an unconscious that constitutes the desire for the social—as a mechanism of self-preservation—in opposition to the *fear* of an "external threat of the non-human or of nature." The political unconscious is the "civilized" heir of this fear. But what if the totality ("the over-arching spirit of the world"), against which fear arises and around which "society organizes itself" is itself only a mechanism for legitimating a *social* totality whose own continuation depends, in turn, on the legitimacy of the fear that spawned and sustains it?

The Political Unconscious is an attempt to provide a rational and enlightened account of the impulse toward the social—an account which thereby serves to legitimate it. The book is an object lesson in the dialectic of myth and enlightenment; in locating the source of the social within a genuine and utopian subjective desire (founded in turn on a supposed legitimate fear of nature, that is, the non-human), it "enlightens" the myth of the social by entrenching and extending it. It is not a diagnosis but a symptom of the postmodern condition.

The program of this "unconscious" and symptomatic book becomes a self-conscious diagnosis of postmodernism in the well-known 1984 essay, "Postmodernism, or The Cultural Logic of Late Capitalism." It is in this essay that Jameson extends the tendency we discerned in *The Political Unconscious* to efface whatever is specific and potentially autonomous in aesthetic artifacts. The subjective totality of meaning only dimly perceived in *The Political Unconscious* becomes explicit and more fully total in the later essay. The essay argues that capital is the source of the totality of opaque reflections. These reflections prescribe a subjectivity that has not yet come about (this is the point of Jameson's discussion of the Bonaventure Hotel). There is then an artifactuality that exceeds what is human. The crucial difference between Jameson's book and essay is that the former disallowed this possibility by locating the source of aesthetic production (form and meaning) within subjectivity. (The "unconscious" is, after all, presumably a human characteristic.) But the essay locates the source of aesthetic production outside human consciousness and unconsciousness; the simulacrum, as that without source, is the best expression of this transformation.

Curiously enough, this transformation to an explicit postmodernism seems to fulfill the sublime desire of modernism to transcend human meaning via aesthetic artifacts. (The judgment of the success of postmodernism is based on the success of this mimicry of modernism.) Given Jameson's argument that all postmodern images are reflections of capital, should we not say that capital has successfully usurped the supposed real source of cultural production: the political unconscious? But perhaps the political unconscious was nothing but capital itself.

Jameson's inclination toward the pre-modern is revealed in *The Political Unconscious* in his positing of the *one* meaning within and behind all artworks, in the overarching meaning of all aesthetic phenomena. This inclination might be seen as the attempted evisceration of any and all meaning except that Jameson insists on positing a meaning (desire) behind all "meaningful" activity. Meaning is then, in the essay, theorized as that which is exceeded only by that structure which is non-human, i.e., capital. It seems that Jameson should then argue that it is capital which truly expresses the genuine collective and utopian impulse.

The Political Unconscious argues that the meaning of all cultural production is accessible via the mechanism of the unconscious. Once the form and location of this unconscious is discovered, the meanings of all cultural artifacts—as utopian aspirations for the collective—disclose themselves. Jameson thus effects a bridging of the distance between artifact and meaning.

Once the principle of mediation between cultural artifact and meaning is explicitly formulated, the relationship between artifact and meaning ceases to be a mediated one and becomes immediate. Paradoxically enough, it is just this immediacy that allows Jameson to state the "meaning" of cultural production in general (thus his appeal to Lévi-Strauss and Turnbull).

In the essay on postmodernism we find Jameson arguing that it is precisely this lack of "depth" between artifact and meaning that characterizes the postmodern. *The Political Unconscious* is a symptom of postmodernism insofar as it generates a false totality of meaning in the effacement of any distance ("depth") between artifact and meaning. Although Jameson argues for the necessity of an allegorical reading—which recognizes the insistence of meaning—his positing of a political unconscious does away with the entire category of specific meanings. The imperialism of Jameson's position here is that he insists on doing away with the very possibility of those cultural artifacts which themselves insist on the specificity and autonomy of their meanings. This latter insistence was perhaps expressed most strongly in modernism, which was nevertheless *not* an expression that avoided the ambivalence and ambiguity inherent to this insistence.

I want to suggest that Jameson's own description of post-modernism reveals it as a successful but unwitting imitation of his notion of a political unconscious. Further, it is in the character of this imitation or reflection that the falsity of the political unconscious is exposed. Finally, does Jameson's diagnosis of postmodernism, as reflection and imitation of Adorno's concepts of the culture industry and totality, succeed in exceeding them?

An earlier version of this essay was published under the title "Jameson and Habermas" in *Telos*, 75 (Spring 1988), pp. 103-123.

The Politics of Fredric Jameson's Literary Theory: A Critique

Philip Goldstein
University of Delaware

In *The Theory of Communicative Action*, Jürgen Habermas suggests that the phenomenological commitments of the original Frankfurt School blunt its political force. I mean to make a similar claim about Jameson's work, which shares both the philosophical assumptions and the political weaknesses of a phenomenological criticism. In a phenomenological manner, Jameson assumes that the interpretations of a reader inextricably weave together the reader's commitments and the text's object; as Jameson says, "Dialectical thinking can be characterized as . . . the study of an object . . . which also involves the study of the concepts and categories (themselves historical) that we necessarily bring to the object" (*PU*, 109). Like Georges Poulet, Wolfgang Iser, and other phenomenological critics, Jameson opens the textual "object" to the reader's methods and practices, breaking with determinate, authorial insight and autonomous, aesthetic structures. In *The Prison House of Language*, for example, he acknowledges the interpretive force of New Critical, semiotic, psychoanalytic, Marxist, structuralist, Derridean, and other approaches, but he re-orients them, displaying their social context, not their textual or authorial truths nor their individual interests. Jameson's is a social, not an individual, approach.

Indeed, Jameson unearths the socio-historical contexts which ahistorical, unself-conscious readers presuppose but fail to grasp. Although this historicizing method endows his criticism with an impressive breadth and depth and returns history to even the most austere, authorial and structuralist criticism, his insistence that, to use his Nietzschean phrase, "the dialectic is 'beyond good and evil'" ("PTI," 62) reasserts what he so radically opposes—the authorial humanist belief that an interpretive stance transcends institutional structures and established discourses and gains acceptance by its own force or, in his terms, its "semantic richness" (*PU*, 10). Poststructuralists, who repudiate such theoretical transcendence, expose the institutional conflicts and divisions undermining conservative notions of aesthetic value, canonical works, objective truth, and political action; Jameson, who believes that only moments of rupture, non-conformity, and utopian vision reveal the future society, shares the Lukácsian belief that capitalism reifies institutional structures, generic types, and textual practices, dividing the individual from the social, the private from the political, and absorbing areas of rebellion and resistance. While this belief endows his faith in ruptures and utopian visions with critical force, the belief pessimistically denies the value of political action, vitiating his forceful and insightful critiques of authorial humanism, scientific structuralism, and postmodernism.

I. Jameson and Authorial Humanism

To an extent, Jameson is committed to the humanist view of rationality—a critical force transcending ideologies and institutions—even though the humanist view erases the institutional politics dividing established, literary discourses. In a negative, paradoxical manner, he critiques the traditional, liberal humanism of E. D. Hirsch, Jr., and Gerald Graff as well as the Marxist humanism of Lucienn Goldmann and Georg Lukács. Even though he is more political than they are, more open to structuralist and poststructuralist theory, he preserves their humanist faith in objective truth. He grants what the traditional humanists demand—a textual object and an authorial or trans-individual subject—but he does not equate textual objects and historical reality in the realist manner; rather, he considers the common objects, shared meanings, and socio-economic homologies required by "objective" understanding of a utopian dream in which, in his terms, "the individual subject would be somehow fully conscious of his or her determination by class and would be able to square the circle of ideological condition by sheer lucidity" (*PU*, 283).

In the modern world of monopoly capital (but not in the rational world of a utopian future), the realism of Hirsch and Goldmann is naive if not simplistic; the object of perception is not the same for all perceivers nor is the text's meaning the same for all critical approaches. The text and the trans-individual subject are, as Goldmann argues, homologous structures, but in the modern world we cannot know that the structure of the one corresponds to that of the other. To identify the one with the other, as Goldmann does, is to arrogantly take for granted what modern society renders impossible—the perfect match of intellectual analyses and historical reality (*PH*, 213-214; *PU*, 43-44).

I grant that, for Jameson as for Lukács, the social conditions implicit in generic conventions and literary techniques give an artist's work its significance. In *Marxism and Form*, for instance, Jameson maintains that only generic conventions can mediate effectively between an artist's work and his society; only these conventions can relate work and social structure in a non-reductive, unmechanical way. However, he emphasizes the productive activity of the artist. Like Raymond Williams, he does not simply extract a kernel of objective insight and dismiss artistic practices as so much chaff: in his terms, "properly used, genre theory must always in one way or another project a model of the coexistence or tension between several generic modes or strands" (*PU*, 141). Such tensions are the peculiar effects of artistic activity. In keeping with the Frankfurt School, he argues that the ability of the work to repudiate "the fallen world of empirical being, of reified appearance and of the status quo," defines the value of the work (*FA*, 19). Moreover, he favors the Althusserian view in which the capacity of the work to distance the reader from its ideologies confers value on it. Distancing the reader is not an intentional act but a peculiar effect produced by the artist's labor upon established forms, codes, and ideologies, by his shaping them into literary figures (*FA*, 21-23). While Anglo-American formal critics deny that "extrinsic" approaches can provide a standard of evaluation, Jameson ensures that they do so, for he shows that the art's points of rupture with or repudiation of its own "reified" genres and codes reveal a critical, utopian insight.

This emphasis on artistic ruptures enables him to appreciate an unusually broad range of generic conventions. Unlike the Lukácsian, who seeks the objective relations of text and society, Jameson's mediations are speculative and hypothetical, for a text embodies a utopian vision breaking with reified social structures —not an objective insight into revolutionary social processes. As a result, Jameson can find a positive social significance in all generic conventions, not just those characterizing the "true" relations of art and society (*MF*, xiv-xv, 306-340). This social significance may be hypothetical and subjective, but it is the possession of all conventions, not the exclusive property of one—traditional realism. In addition to it, romance, fantasy, modernism, comedy, naturalism, and myth also possess a utopian ideal. In *The Political Unconscious*, for example, he argues that the medieval "chanson de geste," which first represents the genre of romance, responds to a historical situation in which marauding bands of violent knights terrorize the countryside. In later eras, when the feudal nobility establishes itself as a class, romance resolves the conflicts of the older "chanson" by representing the foreign, evil knight as a mirror image of the good knight (*PU*, 118).

In addition, he argues that Wyndham Lewis' integrity of style and rejection of "high" or individualist modernism make Lewis' novels valuable even though Lewis is a fascist and a sexist. Lewis' style has the unusual ability to function as "the impersonal registering apparatus for forces which he means to record, beyond any whitewashing and liberal revisionism, in all their primal ugliness" (*FA*, 21). Moreover, his art repudiates the psychological individuality or "monadism" characterizing the fiction of James Joyce and other "high" modernists (*FA*, 14). This impersonality of style and rupture with "high" modernism illustrates the impressive manner in which Jameson finds aesthetic value in an artist's repudiation of generic codes and conventions and not in the objective conformity of his intention and social structures.

While Jameson discovers artistic value not only in realism but also in romance and in modernism, his emphasizing the artist's rupture with and displacement of "reified" codes and conventions minimizes the value of artistic conformity. For example, he believes that Wyndham Lewis both accepts and violates the generic conventions of modernism, but it is the violation, not the acceptance, which makes his novels valuable; in Jameson's terms, Lewis "expresses the rage and frustration of the fragmented subject at the chains that implacably bind it to its other and its mirror image" (FA, 61). His appreciation of rebellion, rupture, or break denies the value which many critics attribute to works unifying artistic practice and social organization, aesthetic commitments, and ideological outlooks. Those critics who believe that oral tales, tribal literature or handwritten, feudal literature identify artistic attitude and social life, or technique and ideology, say that this identity gives the literature value. What would we know about ancient society if we ignored the art of Homer, Virgil, or the Beowulf poet? Would not their work be less valuable if we assume that they repudiate their generic codes and do not affirm their objective truth? Are not these artists too close to the ideologies and conventions of their societies for their works to be valuable in Jameson's sense?

In other words, while literary value may lie in both rebellion and conformity, rupture and solidarity, Jameson confines it to repudiation and non-conformity. The reason why he does so is what he calls the "fragmentation and compartmentalization of social reality in modern times" (FA, 6). This pessimistic view of modern "social reality" restates the Lukácsian belief that the discourses, codes, and theories of capitalist institutions divide the surfaces of life from its depths, efface its "underlying unity," and acquire an obsessive, dominating force. While poststructuralists construe this contest of "reified" discourses as a Nietzschean struggle for power, Jameson complains that the contest creates an impenetrable confusion obscuring the social structure which produces the discourses. In the western university, the commitment to specialized, "scientific" disciplines turns theoretical discourse into reified commodities presenting themselves as *sui generis*, autonomous, and sacred—concealing the mode of production from which they stem (*MF*, 392-416).

As Theodor Adorno and Max Horkheimer suggested, late monopoly capitalism is too "reified," its "established discourse" too "alienated and fragmented," and the ruling "realities" too "unshakeable" to permit change. In other words, like the original Frankfurt School, Jameson believes not only that capitalist classes rationalize society, creating reified institutions, but also that this rationalization dominates both external and internal nature, both institutions and the mind, leaving no room for the resistance and the opposition envisioned by Lukács. However, Jameson traces this all-encompassing reification not to the instrumental rationality characterizing the enlightenment era but to the fragmented subject peculiar to the modernist period. Emerging in this period, the reified structures of modern capitalism have historical, not universal, grounds. During "high realism," Jameson finds the subject unified and his desire or longing elevated. In the modernist era, by contrast, capitalist modes of production degrade the desire of the subject and fragment his psyche, for institutional structures formalize and elaborate the rational faculties but impoverish the sensuous faculties. The postmodern era degrades and fragments the subject in a similar way; in addition, this era, which eradicates the division between elite and popular culture, colonizes art and philosophy too, destroying the last vestiges of the psyche's independence: as Jameson says, "the prodigious new expansion of multinational capital ends up penetrating and colonizing those very pre-capitalist enclaves (Nature and the Unconscious) which offered extraterritorial and Archimedean footholds for critical effectivity" ("PCL," 87).

Insofar as this history of capitalism's reified institutions minimizes the "critical effectivity" of practical or "reformist" action, this history is pessimistic; indeed, as I will shortly argue, too pessimistic. Jameson's faith in utopian vision does offer us hope but not a practical kind—as he says, "even the concept of praxis remains a suspect one" (*PU*, 294). If the reified structures of "high capitalism" obliterate the objective truth of individual life and destroy the possibility of practical action, constructing a

hypothetical whole remains legitimate. A speculative reconstruction of the totality can still take place if the reconstructor
historicizes "partial" approaches. In fact, Jameson reconstructs
the linguistics and semiotics of Saussure, Greimas, Propp,
Hjemslev, and Barthes; the Frankfurt Marxism of Adorno, Bloch,
Marcuse, Benjamin, Horkheimer, and Lukács; and the
psychoanalytic theory of Freud, Lacan, Deleuze, and Guattari. In a
historicized form, these new theories become consistent with (but
do not assert) the humanist ideal, a shared, public object, for
Jameson argues that Marxism, "that 'untranscendable horizon'
that subsumes such apparently antagonistic or incommensurable
operations" (*PU*, 10), exposes what he calls "the 'strategies of
containment' whereby they [e.g., the 'apparently antagonistic or
incommensurable operations'] are able to project the illusion that
their readings are somehow complete and self-sufficient" (*PU*, 10).
At the same time, Marxism does not substitute for the other
methods, for in the present we cannot determine whether or not
their objects are universal. In our "reified" state we cannot see the
way that these theories together constitute one object and express
one objective insight; as he says, his "methodological eclecticism
. . . is unavoidable, since the discontinuities projected by these
various disciplines or methods themselves correspond to objective
discontinuities in their object (and beyond that, to the very
fragmentation and compartmentalization of social reality in
modern times)" (*FA*, 6). We readily shift from the gear of one
approach to that of another, but our system is blindly *ad hoc*, our
method eclectic and irrational, our textual object a thing of shreds
and patches.

In other words, Jameson's historicizing approach leads to a
phenomenological indeterminacy in which the reified state of
capitalist social life precludes practical action but affirms a
moment of hope, a utopian moment in which the humanist ideal
—a common, textual object and objective, shared truth—may yet
prevail. Critics who fault Jameson for permitting too much or too
little interpretive freedom ignore this indeterminacy. For
example, Robert Scholes complains that in Jameson's work the
"text is finally as undecidable as any hermetic critic [one who
favors self-reflexive and non-referential texts] could wish it to be"

(*Textual Power*, 83). By contrast, Samuel Weber complains that in Jameson's work history, which in Weber's psychoanalytic terms, stands for the father's body, contains and limits the text in the same way that the text contains and limits the meaning ("Capitalizing History," 22). In Jameson's work, meaning can be both "undecidable" and limited, both indeterminate and contained, because Weber and Scholes neglect the phenomenological intertwining or "dialectic" of history and interpretation, of method and truth. Jameson permits both the interpretive freedom or undecidable objects of the reified present and the historical determinacy or textual containment of the utopian future.

Although this indeterminacy permits both freedom and containment, the indeterminacy also preserves the humanist notion that "external" institutional discourse ("ideology") obstructs the pursuit of truth and represses the rebel's negativity. In *Marxism and Form*, for instance, thought congealed into positive systems suffers from what Jameson rightly considers "bad" ideology—hardened dogma; such thought breaks a theory into steps, summarizes the "main points," but neglects the critical processes of thought—the ruptures with opposed theories, the "pain of the negative." In *The Political Unconscious*, however, he extends this forceful critique of blindly positive systems to poststructuralist theories as though their institutional commitments impose equally blind obstacles to critical thought. Jameson takes such theories to represent only the "ideological" level of hermeneutics and to block the "higher levels" of hermeneutics and the "communal" truths of social life (*PU*, 282, 291-293). Not only does he fear that institutional contexts and historical conditions "limit" theoretical negativity, he favors what Paul Ricoeur calls positive hermeneutics. As Jameson says,

> Ernst Bloch's ideal of hope or the Utopian impulse; Mikhail Bakhtin's notion of the dialogical as a rupture of the one-dimensional text of bourgeois narrative . . . the Frankfurt School's conception of strong memory as the trace of gratification, of the revolutionary power of the *promesse de bonheur* most immediately inscribed in the aesthetic text: all these formulations hint at a variety of options for

articulating a properly Marxian version of meaning beyond
the purely ideological. (*PU*, 285)

This pursuit of "meaning beyond the purely ideological" commits
Jameson to seeking what he calls "a whole new logic of collective
dynamics, with categories that escape the taint of some mere
application of terms drawn from individual experience" (*PU*, 294).
Although he has forcefully analyzed popular culture, third-world
literature, and radical political movements, his repudiating such
"tainted categories" as the ethical division between good and evil
and the Marxist distinction between the progressive and the
reactionary commits him to disavowing the "merely" progressive
feminist, Afro-American, working class, or third-world struggles
to alter and to expand the traditional canon and conventional
literary study. As an engaged insider, a feminist, an Afro-
American, a working class, or a third-world critic seeks to change
and to improve literary institutions in a "progressive" but not a
utopian direction. In a reformist manner, such scholars ameliorate
the "ideological" present and do not map the utopian future; they
critique their institution's racist, chauvinist, or elitist discourses,
not the irrationality of the whole modern era.

In Jameson's defense, Michael Sprinker says that his method
"cannot be completely evaluated within the present historical
situation, since . . . the present . . . must itself be abolished for the
future to appear" ("Reinventing Historicism," 347). Jameson has
been an outspoken critic of American foreign policy, especially
the involvement in Vietnam and in other third-world countries,
but insofar as this refusal of evaluation depends upon such an
apocalyptic future, Jameson's pursuit of a utopian realm beyond
the ideological or instrumental shows an ultimate indifference to
practical action—its successes and its failures, its achievements
and its frustrations—rendering this pursuit apolitical. His
pessimistic belief that the reified state of capitalist social
institutions precludes practical action or, as he says, imposes
"structural limits" on "praxis" (*PU*, 91) broadens his literary
criticism but weakens his political impact. Institutional practices
are not transcendent but they are not apolitical or uncritical
either. While such structuralist and/or poststructuralist notions as

Althusser's ideological state apparatus, Foucault's discursive formations, Bennett's reading formations, and Fish's interpretive communities do not permit the utopian transcendence which Jameson seeks, these "instrumentalist" notions do not impose mechanical dogmas or obstruct critical thought, as Jameson charges. Habermas has rightly suggested that, to ensure the survival and reproduction of the established disciplines, scholars and critics share a legitimate interest in theorizing and improving their institutional conditions (*Knowledge and Human Interests*, 196-197).

II. Jameson and the Structuralist Approach

Like Jameson's pursuit of a utopian realm transcending ideology or instrumentality, his defense of a structuralism which is scientific yet historical preserves the neutrality of the structuralist project but denigrates the subjectivity of the author. Just as Jonathan Culler justifies the scientific project of structuralism, so too does Jameson consider structuralism scientific but not in a narrowly empirical sense. He rejects the ahistorical stance of Saussure, Greimas, and other structuralists, yet he preserves their scientific neutrality. As a result, he opens structuralist discourse to history but not to the author's subjectivity. In fact, Jameson's version of structuralism condemns the author to blindly repeating antinomies whose historical origins escape his or her "conventional mind" and whose resolution exposes his or her ideological limitations (*PU*, 84-85).

In *The Prison-House of Language*, he complains that Saussure's linguistics restricts language to a positivist framework. The famous distinction between a synchronic or systematic view of language and a diachronic or historical view blinds the linguist to language's historical context. By contrast, Jameson construes structuralism as a scientific "study of superstructures or, in a more limited way, of ideology" and thereby returns the theory of language to society and to history (*PH*, 101). Just as Althusser argued that a scientific Marxism exposes and criticizes ideological practices, so too does Jameson claim that a properly historicized linguistics describes and evaluates cultural models or paradigms. Embedded in the author's unconscious, these models of interpretation "mediate" between theory and society: as he says, history "is inaccessible to us except in textual form" (*PU*, 35). While Barthes abandons the distinction between a model's formal possibilities and its "external," historical context, Jameson retains the distinction not only to bring the repudiated history back into structuralist criticism but to preserve its scientific character, not as a matter of a reader's empirically verified competence but of an interpretation's formal, even mathematical, neutrality.

Like the defense of a utopian vision escaping the ideological or instrumental world of institutions, this "scientific" account of unconscious cultural models mediating between theory and society maintains the neutrality of the structuralist project but in a different way. This account does not dismiss traditional, ethical or Marxian values; this account erases the surface of the text, with its embedded readings and interpretations of the author's values and outlook, as merely subjective, private, or ideological. For example, Jameson reworks A. J. Greimas' structuralist account of narrative in this way: it defines "internal" limits, which are "nothing more than the total number of permutations and combinations inherently possible in the model in question," as well as "external" limits, in which history "pre-selects a certain number of structural possibilities for actualization, while proscribing others as inconceivable in the social and cultural climate of a given area" (*PH*, 128). This contrast between the model's possible "permutations and combinations" and its pre-selected and proscribed possibilities implies that at some points the surface of the text and the schema of the possible permutations and combinations will deviate. In fact, Jameson attributes the value of Greimas' model to its ability to register deviations from the surface text (*PU*, 126). Since Jameson argues that the ideological limitations of what he terms the author's "conventional mind" explain these deviations, this historicized version of Greimas' model critiques the author's ideology by discrediting his or her point of view.

His reading of *Lord Jim* illustrates the way in which this emphasis on deviation reduces Conrad's subjectivity to ideological distortion. According to formal critics, Conrad divides the Marlow of *The Heart of Darkness* into the would-be hero Jim and the contemplative narrator Marlow, and gains, thereby, sufficient aesthetic distance from his characters to make his moral judgments convincing. Conrad's aesthetic devices are, in short, a means of establishing moral standards by which the author judges the characters. According to Jameson, however, Conrad's method of characterization is not a neutral device making ethical judgments convincing but an ideological technique for resolving what are, according to Greimas' semiotics, irresolvable antinomies. Greimas' famous rectangle, which is a four-term variation of a basic structural opposition, reveals the ideological limits that the writer's "conventional mind" imposes on the characters' potential development. The rectangle displays possibilities of development which the writer's ideology will not tolerate.

To describe the limited characterization revealed by *Lord Jim*, Jameson cites two theorists: Max Weber, who analyzes the capitalist "rationalization" divorcing instrumental, active forms of institutional life from the values of institutions, and Nietzsche, who describes the "transvaluation" or changing of religious objects designed for holy worship into autonomous images available for aesthetic consumption. These theories show that the break up of the feudal, cast system and the growth of capitalist markets produces a divorce between value, which becomes "personal," and action which remains public or institutional. Moreover, this antinomy between action and value explains the main features of *Lord Jim's* characters. Thus the gentleman pirate, Captain Brown, signifies action without value; the religious pilgrims, value without action; the deck-chair sailors, valueless inaction; and Jim, the ideal: action of value (*PU*, 46-49).

In this way the antinomy accounts for the characters' opposed features and satisfies Greimas' rectangle; however, it poses an interpretive problem because, as poles of the antinomy, the pilgrims and the sailors are far more important than most interpretations say. Jameson tries to account for their exaggerated significance by invoking the unseen hand of ideology—it may minimize or understate important figures, as, Freud tells us, the censor of dreams does. In this case, ideology encourages Conrad to fill out Jim or Captain Brown but prevents him from developing the religious pilgrims or the deck-chair sailors. The trouble is that the ideological constraint explains what the social theory and not Conrad's "conventional mind" suggested—the exaggerated significance of the religious pilgrims or deck-chair sailors. Ultimately, the constraint only accounts for what the social theory suggested —the exaggerated importance of the pilgrims and sailors.

What is more, the social theory is not neutral: in a radical way it criticizes the emerging capitalist markets. Conrad may not share the radical biases of the social theory, but that fact would only make his outlook ideological and the social theory objective if the formal possibilities envisioned by the structural antinomy somehow acquire a transcendent truth by contrast with which the actual development (surface structure) of the text reveals the merely subjective limitations of Conrad's outlook. Why should the antinomy acquire such an elevated status and Conrad's outlook, such degraded status? Is it not because Jameson assumes that even in historicized form the Gremasian antinomy and structuralism generally remain neutral and objective, just as he assumes that the utopian future preserves the neutral objectivity of the humanist ideal? Berthoud rightly suggests that as a consequence of such assumptions Jameson's structuralist approach renders him "completely incapable of acknowledging Conrad's text as offering . . . a responsible interpretation of the world" ("Narrative and Ideology," 113).

III. Jameson and Poststructuralism

In general, Jameson believes that the mediating, cultural models provided by structuralism, humanism, and other approaches "would remain merely symbolic, a mere methodological fiction, were it not understood that social life is in its fundamental reality one and indivisible, a seamless web, a single inconceivable and trans-individual process" (*PU*, 40). His belief that "social life is in its fundamental reality one and indivisible" sets him against the skeptical poststructuralists, for the belief exacts a mystical faith in an "inconceivable and trans-individual process," preserves the autonomy of the "trans-individual process," and denigrates "subjective" institutional discourses, codes, and practices—what Jameson calls "merely the reality of appearance: it exists, as Hegel would put it, not so much in itself, as rather for us" (PU, 40).

Traditional critics like Jonathan Culler evaluate poststructuralism in similar terms. Culler argues that the poststructuralist critique qualifies but does not destroy the scientific character of the structuralist project; similarly Jameson argues that poststructuralism challenges but does not overturn the transcendental faith of Hegelian Marxism. Culler does not grant that deconstruction has turned the "scientific ambitions of structuralists" into "impossible dreams" (On Deconstruction, 219-220); Jameson does not allow that the poststructuralist critique of Hegelian Marxism reveals anything more than a limitation of the traditional method—it does not respect the autonomy of the levels or the ruptures of historical development.

However, Althusser and Foucault do more than emphasize these ruptures of development or that autonomy of levels; in addition, they repudiate the Hegelian faith in an "inconceivable and trans-individual process." They reject the pursuit of a transcendental reality whose underlying or immanent opposition (the famous "unity-in-difference") can mediate among different discourses and overcome their reified character only by denying the independence of particular discourses as well as their evolution from one period to another. In Reading Capital (1968), for example, Althusser, whose structuralist work has poststructuralist import, argues that the Hegelian approach imposes a self-identical telos preserving historical continuities and repressing historical ruptures. In addition, echoing Friedrich Engel's fear that the Hegelian method mystically deduces the particular from the universal, Althusser complains that the method constitutes the levels of history from the mind's own substance (Reading Capital, 15-17, 131-138). He derides the sleight of hand whereby the totality constitutes them out of itself. Like a magician, totality extracts them from the hat called spirit, reason, or mind and fails to respect the fields, discourses, or topography peculiar to them. As he says, "And Marx is on his guard, because when he inscribes the dialectic within the functioning of the instance of a topography, he effectively protects himself from the illusion of a dialectic capable of producing its own material content in the spontaneous movement of its self-development" (*Essays in Self-Criticism*, 148-149). Not only does the figure of a topography undermine the mystical pretensions of Hegelian dialectic, the figure also subverts the Hegelian faith in an "inconceivable and trans-individual process" underlying fields, discourses, and disciplines. The critique deconstructs the Hegelian fear of fragmentation and brings Marxism back to discourse's historical and institutional contexts, divisions, and disciplines. In *The Archaeology of Knowledge* (1969) Foucault offers a comparable view: contradiction has many levels and functions within and between discursive formations and does not represent a difference to be resolved or a fundamental principle of explanation (*Archaeology*, 149-156). In *Foucault, Marxism, and History*, Mark Poster explains this claim: as an archaeologist studying the discourse of criminals, the insane, and other dispersed subjects, Foucault repudiates the notion of a transcendental reality underlying and unifying diverse discourses and examines a discourse's history, conflicts, and institutional power (Poster, 39).

In a sense Jameson anticipates this critique of the Hegelian method, for he argues that, by destroying social isolation and by democratizing culture, postmodernism leaves the left no room in which to undertake the traditional, Lukácsian analysis of false consciousness. As he says, "[Y]ou have to do it from the inside and it has to be a self-critique" ("RPM," 55). Nonetheless, his responses to the poststructuralist critique preserve the methods and concepts of a Hegelian approach. First, he construes Althusser's critique as Althusser's "unanswerable" repudiation of Stalinism (*PU*, 47). I grant that Althusser meant to attack the Stalinists, but he also repudiated the totalizing approach of Hegel and Sartre. In *Essays in Self-Criticism*, Althusser says clearly enough that the "Thesis that 'men' (the concrete individuals) are the subjects (transcendental, constitutive) of history . . . not only has nothing to do with Marxism, but actually constitutes a quite dubious theoretical position. . . . You just have to read the *Critique of Dialectical Reason* . . . to be convinced of this point" (*Essays in*

Self-Criticism, 98). Here Althusser attacks not only Stalinist versions of Hegelian theory but also the transcendental status of the subject, including its ability to mediate between text and history.

Second, Jameson argues that ultimately the poststructuralist critique only qualifies his account of totality. At best, the critique warns us not to forget the differences between the literary, the political, and the economic levels of society, not to reduce one of these levels to another. At worst, however, the critique disperses basic, methodological unities. It dissolves the historical narrative in which new periods evolve from the old like butterflies from moths. It fragments that underlying, primordial oneness which, because of bourgeois divisions, levels, and disciplines, we see through a glass darkly but will one day discern face-to-face (*PU*, 23-43).

As a consequence, Jameson's approach preserves the differences of interpretive levels or "horizons" but does not abandon the methodological closure or the conceptual language of a totalizing approach. Why else would he say that the "semantic precondition for the intelligibility of literary and cultural texts" and for their "semantic enrichment and enlargement" stems from three "concentric frameworks"—political events, class struggle, and sequential social formations (*PU*, 78-79)? While these frameworks open interpretation to multiple perspectives, the frameworks also fix the points where those perspectives go astray, the limits beyond which he—but not they—can go.

Preserving the autonomy of the levels does not keep Jameson from affirming the transcendental status of his conceptual terms as well as his interpretive "frameworks." While the poststructuralist denies that conceptual distinctions transcend the discursive network in which they are formed and embedded, Jameson assumes that theoretical terms like "class," "value," or "space" escape their disciplinary contexts and acquire a "transcendent" status allowing them to characterize a whole period or to determine political practices or social institutions. How else should we explain that impressive recapitulation of Nietzsche's and Weber's theories enabling Jameson to describe the "antimonies" of *Lord Jim* as an opposition of activity and value?

On what grounds but the transcendental can Frye's account of romance and Nietzsche's account of ethics describe the same binary oppositions? How else can deconstruction and Frankfurt social theory both characterize the "dissolution of the subject" in late monopoly capitalism or the literature, painting, film, criticism, philosophy, and architecture of the 1970s and 1980s share a common, postmodern notion of space?

In addition, his account of postmodernism still seeks to transcend its "subjective" contexts and divisions and to characterize the "dominant" features of this era. In *The Political Unconscious*, for example, Jameson says that the poststructuralist critique of the Hegelian method shows the regressive character of a new period—postmodernism. The poststructuralist critique amounts to what he calls "symptoms of and testimony to a modification of the experience of the subject in consumer or late monopoly capitalism." While he grants that the "psychic dispersal, fragmentations, . . . temporal discontinuities" resulting from this critique imply a "dissolution of an essentially bourgeois ideology of the subject," he refuses to endorse the "schizophrenic ideal" projected by poststructuralism. What is more, he argues that only the "post-individualistic social world" of the future can genuinely fragment or de-center the bourgeois subject (*PU*, 124-125).

In several influential essays, he goes on to describe postmodernism as a "new cultural logic in its own right" ("RPM," 44) but assesses it in equally negative terms. He points out that it breaks with modernism, which lost its oppositional force in the 1960's, when it gained canonical status and institutional position ("PCL," 56). At the same time, postmodernism develops what Jameson calls an "aesthetic populism" effacing the "older (essentially high modernist) frontier between high culture and so-called mass or commercial culture" ("PCL," 54). Jameson denies that his account of postmodernism represents the sort of "moralizing position" which Lukács takes on modernism ("RPM," 51), but he condemns postmodernism's integrating culture into "commodity production generally" in no uncertain terms: "the whole global, yet American, postmodern culture is the internal and superstructural expression of a whole new wave of

American military and economic domination throughout the world" ("PCL," 57).

Although Jameson clearly distinguishes between the socio-economic structures of postmodernism and its cultural theories and practices, his condemnation of it extends to and includes post-structuralist theory. His account of postmodernism's features, such as its pursuit of visual and interpretive flatness, its emphasis on intensities, temporal disjunction, and difference and breaks, its construction of a perspectiveless space, its destruction of cultural autonomy and of individual works, its depersonalization of style, and its use of pastiche and collage, applies to poststructuralist practices, among other theories, practices, and discourses ("RPM," 44-45; "PCL," *passim*). He grants that postmodernism may also reveal "forms of resistance," but his description of the postmodernist alliance with "military and economic domination" emphasizes what he calls the "cultural dominant" ("RPM," 52-53) and minimizes the poststructuralist's radical dimension—its undermining and subverting the conservative, chauvinist subject constituted by popular culture, the canon and other literary institutions.

By contrast, the poststructuralist denies that even such systematizing accounts of an historical period escape institutional codes, discourses, and disciplines and reveal a "fundamental reality one and indivisible." The poststructuralist still resists his or her inevitable complicity with them, but he or she does so by exposing the conservative import of established approaches, not by seeking "independent" territory or advocating alternative practices. Unlike the Derridean Marxists, whose "mise en abyme" dissolves institutional discourse and repudiates established practices altogether, institutional poststructuralism preserves the interpretive force of established approaches but undermines their conservative faith in the status quo. While deconstruction insists that the "mise en abyme" undermines all authoritative discourses, dismissing them as metaphysical quests for absolute meaning, this institutional approach reveals their political import but acknowledges their interpretive power. This approach assumes that interpretation reveals the conflicted, discursive formations or interpretive communities whose conventions and practices constitute the reader as a political subject. In a dialectical but not a transcendental manner, this approach criticizes and preserves authorial and New Critical practices, reader response and deconstructive approaches, and formal and structuralist methods.

Jameson acknowledges that criticism is lost in postmodernism's ahistorical present, but his accounts of authorial, structuralist, and poststructuralist criticism imply that the most valuable politics is speculative and utopian, and not institutional or disciplinary. His Lukácsian fear of reified disciplines and fragmented societies denies that criticism can meaningfully challenge the dystopia of modern life, merge utopia and reality, or open a path from the existential present to the utopian future. If the rational future may permit change but not the dark present, what can literary critics do but wait and hope for the utopian future to reveal itself? The institutional approach of Althusser, Derrida, and Foucault opens a rich, institutional realm of engaged, formal, historical, and political critique; Jameson's historicization of authorial humanism and literary structuralism broadens and deepens both these methods but ends up almost as neutral and as distant as traditional approaches are. Terry Eagleton wisely comments that in this speculative Marxism "the commodity bulks so large that it threatens to obfuscate, not only bourgeois social relations, but a specifically political and institutional understanding in areas of the left" ("Jameson: Politics of Style," 21).

Jameson's Strategies of Containment

Haynes Horne
University of Minnesota

The failure to reflect a hidden commitment to the humanist tradition of the Enlightenment and its "unfinished" utopian project bars Fredric Jameson's attempts to "post-modernize" Marxism, attempts which have generated a great deal of excitement without finally being able to effect the requisite passage out of nineteenth-century philosophy of history in which utopia becomes the dominant topos of a secularized eschatology. Enlightenment: this reading of Marxism—perhaps one of the most fruitful produced under poststructuralism—is only beginning to be fully appreciated. In the following remarks I wish to explore some of its implications, for in his belief in the immanence of reason and the adequacy of communication Fredric Jameson continues the profession of faith in the possibility of maintaining, after the brief hiatus of the 60s, legitimating principles as a basis for historical intervention. That such a faith has justified every revolution, counter-revolution and *coup d'état* since 1789, however, passes unremarked in his writing.

This faith is both the goal and the wreck of Jameson's mission, for the desire to retain the enlightenment heritage of a totalizing philosophy of history within which principles can be theorized and thus universalized blinds him to the results in praxis of such a desire "to seize reality." His pre-critical allegiance to what Lyotard calls "metanarratives of emancipation" obscures all paths leading out of the enlightenment-modernist tradition in which these metanarratives take their pseudo-secular, bourgeois form. Jameson's writings from 1982 to the present (from *The Political Unconscious* through "Cognitive Mapping," several of which I discuss more or less in order of their publication) reproduce in each instance an enlightenment-modernist stance according to which a cognitive-theoretical apparatus in conjunction with a phenomenological account of experience can discover universal meaning "out there." Whether the repository of meaning is "the logic of capital" or Necessity, History's Hermes sense is reconciled with concept, in promise if not in deed. As a result, Jameson's work stands as a fascinating instance of a "late" modernism, for where it is unavoidable, as for example in the phenomenological account of experience of the present, it incorporates poststructuralist elements piecemeal and strategically; but in its cognitive-theoretical underpinnings, Jameson's work continues to posit, finally, a modernist commitment to totality not unlike other enlightenment projects before it. His work remains squarely within the modern, the millenarian, manifesting the desire to represent as whole that which can only be known in shards. Yet in spite of the continuing lament about the lack of an historical sense in the postmodern, Jameson himself fails to note that the desire to represent totality consistently instantiates itself as terror the moment a theory is put into practice in which wholeness of form ceases to be a regulative idea of reason and is made constitutive.

Thus, however desirable the passage of Marx's writings into the postmodern may be, the passage cannot be effected within the same enlightenment philosophy of history in which they took root, nor within any other, for that matter, which refuses to acknowledge both principled limitations to its own authority and the givenness of equally authoritative alternate legends. Only when it will be possible to speak of Marxist *philosophies of histories* and be understood, without being accused of some liberal pluralism, will Marxism have emerged from the hegemony of enlightenment schemes of totality and offered itself anew as a vehicle for transforming—not reproducing—the given social order.

I. The Siren Call of *The Political Unconscious*

Despite Jameson's encyclopedic knowledge of the terms and techniques of poststructuralist analysis, an unmistakably modernist design continues to motivate his work: the attempt to legitimate, in the face of the epistemological break defining postmodernism, political involvement in mass movements. This desire is the unconscious of *The Political Unconscious*—unconscious, however, in the weak sense that it avoids offering itself up to critique; for the reader must go outside of *The Political Unconscious* to find a formulation of it. This work satisfies itself with laying the methodological groundwork for legitimation: the (re-)establishment of the preconditions of a collective which can act as the political consciousness of a new (proletarian?) class struggling against the monolithic hegemony of multinational capitalism. Jameson dissimulates the possibility of attaining this desire through a doctrine of the absolute horizon of history, a history which doubles as the guarantor of both interpretational and communicational adequacy. History becomes the referential bound of language and experience, concept and sense, and as such it is a "functor" of consensus on aesthetic norms and ethical maxims. This program of the "political," which, along with the notion of a teleological philosophy of history, grounds Jameson in the tradition of modernity, forms the interest behind *The Political Unconscious*. It is an interest, however, which is scarcely mentioned in that text itself. One statement of it appears, however, in the critical foreword to Lyotard's *The Postmodern Condition* where Jameson writes

> that the great master-narratives here are those that suggest that something beyond capitalism is possible, something radically different; and they also 'legitimate' the praxis whereby political militants seek to bring that radically different future social order into being. ("FJF," xix)

This motivation for which the "absent cause" of history is tended is only political in that enlightenment-modernist sense which has been dominant from the Convention of 1789 through the Popular

Front to the communal alternatives of the 1960s and which still finds loud support today around academic conference tables: the political as a totalized agglomeration of disparate fields of discourse, among them the aesthetic, economic, and judicial—all circumscribed by an absolute horizon of history, a philosophy of history dominated by ethical discourse which provides a potential basis for legitimate revolutionary praxis. The work Jameson undertakes in *The Political Unconscious* constitutes the founding of a new epic or, better stated, the re-vision of an old one: the epic of the community's struggle for bread, peace, and work. If this is the prevailing though unstated interest behind *The Political Unconscious*, it may prove instructive to consider the text of Lyotard which provokes Jameson to give its full, unabashed statement in the preceding quotation.

Lyotard's *The Postmodern Condition* describes the dissolution of foundational myths or "metanarratives" by positing postmodernity as a position from which such integral myths of modernity can be "re-cognized":

> Simplifying to the extreme, I define *postmodern* as incredulity toward metanarratives. . . . To the obsolescence of the metanarrative apparatus of legitimation corresponds, most notably, the crisis of metaphysical philosophy and of the university institution which in the past relied on it. The narrative function is losing its functors, its great hero, its great dangers, its great voyages, its great goal. It is being dispersed in clouds of narrative language elements— narrative, but also denotative, prescriptive, descriptive, and so on. Conveyed within each cloud are pragmatic valences specific to its kind. Each of us lives at the intersection of many of these. However, we do not necessarily establish stable language combinations, and the properties of the ones we do establish are not necessarily communicable. (*Postmodern Condition*, xxiv)

In condensed form this passage could be said to contain the bulk of the poststructuralist "program" Jameson hopes to contain. First and foremost Jameson propounds the utopian ideal or promise, which provides his project with its *telos*, its meaning and its justification. The path toward this utopia is linear and narrative and may thus be literally read in such forms as the history of productive forces, and the story of necessity and class struggle, all co-extensive with the *grand récit* of "the logic of capital." And although Jameson does not acknowledge the fact, having once posited the contours of a history within which a single narrative of liberation arises, he simultaneously gets, along with the narrative, its subject of elocution, the heroic revolutionary subject which remains capable of the "dangerous voyages" and the heroic action. Jameson's writings are concerned almost exclusively with the pragmatics of theorizing this revolutionary subject, and although his task leads him into many disparate fields of discourse, any comparatist gleanings are obscured by the unflagging effort to subsume their diversity under a transcendent notion of history as a unified field for the playing out of the logic of capital.

Lyotard, on the other hand, sees the possibility of writing the *grand récit* out of the script of a "new" modernity. Indeed the postmodern, for Lyotard, is no more than that moment of continual renewal of modernity itself in which we are presently called to intervene: not with a program which would merely reproduce the terror already inscribed on us by the last two centuries, but rather with a program in which a new toleration acknowledges the principled incommensurability of language games and their contestants. Such an endorsement of diversity could inscribe an entirely new modernity. Lyotard's version of a new "modernity" is stripped of the enlightenment characteristics of the one it seeks to replace; it is one in which utopian visions and the "final solutions" upon which they have always ultimately been based would be stripped of their claims to ethical pre-eminence, a modernity in which a principled endorsement of agonistics supplants the sentiment for consensus, a modernity in which the indefinite postponement of a totality of meaning allows for a proliferation of stories, temporalities, spaces.

Jameson, on the other hand, assumes that the fact of the radical dissolution of metanarratives which Lyotard describes can only be endorsed when this dissolution functions within programs which serve as a merely strategic component of a politically conscious telos operating within the movement of History. How such a description as Lyotard provides—aleatory and non-programmatic—could be itself of interpretive value and political utility does not occur to him, for in the modernist sense of the term it can be recognized as neither interpretive nor political. Indeed, Jameson seems to hold to the "with me or agin' me" idea, thinking that the only alternative to a markedly oppositional role is co-optation. Yet this stance ignores the capacity of institutions to thrive on oppositional movements. Such movements remain trapped in an identity logic according to which they necessarily remain fully determined by the existing system through the attempt to negate the characteristics of that status quo. Thus, although they nominally oppose the status quo, through their opposition they can only reproduce the existing social order. This can be readily seen within the academy: if a professor publishes a particularly powerful, oppositional critique of the system, s/he most often gets a pay increase for this labor; and the more powerful the critique, the larger the raise. With a larger office and more numerous research assistants, the institution increases its power over the thought and production of its nominal "opponent," recontaining the professor in its system of patronage, gaining increased power through its show of tolerance. Yet Jameson's commitment to a modernist totalizing program blinds him to the possibilities offered by the postmodern condition as Lyotard describes it, for opposition is the only role for the political Jameson's commitments allow, and unfortunately, all possibilities of resistance are collapsed into it. Lyotard, on the other hand, himself no stranger to big paychecks or to oppositional politics in the modernist tradition, proposes a strategic endorsement of the postmodern condition, an endorsement in which the dissolution of metanarratives and the corresponding corrosion of the concept of totality is seen as liberatory. Although opposition in the modernist fashion becomes no longer tenable, the possibilities for resistance proliferate by means of the very fragmentation of social life itself.

Lyotard has mobilized a powerful and unexpected ally for his attack on totality in the Kant of the *Third Critique*, a text lying close not only to the surface of Lyotard's work on postmodernism but, in the caption bequeathed us by Schiller, a text fundamental to the conception of modernity as it is known in the West as "enlightenment" (de Man, "Kant and Schiller"). Lyotard's is a Kant who demarcates very carefully between types of judgments, epistemological, ethical and aesthetic, a Kant for whom the imperative of holding these realms apart cannot be overstated, a Kant for whom the derivation, even by negation, of a form of civil society from a phenomenological description of existence is clearly marked as dogmatism.

Lyotard shows us a Kant in which the critique of totality is by no means a mere postmodern fashion, as Jameson has a way of suggesting. Jameson writes as if he can construct a non-cognitive framework; i.e. "the absolute horizon of history," within which a specific ethic, in this case "the praxis whereby political militants seek to bring *that* radically different social order into being," can derive its legitimation. In other words "the great master narratives"—translate, the history of class struggle—which have, for the present at least gone into hiding in the political unconscious, can secure us an "is" from which at our hour of need an "ought" can be derived.

It is disturbing that such an argument as this for tending the master narratives is hardly present in *The Political Unconscious*, for we ought to expect rigor from modernist political theories; they should at least acknowledge their fundamental narratives. Instead, as Sam Weber has pointed out, Jameson's text is aimed at a notoriously apolitical audience of professional academicians with arguments for a methodology which can be reduced in part to what amounts to an appeal for upholding the status quo of the institutional framework of intellectual life (see "Capitalizing History"). Before examining these points further, I would like to continue with what I would call his misreading of Lyotard and Kant, a misreading which causes him to rely on history as the "absent" referent which nonetheless is capable of anchoring the signification required for the revolutionary praxis prescribed by modernist millenarian versions of Marxist theory.

In the following passage from an essay appended to *The Postmodern Condition*, "Answering the Question: What is Post-modernism," Lyotard presents a striking denouncement of enlightenment humanism, whether of Jameson or E. D. Hirsch:

Finally, it must be clear that it is our business not to supply reality but to invent allusions to the conceivable which cannot be presented. And it is not to be expected that this task will effect the last reconciliation between language games (which, under the name of faculties, Kant knew to be separated by a chasm), and that only the transcendental illusion (that of Hegel) can hope to totalize them into a real unity. But Kant also knew that the price to pay for such an illusion is terror. The nineteenth and twentieth centuries have given us as much terror as we can take. We have paid a high enough price for the nostalgia of the whole and the one, for the reconciliation of the concept and the sensible, of the transparent and the communicable experience. Under the general demand for slackening and for appeasement, we can hear the mutterings of the desire for a return of terror, for the realization of the fantasy to seize reality. The answer is: Let us wage a war on totality; let us be witness to the unpresentable; let us activate the differences and save the honor of the name. (*Postmodern Condition*, 80).

There is hardly room in such an account of "the postmodern condition" for a doctrine of a master narrative, wrapped in the guise of an "absent cause" or not, and it is unfortunate that Jameson does not address these remarks in his introduction. Jameson approaches this theme, which accuses totality *qua* totality of leading to terror, only very indirectly by referring to it as "instinctive" and somehow vaguely fashionable ("FJF," xix). But this is a theme which is by no means confined to the short essay of Lyotard's quoted here.

It is a realization fundamental to Lyotard's postmodernism that any theory or concept capable of justifying "the praxis whereby political militants seek to bring that radically different future social order into being" is equally capable of bringing a reign of terror—indeed, that the two may not even be objectively distinguishable. Lyotard insists on reminding us of what has gone on before in the name of reason. He recalls for us the Kantian distinction among the realms of knowledge, ethics, and aesthetics in order to support his argument against any totalizing system which claims to be the final adjudicator of conflicts between the faculties of the mind or, as could be said, language games. Lyotard's interest in postmodernism is very close to the surface in this final statement just cited. He sees in the fractured and fragmenting activity of postmodernism an expression of unbridgeable chasms between the faculties of the Kantian subject, and in them a form of resistance to any system under which "the fantasy to seize reality" might become an instance of practical action.

Jameson realizes that in the absence of such maxims, and in the absence of communities which make general agreement about them possible, there can be no class or class organ capable of legitimate revolutionary praxis. But this position takes into account only half of the problem of justifying political praxis, the empirical absence of a community of shared values—which in any case is and was almost certainly only a mythical community. Jameson ignores the problem to which Lyotard's Kant points: the logical chasm which separates ethics from knowledge. Only this fundamental omission can account for the modernist's single-minded drive to re-establish a binding connection between "is" and "ought." Jameson ignores the possibility that revolutionary praxis is not necessarily weakened by acknowledging that its justification resides solely in the local actions of those who are moved to revolt in a certain place and time. And yet how much more successful might revolutionary praxis have shown itself to be if the banners under which it marched had been more modest than to read FREEDOM, TRUTH, HUMANITY? To move incrementally toward such goals is, as Kant suggests, a requirement of the faculty of reason which he calls *streben*; but to act in the name of them, as if they were secured and contained within some set of principles written by a world-historical subject in a declaration, betrays the "fantasy to seize reality" of which Lyotard warns.

While Jameson's emphasis on a political program manifests itself openly in the introduction to Lyotard's work, in *The Political Unconscious* he describes the totalizing system as a liberal one. (However, this is a liberalism paradigmatic of the term's absolutist-americanist sense described by Louis Hartz.[1]) Instead, Jameson's goal seems to be to convince his readers of the utility of such a comprehensive system for literary interpretation and for the communicational adequacy of the larger social body. His work, he says,

> seeks to argue the perspectives of Marxism as necessary preconditions for adequate literary comprehension. Marxist critical insights will therefore here be defended as something like an ultimate semantic precondition for the intelligibility of literary and cultural texts. (*PU*, 75)

Thus, Marxism, according to Jameson, offers the necessary perspective from which "the inert givens and materials of a particular text" can be semantically enriched, and this semantic enrichment of inert givens becomes the "adequate literary interpretation" provided by the Marxist perspective he offers. Only the Marxian method can offer an "untranscendable horizon" because, says Jameson, the plethora of alternative critical approaches are merely "local" (should we read anarchic?) in their claims and are involved in rhetorical strategies which make them seem more comprehensive than they really are. In *The Political Unconscious* he proposes to demonstrate by comparison the absolute strength of the Marxist approach:

> Their [the 'alternative approaches'] juxtaposition with a dialectical or totalizing, properly Marxist ideal of understanding will be used to demonstrate the structural limitations of the other interpretive codes, and in particular to show the 'local' ways in which they construct their objects of study and the 'strategies of containment' whereby they are able to project the illusion that their readings are somehow complete and self-sufficient. (*PU*, 10)

As Weber has pointed out, Jameson is quick to say, however, that the "local" operations of the myth-critical or psychoanalytic interpretive methods, to cite two of his examples, do not warrant being discarded, and thus no threat is implied to their professors. Indeed the variety of methods current "in the 'pluralism' of the intellectual marketplace today" are of at least sociological interest, Jameson implies, even if their actual interpretive utility can be shown to be limited, for

the authority of such methods springs from their faithful
consonance with this or that fragmented law of social life,
this or that subsystem of a complex and mushrooming
cultural superstructure. (*PU*, 10)

Thus these competing interpretive codes, Jameson argues, have a
local utility and need not fear acknowledging the Master
Narrative of Marxism since each will be assigned "an undoubted
sectoral validity" within it, "thus at once canceling and preserving
them." Paradoxically then, Jameson argues for the adoption of
Marxist interpretive methods as a kind of guarantor of the
institutional status quo which can insulate the "local" operations
of various critical schools from the cutthroat competition of the
"intellectual marketplace today." Between Jameson's entrapment
in the identity logic of opposition and the almost physiocratic
argument for Marxism as interpretive master narrative found
here, the suspicion that Jameson's Marxism has more to do with
the reproduction of the institutional status quo than its transformation begins to take on a more definite contour. It remains to
be discussed, however, how Jameson argues for such an
interpretive master narrative.

Jameson proposes what he calls a "social hermeneutic," a
term which clearly displays the link between interpretive
adequacy in the cultural sphere and the restoration of an organic
character to the body politic. Repeating the gesture of an earlier
phase of *Weltmüdigkeit*, Jameson follows the movement well-
represented by the generation of T. S. Eliot when he takes the
purported wholeness of a mythic medieval society as his model:

A social hermeneutic will . . . wish to keep faith with its
medieval precursor . . . and must necessarily restore a
perspective in which the imagery of libidinal revolution
and of bodily transfiguration once again becomes a figure
for the perfected community. The unity of the body must
once again prefigure the renewed organic identity of associative or collective life. . . . Only the community, indeed, can
dramatize that self-sufficient intelligible unity (or 'structure') of which the individual body, like the individual

'subject' is a decentered 'effect,' and to which the
individual organism, caught in the ceaseless chain of the
generations and the species, cannot, even in the most
desperate Renaissance or Neoplatonic visions of herm-
aphroditism (or in their contemporary counterpart, the
Deleuze-Guattari 'bachelor machine'), lay claim. (*PU*, 74)

This statement is part of an acknowledgement of "debt" Jameson
says he owes "to the great pioneers of narrative analysis" (*PU*, 12).
Indeed the medieval interpretive model and its political
counterpart are intended by Jameson to parallel his own proposals.
In this acknowledgement of "debt" the continued reliance on the
classical understanding of the individual's subjectivity is
maintained and restored to the extent that the possibility of a
perfected individual is rendered again as a function of a "perfected" polis or Utopia, a possibility rendered through a "social
hermeneutic."

In Jameson's striking renewal of the analogy of the social to
the organic form of the body, the recollection of the price paid for
such a harmonious "organic identity of associative or collective
life" goes without mention: the inflexibility of the caste-like
system of guilds, the ineluctable demand for conformity to
custom, and the principled barbarism of the Inquisition which
terrorized both the high and the low when the strains within the
system could no longer be contained. These are the terrors, even if
quaint by the standards of the Twentieth Century, of which such
thinkers as Lyotard warn in their resistance to closed systems.
Jameson misses an opportunity to address the issue which he
himself brings to the surface of his argument. Not withstanding
his failure to mention its problematic aspects, Jameson gains a
great deal from the analogy. As God functions for the medieval
theologian as The Untranscendable but Benign Other—a horizon
of biblical hermeneutics which guarantees the limits within
which meaning can be collectively established—in the same way
History (now capitalized, of course) acts as the untranscendable
horizon. For a thinker whose slogan is "Always historicize!" this
call for a "social hermeneutic" which promises a renewal of
"organic identity of associative or collective life" remains

strangely isolated from any resonance with its corporatist analogues. This is the analogue Lyotard would not have us forget.

Having proposed this ideal of a "social hermeneutic," Jameson continues with an overview of his method of literary interpretation which assumes

> three concentric frameworks, which mark a widening out of the sense of the social ground of a text through the notions, first, of political history, in the narrow sense of punctual event and a chroniclelike sequence of happenings in time; then of society, in the now already less diachronic and time-bound sense of a constitutive tension and struggle between social classes; and ultimately, of history now conceived in its vastest sense of the sequence of modes of production and the succession and destiny of the various human social formations, from prehistoric life to whatever far future history has in store for us. (*PU*, 75)

On this third level, we are invited to entertain the "sequence of the modes of production" and the "succession and destiny of social formations" moving purposefully toward that "far future history has in store for us" as the "absent cause": History. Transcending the tendentious plurality of discourses, history only reveals itself to us as the "mystery" in a master narrative which becomes textualized in the *homo sapiens'* experience of necessity (*PU*, 19). The phrase, "the sequence of modes . . . and the succession and destiny" strikes a totalizing note, for this phrase excludes the possibility of multiples: the *sequences* of modes of production, or the *successions* and *destinies* of the various human social formations. Beneath the surface of this apparent stylistic quibble lie four hundred years of Western nationalism and imperialism, resident now in the very discursive structures of theory. In keeping with his rhetoric of restoration, Jameson tells us that by means of the adequacy of Marxist interpretation "this mystery can be reenacted. . . ." Safely contained within such an absolute referential boundary in which all truth value returns to apparent simplicity on the model of an oral culture—indeed in Jameson's remark explicitly on the model of cult practice—all interpretation can be grounded in sense by an interpretive process of "semantic enrichment."

Apparently untroubled by the mythic resonance of his proposal, Jameson argues for the necessity of a conception of the movements within history "conceived in its vastest sense" to provide the "ultimate" boundary of interpretation, a history which can act therefore as guarantor of interpretive validity and communicational adequacy. And the reader is not alone at fault if s/he hears the sound of a palliative offered to an age grown weary of the agonistic character of a cultural politics in which difference brackets meaning. Jameson's attempt to recuperate meaning takes an ill-chosen path, however, and his exploitation of the medieval as a model for the wholeness of the body politic aligns him with the Southern Agrarians, for example, who ought to be very disagreeable to him (see Karankas, *Tillers of a Myth*, esp. Ch. 5).

Like the Agrarians, Jameson hopes to secure the recognition of an outer limit of meaning beyond which we may not pass in order to establish communicational adequacy under the paradigm of literary interpretation. Unlike the Agrarians, and with a more liberal gesture, Jameson would reconstruct "the renewed organic identity of associative or collective life" within which individual schools of interpretation maintain their utility and their local autonomy without a disruptive divergence of meanings or an unbounded agonistics which would threaten the contours of the collective itself. These outer limits, furthermore, securely anchor the sense and reference of the texts themselves by establishing in them a symbolic re-enactment of the movement of productive forces, a movement which then acts as a common fundament for the various interpretive schools. Without this common fundament, Jameson apparently fears the reign of anarchy over the interpretive community and thinks this must necessarily bring in train the further splintering of schools of interpretation into irreconcilable camps, making community in the sense of communicational adequacy impossible.

For the loss of this transparency of meaning which disrupts (re-)building a collective goes hand in hand with the loss of "the imagery of libidinal revolution." This in turn entails the loss of a community which can be construed as a revolutionary subject of history, a problem Jameson points to in the foreword to *The Postmodern Condition* when he writes, "More orthodox Marxists will agree with the most radical post- or anti-Marxist position in at least this, that Marxism as a coherent philosophy (or better still, a 'unity of theory and praxis') stands or falls with the matter of social class" ("FJF," xv). By stipulating the mythic history which is to serve *in potentia* as the bound of sense, Jameson is simultaneously stipulating the possibility of a subject of that history, one which remains theoretically capable of, and capable of justifying, revolutionary praxis. The effort to construct a socially organic whole within which communication can be, as Habermas has said, "noisefree," finds here its own telos "within the unity of a single great collective story."

Thus while Jameson claims to be following the path of the subject and its modes of interpretation through his method of historicizing, this path turns out to be derivative and dependent on establishing a history capable of comprising the object (*PU*, 9). The fact that he locates the object in the political unconscious is a necessity of the current critical climate, and it is a climate which he argues forcefully to change. Yet the direction of the change must be viewed with skepticism; all the more so given the tenor of Jameson's remarks and examples.

In the closing section of his introductory chapter, Jameson characterizes the "final horizon" of history in the same categorical terms he has been using up till now:

> With this final horizon, then, we emerge into a space in which History itself becomes the ultimate ground as well as the untranscendable limit of our understanding in general and our textual interpretations in particular.
> (*PU*, 100)

While such a passage no longer arouses dismay, the juxtaposition of this Marxist absolutism with the very insights of postmodernist critique—though in the form of mere alternative absolutisms of Eco and Habermas—must give cause to wonder how Jameson manages to avoid the conclusions which could be drawn from his own juxtaposition. He is very well aware that

> some practitioners of alternate or rival interpretive codes—
> far from having been persuaded that History is an inter-
> pretive code that includes and transcends all others—will
> again assert 'History' as simply one more code among
> others, with no particularly privileged status. (*PU*, 100)

"Practitioners of alternate codes" is not really the issue; rather there is a less academic question Jameson utterly fails to ask, namely, "*Whose* history?" Africa's or China's? No, Euramerika's! Blacks' history or Orientals'? No, Caucasians'! Women's History? No, Men's! What Jameson reduces to "practitioners of alternate codes" are more properly in his own terms "livers of alternate histories." As such they have every reason to expect that their histories be taken seriously by Jameson, which, however, will not be possible under the regime of a master narrative in which the single "logic of capital" dictates the temporality as well as the space of each narrative.

Dismissing such a possible avenue of interrogation as relativism, Jameson himself attempts to relativize the alternative models by citing examples which make the same absolutist claims as his own arguments. In such a way he seems to offer his readers a most reasonable choice: since "nothing is to be gained by opposing one reified theme—History—by another—Language—in a polemic debate as to the ultimate priority of the one over the other" (*PU*, 100); why not, runs the implicit argument, choose this form of Marxist interpretation which is here shown capable of leaving the institutional framework, the pluralism of the intellectual marketplace intact? Under the umbrella of History all interpretive schools find their justifiable place (in my Father's mansion?), and be assigned a "sectoral validity" by the master narrative. This would be the most stable and convenient arrangement all around, wouldn't it?

Jameson ignores the strongest argument against the adoption of History as absolute horizon by characterizing the decision as one to be made between various absolute systems. Thus he makes such a decision into a merely utilitarian one. The position which he ignores is one which suspects all claims of absolutes and one which, as Weber suggests, ought to recognize the frameworks of interpretation themselves as already the product of an interpretive process ("Capitalizing History"). Such a recognition Jameson is in no way prepared to make, and indeed he spends the first one hundred pages of *The Political Unconscious* arguing that it is unnecessary and impossible to subject the framework of history itself to interpretation.

History, he says, is beyond our critical powers; it is present to us only as Necessity, which we all experience as "the inexorable *form* of events" (*PU*, 102). Thus History, finally, is present to us through the shared experience of necessity, and "can be apprehended only through its effects." "This is indeed the ultimate sense in which History as ground and untranscendable horizon needs no particular theoretical justification: we may be sure that its alienating necessities will not forget us, however much we might prefer to ignore them" (*PU*, 102).

Thus Jameson hypostatizes, in terms of the Kantian antinomies, the understanding, whose requirement of a first cause as necessary for the teleological movement of nature choreographs nature with man in a unity as only the Enlightenment could project it. Jameson has forgotten, however, the conflicting tendency of a not yet fully instrumentalized reason which cannot rest satisfied with any final cause, and whose power of analysis refuses to recognize boundaries of any sort. In his call for a return to a neo-Enlightenment historiography, Jameson can be sure of finding a ready audience, one wearied of the uncertainties of its age and of the ceaseless movement of signification. The call tantalizes us with its project of building a community capable of acting as the revolutionary subject, a project Jameson invites us to join. But finally this call must be understood as the one Lyotard warns of, the call of "a nostalgia of the whole and the one, for the reconciliation of the concept and the sensible, of the transparent and the communicable experience" (*Postmodern Condition*, 82). As such, the call is that of the Sirens, luring us with "the fantasy to seize reality"—a fantasy behind which stands, as Lyotard points out, "the desire for a return of terror."

II. Dialectic as Inoculation

In the essay, "Postmodernism, or The Cultural Logic of Late Capitalism," Jameson develops an exposition of postmodernism which attempts to deflect criticism of his project as totalizing and marxizing. The "Postmodernism" essay acknowledges and incorporates as many elements of poststructuralism as possible into a text which seems constantly to problematize its own quasi-postmarxist tenets. While this was indeed already the case with certain elements of *The Political Unconscious*, the "Postmodernism" essay is quite literally a montage of postmodernist themes. With this strategy Jameson acknowledges the historical fact of postmodernism at the phenomenological level, yet in the same essay he offers an initial sketch of its periodization, a sketch fully formulated in "Periodizing the 60s." But despite his encounter with postmodern phenomena and the attempt to come to terms with current critical and cultural tendencies, he shows himself finally unwilling or unable to draw out their implications. For his primary concern is to provide arguments for theorizing an agency capable of a modernist political praxis. It is important to discuss the method by which Jameson seeks to incorporate, or better yet, sublate, poststructuralist elements into his overall attempt at theorizing such a praxis.

A significant motivation for this strategy is the notion of the dialectic itself. Jameson tells us that "moralizing condemnations of postmodernism" must be rejected, even as he constantly gives us grounds for such judgments. He writes, for example, about the cultural critic in "postmodern space," who is "*infected* by its new cultural categories" ("PCL," 85). Furthermore, we read that in relation to "Utopian 'high seriousness,'" postmodernism can rightly be faulted for its "triviality." And most significantly, in terms of Jameson's sympathy for collectives, we are given to understand that "for political groups which seek to intervene in history . . . there cannot but be much that is deplorable and reprehensible in a cultural form of image addiction which . . . effectively abolishes any practical sense of the future and of the collective project" ("PCL," 85). This "collective project" is indeed what Jameson seeks to legitimate; one needn't strain to find Jameson's own sympathies. Yet his dialectician's sense occasionally gets the better of him when he writes: "Yet if postmodernism is a historical phenomenon, then the attempt to conceptualize it in terms of moral or moralizing judgments must be finally identified as a category-mistake" ("PCL, " 85). In spite of the fact that Jameson generally allows his epistemology to be lead by his ethics, at times at least, he is saved from his own beliefs by the recognition of a transcendental obstruction in their logic. He seems to draw back from legitimating a moralistic approach to the phenomenon of postmodernism because it is a historical fact not to be done away with. And instead, he claims to embrace it in the terms of a dialectic whose model he finds in the *Manifesto*:

> We are, somehow, to lift our minds to a point at which it is possible to understand that capitalism is at one and the same time the best thing that has ever happened to the human race, and the worst. The lapse into the more comfortable stance of the taking of moral positions is inveterate and all too human: still, the urgency of the subject demands that we make at least some effort to think the cultural evolution of late capitalism dialectically, as catastrophe and progress all together. ("PCL," 86)

Clearly, despite his druthers, Jameson recognizes something like a "categorical imperative" of historical materialism which requires us to think the postmodern dialectically, that is, both its good points and its bad must somehow be thought together.

Having stated—if not entirely fulfilled—his obligation to refrain from moralizing, Jameson attempts to expand the notion of culture to include the productions of the postmodern. He needs this expanded notion of culture badly, for under the thoroughly aestheticized regime of the theory/praxis bifurcation, the applicability of Marxist interpretative methods such as Jameson's semantic enrichment fails to be applicable to current production. Yet it's clearly trying to him to discuss Warhol's painting "Diamond Dust Shoes" in the same section as van Gogh's "Peasant Shoes." Jameson is able to do this, but not without a few nasty remarks about soup cans and tinsel.

Jameson titles this section "The Deconstruction of Expression," which he begins with the warning that if van Gogh's "often reproduced" image is not to "sink to the level of sheer decoration," he must perform something he calls in *The Political Unconscious* "semantic enrichment": "Unless that situation—which has vanished into the past—is somehow mentally restored, the painting will remain an inert object" ("PCL," 58). So it would appear that even works of high modernism face the fate of having their expression deconstructed, not just by the critical climate of the age, but merely by the passage of time itself. Jameson seeks to restore the "whole object world of agricultural misery," thus creating without acknowledging it, a text of the painting which is extended to the sociohistorical. Thus it regains its "expression," which is one of "backbreaking peasant toil, a world reduced to its most brutal and menaced, primitive and marginalized state" ("PCL," 58), a world Jameson fails to recognize as based largely in the text created by his own semantic enrichment.

Claiming to have thus restored the expression of van Gogh's painting, Jameson turns to that of Warhol, of which he says in a moment doubtful of the dialectic imperative: "I am tempted to say that it [Diamond Dust Shoes] does not really speak to us at all" ("PCL," 59). Nor does this painting seem to leave space for the viewer, he thinks, and its thematic level is one of mere fetish. Jameson thinks Warhol's shoes closer to the object world of nature than human artifact, and he likens them to shoes stacked outside an Auschwitz oven, so bereft are they of the life-world which filled them. But here we might wonder why the life-world of the Auschwitz shoes might not be semantically enriched following the same "mental" procedure he performs with "Peasant Shoes," and why Warhol's painting cannot likewise have some expressiveness restored. Jameson claims he can find no "lived context" in Warhol's paintings, nothing upon which to perform a hermeneutical operation. The reason for Jameson's impotence in the face of these shoes is not far to seek: "Warhol's work in fact turns centrally around commodification . . . " ("PCL," 60); thus it has no expression, at least none outside of the reified realm of commodity fetishization. But if commodification destroys "expression" in cultural artifacts, then only those archaically produced under precapitalist modes of production can be considered of interest with the catastrophic result that our present cultural sphere falls into the mute world of nature. Yet the production of commodities is still—perhaps even more so than in the past—*social* production which re-presents the social world out of which they derive.

The final condemnation of Warhol's work is expressed, despite his methodological intentions, by the fact that these images somehow forgo what potential expression they might have:

> the great billboard images of the Coca-cola bottle or the Campbell's Soup Can, which explicitly foreground the commodity fetishism of a transition to late capital, *ought* [Jameson's italics] to be powerful and critical political statements. ("PCL," 60)

Of course, the implication is that Warhol's work is simply another instance of what Jameson calls "image addiction." Its critical potential is read out by Jameson on the grounds that the image does not explicitly condemn or reject commodification, but merely thematizes it. It must be asked whether such a reading qualifies as "dialectical," even under Jameson's own criteria of thinking the good with the bad in a single thought. He might have spoken, for instance, of the depthless surfaces of the image as a "statement" against the re-presentation of dimensionality as the tradition of oil painting knew it. Surely the technique of silk-screening itself can be read as an "expression." Instead Warhol's surfaces are "debased and contaminated in advance by their assimilation to glossy advertising images," and their explicit, highly reflected "dis-representation" robbed of significance.

Thus the sublation of a poststructuralist notion of culture, one which expands the use of the term beyond the humanistically accepted genres, never succeeds in transforming the late modernism of Jameson's cultural prejudice. The notion of ideology as "false consciousness" is not overcome, as Jameson promises, by tolerating the mutual contradiction of dialectic, by thinking the "good" with the "bad." The analysis of culture Jameson gives in "Postmodernism" remains intolerant of the expansion of the idea of culture under postmodernism.

III. Periodization as Theoretical Prophylaxis

In these late years of the Reagan/Bush decade, we find ourselves confronted with a startling, massive public education campaign promoting, of all things, "safe sex." A virtual parade of major figures in public health in this country are publicly agitating for the use of condoms, and a Reagan appointee himself has argued before Congress, against the resistance of the media executives, for condom ads on television. Colleges and universities, meanwhile, sponsor National Condom Week, during which condoms are given away free to the nation's best and brightest. But perhaps even more surprising than the appearance of a "safe sex" campaign during the height of the Right's program for moral renewal is the appearance in the writings of Fredric Jameson, perhaps the foremost Marxist literary critic in the U.S. today, of a figure equivalent to the *cordon sanitaire*, which is of course only the late, institutional offspring of the far more ancient and venerable condom. Thus prophylaxis is mobilized not only as a technical means for fighting the spread of AIDS—an increasingly essential aspect of public health policy—but in the openly ideological sphere of hermeneutics as well, the notion of a *cordon sanitaire* appears in the guise of periodization. Health officials seek to contain the spread of the AIDS virus in a way similar to that in which Jameson's strategy of periodizing seeks to contain the dissemination of poststructuralist theory, which in its solvent form endangers the project of reviving the revolutionary subject.

By "Periodizing the 60s" Fredric Jameson thinks he can isolate, categorize, and neutralize this epistemological epidemic, the "origin" of which he finds in the 60s. Theory in its poststructuralist form thematizes the principled shifting of signification, undermines theory, and derivatively, any universalized form of meaning and purpose; such attacks decenter any locus of world-historical agency, thereby delegitimating forms of revolutionary praxis seeking justification within a logocentric framework. By periodizing the 60s within the brackets of a time-table (appended conveniently to the end of the essay), Jameson attempts to construct a *cordon sanitaire* around the decade, a prophylactic maneuver which he thinks can restrict the temporal range of application of the theoretical movements which Jameson thinks first make their appearance there, and simultaneously he restricts the period during which traditional Marxist theory, as he admits himself, was inapplicable.

In "Periodizing the 60s" Jameson writes as if he were the Surgeon General of Ideological Public Health seeking to avoid panic in a population faced with disaster. The situation, he seems to say, while serious, need not be as threatening as it appears, given appropriate counter-measures. For poststructuralism is only an ephemeral *Nachleben* of the 60s. Recognized as such, it can be safely re-contained within the figure of periodization, which functions, like the condom, to stymie the spread of contagion. Once contained, poststructuralist readings become hygienic laboratory specimens, of interest for historical research:

> There is of course no reason why specialized and elite phen-
> omena . . . cannot reveal historical trends and tendencies as
> vividly as 'real life'—or perhaps even more visibly, in their
> isolation and semiautonomy which approximates a
> laboratory situation. ("PTS," 179)

Thus would Jameson achieve the aims of theoretical prophylaxis: by the containment of non-traditional theory in a scheme of periodization which need not deny those theories nor ignore them, having put them safely in petri dishes in the refrigerator.

I do not wish these remarks to leave the impression that I think Jameson's efforts are insincere or his problems illusory. Nor do I think Jameson is maneuvering solely in order to resuscitate his own creed—a creed he openly admits is in crisis—for efforts to restore meaning and value to their pre-World War I position are occurring across the political spectrum. There is no sense in which this effort is merely a concern of the left. Much more is at stake—about this there is general agreement. The stakes are the very possibility of some legitimate form of revolutionary social praxis—whether of reformist or utopian character. Here we must be clear that we speak of the possibility of mass-movements which would be capable of transforming the status quo. These are no trifling matters, for today few remain unaware of the difficult question of mass-movements and how they are to be theorized and legitimated. But these are matters which must be scrutinized without sentimental feelings for a world which has passed by, a world in which instrumental reason successfully dissimulated a self-knowledge by which it seemed able to calculate its own future. This is not our time, and we seek to restore it only at the expense of unduly privileging the very categories we claim to examine: first and foremost a concept of meaning which can bridge the chasm between concept and sense, or in Jameson's terminology, between language and history.

In the first section of this essay, I argued that *The Political Unconscious* was an attempt to reconstitute meaning within the absolute boundaries of history, that such a historical totality was a methodological necessity for halting the shift of signification which renders meaning problematic, community impossible, and thus mass revolutionary praxis illegitimate. In "Periodizing the 60s," periodization is a substitute for totalization: it attempts the same goal, namely rendering transparent the lessons of the past, even though its scope is of a less cosmic scale than History writ large. In terms of the proportions of *The Political Unconscious*, "Periodizing the 60s" is an attempt at intervention at the level of micro structures.

I wish to sketch the opening and closing punctuation of Jameson's periodization scheme, and then address the question of signification which he hopes to contain within it. In a brief introduction he offers an apology for his periodizing concept, admitting it to be "unfashionable," and thereby forestalling any principled critique of his plan. He attempts to distance himself from earlier periodization schemes by seeking "breaks" (*coupure*: "this break is most often related to notions of the waning or extinction of the hundred year old modern movement" ("PCL," 53) which stand in some homological relationship to one another. By concentrating on these breaks he hopes to avoid what he himself criticizes as the "older organic history which sought 'expressive' unification through analogies and homologies between widely distinct levels of social life" ("PTS," 179). But mustn't we ask whether the positing of relations between the "breaks" is any less expressive than the positing of relations between unities as in the earlier model of periodization? It would seem that the homological relations between breaks just as much as those between unities are no less relationships of the logos under Jameson's description, that is, the relations he wishes to establish speak from a transcendental plane of History, a plane beyond quandaries raised by theory. We recall from *The Political Unconscious* that history, the subject of Jameson's "Periodizing the 60s," is beyond theory—it reveals itself to us only as necessity.

Out of the internal relations of history's necessities which Jameson offers, lessons unobstructed by interpretational frameworks which cannot be theorized may be read. The text is thus an unimpeachable veracity, our readings capable of verification ("PTS," 179). There is a clear statement of the value of history in Jameson's essay "The Ideology of the Text," published in 1975:

> Each moment of the past . . . has a very special sentence or judgment to pass on the uniquely reified world in which we ourselves live: and the privilege of artistic experience is to furnish something like an immediate channel through which we may experience such implicit judgments, and attain a fleeting glimpse of other modes of life. ("ITT," 235)

The "moment of the past" passes judgments or sentences in what—given "the immediate channel"—could only be a transcendental manner on the "reified" present. And by opening and closing a period of history, these judgments—untheorized and uninterpreted—provide the basis for evaluation, for meaning, and finally for revolutionary praxis.

Jameson opens the period of the 60s with the decolonization struggles in British and French Africa, specifically—on his time line—with the Battle of Algiers in 1957. The arbitrary character of this "origin" is thinly masked by the introductory sentence:

> It does not seem particularly controversial to mark the beginnings of what will come to be called the 60s in the third world with the great movement of decolonization in British and French Africa. ("PTS," 180)

But this statement is not controversial only to the extent that it is utterly arbitrary, for to speak of the beginnings of decolonization without reference to Mahatma Gandhi, the 20th Century prophet of non-violence, or the Jeffersonian idealism of Ho Chi Minh, is to emaciate any historical understanding of the struggles in Africa. The problem is only further exacerbated by the ellipsis in which Gandhi's own experiences in South Africa as a young man contribute to the goals and strategies of his later efforts on the subcontinent. Against the suppression of this arbitrariness—which I submit is a principled arbitrariness—methodological objection must be taken. No one can really avoid, much less seriously object to, periodizing as long as the procedure remains aware of its own arbitrariness. It may be that valuable readings of phenomena are gained by organizing them in this way or that. But when the essential arbitrariness of historical delineation as such is not reflected, when it is not admitted that the selection of boundaries is in all cases itself already an interpretive act, suitable only for particular and always limited tasks, schemes of periodization guise themselves as transcendental parameters which are beyond the reach of reflection and which do not admit to their social origin in an underlying act of interpretation. The result is a reflective closure which, if it is widely accepted, must finally obscure more than it can reveal.

Jameson closes the period of the 60s in an equally arbitrary way, this time, however, motivating his closure in the basis not the superstructure, namely, with the "oil crisis" of 1972-74. The title of this section, "Return of the 'Ultimately Determining Instance,'" suggests again the transcendentality of the underlying structure. Here Jameson fastens on to a notion of business cycles of thirty to fifty years, theorized by Ernest Mandel, with the end of the latest of these cycles falling around Jameson's dates. Also associated with this cycle is what Mandel calls "generalized universal industrialization" which he opposes to the idea of a post-industrial period. Jameson interprets Mandel's description of this latest transformation of the base as follows:

> Late capitalism in general (and the 60s in particular) constitute a process in which the last surviving internal and external zones of precapitalism—the last vestiges of non-commodified or traditional space within and outside

the advanced world—are now ultimately penetrated and colonized in their turn. Late capitalism can therefore be described as the moment in which the last vestiges of nature which survived on into classical capitalism are at length eliminated: namely the third world and the unconscious. The 60s will then have been the momentous transformational period in which this systemic restructuring takes place on a global scale. ("PTS," 207)

In addition to the power of his apocalyptic vision of world domination, Jameson heaps incident upon incident to prove that there is something significant enough about the years 1972-74 to warrant selecting them to close the period of the 60s: the founding of the Trilateral Commission, the fall of Allende, the Green Revolution, and Lionel Trilling's *Sincerity and Authenticity*. Despite the amassing of particular incidents and their apparent subsumtion under powerful business cycles, the closure remains in principle arbitrary, as even Jameson's appended time-line reveals, for it continues until 1976 with the death of Mao, the Soweto rebellion and the victory of *Parti Quebecois*.

The classical argument about base-superstructure relationships finds a fertile field in Jameson's essay, but his attempt to finesse this problem by means of homological relationships between breaks does not go far at all with solving what is, in the framework of his essay itself, the larger problem. Granting that the oil crisis is somehow related to the founding of the Trilateral Commission and that the withdrawal of U.S. forces from Vietnam hangs together with the role of I.T.T in Chile, all incidents cited by Jameson, why should these events in this time-frame mark the end of the 60s and not some prior or some subsequent set of events? In fact, I suggest it would not affect his argument in the least, for it is an argument which depends on closure alone. It is largely irrelevant when the closure takes place: the collapse of the Paris barricades, the break-up of the SDS or the election of Jimmy Carter, for that matter, would all serve Jameson equally well. I suspect that he would indeed be quite flexible and generous about when the 60s ended, but I'm convinced that he would be vociferous about the fact that they did.

One of the principle elements Jameson wishes to contain, a topic which recurs in many recent works, is the problem of signification. In section five of his essay on periodizing the 60s called "The Adventures of the Sign," Jameson speaks of the "reification" of the sign and the consequent mythification of the referent:

> in a first moment, reification 'liberated' the Sign from its referent, but this is not a force to be released with impunity. Now, in a second moment, it continues its work of dissolution, penetrating the interior of the Sign itself and liberating the Signifier from the Signified, or from meaning proper. This play, no longer of a realm of signs, but of pure or literal signifiers freed from the ballast of their signifieds, their former meanings, now generates a new kind of textuality in all the arts . . . and begins to project the mirage of some ultimate language of pure signifiers. ("PTS," 200)

This is one of the main effects of the 60s that Jameson is at such pains to locate and isolate—although something quite similar could be read in Benjamin's "Task of the Translator," dating from the 20s.[2] Within a closed historical period—i.e., within the petri dish in the social laboratory—Jameson as *Literaturwissenschaftler*, can safely study the phenomena or contagion and lessons can be drawn. If it gets out of the laboratory, on the other hand, the "play of signification" must result in radical skepticism toward basic premises of bourgeois culture by playing havoc with meaning. Such a threat to the ethical subject in whom Jameson vests his Humanistic faith cannot be tolerated, for with the loss of meaning goes the possibility of community and thus any form of legitimated revolutionary praxis.

To show just how inimical Jameson is to the ellipsis semiotics describes language to contain, he links the inhuman power of the unfettered signifier to capital itself:

> I will suggest that this process [of absolute self-referentiality], seemingly internal to the sign itself, requires a supplementary explanatory code, that of the more universal logic of capital itself. ("PTS," 197)

In this way the excesses of semiotics are linked with the excesses of capital, and the social control of both becomes the implicit proposal of Jameson's argument, a proposal which offers to halt the indeterminacy of meaning which paralyzes revolutionary praxis. This motivation lies very close to the surface of the concluding remarks to "Periodizing the 60s."

Jameson opens the concluding paragraph with a litany of the successes of the 60s: "an immense freeing or unbinding of social energies, a prodigious release of untheorized new forces . . . the development of new and militant bearers of 'surplus consciousness,'" most of which, he continues, do not seem "to compute in the dichotomous class model of traditional Marxism" ("PTS," 208). Here Jameson seems to endorse, as he must, the factual accomplishments of the period. But immediately this endorsement is undercut by an analogy which attempts to underscore its ephemeral nature:

> The 60s were in that sense an immense and inflationary issuing of superstructural credit; a universal abandonment of the referential gold standard; an extraordinary printing up of ever more devalued signifiers. ("PTS," 208)

Fortunately, there is a rich, wise uncle who has apparently kept his gold in a sock in the mattress and avoided the crisis of Jameson's referential inflation. Now, in the 80s, when the completed form of multinational capital stands at the door waiting to dun us, we can call on him:

> 'Traditional' Marxism, if 'untrue' during the period of a proliferation of new subjects of history, must necessarily become true again when the dreary realities of exploitation, extraction of surplus value, proletarianization and the resistance to it in the form of class struggle, all slowly reassert themselves on a new and expanded world scale, as they seem currently in the process of doing. ("PTS," 209)

Here is Jameson at his best, offering us, in the face of crisis, a tradition of interpretation which clarifies the messy problems by having them liquidated by History. One example of this might be that the untheorizable trans-class feminist movement of the 60s has now been nicely quartered into a subcultural component, lesbianism, a middle class component in NOW, and its academic component in the university system. We are not expressly told what to do about the "inflationary" flight of signification, but, we have been shown what is for Jameson, perhaps, the less treacherous option: we can dismiss it as an epiphenomenon of a by-gone age, leaving our attention focused on the new configurations of the basis which can be traditionally theorized and which can therefore provide an object for analysis capable of a reorientation to a humanistic, utopian future.

IV. A Preference for Beauty

One of Jameson's most recent articles is "Cognitive Mapping" (1987). Here we are invited to join in the task of imagining utopia, a basic element of which will be an aesthetic of cognitive mapping. One is inclined to suppose that Jameson has been reading Lyotard, for there seems to be a certain resonance between Jameson's phrase, "to produce the concept of something we cannot imagine," and Lyotard's call, quoted earlier, "to invent allusions to the conceivable which cannot be presented." Unfortunately, Jameson's preference for the beautiful over the sublime can already be read from the above injunction, for the ability *to produce* a concept of something is the very crux of Kant's distinction between the beautiful and the sublime: the resistance of something to subsumption under a concept of the faculty of understanding compels the perceiver to turn to the faculty of reason, which faculty, while capable of subsuming the thing under a totalizing concept, resists—unfortunately for Jameson—the reconciliation of this totality to sense experience. Thus an aesthetics of cognitive mapping—in spite of its gesture towards a language of the sublime—turns out to be yet another aesthetics of the beautiful. Indeed Jameson foregrounds the enlightenment character of this aesthetic by citing its tasks: "to teach, to move, to delight." Iffland and Kotzebue would certainly agree. In their efforts to train an emerging bourgeoisie how to ape the affects and sentiments of an aristocratic ethos, an aesthetics reconciling form and content, i.e., that of the beautiful, was the foundation of their craft. Here one can read what the reconciliation of concept and sense produces: art reduced to the utilitarian function of reorienting an emergent class from its traditional, late medieval social model based on craft affiliation and hierarchy to a model of the polis with a single, abstract and universalized concept of citizen.

To take this analogy a bit further, Jameson's aesthetic of cognitive mapping is charged with the explicit function of providing orientation to a postmodern space of late capitalism:

> the new space involves the suppression of distance . . . and the relentless saturation of any remaining voids and empty places, to the point where the postmodern body—whether wandering through a postmodern hotel, locked into rock sounds by means of headphones, or undergoing the multiple shocks and bombardments of the Vietnam War as Michael Herr conveys it to us—is now exposed to a perceptual barrage of immediacy from which all sheltering layers and intervening mediations have been removed. ("CMP," 351)

Jameson calls postmodernism "a new and historically original dilemma, one that involves our insertion as individual subjects into a multidimensional set of radically discontinuous realities." Yet the transition to modernity in the late Eighteenth Century is less a dilemma than the transition to postmodernity only because we know it as it is contained in narrative form, without the unrecoverable phenomenological experience of it. Consider, on the other hand, a remark of Goethe's written to Schiller in 1797:

> the location of my grandfather's house, courtyard and garden, a location which consisted of the most limited and patriarchal circumstances imaginable in which an old mayor of Frankfurt lived, was transformed by smart entrepreneurs into the most useful warehouse and marketplace. The building was, through unusual circumstances, destroyed in the bombardment and is now, largely as a pile

of rubble, still worth twice what the present owners paid
my family twelve years ago.[3]

The historical singularity ascribed to the postmodern by Jameson
is, at best, debatable, for in Goethe's amazement that "a pile of
rubble" is worth more than an intact, though modest residence is
a clear indication that the disorienting colonization of use value
by exchange value has long since left its mark. Whether or not the
greater speed characteristic of the transformations marked by
postmodernizing relative to modernizing constitutes an absolute
difference between the two, one thing seems clear: the reaction to
the transformation of social life found in an aesthetic of cognitive
mapping shares with its enlightenment analogue, an aesthetic of
the beautiful, a common reliance on totality to reorient, i.e.,
reshape subjectivity to the features of the present. For whether in
the symbol-concept of German Classicism or the cognitive
mapping of postmodern space in Jameson's proposed aesthetic, the
logos becomes sensible, concept is reconciled with experience,
and an aesthetic of the beautiful becomes the functor for the *grand
récit* of emancipation.

V. Conclusion

Jameson's texts discussed in this article all contain the
methodological prerequisites for the (re-)establishment of a
Marxist Humanism. From the orthography in which Jameson
regularly capitalizes history and utopia to the theoretical
adroitness with which he maneuvers the totalizing perspective of
a modernist philosophy of history into "postmodern space," these
texts promise purpose, meaning, and program. The repudiation of
such promises must jar Right Reason and offend all sensibility for
the injustices of the present out of which the utopian takes its
power. And yet the incestuous relations between reason and
utopia have themselves no claim to innocence, for the instrumental form in which reason presently resides leaves none of its
consorts unblemished. The postmodern "pathology of communication" would be barred from utopia and only wordless signals,

freed of indeterminacy and reflexively instantiating disembodied reason, could take its place. This is the utopia reason has shown us already: in speechless monasticisms and in the compulsion of transubjective feeling of the beautiful in an enlightenment Kant. I suggest neither instance recommends itself. Rather than laying the foundation for a millennial kingdom in which reason banishes force, the present moment—as moments of upheaval before it— offers us the rare prospect of revealing force itself as but one of a myriad of reason's own guises. We do not know what "lines of escape" the pathology of our present discursive practices may reveal; even so the reactive path which claims to (re-)construct meaning and (re-)establish community is all too well known. After the experience of the 20th Century, the unpresentable cannot hold more terror for us than the known; the unpresentable has become the salvational, if only through default.

Notes

1. In this work, *The Liberal Tradition in America*, Hartz describes the effect of transplanting liberalism from its European environment to an America without the same established feudal structure. One consequence of this transplantation is the creation in America of a kind of liberal absolutism in which any critique can be tolerated so long as it does not come from outside the system.

2. In Benjamin's essay, there seems to be something like a "reine Sprache" toward which all empirical languages move. This inference is justified by his assumption that all languages desire to express the same thing.

3. Quoted from Heinz Schlaffer, *Faust Zweiter Teil: die Allegorie des 19. Jahrhunderts*. (Stuttgart: J. B. Metzler Verlag), p. 15. The translation is mine.

Poststructuralist Politics—
Towards a Theory of Coalition

R. Radhakrishnan
University of Massachusetts

"Ideology" we now know is no more a dirty word. It is no more that pejorative epithet that we apply to the adversary while congratulating ourselves on our scientific objectivity and disinterestedness. We are all aware that all theories are profoundly and constitutively ideological. But this awareness precipitates an entire range of questions and issues. If ideology is that authorizing and legitimizing horizon that enables and accommodates certain kinds of "meaning" and "value-production," and, if, furthermore, this horizon can only be posited *aprioristically* as a kind of moral, political, and categorical imperative, we are then faced with the problem of the incommensurability of the "descriptive" with the "axiological," and analogously, of the "theoretical" with the "ethical" and the "political." My purpose in this paper is to bring into mutual focus Fredric Jameson's brand of Marxist theory and the poststructuralist critique of "identity" and its consequent advocacy of "difference." It seems to me that there are interesting similarities and divergences between these two bodies of thought, and both stand to gain from a critique by the other. Both address a number of common issues and themes with great polemical skill and intensity. But when it comes to crucial choices and determinations, Jameson's critical theory and poststructuralism begin to diverge significantly and move beyond reconciliation—in spite of

Jameson's diligent efforts to contain this divergence. I shall be arguing that the poststructuralist project is something "other" than Jameson reads it to be and that contemporary realities themselves are marked by a certain poststructuralist "difference."

Poststructuralist thought has done an impressive job of unmasking the ideological underpinnings of systems of thought and uncovering the "will to power" that underlies all theory that is inevitably exclusionary and hegemonic. Chastened by the realization that human civilization is coextensively a document of barbarism, poststructuralist thought eschews, by way of what Jacques Derrida terms "protocols of vigilance" the enunciation of any new truths, originary principles, and a new axiomatics ("The University in the Eyes of its Pupils"). Instead, it devotes itself indefatigably to the task of deconstruction and a negative *écriture*. It has to, by design, fall short of an affirmative programmatic, for, the very structure of affirmation is ineluctably complicitous with those very repressive modalities and algorithms that deconstruction seeks to put in question.

But, if it is to remain consistent with its own findings, deconstruction has to come to terms with the insight that its own critical or micrological operations too are, and can be, only ideological. Should deconstruction then assume responsibility for its own anti-ideological ideology and thus project its own identity in the form of an intentional trajectory, or should it radicalize itself as the ultimate unwilling of the will and opt out of all worldly intentionality? To state this differently, now that ideology-as-such has been exposed, is there a difference between being self-consciously ideological and ideological in the name of some transcendent Truth? In theory, there seem to be two possible alternatives: 1) the kind of theory that believes in itself in the name of an overarching ideology and consequently identifies and valorizes itself, and 2) the kind that would rather exist and function as "pure difference" without intentions of shoring up for itself any kind of identity, authority, or domain. The latter choice is exemplary of Derridean deconstruction and is altogether admirable in its single minded resistance to "authority" and official accommodation. And yet, the question remains: what does or can it mean to espouse "difference" auto-syntactically, i.e., in a semantic and historical vacuum? Are not all acts of advocacy and partisanship always "in the name of?" And moreover, how does one advocate "difference" intransitively without at the same time believing in it, and if it is indeed a matter of choice based on belief, have we not already capitulated to the pre-scriptive discourse of "value?"

Fredric Jameson, more seriously than most other Marxist theorists, has negotiated in good faith with the massive aporias and indeterminacies of poststructuralist thought, but having done so, he still feels the need to posit a Utopian (and, in his case, Marxist) hermeneutic horizon that in effect disarms the radicality of the poststructuralist threat to the Marxist enterprise. Jameson is in an intriguing situation where he cannot but take into account the reality of the poststructuralist and the deconstructive intervention and at the same time not credit that reality with the capacity to decenter his own Marxist sense of destiny and anchorage. His identity as "Marxist" also poses another problem, i.e., the problem of demonstrating both the propriety and the exemplarity of the Marxist model *vis à vis* reality. Jameson then has to argue concurrently both for the systemic superiority of the Marxist hermeneutic horizon and the "referential" and interpretive adequacy of this horizon. In other words, Jameson is constrained by his own affirmative Marxian hermeneutics to disallow the indeterminate decenterings that different versions of poststructuralist thought offer by way of political and theoretical radicality. The question then clearly arises: what will it take to disengage Jameson from his Marxist moorings, and if the answer is "nothing will," then are not his efforts to galvanize, on behalf of Marxism, possibilities for auto-critique condemned not to take that step that poststructuralism at its very best contemplates?— the step beyond "identity" and semantic closure? Also, may not Jameson's project be interpreted as a commitment not to the "political unconscious" but to the rectitude of the Marxist model of the political unconscious?

My suggestion is that we take Jameson's concern seriously but at the same time be wary of a certain totalizing, evangelical, and apologetic tendency in his rhetoric. For, in an attempt to secure the political horizon—i.e., the Marxist determination of the political horizon (a determination that Jameson will neither relativize nor problematize)—Jameson renders the processes of critical epistemology heteronomous and subservient to an essentialist macrology. He has to resort to 1) the concept of "a single, unfinished plot" for all humanity, and 2) to a hermeneutic value of interiority that, in spite of a certain secularization, is still a return to an allegorical and monocentered consciousness. Both these moves are inherently (in spite of Jameson's intentions) quite repressive; for the single narrative can be realized only through a monologic determination of multiple and heterological realities, and the very structure of an allegorical hermeneutics, that Jameson invokes so confidently, belies history-as-process.

The notion of "allegory as interpretive code" constitutes a definitive and authoritative scission between "history" and the "meaning of history." Though Jameson takes great effort to acknowledge and incorporate the many poststructuralist critiques of teleology and interiority, he is fundamentally uneasy with the idea of producing what Foucault would call "the history of the present" and the radical valorization of "discontinuity" that such a counter-mnemonic production would demand. His critical epistemology finds its resonance within the binary structures of immanence and transcendence. Given this binary axiology, to historicize is to rescue history from the meaninglessness of immanence by way of the morality of an allegorical semantics. What Jameson forgets, in spite of his academically cultivated sensitivity to poststructuralist formulations of discontinuity and difference, is that the allegorical code can only be "always-already" unmastered, if not altogether question-begging. For, if the code is part of what is to be explained, then it can have no interpretive authority; but on the other hand, if the code is at a panoptic distance from what it is supposed to explain, then it tends to explain away, or, at the very least, do epistemic violence to its object. In other words, allegories succeed only as arbitrary interventions of hermeneutic authority that will not, by definition, contextualize or historicize themselves. The allegorical mode functions within a plenary and hierarchic space where sub-spaces are acknowledged but only to be sublated within a totalized semantic horizon. It is only by concealing its own contingent perspectivity that allegory gains its exemplarity as universal trope.

When Jameson argues that "allegorical narrative signifieds are a persistent dimension of literary and cultural texts precisely because they reflect a fundamental dimension of our collective thinking and our collective fantasies about history and reality" (*PU*, 34), it is not clear what universal and anthropological Subject of history is speaking in the voice of the "collective we." The one collective allegory that Jameson prefers in the name of a sharable progressive history ironically disallows the realities of different and globally unequal histories. Though in a footnote to his *The Political Unconscious* Jameson does talk approvingly of "alliance politics," he is deeply distrustful of modes of theory and practice that are anything but identitarian. The heterogeneous fall-out ushered in by feminisms, ethnic movements, gay and lesbian politics, non-Western, subaltern and post-colonialist elaborations is still subsumable, by Jameson's logic, under the capacity of dialectical thought to think "identity" and "difference" together. It is not surprising then that Jameson's versions of poststructuralism do not take seriously those aspects of poststructuralist thought that run counter to the Marxian axiology. Jameson fails to perceive that a number of these poststructuralist projects (deconstruction, schizo-analysis, a counter-menmonic genealogy, for example) are concerned with transforming not just the "contents" but the very "forms" of history. It is, for example, quite misleading when Jameson claims that "the thrust of *Anti-Oedipus* is, to be sure, very much in the spirit of the present work" (*PU*, 22). Nothing could indeed be more different from Jameson's macropolitics than the micropolitical analysis of desire that Deleuze and Guattari are interested in; as a matter of fact, they perceive the thrust of their own work as decidedly anti-Marxist, and yet Jameson thinks nothing of appropriating them to his evangelical and anthropological Marxism.[1] Jameson's globally allegorical Marxism is incapable of calling into question its own "high seriousness."

This epistemological/cognitive failure on the part of Jameson's critical Marxism has serious political implications too. Thus, when Jameson, with the best of intentions, and what I

would call a rare, inaugural hermeneutic generosity, begins
talking about Third World literatures and nationalism out there in
far-off places, he ends up, quite inevitably, committing an act of
aggression.[2] It is not Jameson's intentionality that is at fault here,
but the model that he in all good faith follows. The allegorical
mode in assuming a putative one world just fails or forgets to raise
the question of "who is speaking, why, and on whose behalf." We
can perceive a strong conflictual tension here in Jameson's
thought between two aspects of the "one, unfinished" Utopian
plot: on the one hand, the progressive "non-closure" of a radical
Utopian thought and, on the other hand, the magisterial
imposition of the value-free facticity of the one world.[3] This
tension is the "unconscious" of Jameson's own theory; for,
nowhere does he explicitly raise the issue of global exemplarity
versus perspectivity or that of representation versus post-
representational politics.[4] What is missing in Jameson's critical
thinking is a more nuanced and differentiated awareness of the
mutual interplay of deferral and nihilation between regional and
global trajectories or impulses. Unfortunately then Jameson ends
up dehistoricizing the very constituencies that he had set out to
befriend and understand.[5]

My diagnosis of this lapse is simply that it is in the nature of
Marxist thought to assume that its revolutionary subject is
simultaneously the global subject of history. Also, Marxism as the
expression of an adversarial and revolutionary subject-position all
too easily arrogates to itself the authority of the *Subject Position*
of all insurgent subject-positions; that is, it sets the agenda as
though it were the quintessential and totalized expression of all
possible and potential subsets of opposition. Jameson's own
response to the poststructuralist threat is merely to restate the
primacy of the Marxist semantic/political horizon. He also credits
Marxist theory with the ability to axiomatize its own
perspectivity as *P*erspectivity and to historicize its own identity
without any damage to its primary or originary historicity.[6]
Jameson sees no reason, historical or structural, to question the
efficacy of the Marxist model. In sharp contrast to such faith, we
have the anxiety of a Michel Foucault who, although appreciative
in general of what global Marxism has achieved as a model, finds

it politically more relevant to question the mastery of Marxism. And it is interesting that Foucault should pose this unease in terms of the politics of location. Foucault talks about geographic and geopolitical discontinuity and articulates the fear "that as soon as we struggle against exploitation, the proletariat not only leads the struggle but also defines its targets, its methods, and the places and instruments for confrontation; and to ally oneself with the proletariat is to accept its positions, its ideology, and its motives for combat" ("Intellectuals and Power," 216). Foucault concedes that struggles, whatever their regional autochthony, need to enter into a progressive alliance with the proletariat, but is at the same time wary of a total or preemptive identification with the perspectivity of the proletariat. Foucault's concern here is with "difference" and he is solicitous of the need each subject-position has to enter history in its own specific way.[7]

Foucault's critique of Marxian avant-gardism and scientificity raises a number of fundamental questions concerning the nature of "the world out there," our modes of critical perception and paradigms of thought, and the relationality between the two.[8] How are we to get a world picture by way of the internal and systemic adequacy of the paradigm that we have settled for?[9] Is the world one or not one? What is the ratio of the interplay between "identity" and "difference?" Are we to assume that differences are to be subsumed within a given identity or are there as many versions of "identity" as there are points of view that present such versions? At the present world-historical conjuncture, is there a painful incommensurability between the epistemological, theoretical, and cognitive realization of unbounded heterogeneity and the political need for collective, unified and solidary action? The borderlines where Jameson's Marxism adjoins poststructuralist thought are fraught with the intensity of these questions. As we juxtapose these two bodies of theory, we are immediately aware that their mutual relationship is in the form of a challenge. Jameson challenges poststructuralism to generate a genuine macropolitics from its micropolitical operations and protocols. Underlying this dare is Jameson's calm conviction that it is not possible to generate such a change, for there is nothing "semantic" at the level of the "micro-" that can make possible the qualitative transformation from the "micro-" to the level of the "macro-." Jameson's assumption is that one needs the apriorism of macrology to set in motion a directed micrological praxis. He also dares poststructuralist thought to find a "politics of difference": here again, Jameson's tacit certitude is that such a politics is not feasible and, indeed, that politics is still done the old-fashioned way despite the second-degree complications introduced by theories of difference or deconstruction. The poststructuralist challenge to Jameson is to reconcile the orthodoxies and verities of Marxism with the dynamics of the "post-" and to demonstrate that Marxism is somehow the long *dureé* that contains the politics of location as well as the problematic of the "post-political."[10] The very fact that there are possibilities for mutual interrogation between poststructuralism and Jameson's Marxism points up a potential common space where the similarities and the dissimilarities between the two can be played out.[11]

I would now like to indicate selectively that common space even as I suggest a number of active differences between these two projects. In general, it would seem that these two endeavors are not all that dissimilar in their "ends." It is at the level of the modality of "the means" that crucial differences emerge. In Jameson's case, "the ends" are a form of the *telos* that guards against "the immanentist fetishization" of "the means"; whereas a number of poststructuralist practices, Derridean deconstruction and Foucauldian resistance and poststructuralist-Marxist-feminism in particular,[12] seem concerned in changing the very "means" and thereby the very nature of the so called "ends." I begin then with the space known as "ideology." I would like to examine how in different but related ways Jameson's affirmative hermeneutic procedures, such as his ideology-critique, and the energies of deconstructive thinking take on the problems of false consciousness and mythified centralities. It seems to me that what is at stake in this encounter is the very status of "affirmation," and, with it, the politics of a post-deconstructive horizon.[13]

The ineluctable first question is: how then do we deal with ideology? Are we "always-already" co-opted by ideology, and how do we empower critiques of ideology if the very structure of empowerment is an ideological effect;[14] and, furthermore, are there strategies to effect the disengagement of modes of libertarian and emancipatory truth from ideological interpellations? The critic is caught up simultaneously in multiple economies and multiple temporalities: knowledge as ideology, the critique of knowledge-as-ideology, and the meta-critique of the primary critique. And, if the critic's concern is not merely the infinite regress of an epistemological recursiveness—but the effect of such a recursiveness on the ethics of choice (i.e., how does one adjudicate among different, and often mutually exclusive ideologies)—the problem mounts in complexity. Now that it is untenable to equate "the good" with the non-ideological and "the bad" with ideology, we are left with a different problem: what is good, and what is bad ideology? How do we make the choice? What is significant and irksome is that the terms "good" and "bad" survive the operations of the critique. The problem is further exacerbated by the non-availability of an inclusive or meta-narrative or field theory to help us in the task of adjudication (cf. Lyotard's *Postmodern Condition*). How do we legitimate our choice of one ideology over another? Is that choice somehow incontrovertible in its existential / experiential / historical authenticity? If the legitimacy of this choice is determined outside the actual operations of critical theory, how should critical theory formalize its relationship to an axiological determination over which it has no jurisdiction? How well can critical theory deal with the "interestedness" of its own formation and genealogy even as it envisions a "trans-interested" production of knowledge-as-lived reality (see Habermas, *Knowledge and Human Interests*)? Analogously, how best can such a theory (of whatever persuasion or provenance) make instrumental use of its own categories of analysis, interpretation, and intervention without degenerating into what Nietzsche would call the self-adequating narcissism of methodology?[15]

The choices seem to be: 1) Having assumed our perspectivity in the form of a suitable ideology, we proceed to unpack and elaborate a certain kind of critical *praxis*, which is to say that once we have assumed our macropolitical stance we will not submit that stance to a recursive analysis. This option results in the universalization or naturalization of one's own perspectivity. 2) The critical theorist takes up responsibility for a determinate ideological position but with an awareness that no one ideological perspective is privileged or putative, and, therefore, remains open to contestations by opposing political and theoretical positions. 3) The critic assumes responsibility for her choice but at the same time does not abdicate the second-order responsibility of submitting the "correctness" of her position to a deconstructive critique whose legitimacy is not necessarily complicitous with the macrology or the *telos* of the critic's primary commitment.

The first option is an old-fashioned evangelism that sanctions its own didactic claims in the name of some natural and trans-historic truth. The second choice acknowledges real oppositions and conflicts but is incapable of accounting for qualitative differences among ideologies or offering reasons why one is better or more ethical than the other. In this battlefield where each clashing ideology is internally self-consistent and thus generative of its own truth claims, the winner, in the absence of a magisterial *nomos*, is literally the one who wins. The contestation for hegemony is exactly and quite literally what it is: a Nietzschean arena where dominance is its own explanation. And besides, there is very little translatability of meanings and valences across systems; nor are there possibilities of persuasion across boundaries, for, in spite of relativism, each ideological system reproduces within the relativist *episteme* the dream of its own absolute authority. The third option is, generally speaking, the poststructuralist option with its strong emphasis on a deconstructive *rationale*. According to this *rationale*, the affirmative project is "always-ready" called into question by its own inadequacy or potential errancy.[16] To state this more programmatically, the deconstructive critique will have to commit itself to a contingent identitarian politics even as it engages in the namelessly permanent revolution of the "post-identical."[17] A basic feature of the deconstructive critique is an unavoidable "doubleness" whereby the critique operates parasitically and "supplementally" (as in, for example, Derrida's forumlation of the "dangerous supplement") and disallows the progressivist desire to abstract away the reality of affirmative modes from the temporality of their antecedent modes.

This critique, like the dialectical method, is relational in its operation; but it goes a step beyond by valorizing the epistemological "break" from the past as a form of inter-temporality that is neither purely negative nor entirely affirmative. The desire or the force of a differential-deconstructive thinking is to enfranchize and historicize the liminal temporality of the "post-" beyond the authority of the dialectic which, even in the hands of an Adorno, in the ultimate instance, has to follow the pre-given Marxian macrology. Differential thought on the other hand loosens up the very notion of determination, i.e., it enables possibilities of multiple and uneven determinations as well as impure and contradictory interruptions (see Spivak, *In Other Worlds*) and is not afraid of employing *bricolage* and of being redefined and constituted by this very *bricolage*. Strange as it may sound, my claim is that a differential critical thinking has greater potential than an ideologically programmatic thought to realize and activate that exilic or marginal space characterized so eloquently by Edward Said as the space "between Culture and System." The poststructuralist attack on identity and totality realizes a) the need *not to* privilege any one system or mode of intervention as the authentic mode, and b) the urgent need to open up what I call an actively "null space" where different constituencies and histories and emergences could negotiate with one another without fear of mutual pre-emption or betrayal. The attack on totality is thus not an end in itself; it is a means to a coalitional politics.

Jameson is quick to recognize the importance of the poststructuralist assault on totality, but his reading of these repudiations of totality is insistent on resuscitating the totality. Thus, when he talks about "difference," "dissemination," "heterogeneity," "Deleuze's conception of the schizophrenic text and Derridean deconstruction," he is really celebrating the power of a pre-existing totality to withstand and nullify these repudiations. This is what Jameson has to say of these philosophies after having considered their impact on the totality:

> We will therefore suggest that these are second-degree or
> critical philosophies, which reconfirm the status of the
> concept of totality by their very reaction against it; such a
> movement is worked out even more explicitly in Adorno's
> 'negative dialectic,' with its counteraffirmation—'the whole is
> the untrue'—in which the classical dialectic seeks, by biting
> its own tail, to deconstruct itself. (*PU*, 53-54)

I think Jameson is absolutely right to point out some of the
similarities between deconstruction and Adorno's "negative
dialectic," a connection which Derrideans in their apostolic
enthusiasm to establish the singularity of Derrida, all to often
forget to make. But having said this I would still maintain that
Jameson's reading of these "second-degree critical philosophies" is
wildly off the mark. To put it more simply, Jameson's argument
that these philosophies "reconfirm the status of the concept of
totality by their very reaction against it," is no more convincing
than the theist's contention that atheism merely confirms the
reality of god, for don't we all know that the very proposition
"there is no god" contains the term "god" and *ergo* demonstrates
the ontology of god. Here, I believe, Jameson is not giving us an
argument; he is merely asserting his bias and demonstrating to us
how passionately he wishes that no critical philosophy be capable
of unseating the totality. If nothing by definition can question the
totality, then, by Jove, nothing will.

Jameson's reading here misreads the force of desire behind
these critical philosophies. That indeed they desire to have
nothing more to do with the sclerotic authority of the dialectic or
that there may be a different sense of constituency driving these
philosophies is virtually unthinkable to him. Paradoxical as it
may seem, it is Jameson, with his strong belief in "historicizing,"
who will not participate in historicizing the dialectic itself to "its"
second degree; for such participation may damage the dialectic
beyond repair. It is no wonder that he contains the energies of
these critical philosophies as epiphenomenal, secondary, and, in
some sense, even unreal. By effecting a clear-cut division between
primary orders and critical orders he creates a scenario where the
"totality" is made to seem as inherent in reality and therefore

beyond all critical interrogation. This "totality" must be preserved at all cost, for, it is "real," and no maverick or upstart thought can dislodge it or question its status. What we are witnessing here is the essentialization of the dialectic—the ideological shoring up of the dialectic as truth, as *its truth*. The confident reference to Adorno seems to suggest that all of this "second-degree" stuff has been done before. The omniscience of the dialectic cannot be "gone beyond."

My criticism of Jameson's reading of poststructuralism is two-fold: 1) Jameson merely asserts his bias when he argues for the anterior reality of the totality. He does so because he has to; his commitment to his teleology will not have it any other way. He thus negates the very possibility, epistemic, theoretical, and historical, of de-totalized visions of accounting for reality. 2) Scotomized by the ideological plenitude of his own vision, he cannot see that the rhetoric of totality is the effect and not the cause of perspectivity. He shores up absolute authority for Marxism by denying it its own specificity as well as historicity. I will merely say that this is a classic case of a defensive reaction on the part of Marxism whose monopolistic hold on revolutionary subject formation is being challenged seriously by other discourses based on gender, sexuality, ethnicity, and the politics of location. Marxism cannot but acknowledge the historical reality of these diverse determinations, and yet, it cannot easily let go of the desire to prolong its role as *primus inter pares*. Indeed, there are contemporary realities undreamt of by Marxist philosophy, but Marxist philosophy, to remain *itself* has to lay claims to a long *dureé* and thereby annex all formations within its proper semantic horizon. It is, if anything, quite characteristic of the omniscience of Marxism to be aware of all developments, but such an awareness is not easily influenced or transformed by the developments. Instead, this awareness seeks to claim these developments as its own. This take-over typically is in the name of political authenticity.[18] A case in point is the passage in *The Political Unconscious* where Jameson emphasizes the point "that the process of totalization outlined in our opening chapter offers no way out of this 'the labor and suffering of the negative,' but must necessarily be accompanied by it, *if the process is to be authentically realized"* (*PU*, 284, my emphasis). This certainly is sound relational and dialectical thinking, but it is also teleological thinking at its very best: dialectics without "difference." The "authentic" beckons from afar and insists on its self-presence: the reference to "process" is half-hearted. The insight of the "authentic" is co-extensive with a blindness to the possibility that "the realization of the authentic" and the dynamic of process may be mutually exclusive and/or incommensurable.

A word here is in order about the nature and function and formation of "ordinal" discourses in the production of knowledge, particularly since Jameson and poststructuralist theorists are interested in the notion of the critique. The important question is: How do critiques and meta-critiques acquire their valence and what is their status within the hierarchized epistemic space of knowledge? As critical theory becomes conscious of itself as a critique of knowledge, it secedes from its position of explanatory or exegetic secondarity and establishes itself as an autonomous interpretive order and sets in motion an ordered sequence of discourses that were never *in* the original body of knowledge.[19] We might say that each order generates *its* second order formation, but in doing so loses its own identity and sense of self-mastery. It becomes profoundly vulnerable to the logic of the supplement;[20] the second order does not belong to the prior order any more, for, the prior order has no binding claim or jurisdiction on "its" second order. The concept of the supplemental series radically re-proposes the identity-difference nexus (see Foucault's "Theatrum Philosophicum" for an eloquent reading of Deleuze's philosophy of "difference and repetition"). By demonstrating that the so-called putative identity is nothing but the effect produced by the structure of iterability, the logic of the supplement de-recognizes the authority of "the antecedent," of *antecedence-as-such*. This does not result in the denial of history, as politically oriented critics of deconstruction are fond of claiming. What it does result in is the denial of a particular kind of history (with its absolute trust in immutable "befores" and irrefragable "afters" and teleological narratives) and its hegemonic hold over the signification of reality. The term "post-historical" would refer then not to a glib transcendence of history but to a complex

second-order questioning of received historiographic imperatives[21] and the revisionism that is to be enabled by such an
interrogation.[22] Whereas Jameson's critical narrative belongs to a
proper / centered / official history, a deconstructive history is an
orphaned or a maverick project.[23]

Derrida's grammatology seeks to locate, enliven, and
perennially maintain this orphan status in opposition to logocentric inscriptions of power, belonging, and home (cf. Spivak's
"Introduction"). Being orphan to Derrida is a form of weak-phil-
osophizing that in reality has far-reaching subversive capability.
Writes Derrida:

> That status of this orphan, whose welfare cannot be assured
> by any attendance or assistance, coincides with that of a
> *graphein* which, being nobody's son at the instant it
> reaches inscription, scarcely remains a son at all and no
> longer *recognizes* its origins, whether legally or morally. In
> contrast to writing, living *logos* is alive in that it has a
> living father (whereas the orphan is already half dead), a
> father that is *present, standing* near it, behind it, within it,
> sustaining it with his rectitude, attending it in person in his
> own name. (*Dissemination*, 77)

The strength of the orphan lies in her/his[24] ability to *de-recognize
not the reality but the authority of origins*. If we do not make this
vital distinction between "the reality of origins" and "the
authority of origins," we will end up repeating the lame and
careless criticism that deconstruction is ahistorical. As we look
critically at the passage quoted above, we can discern a number of
substantive differences between Jameson's ideology critique and
Derridean grammatology. Whereas Jameson perceives no
difficulty in contributing to the history of identity, Derrida pits
his "writing" in opposition to the regime of identity. Derrida's
project has a great deal in common with Walter Benjamin's
commitment to "brushing history against the grain": both these
endeavors take seriously into account the reality that "there is no
document of civilization which is not at the same time a
document of barbarism" ("Theses on the Philosophy of History,"
256). In contrast, Jameson is persuaded by the ability of the

dialectic to correct itself in the name of a correct, just, and desirable identity. (It is not surprising that Benjamin does not play a vital role in Jameson's framework).

The graphein or the "orphan" is what is missing in Jameson's account of the dialectic. To Jameson, the dialectic process is both the historicity of process as well as the *telos in the name of which* the process is to be "authentically realized." Derrida's position, however, is quite different; he has a quarrel with the category of the "name" in all its omni-historical generality. The *graphein* is that differe(a)nce whose namelessness shakes up the authority of all systems of thought, the dialectic included. To put it reductively, the normative progressivist in Jameson believes in the legality of "names" and in the reliable adjudication between "right / proper / correct names" and "improper / wrong / incorrect names." In other words, Jameson does not object to the history of the *name-as-such*. On the contrary, Derrida's attack is not merely on the oppression brought about by any one name but on the very economy of "naming." Derrida, quite literally, de-capitates the "subject" (not any particular subject such as "man," "woman," "the proletariat," etc., but the very structure of "the subject" in historiography). In this sense, Derrida's practice resembles Althusser's category of "process without Subject or goal(s)."

In all fairness to Jameson, he does take into account Althusser's structuralist redefinition of Marxism; but there is a point beyond which he will not go. Thus, the Althusserian "anomie of process" will not work for Jameson because, to Jameson, the Althusserian formula comes across as a dangerous celebration or fetishization of immanence. Jameson would rather have "the dialectic as process" *centered* in the dream of total and identical realization. In other words, "the motor of history" has to be yoked to a trans-historical terminus which is the transcendent "subject" of the motor. Not that Jameson is disinterested in possibilities of a permanent revolution. His interest is in removing the notion of the permanent revolution to an absolute distance; i.e., he will not allow it to interrupt (or be inmixed with) the positivity of the agenda on hand. From Jameson's perspective, the idea of the dialectic alienated or "differentiated" or "deferred" from *its truth* accords to "process" a kind of micrological open-endedness that is in direct semantic conflict with the notion of "authentic realization." Similarly, the capacity of the structures of interpretation to secede from structures of meaning, and, the potential that "supplemental" philosophies have to actualize themselves "intransitively" are dire threats to the dialectical regime of meaning. Strangely enough then, it is the anti-structuralist in Jameson (although he is altogether convincing in his critique of structuralism on other grounds) that will come in the way of his appreciation that what the poststructuralists are proposing is a second-order transformation. Their concerns are not with "meaning," but with the "meaning" of meaning (not just "history," but the "history" of history). Jameson's valorization of history as primarily content and only epiphenomenally as structure/form results in his conviction that history is essentially semantic and centered. The potentially insurrectionary possibilities of structure are immediately devalued and the semantic horizon begins to loom more and more definitively.

Unlike Jameson's dialectical critique that accommodates all manner of contradiction, negativity, and second-order uprisings in incrementation of its own centered authority, the Derridean critique takes a very different path. The aim of the Derridean critique is to "show up" totality and demonstrate the incoherence of the center. Derrida's diagnosis runs thus:

> The center is at the center of the totality, and yet, since the center does not belong to the totality (is not part of the totality), the totality *has its center elsewhere*. The center is not the center. The concept of centered structure— although it represents coherence itself, the condition of the *episteme* as philosophy or science—is contradictorily coherent. And as always, coherence in contradiction expresses the force of desire. *The concept of centered structure is in fact the concept of a play based on a fundamental ground*, a play constituted on the basis of a fundamental immobility and reassuring certitude, which itself is beyond the reach of free play. (*Writing and Difference*, 279, my emphasis)

It must be remembered that Derrida's reading of the center is produced in opposition to the structuralist *episteme* and its notion of centered structures. It is precisely by taking structuralism seriously that Derrida is able to submit it to "its own" second-order critique and thereby destabilize its truth claims. But before getting into the nature of the decentered critique, I would like to digress a little and say something about the center in general.

The critique of the center as organizing principle brings together a number of poststructuralist thinkers who in many ways are dissimilar: Althusser with his notion of "excentration," Derrida's interrogation of the center, the Deleuzian "meaning-event" in search of a decentralized historiography, and Foucault's whole-hearted endorsement of Deleuze. The opposition to the center is often specific as in the repudiations of *phallo*-centrism, *photo*-centrism, *phono*-centrism, *ethno*-centrism, *logo*-centrism, *andro*-centrism, *gyno*-centrism, etc. Often, the contestation is indeterminate and algebraic as in the quarrel with *centrism as such.* The underlying conviction is that the *dureé* of the center is politically and theoretically bankrupt. The center is neither real nor authoritative. As Derrida shows us, the trope of the center effects its reality as a reality of power and control. Reality seems centered only because a certain system of thought has made it mandatory that we think in centrist terms. Just as Foucault demonstrates, with the help of Bentham's Panopticon, the ease with which hegemonic regimes impose their contours on reality and thus occlude the possibility of other modes of living, Derrida argues how a centrist morphology of philosophy developed and ideologized over two millennia has made it virtually impossible for thought to think in other forms and patterns. Quite literally, we have been mystified into believing that "if the center will not hold, mere anarchy will be loosed upon the world" (Yeats). The Derridean critique consequently has to maintain a delicate balance between asserting on the one hand that the history of the center has been real and contending on the other hand that this very history of truth is, to follow Nietzsche, the history of a lie. The contemporary moment accordingly is the orphan who in inheriting the *dureé* of the past, in fact, disinherits it through the use of "a double gesture, according to a unity that is both systematic and in and of itself divided—a double writing, that is, a writing that is in and of itself multiple" (Derrida, *Positions*, 41).

This double-writing or this double-science is characterized by an impure or liminal temporality, that is, it is not centered in its own proper temporality. It quite simply calls into question the "center" and the notion of "propriety." The "double writing" as critique "plays" with the center thus de-pedestalizing the center and historicizing the center back into the play. The center itself is in play. Unlike a centered critique that acquiesces in the normativity of the center, a decentered critique empowers critical reflexivity to deconstruct "that which it reflects upon." Both Derrida and Foucault (in his famous "analytic of finitude" in *The Order of Things*), albeit in different ways, are invested in the task of enabling recursive thinking to go beyond the legalities of beginnings and ends. I will just mention in passing that there is an analogous moment in contemporary mathematical theory: the concept of axiological undecidability and systemic incompleteness as postulated by Kurt Gödel. This theory, in short, proves that no system of proofs is complete and demonstrates that the correctness of any axiom is undecidable within the order of complexity opened up by that axiom; it is decidable only at the next order of complexity, *ad infinitum*. This problematic proliferation of recursivity towards infinite regress which Derrida and Foucault find exhilarating and politically valuable is, if anything, pre-empted and/or aborted by Jameson's macropolitical ideology. Derrida and Foucault, despite their differences, are in revolt against the law of the Same and the Identical—i.e., they are interested in forms of alterity and heterogeneity repressed by identical thought. Jameson's investment in centered dialectic, on the contrary, results in an omniscient single model that takes care of and speaks on behalf of all possible differences and heterogeneities. Jameson does not ever deny the reality of multiple histories, constituencies, and trajectories: what he does deny is the possibility that "difference" can be practiced differentially and heterogeneity theorized heterogeneously. Jameson's critical thinking requires an identitarian umbrella.

Otherness, difference, subject-position, and the critique of representation: these are some issues that do not quite make it to

Jameson's agenda except through a process of reformed representation. With these themes in mind, I now turn to Foucault and his particular manner of enfranchising "difference." I have attempted elsewhere[25] a critique of Foucault from the point of view of Gramscian Marxism; but for my purposes here, I will be in strategic agreement with Foucault in opposition to Jameson's canonical Marxism. Foucault in strong support of Deleuze, dares thought to conceive "of difference differentially, instead of searching out the common elements underlying difference. Then difference would disappear as a general feature that leads to the generality of the concept, and it would become—a different thought, the thought of difference—a pure event. As for repetition, it would cease to function as the dreary succession of the identical, and would become displaced difference" ("Theatrum Philosophicum," 182). To liberate "difference" from its secondary and heteronomous status within the logic of Identity, and to inaugurate a "different" history—that is Foucault's project as he blends his genealogical thinking with Deleuzian phantasmatology and rhizomatic thought. Foucault's concern here is the way in which received forms and categories of thinking betray and misrepresent the specific temporality of the event: the event that cannot be parsed and recuperated within official historiographies. It is true, however, that nowhere does Foucault submit Marxism to a sustained and systematic critique; but this fact does not seriously impair the value of his non-acceptance of the dialectic, especially when this non-acceptance is prompted by Foucault's advocacy of the "specificity" of events, positions, the intellectual, and the theoretical commitment to non-authoritarian practices. Here then is Foucault as he differentiates the "practice of difference" from the dialectic:

> The freeing of difference requires thought *without contradiction, without dialectics*, without negation; thought that accepts divergence; affirmative thought whose instrument is disjunction; thought of the multiple—of the nomadic and dispersed multiplicity that is not limited or confined by the constraints of similarity; thought that does not conform to a pedagogical model (the fakery of prepared answers), but

that attacks insoluble problems—that is, a thought that addresses a multiplicity of exceptional points, which are displaced as we distinguish their conditions and which insist and subsist in the play of repetitions. Far from being the still incomplete and blurred image of an Idea that eternally retains our answers in some upper region, the problem lies in the idea itself, or rather, the Idea exists only in the form of a problem: a distinctive plurality whose obscurity is nevertheless insistent and in which the question ceaselessly stirs. What is the answer to the question? The problem. How is the problem resolved? By displacing the question. ("Theatricum Philosophicum," 185)

Affirmation through disjunction, multiplicity, exceptional points, the acceptance of divergence: these issues constitute Foucault's politico-epistemic platform. Jameson, I am sure, would not gainsay the material and historical reality of these issues, but he would certainly not allow these issues to weave together a politics of their own. He would maintain that the existing Marxist platform can fully take care of these sub-issues. In the passage quoted above, Foucault is deconstructing a number of assumptions cardinal to the efficacy of the dialectic: the "negation," the "negation of the negation," the sublation of contradiction, and finally, the legislative and problem-solving nature of the model. "By displacing the question," Foucault is attempting to think a thought that is beyond the finality of the dialectic.

Derrida's double writing and Foucault's "acategorical thought" are improper modes from Jameson's perspective since they seek to derive their authority from their "difference from" what they critique. A proper critique by contrast is characterized by a sense of filial/dynastic/familial/genetic belonging with its pre-history. Furthermore, a proper critique has a "name" and an "identity" that is conferred upon it by its primary order. The primary order "begets" its own critique which attests to its parentage. In theoretical/epistemological terms, the "time" or the temporality of the primary discourse regulates (to repeat a point I made a while ago in the context of Jameson-Derrida) and synchronizes the departures and disjunctions of "critical and second-degree philosophies." We can now see how it is possible for Jameson to talk of "one humanity" coordinated by one undifferentiated *chronotope*. By refusing to take into account the "critique of representation" and the reality of "the politics of location," Jameson enforces a common world, and, by disallowing the historical and epistemological status of discontinuity," he condemns narrative to the burden of "continuity." In the final analysis, Jameson's sense of history is monothetic and synchronic. The "improper critique," on the contrary, occupies contradictory spaces and times, testifies to a multiple and nameless parentage, denies the authority of genetic/dynastic logic and manifests a "will to signification" that is revisionist and counter-mnemonic.

One could go on elaborating the differences between Jameson and poststructuralism without ever being able to generate a set of criteria to help us choose between the two. After all, when we are talking "politics" and "ethics" we are certainly talking about choice. What more can one say except that each mode of thought is "true" to itself and its sense of self-formation? I think we can, however, by making reference to the "world out there." It seems to me that in a "global" conjuncture where the very term "global" is suspect, where determinations are multiple, where so-called "identities'" and "constituencies" turn out to be the over-simplified expression of contradictorily and unevenly cross-hatched subject positions, Jameson's Marxism is extremely inadequate and unsatisfying. I do not see how it can contribute to an understanding of a coalitional cultural reality beyond offering formulaic Marxist diagnoses and resolutions. Jameson's discourse is virtually silent on a whole range of formations such as feminism, ethnic studies, discourses of sexuality, etc., and yet makes total and global claims. This in some sense is the tragedy of a world-philosophy like Marxism which gets so caught up in its own axiomatics that it virtually denies the experiential and phenomenological reality of worlds that do not abide by its axiomatics. As one reads the long introductory chapter to *The Political Unconscious*, one is immediately aware of the extent to which Jameson tries to reconcile Marxism with rhetorics and discourses that are a critique of Marxism. The result is an unconvincing ecleticism. In my perception, Jameson oscillates between offering us a "strong Marxism," i.e., a Marxism that retains and preserves its official and denominational sense of self-identity in the face of a protean and polymorphous reality, and, a "weak" or "figurative" Marxism that functions as a general and blanket space for progressive political thinking. In the end, it is the desire to validate a strong Marxism that prevails.

I wish to argue that the path Jameson charts for Marxism is not the only way. There are a number of powerful and influential contemporary practitioners of Marxist theory (I have in mind people like Gayatri Chakravorty Spivak, Nancy Fraser, Cornel West—to name just a few), who have created a new and different space where Marxism enters into negotiation with deconstruction, feminism, post-colonialism, etc., without the imperative to take over and authentically interpret these more recent discourses. We now have a generation of critics who can only be classified with the help of a number of clumsy hyphens: Marxist-Feminist, Marxist-New Historicist, Marxist-Deconstructivist-Feminist, Marxist-French Feminist, Marxist-Afro-American, Post-Colonial-Subaltern-Deconstructive-Marxist, Psychoanalytic-Marxist, Foucauldian-Revisionist, and so on. It is indeed surprising, and, in some sense, disappointing, that while all of these improper formations are taking place, that someone as brilliant and learned as Jameson should seek authority in a monologic Marxism. It is the denial, in Jameson's theory, of a differently coordinated coalitional or "axial space" that I find most disturbing. In a contemporary socio-political-and-cultural situation where there is a need, more than ever before, for the creation of a non-aggressive, non-coercive, and generous space where different and multiple constituencies may meet collectively without the fear of being already spoken for or pre-defined, Jameson's critical framework, whose space is already hardened into official themes, categories, and values, seems out of sync. Surely, Jameson is to be credited for the honesty with which he styles himself and the courage with which he speaks out even on issues that are not "organically" his, especially at a time when it has become easy to take refuge in theory to avoid explicit political commitment. But then, on the other hand, one cannot but help noticing how, in the name of non-equivocal political engagement, Jameson's "cognitive map" blocks out "other spaces" that are working out "other" destinies based on "other" desires. I am not suggesting for a moment that a certain kind of feminism, or deconstruction, or a Foucauldian resistance has already succeeded where Jameson has failed. My point is that a certain kind of *bricolage* made up from a number of current poststructuralist practices has greater potential as well as relevance in "our" present day context.

I will conclude my essay with a brief analysis of what I consider a truly historic development in "our" own time; I am indeed referring to the "rainbow coalition" headed by Jesse Jackson, and a claim that there is a real and historical connection between the dynamics of the "worldliness" of the rainbow coalition and the elaborations of "difference" that we find in poststructuralist theory. My chief point here is that "a politics of difference" is appropriate and valid not because theory says or wills so in abeyance of reality, but rather that such a politics is already afoot. My position is that much of poststructuralist cultural theory is in response to changing times and realities: a sensitive and nuanced understanding of what the rainbow coalition is all about requires a different theoretical model.

The amazing thing about the rainbow coalition is the fact that it is not "doable," and yet it is being "done." Given the two party system and the basic ideological "sameness" that underlies this binarity, the phenomenon known as the "rainbow coalition" literally does not have a space to occupy and exist in: it has no official reality. Much of the incredulity and surprise reported by the press about the growing momentum of the Jackson campaign has to do with the fact that the campaign was transforming not merely the contents of the political agenda, but the nature and the very form of the agenda. Here is a campaign that attempts to effect a "second order" transformation even as it is pitched at the level of the "immediately" political. The campaign is a phenomenon that is not intelligible within the authority of existing categories and political values. This campaign in many ways is like revolutions, to quote from a title of a powerful essay by Gayatri Spivak, "that have as yet no model." To be valorized in its "own most" way, the coalition has to create its own space both in a historical and in an epistemological sense: historically, since it is by now demonstrably true that this "space" has succeeded in bringing people together and collocating them within an emerging solidarity that cuts across and defies "given" boundaries and proprieties such as, race, gender, sexuality, ethnicity, economic, and academic status, class, etc.; and epistemologically, since the theoretical expression of this space goes beyond the existing dominant "identitarian" categories. In other words, a coalitional politics necessitates the creation of coalitional space, and this space has to be coordinated, by way of a "double science," in transgression of the hegemonic political space.

Since no revolutions can be worked out *ex nihilo*, they find themselves disposed ambivalently towards the material mediations that are available at that time. Lacking in a pure model, these revolutions cannot but make use of existing mediations and structures, but in doing so, they transform the very nature of these mediations. In other words, the legality of the revolution uses and works through the means available, but is not determined or bound by the axiology that underwrites these mediations. In terms of the Jackson campaign, the campaign has a "double locus": 1) the here and now where the reality of the two party system and the appropriateness of the Democratic platform and candidacy has to be accepted and used as mediation, and 2) a future and as yet an indeterminate and nameless time that has very little to do with the present arrangement. The Democratic party is a means to an end; the party is not to be fetishized as an end in itself. Obversely, the Democratic party does not have the moral or the theoretical authority to definitively "identify" and thereby exhaust the sense of constituency that underlies the coalition except in the short run of the 1988 presidential elections. What is different, and therefore challenging, about the Jackson campaign is its insistence that the "short run" and the "long run" be articulated together within the reality of a determinate political platform. Thus, the campaign as the expression of a permanent revolution, lives on even after Jackson lost the nomination.

It must by now be clear that the political valence of the rainbow coalition is organically related to its theoretical and epistemological valence. To spell out this connection a little more in detail:

1) the coalitional campaign revolutionizes our understanding of categories such as "identity," "cause," and "constituency." Though it does not explicitly say so, its commitment is not to essentialized "identities," but to itinerant "subject positions" that are constantly shifting, re-affiliating, and transforming themselves within a collective, differential, and relational field. Thus, for example, to be a "black" within the rainbow coalition does not confer on the black constituency an exemplary value, and the fact that the leader of the coalition happens to be a black man does not define the "rainbow" as "black." There is no axiomatic one to one correspondence between the political ethic of any one of the components of the rainbow and that of the rainbow as such. Values, valences, and priorities are established as part of an ongoing negotiation where the regional interests of a particular group within the coalition are read in terms of the other interests that make up the ever expanding rainbow. The imbalances within the rainbow make it imperative that flows of generosity reach beyond the specificity of one's own narrow sense of belonging, such as, Chicano, Jewish, lesbian, gay, etc. Both global and regional impulses are registered and acknowledged by this model, for the delicate task is to produce a double reading that in enfranchising the rights of one group will not deny the connectedness of that group to other groups. What such a reading produces is not an oppressive version of "globality," but a global possibility indicated as an ever-changing "space," and not as a given "content."

2) In rethinking the world coalitionally—i.e., in mapping it cognitively as shifting positions within an ever-changing space— this model denies the world as it is. Briefly, we understand coalitions to be opportunistic structures that are to be used and discarded as soon as power is seized, and the end is realized. Coalitions do well as instruments of resistance, but not so well as dominant formations. But if one's cognitive model of the world itself were coalitional, then there are possibilities of realizing coalitional strategies as agents of a "permanent revolution." Built into the coalition is the insight that a common world is thinkable

only when we can divest ourselves from interests that are merely and obsessively regional and that it is the ethical and political responsibility of the advanced and developed sectors within a country or the world to practice some form of sacrifice and *askesis* so that the underdeveloped sectors may catch up and be redressed of their grievances. I say "responsibility," since underdevelopment in one area has always the result of overdevelopment elsewhere; we need only look briefly at the history of colonialism, imperialism, racism, and sexism to reach this conclusion.

In a world-historical context where every theory has the moral obligation to prioritize the problem of an uneven global development, it is all the more urgent to bring together the "spatiality" of the coalition with the "semantics" of subject positions in search of new and different forms of moral, political, and theoretical persuasion. And here, there is a strong connection between the poststructuralist reading of the Saussurean linguistic model and the geopolitical syntax of the rainbow coalition. In both cases, identity is an effect of subject positionality and is therefore not ontologically inevitable. Both models are based on the principle of collective mobility and reciprocal readability that is dependent on the dynamic of the signifying field and not on the authority of any one element or constituent that is a participant in the field. In the same way that identity is unpacked as "identity effect" or subject position, the "signified" is understood as an effect that is "always already" functioning as a "signifier" that points to another "signified," *ad infinitum*, within the linguistic chain. Translated in political terms, any one constituent of the coalition enjoys the "signified effect" only because it has been "signified" by another constituent in the coalition. The dynamics of signification is in the form of a perpetual relay where no one position is definitively inaugural or terminal. But the conduct of the relay does not militate against the possibility that, given historical determinations, any one particular element within the relay could play a major role at a particular conjuncture. The major role could be played by the Civil Rights Movement, or Feminism, the Gay Alliance, immigrant populations, etc., but this role itself is not a constant. The meaning of the word (in Saussure), and analogously, the meaning of the constituent in the coalitional chain, is the result of its difference, and its openness to forms of "otherness" made possible by the signifying network.

To pursue this line of reasoning further, the meaning, for example, of "being Indian" within the signifying coalitional chain is "not being Chicano," "not being Chinese," etc. If the positive experience of "one who is" is the effect of a differential transfer whereby "who one is not" determines one's awareness of one's identity, it follows then that the "identical one" does not really exist except in terms of relationality. If identity effects such as "being Indian," "being Chicano," "being Chinese," etc. are characterized by structural equivalence within the signifying chain, it follows then that the differential logic that "one" employs in identifying one's self, e.g., my "self" is "not other," or not the "other 's self," has to be extended to "one's own self." My "self" is someone else's "other," or "not-self," and since all "selves" are subject to this exotopic[26] "field logic" (where there is a structurally symbiotic relationship between my being my "self" and the availability of this self as "other" to the "self" of the "other": if the "other" did not recognize me I would not be a "self"), any self is always already alterior to itself. By persuading every self to acknowledge "the other within" and "self in the other," this model of human interaction and signification gives rise to a politics of "alterity," that allows us to celebrate the legitimacy "of what we are not in us."[27]

Strange as it may seem, it is the commitment of poststructuralist theory to issues such as "difference," "otherness," "heterogeneity," and "indeterminacy," issues that are deemed politically dead or counterproductive by aggressive libertarian political philosophies such as canonical Marxism, that make it more capable of a more generously transformative politics: the politics of "letting other worlds be" (cf. Spivak, *In Other Worlds*), wherever and whenever they are.

Notes

1. I use the term "anthropological" in a critical sense to indicate how anthropology as a "science of humankind" is guilty of ethno-

centric, imperialist, and often, racist totalization. I am profoundly indebted to Johannes Fabian who in his *Time and the Other* takes anthropology to task for "denying coevalness" to other cultures and their temporalities. Marxism, like anthropology, in so far as it is committed to producing globally representative "theories of the human," is vulnerable to a similar *hubris*.

2. See "Third-World Literature in the Era of Multinational Capitalism." During the course of this essay, Jameson talks all too glibly about "the return of nationalism" in the Third World as though nationalism were enjoying a re-run in the Third World. The confident use of the word "return" suggests that within the universal synchronicity of Western time, nationalism is repeating itself in the Third World, whereas, historically "nationalism" is new to the Third World. Throughout this essay (in spite of an initial gesture of unease), Jameson has little difficulty in maintaining his official conviction that the Third World histories are a predictable repetition of the histories of the "advanced world"; hence, the masterly confidence with which he "allegorizes" the Third World on its own behalf. In insisting that, unlike the first two worlds, the Third World enjoys a politico-cultural milieu where the "political" and the "libidinal" are "always already" in a state of mutual cathexis, Jameson belittles the problem of being "political" in a Third World context. The allegorical-romantic lenses through which he perceives the Third World will not let him see the devastation in the Third World, a devastation brought about by Western Imperialism and Colonialism. Also, his reading of the Third World, by effecting a felicitous equation between the individual consciousness and a macropolitical consciousness in the context of Third World nationalism, fails to realize how problematic "nationalism" is in Asia and Africa. Moreover, in focusing all too earnestly on the Third World "out there," Jameson's discourse fails to account for "the third world" that is "within" the so-called "First World."

3. See my essay, "Traveling Theory and the Professional Intellectual: In Search of a Common World," forthcoming in a collection of essays, eds. Elizabeth Meese and Alice Parker.

4. Though Jameson is on to the critique of representation offered by poststructuralism, his appreciation of it seems partial. Of the two aspects of this critique: a) the problematization of reality and b) the quarrel with the problem of "being spoken for," it is the former that claims his attention. He does not take seriously into account the

extent to which a representational epistemology is at the service of the dominant ideology.

5. Please refer to Aijaz Ahmed's critical response to Jameson's essay on Third-World literatures in *Social Text*, 16 (1986).

6. The entire prolegomena to *The Political Unconscious* where Jameson offers us his perspective "On Interpretation" is geared toward recuperating the dispersed or disseminated energies of interpretation within the Marxist hermeneutic horizon.

7. The very notion of the "specific" takes on great political resonance in Foucault's political thought. Whether it be the "specific intellectual," or the specificity of the event and its location, "the specific" is a mode of operation whereby "popular" and "insurrectionary" knowledges achieve their own epistemological and historical thresholds without the need to conform to a global platform or a Utopian program.

8. Here I refer to Foucault's critique of the Althusserian model of "scientific" ideology critique. Jameson too has argued dialectically against the false rigors of scientific Marxism; but, Foucault's criticism is even more telling. For, he is not merely concerned with the formal limitations of scientific rigor, but with the *scientificity as such*. He is concerned on behalf of "other" knowledges that will find themselves denied within the scientific paradigm.

9. The "worldliness" I invoke here is derived from Edward Said's notion of "worldliness" in *The World, the Text, and the Critic*.

10. See Gregory S. Jay's essay, "Values and Deconstruction," for a spirited "revaluation of value" and the category of the "political" in the context of Derridean deconstruction.

11. Michael Ryan's *Marxism and Deconstruction* is a notable attempt in this direction. But Ryan does not satisfactorily resolve the "hierarchic" relationship between Marxism and deconstruction. The "and" in the title of his book suggests a symbiotic coordination between the two; but the actual relationship is much more controversial and contestatory.

12. See *Feminism as Critique*, eds. Drucilla Cornell and Seyla Benhabib, for a rich and varied range of positions and options in relation to the politico-cultural field.

13. See my essay, "Ethnic Identity and Post-Structuralist Differance," *Cultural Critique*, 6 (Spring, 1987), pp. 199-220.

14. I take up this question of the "ideological effect" more elaborately in the context of Althusserian Marxism and the post-structuralist theory of the "subject" in a forthcoming essay, "Subject,

Structure, Ideology: Notes towards a Theory of Change," eds. Mas'ud Zavarzadeh and Teresa Ebert.

15. The Nietzschean impulse in poststructuralism is considerable. Though references to Nietzsche are bound to be controversial and ambivalent, I would like to suggest that the Nietzsche who inveighs against the blind and self-adequating arrogance of anthropocentric thought is certainly a progressive political thinker. Not unlike the equally controversial Martin Heidegger, Nietzsche tries to free the processes of knowledge from the tyranny of Truth.

16. For an interesting analysis of the relationship of poststructuralist errancy to Marxist theory, see Andrew Parker's essay, "Futures for Marxism: An Appreciation of Althusser."

17. French feminisms, and in particular, the contributions of Hélène Cixous and Luce Irigaray are uncompromising in their rigor against normative identification. Also interesting is the work of Julia Kristeva who maintains that succeeding generations of feminists need to engage as much with the "symbolic" as with the overtly political.

18. I cannot but recall the dangerously charismatic nature of the word "authenticity" and Adorno's incisive repudiation of Heidegger's "jargon of authenticity."

19. Whether the "latter knowledges" are the "unconscious" of the so-called "primary knowledges," or "something other" altogether is a hotly contested issue in contemporary theory.

20. The trope of the supplement in Derrida, the "phantasmal" in Deleuze and Baudrillard's "simulacrum" are all critical formulations calculated to deny authority to the regime of Identity. In my reading however, Derrida and Deleuze come across as politically "interventionary" thinkers whereas Baudrillard's acquiescent rhetoric does not quite take off beyond description.

21. The work of Hayden White, with its emphasis on "metahistory" and historiographic tropes comes to mind here. More than Jameson, White pays scrupulous attention to the "forms of content," but then, on the other hand, he does not explicitly raise questions concerning ideology.

22. The fictional text that I have in mind here is Donald Barthelme's *The Dead Father* that generates, by way of an acute countermemory, a sense of "break" from an oppressive prehistory. My general point here is that all contemporary emergences are a form of revisionism against the past.

23. Both Althusser and Gramsci, despite their many differences, testify against a philosophic tradition that loves to regularize and

normalize revolutionary thought in the name of proper parentage. Gramsci's "inventory" of one's history reveals multiple trajectories and Althusser's epistemological "break" rejects "proper" filiation.

24. The orphan in Derrida cannot be gender-free or neutral. My interpretation is that despite Derrida's alliances with Feminism, the orphan is a "he."

25. See my essay, "Towards an Effective Intellectual: Foucault or Gramsci?" forthcoming in *Intellectuals and Social Change*, ed. Bruce Robbins, University of Minnesota Press.

26. The reference here is to Mikhail Bakhtin: "exotopy," "heteroglossia," "dialogism," "the carnival," etc. are some of his unique formulations. The philosophical anthropology he offers transcends the limitations of Western Marxism. His preoccupation "with the other in the self" and his version of human socialization sets him apart from the canonical Western Marxists. It is interesting, but not surprising, that Bakhtin is not a strong influence on Jameson.

27. I refer here to Adrienne Rich's poignant and powerful phrase, "the lesbian in all of us." The politics of subject positions has to acknowledge various forms of alterity that are in us: often suppressed and brutalized beyond recognition.

Jameson, Totality, and the Poststructuralist Critique

Steven Best
University of Chicago

> There is no single tendency in the history of modern thought more remarkable in its persistence or more far reaching in its influence than the struggle to formulate a plausible version of the idea of totality.
>
> —R. M. Unger[1]

In the foundational text of "Western Marxism," Georg Lukács argued, "It is not the primacy of economic motives in historical explanation that constitutes the decisive difference between Marxism and bourgeois thought, but the point of view of totality" (*History and Class Consciousness*, 27). Taking up this position as his own, Fredric Jameson has claimed that totality is "the most dramatic battleground of the confrontation between Hegelian and structural Marxisms" (*PU*, 50). More recently, totality has been a central target of attack by poststructuralism and post- and anti-Marxisms of various types. Indeed, since its explicit theorization within the Western Marxist tradition itself, the concept of totality has been a central focus of debate. While theorists such as Korsch, Gramsci, Marcuse, Lefebvre, and Habermas have defended its importance, others such as Adorno, Horkheimer, Benjamin, and Della Volpe have problematized and/or rejected different aspects of this complex and multivalent concept.

In these debates and hostile face-offs, the stakes are high and involve issues concerning what type of society and culture we live in and what modes of theoretical comprehension and political groupings are possible and desirable. In this paper, I discuss Jameson's interventions in the debates over totality and attempt to render the complexity of his position which poststructuralists have consistently obscured (and which Jameson has repeatedly tried to bring out in various texts and interviews). While I will criticize aspects of Jameson's work and point to places where, in fact, he is too "totalizing," I will argue that the poststructuralist critiques of totality and of the alleged theoretical sins in Jameson's neo-Hegelian totalizations are based on misunderstandings and are for the most part inadequately theorized.

I. Marxism / Poststructuralism / Postmodernism

We live today in the age of partial objects, bricks that have been shattered to bits, and leftovers.
—Deleuze and Guattari, *Anti-Oedipus*, 42

The philosophical repudiation of Marx has been under way in France for some time, beginning with the rise of structuralism and accelerating with poststructuralism and the so-called "new philosophers." In public ceremonies sanctified by the media, the figurehead of Marx has been burned in effigy and replaced by the new idol of Nietzsche. With the Foucauldian emphasis on power as the primary structuring principle of society and discourse, dialectics and totality are equated with a repressive "identity theory," a "master discourse" whose will to power is manifested in the reduction of complex differences and particulars to some fundamental category or code.

It comes as no surprise, then, that the dissemination of poststructuralist philosophy in the U.S. has prompted an attack on Fredric Jameson, perhaps the foremost North American representative of the Hegelian-Marxist tradition. Common to all the philipics is the accusation that Jameson, in both his earlier and later work, is too reductive, essentializing, and "totalizing."

Frequently, poststructuralist critics (see Radhakrishnan and Horne in this volume) begin by trying to understand his concerns, acknowledging the positive aspects of his Marxism and paying homage to the impressive breadth of his work and his daunting encyclopedic knowledge. That said, they argue that Jameson's "pluralism" is only a façade for a relentlessly totalizing problematic. They excoriate him for reputedly reductive and terroristic totalizations, seeing him, with Habermas, as a dinosaur of paleolithic Marxism and modernism trying to foist a repressive Enlightenment scheme upon denizens of the postmodern scene. Jameson, they argue, fails to grasp the full radicality of the poststructuralist critique which, if properly understood, would compel him to abandon Marxism and utopianism. With Lyotard, they inveigh against "the fantasy to seize reality" and equate any attempt to map an "unrepresentable" socio-historical reality as a "return to terror" (*Postmodern Condition*, 81-82).

While there have been attempts to reject Marxism in favor of poststructuralism (see Baudrillard 1975; Laclau and Mouffe 1985; Kroker/Cook 1986), there have also been efforts to effect some sort of *rapprochment* (Eagleton 1981; Ryan 1982; Spivak 1987; Kellner 1989). Indeed, Jameson's own work has been concerned with appropriating the insights of poststructuralism—in addition to virtually all other contemporary critical discourses—and the two problematics are not altogether dissimilar. Both Marxism and poststructuralism, for example, are radically opposed to traditional dualistic, a-historical, and essentializing philosophies; both critique the ideology of the natural and self-evident character of knowledge; and both decenter the subject in relation to larger processes which precede and condition it. But there are also strong differences between these two discourses that preclude any easy "synthesis" and have generated the contemporary debates and conflicts that I am concerned with addressing.

In general, as dramatically argued by Baudrillard in *The Mirror of Production* (1975)—who follows a strategy antithetical to Althusser's and Balibar's attempt in *Reading Capital* (1970) to ground Marxism as a revolutionary break from classical philosophy and political economy—poststructuralism believes that Marxism is insufficiently radical, that it has not truly broken with a-historical, metaphysical, and idealist problematics. In Foucault's image, Marxism is said to be nothing more than a ripple in the pond of nineteenth century thought (*Order of Things*, 262). Indeed, from a critical standpoint such as Baudrillard's, it is believed that Marxism cannot overcome these problems because its "productivist" categories are inherently reductionist.

Poststructuralist critiques have charged Marxism with the following discursive crimes—crimes in which Jameson is frequently implicated: (1) humanism, which believes in a human essence and a founding subject; (2) geneticism, which seeks ultimate origins; (3) teleology, which asserts direction, rational purpose, and pre-ordained goals in history; (4) historicism, which adheres to a linear and evolutionist conception of historical time; and (5) reductionism, which subsumes difference and plurality to a false unifying scheme and center.

Charges (1) – (4) are related to (5), the central concern of this essay. Against Hegelian-Marxism (Lukács, the Frankfurt School, Sartre, et al.), poststructuralism has vehemently rejected every conceivable form of totality, such as textual, the (literary) text as an organic whole which expresses authorial intentions; subjective, the subject as a unified consciousness or ego; synchronic, society as a system, structure, or mode of production; diachronic, human history as a coherent process or narrative. Whereas dialectical, totalizing Marxism begins with the assumption that reality, despite its dynamic, contradictory nature, is ultimately an intelligible whole comprehensible through a scientific or theoretical discourse, poststructuralism proceeds on the belief that all "texts" are constituted of incommensurable fragments and particulars which cannot, without a reductive violence, be assimilated to some larger whole. There is no underlying essence which can be appealed to in the unification of particulars, no grand abstraction common to all terms to sew up difference within a final identity. This position is evident in Foucault's *Archaeology of Knowledge* which deconstructs historical totalities (such as epoch, civilization, and history itself), in Barthe's *S/Z*, which explodes Balzac's novella into a multiplicity of disconnected codes, or in Deleuze and Guattari's *Anti-Oedipus*, which seeks the deterritorialized "lines of escape" for a micro-politics of desire.

Thus, unlike classical Marxism, the central methodological move of poststructuralism is to assume discontinuity and difference from the start and begin by undoing false conceptual abstractions and unities to resolve them into the irreconcilable particulars that constitute society and discourse. Following Nietzsche's lead, poststructuralism refuses systematic philosophizing and the very idea of systemic connections (which, it is thought, implies some underlying center or essence). It refuses totalizing, global, or even "general" theories (Hindess and Hirst 1975).

Just as Marx saw capitalism as a demystifying movement where the real forces and relations of society became visible (at the same time as they are fetishistically occluded), postmodernism is conceived as the period in which we finally see totalizing myths for what they are and "re-cognize" them. In Lyotard's words, "Simplifying to the extreme, I define postmodern as incredulity toward [totalizing] metanarratives" (*Postmodern Condition*, xix). Lyotard understands postmodernism as a new era marked by sensitivity toward difference and toleration for the incommensurability of language games, where agonistics replaces the (repressive) desire for consensus.

And here we need to note a significant elision and shift in perspective: from the *description* of difference and discontinuity to its *celebration and affirmation* as a normative principle and goal, and not only for theory, but for the body and psyche itself. Any limitation of the radical and infinite play of difference is considered to be a repressive, artificial, and ideological construct. As Christopher Norris has stated, "deconstruction is inimical to Marxist thought at the point where it questions the validity of any science or method set up in rigid separation from the play of textual meaning" (*Deconstruction: Theory and Practice*, 83). Thus, unlike Foucault who in *The Archaeology of Knowledge* deconstructs totalities and ordering procedures in order to reconstruct them in a more satisfactory model and then in his later work to reconstruct the radical political project, Lyotard, in his "war against totality" and the Habermasian ideal of rational consensus, calls for the proliferation of language games, not merely to throw off the modernist straightjacket of universal ideals, but to disseminate for the sake of dissemination itself, to reside in that limitless, agonistic space where we are all "just gaming" (Lyotard/Thebaud 1985). Indeed, in deconstructionist appropriations of poststructuralism (Paul de Man, et al.) the modernist project of human emancipation has given way to a frivolous and depoliticized play of textuality. In this vein, Baudrillard defines the postmodern subject as one who "plays with the pieces." Not to be outdone, and taking this line to its logical conclusion, Deleuze and Guattari celebrate schizophrenia as a revolutionary mode of being and espouse libidinal pleasures in disjointed encounters with partial objects (see *Anti-Oedipus*).

The rejection of totality is inevitably accompanied by a rejection of "meaning" itself. If meaning is context-bound, and there is no identifiable whole which can serve as the context, then there can be no "meaning" (a very under-theorized term), only endless permutations of signifying chains which cannot be stabilized with artificial totalizing schemes. Thus, Derrida in *Dissemination* proclaims indeterminancy, dissemination, and undecidability; and Baudrillard in *Simulations* and *In The Shadow of the Silent Majorities* upholds aleatory schemes and the death of meaning, the social, and reality itself. This, of course, forestalls any possibility of collective political praxis. In general, poststructuralism is characterized by extreme skepticism, relativism, nihilism, and irrationalism. In its "absolutization" of language it has privileged signs, codes, and discourse and conflated significant differences between language and social institutions (Anderson 1983). The loss of representability (the ability to conceptually "map" the world), meaning, commmunity, and reality has been accompanied, not surprisingly, by a general sense of paralysis (no doubt linked to the defeat of the Left in post-1968 struggles). But far from suffering nostalgia or melancholy, many poststructuralists have aggressively assumed an Adornoesque stance of absolute negativity, believing that to take some positive stance is to fall into a debilitating ideology or to become ensnared in the will to power and its ruse of valuation (see Kroker/Cook 1986). It is in response to these current crises and challenges and in opposition to the pessimistic strain of Western Marxism (most notably Adorno and Horkheimer), that Jameson, like Habermas, attempts to revive traditional Marxist concerns with truth, totality, representation, community, and revolutionary praxis.

II. Narrative, History, and Hermeneutics

> Familiar though his name may be to us, the storyteller in his living immediacy is by no means a present force. He has already become something remote from us and something that is getting even more distant.
> —Benjamin, *Illuminations*, 83

The Political Unconscious is about the history of inter-pretation and the interpretation of history. Jameson interprets cultural texts as he reflects on the operations of the interpretive act, the codes through which texts are read and received, and the monumental history to which they belong. Following the lead of Heidegger (1962) and Gadamer (1975), who emphasized the un-avoidably "forestructural" and "prejudicial" nature of human understanding, Jameson renounces any vulgar realist approach which asserts some un-mediated access to the text in a favor of a "historicist" approach (in another of its many senses) where interpretation always proceeds through pre-given historical categories and so never confronts the *Ding-an-sich*. With Althusser, Jameson sees history as an "absent cause" which, while not itself a mere "text," is available only indirectly, through the mediation of texts and their hermeneutical framing. But Jameson does not simply re-hash standard hermeneutical arguments with-in a Marxist problematic. Synthesizing the contributions of Marx, Lukács, Althusser, Freud, Lévi-Strauss, Greimas, Frye, Lacan, Deleuze and Guattari, and others, Jameson attempts to construct "a new *hermeneutic*" (*PU*, 21), "an outline or projection of a new kind of critical method" which attempts "to restructure the problematics of ideology, of the unconscious and of desire, of representation, of history, and of cultural production, around the all-informing process of *narrative*" (*PU*, 12-13).

Following the lead of Lévi-Strauss, Jameson sees narrative as a "socially symbolic act" where social conflicts and contradictions are given a pseudo-resolution in aesthetic form. This process is broadly defined as ideology, but Jameson re-defines ideology such that it refers not simply to the more traditional "false consciousness," but also includes the more positive Blochian perspective that seeks to uncover a trans-historical utopian longing for unalienated social life. All literary texts, therefore, contain the imprints of social and historical existence and are to be critically deciphered in a hermeneutical operation which attempts to uncover their multi-dimensional "political unconscious." Jameson's hermeneutic breaks from all idealist and formalist methods that reify the text as a frozen artifact by situating it within an ever broader framework that includes the social, political, and historical conditions of textual production.

This last, diachronic dimension of textuality—"the whole complex sequence of modes of production" (PU, 76) to which a text ultimately belongs—takes on a decisive importance in Jameson's work. With Marx and Lukács, both of whom accepted Vico's dictum that human beings create their own history and therefore can comprehend it, Jameson sees history as an intelligible and meaningful whole which can be retrospectively grasped in its "totality," within a single narrative. As most forcefully articulated by Marx, this is the (Enlightenment) story of the gradual triumph of the subject over the object, of the slow transition from the realm of necessity to the realm of freedom, of the progressive augmentation of the productive forces and the parallel evolution of the human subject in its manifold aspects.

Writing late in this unprecedented century of disaster, Jameson can hardly hold to the letter of a (widely imputed) Lukácsian optimism of a final subject-object reconciliation in history, but, despite this and his rather awkward assimilation of aspects of postmodern pessimism, he remains wedded to the spirit of the Marxian-Lukáscian narrative, which, in stark contrast to the tragic narratives of Marxists such as Adorno, Horkheimer, and Benjamin, or postmodernists such as Kroker, affirms history as a dialectic of liberation and domination and emphasizes the emancipatory possibilities within the present age, as well as the importance of totality as a normative and utopian goal.

Since, for Jameson, Marxism is the only discourse which

uncovers the full scope of historical development in its brute material reality, it becomes the hermeneutical epicenter of all possible historiography, social and cultural theory, and literary criticism. Thus, psychoanalysis, structuralism, myth-criticism, etc. are merely "local" and auxiliary methods which at best supplement the "semantic richness" of Marxism and at worst pose dissemblingly as autonomous, self-sufficient discourses. Marxism is the "untranscendable horizon" of interpretation that, in a dramatic *Aufhebung*, cancels, preserves, and transforms these secondary discourses "within the unity of a single great collective story" (*PU*, 19) of material production, human desire, and class struggle. "It is in detecting the traces of the uninterrupted narrative, in restoring to the surface of the text the repressed and buried reality of this fundamental history, that the doctrine of the political unconscious finds its function and necessity" (*PU*, 19-20).

Hermeneutics, therefore, has an explicit task: "Interpretation is here construed as an essentially allegorical act, which consists in rewriting a given text in terms of a particular interpretive master code" (*PU*, 10). Thus, with full knowledge of the "anti-hermeneutical" critiques of theorists such as Sontag or Deleuze and Guattari, Jameson aggressively reasserts hermeneutics as an allegorical act of textual rewriting which reorganizes texts and their social histories within the unity of a narrative form that recuperates the "truth" of the historical past (for a defense of Jameson's hermeneutics, see Best, "After the Catastrophe").

The valorization of narrative and Marxist hermeneutics leads us to the central issue of this paper insofar as it immediately entails a defense of "the necessity of and priority of totalizing thought" (*PU*, 21). For Jameson, "the problem of representation, and most particularly of the representation of History . . . is essentially a narrative problem, a question of the adequacy of any storytelling framework in which History might be represented" (*PU*, 49). The key term here is "adequacy." For poststructuralists and others, traditional narrativist categories—actors, plots, characterization, and a linear time scheme of beginning, middle, and end—are immediately bound up with the metaphysics of subject, teleology, and continuity which they reject. For some historiographers and literary theorists (Sprinker 1986), history must be constructed on the basis of a "science" and literary-narrativist categories are "unscientific" (see Ricoeur 1984, vol. 1).

The question becomes: can a narrative framework be reconstructed to avoid these problems and what shape would this take? Clearly, teleological narratives, Cartesian subjects, and Aristotelian schemes are inadequate devices for rendering the complexity of history, but it is arguably a mistake to dispense with narrative categories altogether. If the argument that human beings structure their reality in a narrativizing way is correct, as Jameson, following Lévi-Strauss and Ricoeur, asserts,[2] or that history has a structure and trajectory which can be analyzed on a narrative scheme, then there is a case to be made for the legitimacy of narrative analysis. As Ricoeur (1984) suggests, narrative categories can be effectively retained even though "decentered" and re-written in a non-metaphysical way. Jameson himself attempts to avoid false closures, to employ a de-centered "collective subject," and to break with simple "historicist" schemes by emphasizing historical discontinuities, overlapping modes of production, and uneven development.

Yet one of the central moves of *The Political Unconscious* is to defend the importance of diachronic narrative against a hasty Althusserian dismissal of narrative as a reductive device which succumbs to the idealist logic of humanism, historicism, and expressive causality. While Jameson otherwise accepts the full force of Althusser's critique of mechanical and expressive causality (see below), in this case he argues that history is constituted as a type of allegorical form which can only be interpreted textually through a particular (Lukáscian) narrative (*PU*, 34ff). History, therefore, is "a single great collective story" (*PU*, 19) and the unqualified repudiation of allegory and master narratives occludes a critical reading of the political unconscious of history, "just at the moment when increasing privatization has made that dimension so faint as to be inaudible" (*PU*, 34).

One sees, therefore, how narrative becomes Jameson's key concept and how the Lévi-Straussian conception of narrative as ideology is synthesized with a Lukácscian conception of narrative as totality. Narratives make connections and contextualize events within a unified whole of the storytelling framework. Narrative projects interrelationship as an aesthetic by way of the tendential sense that in order to show what a given event is in reality, the novelist must somehow overcome the presentational constraints of the immediate, and somehow suggest the active influence and effects of that whole range of social and historical forces without which this unique event is finally inconceiveable. ("HCC," 55)

For Lukács, a literary narrative has merit to the extent that it provides both a critical and totalizing perspective on bourgeois society, that is, to the extent it reveals the workings of class domination and its systemic nature.

Agreeing with Lukács on the potentially critical function of literary narrative and expanding this role to theory itself, Jameson applies narrative, synchronically, toward a restoration of "the lost unity of social life, and [to] demonstrate that widely distant elements of the social totality are ultimately part of the same global history" (*PU*, 226) and, diachronically, toward a contextualization of synchronic narrative within the full sequence of historical modes of production. For Lukács and Jameson alike, narrative is a fundamental expression and realization of the "aspiration to totality" (Lukács), a yearning that Jameson's later work reconfigures as "cognitive mapping."

Since there can be no question that Jameson is "totalizing," the issue becomes this: in what ways is he totalizing and is totalization always and necessarily a bad move? These are the crucial questions poststructuralists generally fail to address in their indiscriminate attack on dialectical and totalizing thought. Consequently, we must provide some initital clarification of the concept of totality and distinguish between acceptable and unacceptable uses of the concept. First, it must be emphasized that totality is not simply a concept but points to concretely existing structures. The holistic assumption guiding Marxism is that history and society are constituted as types of totalities. A "totality" can be defined as a structure or system comprised of parts that are constituted by the whole system to which they belong and which interrelate within that system. In this emphasis on system and relationality, holism is a rejection of the empiricist philosophy which holds that reality is constituted of isolated, self-sufficient particulars. The general argument for totality is plausible to the extent that (1) things are relational and systemic in character, and (2) a method exists whereby these relational entities can be theorized and grasped.

If the fallacy of empiricist methods is to reify and hypostatize real entitites as autonomous in nature, then the potential danger of a totalizing analysis is to overemphasize system, unity, and coherence, to the extent that empirical complexity is reduced and forfeited to the *a priori* demands for "system." But unity need not entail uniformity, totality need not be totalitarian, and systemic outlook is not the same as systematic philosophy. The viability of Jameson's work and, more generally, the totalizing standpoint of the Hegelian-Marxist tradition, depends on developing a concept and practice of totality which negotiates between the extremes of an overly rigid system and an anarchic pluralism, and articulates, to use Lefebvre's distinction, an "open" totality, always contingent and in process (*Dialectical Materialism*, 111), rather than a "closed" totality, predetermined and finalized.

Thus, a major distinction I shall rely on throughout this paper is between totalization as a contextualizing act which situates seemingly isolated phenomena within their larger relational context and draws connections (or mediations) between the different aspects of a whole and totalization as a reductive analysis which forces all particulars within a single theoretical perspective at the expense of "textual" difference and complexity. The poststructuralist critique of totality, as I will attempt to demonstrate, is properly aimed at the latter type of totalizing analysis, rather than the former, which grasps systemic relationships while respecting difference, discontinuity, relative autonomy, and uneven development. These terms, and the revaluation of totality that I am calling for, demand a reconsideration of a key Marxist theorist, Louis Althusser, who greatly influenced Jameson and who himself stands in an ambiguous relation to poststructuralism.

III. Jameson's Marxist Triumvirate: Althusser, Lukács, Sartre

[T]he apparently simple contradiction is always over-determined.

—Althusser, *For Marx*, 106

The only totality the student of society can presume to know is the antagonistic whole, and if he is to attain totality at all, then only in and through contradiction.

—Adorno, "Sociology and Psychology," 74

Terry Eagleton once remarked that Jameson is a "shamelessly unreconstructed Hegelian Marxist" (*Against the Grain*, 58). Given Jameson's defense of diachronic totality and certain "religious" themes throughout his work (see Flieger 1982; O'Neill in this anthology), one can see some truth to this claim.[3] But it is also a misleading and careless remark which altogether ignores the extent to which Jameson has assimilated the Althusserian and poststructuralist challenges to Hegelian-Marxism and revised the tradition through this encounter. In the Jamesonian kaleidoscope, the most vivid (Marxist) colors are those of Althusser, Lukács ("the greatest Marxist philosopher of modern times" (*PU*, 13)), and Sartre. While the Lukáscian influences on Jameson's work—the concepts of narrative totality and reification—are familiar to most of Jameson's critics, what seems less understood is how Jameson appropriates Althusser to rewrite the Lukáscian totality as a "structure-in-dominance" and how he uses Sartre to recast the Althusserian totality as a "transcoded" whole rich in mediations.

Whatever the problems in Althusser's rejection of subjects as real social actors, his tortured distinction between science and ideology, and his rigid bifurcation between an early and late Marx, his significant contribution was to recover the complexity of key Marxist concepts (totality, causality, and contradiction) and to develop this complexity in a more explicit philosophical theory based on the categories of "overdetermination" and "structural causality" (see *For Marx*; Althusser and Balibar, *Reading Capital*).

On Althusser's conception, each historical mode of production is a "structural totality." For Althusser, this notion is premised on a break with the Lukáscian (and Gramscian) notion of "expressive totality," which Althusser sees as a Hegelian, non-Marxist, pre-scientific, idealist, and metaphysical conception that, unlike the notion of "linear totality," grasps the reciprocal interrelation of parts (social levels) within a whole (mode of production), but theorizes them as nothing more than expressions of an underlying essence that informs the whole.

Repudiating what he understands as a simple "materialist" rewriting of the Hegelian conception of totality, and its simplistic and deterministic concept of causation, one of Althusser's key characterizations of the structural totality is that it is a "de-centered whole." For Althusser this means that the totality is a differentiated whole comprised of multiple, relatively autonomous, unevenly developing, and complexly interrelating levels. Overdetermination is the logic governing the decentered whole: each level of a social formation—political, ideological, economic, and, a later addition, theoretical—has its own specific character and each determines, and is determined by, the other. As opposed to the economism of orthodox Marxism, therefore, the economic, while still "ultimately determining" all other levels, does not directly or fully determine other social levels, nor do they, in some strict scheme of "homologies," develop in an exactly parallel path and manner. Each social level has its own trajectory and history.

In his dismissal of anything smacking of humanism, historicism, or telology, and in his emphasis on plurality, complexity, decenteredness, discontinuity, and uneven development, Althusser's reformulation of totality has strong similarities to poststructuralism. (Not coincidentally, Althusser and some post-structuralists, such as Althusser's student, Foucault, come out of the same historiographical tradition of Bachelard and Canguilhem.) Of course, these emphases are more pronounced in poststructuralism, to the point of rejecting *any* version of totality as a repressive and reductive concept (although this certainly does not prevent them, as I will suggest, from their own form of "totalizing" theories). But while both Althusser and poststructuralists emphasize the heterogeneous complexity of the social field and discursive practices, Althusser rightly insists that these phenomena do *not* entail or allow the rejection of totality as a valid and necessary concept. For Althusser, the *de-centered* whole is a de-centered *whole*; the unevenly developing totality is still a "unity," but no longer "the unity of a simple, original and universal essence"—be it *Geist* or Economics.[4] For "the unity discussed by Marxism is *the unity of the complexity itself . . .* the mode of organization and articulation of the complexity is precisely what constitutes its unity" (*For Marx*, 201-202). For Althusser, as for Jameson, unity is achieved only *through difference*, and a "totalizing" analysis attempts to preserve differences, dispersions, and discontinuities while also supplying the general context of determination common to every aspect of the whole.

The poststructuralist challenge to a Marxist theory of totality, therefore, quite apart from a repudiation of the Hegelian model, involves a radicalization of the more sophisticated Althusserian model, and explodes the emphasis on difference and discontinuity beyond the boundaries of any theorizable totality, into a Leibnizian space of radical seriality and "pure difference" (Lyotard). If we accept the poststructuralist theorization of dissemination and *différance*, we could still reject the claim that textuality is so radically de-centered as always to prevent any form of totalizing analysis.

While Althusser remains at the level of abstract argumentation and polemic, it is the considerable value of Jameson's work to demonstrate in concrete analyses that a sophisticated use of totalization is both valid and necessary for textual and social analysis. Following Althusser, he applies a decentered and discontinuous perspective toward a non-reductionist and non-essentialist rehabilitation of totality in its various aspects.

But while Althusser serves the important function of qualifying aspects of Lukács and the Hegelian-Marxist tradition in Jameson's work, Jameson also attempts to defend the basic Lukáscian project—aspects of his theory of literary realism and his category of totality—and uses Lukács (and Sartre) to criticize aspects of Althusser's project. The defense of Lukács is carried out not only in *The Political Unconscious*, but more dramatically, in the recent, "*History and Class Consciousness* as an 'Unfinished Project,'" which applies Habermas' notion of modernity as an "unfinished project" to Lukács' project as developed in *History and Class Consciousness.* Examining "the doxa and prejudices at work in Lukács' reception" ("HCC," 51), Jameson argues that Lukács—and Hegel for that matter—had a considerably more complex account of subject and object than some simple theological narrative of alienation and reconciliation.[5]

Jameson also sees Althusser as a historical regression from one of Lukács' central contributions—the development of a complex theory of mediations ("HCC," 63). Jameson argues that Althusser wrongly dismissed the concept of mediation—which draws connections among social levels and seemingly isolated social phenomena while articulating the indirect influence of the economic—as an idealist and reductionist device which conflates the relative autonomy of social levels. Jameson grants Althusser's point that mediation is a potentially metaphysical conception which only displaces the problem rather than solving it—deferring the attainment of an abstract, non-differentiated structural identity ("expressive causality") through a pseudo-differentiation of social levels. But he argues that mediation is not logically tied to expressive causality, that Althusser's differentiating structural causality is itself a form of mediation, that its true critical target is the structural category of "homology" or the "unreflected immediacy" of an abstract totality and that mediation is necessary for a Marxist theory of totality.

Because Althusser sees mediation only as an external force—"where mediation passes through the structure rather than a more *immediate* mediation in which one level folds into another directly" (*PU*, 41)—Jameson points to a potential problem in his conception of totality. The Althusserian emphasis on relative autonomy "has to *relate* as much as it *separates*" (*PU*, 41) and the danger is that it will only separate and leave each level independent from the other. Hence the importance of the concept of "relative autonomy," which some critics wrongly reject as a redundancy, and theorizing not only difference but also "identity." Althusser's failure to achieve adequate mediations between social levels leads—at least in some theorists such as Hindess and Hirst—to what Jameson later calls the "'meltdown' of the Althusserian apparatus" where "semi-autonomy relax[es] into autonomy *tout court*" ("PTS," 192) and the various struggles waged against the totality of capitalism lose all connection to one another.

This reification can be broken only through a sophisticated concept and practice of mediation which identifies systemic interrelation within a general context of overdetermination:

> Mediations are . . . a device of the analyst, whereby the fragmentation and autonomization, the compartmental-ization and specialization of the various regions of social life (the separation, in other words, of the ideological from the political, the religious from the economic, the gap between daily life and the practice of the academic disciplines) is at least locally overcome, on the occasion of a particular analysis. (*PU*, 40).

Jameson's approach, therefore, is to grant relative autonomy *and* to grasp the interconnections occurring among these levels, to combine the Althusserian and Lukáscian approaches to social totality, to unite analytic and synthetic mental operations:

> I have found it possible without any great inconsistency to respect both the methodological imperatives implicit in the concept of totality or totalization, and the quite different attention of a 'symptomal' analysis to dis-continuites, rifts, actions at distance, within a merely apparently unified cultural text." (*PU*, 56-57)

To show that such an articulation is possible, Jameson refers us to Sartre's *Search for a Method* (1968). Here Sartre attempted to develop a syncretic theory which mediated between the objectivistic account of Marxism and the subjectivistic accounts of existentialism and psychoanalysis, showing how the individual experiences are decisively determined by the economy and its class structures, yet how this determination reaches the individual through the filter of the family. Jameson sees the Sartrean model as "an identificatory transcoding which requires you at one and the same time to maintain these three 'levels' at some absolute structural distance from one another" (*PU*, 43), while grasping their structural interrelation. While never losing sight of the powerful determination of the capitalist economy on society and individual experience, Sartre also showed the oblique path this determination takes and how individuals can in turn react against it (see also Adorno, "Sociology and Psychology").

Following the lead of Sartre, Jameson attempts to employ a complex theory of mediations and he does so by elaborating on the Greimasian notion of "transcoding": "the invention of a set of terms, the strategic choice of a particular code of language, such that the same terminology can be used to analyze and articulate two quite distinct types of objects or 'texts' or two very different structural levels of reality" (PU, 40). Here Jameson articulates the aspect of mediations normally associated with a totalizing analysis, its ability to grasp systemic relations within a given structure. But this is only the unifying aspect of an operation which also includes, just as much, a decentering and differentiating movement. Thus, Jameson tries to recover a supressed logical possibility, another aspect of mediation which has been under-emphasized, ignored, or dismissed in the recent critiques of totality—its capacity to register *differences*:

> To describe mediation as the strategic and local invention of a code which can be used about two distinct phenomena does not imply any obligation for the same message to be transmitted in the two cases. . . . We must therefore repudiate a conception of the process of mediation which fails to register its capacity for differentiation and for revealing structural oppositions and contradictions through some overemphasis on its related vocation to establish identities. (PU, 41-42)

Throughout *The Political Unconscious*, Jameson tries to grasp the ways in which economics and social class affect the form and content of literary production. He articulates the mediations between stages of capitalist development, forms of subjectivity, and types of literary genres, styles, and narrative categories. But it is clear throughout this text that these mediations are very complex relations and not simple "homologies."[6] As the term implies, transcoding involves a trans-positional movement from cause(s) to effect(s), a trans-lation which is always a *transformation*. Transcoding allows us to identify "the relationship between the levels or instances [of a social whole], and the possibility of *adapting* analyses and findings from one level [e.g., art] to another another [e.g., the economy]" where these levels do not develop in any simple one-to-one correspondence with one another or the economy (*PU*, 39, my emphasis).[7]

Following Althusser, Jameson attempts a dramatic escape from reductionism by transcribing Marxist discourse within the categories of psychoanlysis. Eschewing the traditional language of reflection or representation, which assumes the text to be a passive mirror of larger processes, Jameson tries "to grasp the mutual relationships between [the various] dimensions of the text and its social subtext in the *more active terms* of production, projection, compensation, repression, displacement, and the like" (*PU*, 44). These terms represent the "various dynamic possibilities" (*PU*, 49) of a literary text or human society. Modernist texts, for example, do not simply mirror and reproduce reification, as Lukács argued, they also contain a "revolt" against reification and contain "a whole Utopian compensation for increasing dehumanization on the level of daily life" (*PU*, 42).

By rejecting the idea of the social as a seamless whole where all the parts express some inner unified truth, by absorbing positive elements of Althusser and poststructuralism and employing a model of totality which is decentered and overdetermined, and by providing numerous and detailed examples of types of structures and mediations which can be theorized through a systemic analysis that privileges economic production as the central determinant in capitalist society, I suggest Jameson goes a long way toward constructing a "plausible version" of totality which deflects the main thrust of poststructuralist attacks. Rather than pursuing the applications of this philosophical framework in *The Political Unconscious* in his detailed readings of Balzac, Gissing, and Conrad, let us instead turn to Jameson's later work and show how he applies the philosophical model of totality articulated in *The Political Unconscious*, in an even more refined manner, toward the development of a theory of postmodernism.

IV. Postmodernism as Cultural Dominant

> I have felt . . . that it was only in the light of some conception of a dominant cultural logic or hegemonic norm that genuine difference could be measured and assessed.
> —Jameson, "PCL," 57

In interviews and key essays, Jameson attempts to elaborate a theory of postmodernism as "the cultural logic of late-capitalism," a distinct moment in the development of the capitalist mode of production. The effort to delineate historical stages and theorize the mediations at work within a synchronic totality, however, makes him vulnerable to the following objection:

> As for periodization, its practice is clearly enveloped by that basic Althusserian conceptual target designated as 'historicism'; and it can be admitted that any rewarding use of the notion of a historical or cultural period tends in spite of itself to give the impression of a facile totalization, a seamless web of phenomena each of which, in its own way, 'expresses' some inner unified truth—a world view or a period style or a set of structural categories which marks the whole length and breadth of the 'period' in question. (PU, 27)

Is it possible, then, to construct a synchronic totality that avoids a state "in which everything becomes so seamlessly interrelated that we confront either a total system or an idealist 'concept' of a period" (PU, 28)? Indeed, Jameson's critics (e.g., Sprinker 1982; Davis 1985) have charged him with precisely these crimes. They have argued that he operates with a metaphysical and reductionist "homology" scheme which posits overly strict correlations between the three general moments of capitalist economic development (market capitalism, monopoly capitalism, and multinational capitalism) and three corresponding cultural levels (realism, modernism, and postmodernism).

I have already suggested how Jameson might respond to such critiques. In his recent interviews and articles, Jameson takes a number of opportunities to clarify gross misunderstandings of his position and to recapture the specificity of his analysis which is overlooked in the poststructuralist critique. In "Periodizing the 60s," for example, he states, "there is a fundamental difference between the present narrative and those of an older organic history which sought 'expressive' unification through analogies and homologies between widely distinct levels of social life" ("PTS," 179). In his interview with Anders Stephanson, Jameson reiterates the fact that he "make[s] a place for over-determination," discontinuity, and uneven development: "I find it paradoxical that a discontinuous and dialectical model of something can be criticized for being an idealist continuity which includes a telos. Each of these moments [in a mediated totality] is dialectically different from each other and has different laws and modes of operation" ("RPM," 52). More than once in this inter-view he insists on the irreducible heterogeneity of postmodern culture and the qualifications this requires of a totalizing method: "I picked emblematic things and by no means everything can be analyzed in that vein. . . . My concept of postmodernism is thus not meant to be a monolithic thing but to allow evaluations of other currents within this system [capitalism]—which cannot be measured unless one knows what this system is" ("RPM," 48-50).

This type of qualification is visible in the seminal essay to which Jameson here refers, "Postmodernism, or The Cultural Logic of Late Capitalism." His idea of "cultural dominant" is a differentiating notion which attempts to discriminate among different types of cultural artifacts: "I am very far from feeling that all cultural production today is 'postmodern' in the broad sense I will be conferring on this term" ("PCL," 57). While discussing the new type of image production characterized by a lack of expressive emotion or depth (as paradigmatically represented by Warhol's work), for instance, Jameson notes that "it would be inaccurate to suggest that all affect, all feeling or emotion, all subjectivity, has vanished from the newer image" ("PCL," 61). While this new sort of image is "dominant," it is not the sole type of image production in a complex "force-field" where counterveiling logics prevail.

By turning to Jameson's theory of postmodernism we have an even better test case for his theory than the modernist texts of Balzac, Gissing, and Conrad. For postmodernism is frequently characterized in terms of its extreme eclecticism and hetero-geneity and Jameson attempts to develop a theory which registers this. The first task is grasping "postmodernism" not simply as an aesthetic style, but as a new cultural logic in its own right. This very move is non-totalizing (in the reductive sense) insofar as Jameson, in a manner similar to Foucault, is sensitive to historical discontinuities and attempts to break up abstract monolithic periods—such as "capitalism" or "modernity"—into their differentiated stages, while mapping the specific aspects of each. The function of the concept postmodernism is "to correlate the emergence of new formal features in culture with the emergence of a new type of social life and a new economic order—what is euphemistically called modernization, post-industrial or consumer society, the society of the media or spectacle, multi-national capital" ("PCS," 113). It is not, therefore, that the very notion of "period" is a reductive and "totalizing" notion, creating expressive unities; rather *not* to use it, when justified, is reductive insofar as one fails to grasp qualitatively different levels of histor-ical development. Subsequently the focus must shift to *how* periodizing categories are used in particular instances.

In Jameson's case, he defends his use of postmodernism as non-reductive and he does so on the basis of his sensitivity toward differences. In "Periodizing the 60s," Jameson states:

> the 'period' in question is understood not as some omni-present and uniform shared style or way of thinking and acting, but rather as the sharing of a common objective situation, to which a whole range of varied responses and creative innovations is then possible, *but always within that situation's structural limits. . . .* What is at stake then is not some proposition about the organic unity of the 60s on all its levels, but rather a hypothesis about the rhythm and dynamics of the fundamental situation in which those very different levels develop according to their own internal laws. ("PTS," 178-179, my emphasis).

The "limits" Jameson refers to are, of course, those set by the capitalist mode of production. In this essay, Jameson charac-teristically ranges across the whole map of a historical period and examines "the 60s" from the diverse perspectives of philosophy, politics, culture, and economics. While describing the specific aspects and temporalities of each social level and practice, moving from the streets of New York to the forests of the Sierra Maestra, Jameson also attempts to show how they are all part of the same system of global capitalism. Rather than a simplistic "homology" scheme, what we find in this essay is a complex dialectic of unity and diversity within a decentered totality.

The strength of Jameson's analysis is demonstrated in his contextualization of poststructuralism itself and the sign system it theorizes (frequently ahistorically) within the larger systems of postmodernity and late-capitalism. Jameson interprets post-modernity (in part) as an intensification of the reifying logic of industrial modernity rooted in the capitalist economy and its relentless commodification of the social totality. As capitalism attains an increasingly abstract, imagistic, and reified mode of existence, language itself becomes increasingly abstract, event-ually throwing off the burden of referentiality and attaining self-referential status, such that we are "no longer of a realm of signs, but of pure or literal signifiers freed from the ballast of their signifieds, their former meanings" ("PTS," 200). In this essay as well as in "Postmodernism," Jameson shows how a new social logic emerges, affecting many areas of social existence. Thus, the new culture of images and signs registers not only in the arts and the psychic structure itself, it drastically modifies the realm of theoretical production. Nihilistic punks and the rejection of the great hermeneutical systems and their depth models are quite different phenomena, but they ultimately must be understood as parts of the same general system—most immediately of the new postmodern culture and its "dominant" forces, but more generally as part of the late-capitalist economy, its hyper-abstract logic of commodification, and its all-embracing mode of reification (see Best, "Commodification of Reality" 1988).

Thus, immense plurality and sundry differences, but within a *systemic context* where one finds not *simply* differences or random developments, but also "striking analogies or homologies in very different and distant areas of social practice . . . [a] replica-tion of a common diachronic rhythm or 'genetic code'" ("PTS,"

201). Within the very narrow conditions of human possibilities provided by a homogenizing global capitalism, the "infinite play of difference" celebrated by poststructuralists becomes a more naive and utopian notion than anything to be found in the Marxist tradition. The theory of radical dissemination is perhaps more accurate as a theory of textuality—in a narrow, literary sense— than as a social theory. For "the unifying force here is the new vocation of a henceforth global capitalism, which may also be expected to unify the unequal, fragmentary, or local resistances to the process" ("PTS," 208-209).

If postmodern culture is "a system involving a whole range of things" ("RPM," 70), the differences to be gauged include not only the diversity of new cultural elements which could properly be termed postmodern, but also the different and (sometimes) conflicting intersection between the modern and the postmodern, the continued (or "residual") presence of "modern" elements within the new era of modernity. A more totalizing theory of postmodernity, such as we find with Baudrillard or Kroker/Cook, posits a dramatic break in history which instantiates the new "postmodern scene." It analyses the shift from modernity to postmodernity only in terms of radical discontinuity. The result is that everything in the new social epoch is seen as "postmodern" and "postmodernity" becomes the very "monolithic thing" that Jameson has attempted to avoid.

A more satisfactory and less totalizing theory of post-modernity would grasp not only the lines of discontinuity, but also the lines of continuity, accounting for the ways in which key dynamics of modernity abide, albeit in modified (and intensified) form. In order to theorize this dialectic of continuity and discontinuity, Jameson draws on Raymond William's distinction between dominant and emergent (*Marxism and Literature* 1977). In doing so, he augments the philosophical framework of *The Political Unconscious* in an important way and he provides a much more fruitful way of conceiving the concept of historical break ("*coupure*") than do radical postmodernists:

> radical breaks between periods do not generally involve complete changes of content but rather the restructuration

of a certain number of elements already given: features that in an earlier period or system were subordinate now become dominant, and features that had been dominant again become secondary. In this sense, everything we have described [as postmodern] can be found in earlier periods and most notably within modernism proper: my point is that until the present day those things have been secondary or minor features of modernist art, marginal rather than central, and that we have something new when they become the central features of cultural production. ("PCS," 123)

Both Jameson and radical postmodernists understand postmodernism as an historical "break," but Jameson sees the transition as an *ab utero* shift within the general conditions of capitalism while they see it as a rupture which emerges *in vacuo*. Thus, rather than arguing for "the end of political economy" (Baudrillard), Jameson, following Mandel, sees its continuation and intensification in postmodernity.

Ultimately, the response to the argument against totality and "homology" must proceed with a reassertion of the most basic materialist principle: it is not a question of whether or not "cultural" production is influenced by "economic" production (to use a familiar but problematic distinction), but rather to what degree and through what *mediations* this determination occurs. If social being is indeed materially determined then, necessarily, some types of inter-connections between the economic and the cultural will exist.

The theory of transcoding allows Jameson to register the determination of the economy on the social totality through a complex series of mediations, to grasp a systemic web of over-determined practices. To object to transcoding as an essentialist device which conflates differences and reduces the radical heterogeneity of the social field, as some poststructuralists do, one must address Jameson's counter-argument that these differences are not so extreme as to prevent structural inter-connections and "analogies" and to stand outside of a systemic context within which they receive their general character and, indeed, their very nature as particulars.

If we are going to throw around the stigma of idealism, it would seem to be a more accurate characterization of the post-structuralist position which, in effect, severs the connection among social levels. Objections to a sophisticated periodization scheme governed by the logic of overdetermination and uneven development depend on the dubious assumption that there are no correlations or inter-connections among social levels whatsover. Without some way to register not only the differences between social levels (relative autonomy) but their interrelation and general points of "correspondence," we are left with only a purely contingent series of events: "we fall back into a [poststructuralist] view of present history as sheer heterogeneity, random difference, a co-existence of a host of distinct forces whose effectivity is undecideable" ("PCL," 57). We do not then show how Wallace Stevens and Che Guevara are "somehow 'the same'" ("PCL," 179), a ludicrous proposition, but how the *same system* of global capitalism affects both of them in quite specific ways and how their quite different practices and ideologies ultimately share the same historical context and referent.

To summarize, the problem is not with utilizing a totalizing mode of analysis, but rather with instantiating a too abstract totality and constructing inter-connections which are too simple, direct, and unmediated. The real issue then concerns the use of adequate mediations, of constructing a sufficiently sophisticated framework which can map the full complexity of cultural texts and social practices in a non-reductive way. Drawing from the problematics of Marxism, psychoanalysis, poststructuralism, etc. and employing categories such as overdetermination, relative autonomy, and transcoding, Jameson has, I suggest, the necessary tools for a theory of mediation which grasps important social inter-connections and avoids any "facile totalization." Over-determination, for example, assures that no single causal center with a unidirectionally determining logic is posited. This immediately allows for the relative autonomy of social levels, and hence for their uneven development, freed from the mechanistic dependence of a one-to-one correlation with the economic.

Of course, this by no means ensures that Jameson always uses these tools unproblematically. Indeed, as I shall show in the concluding section, he often falls into excessively totalizing practices. But the poststructuralist argument is not that Jameson does not use his eclectic tools in a satisfactory way, but rather that he cannot, because a totalizing analysis is *ipso facto* reductive. This argument itself, I have argued, is totalizing insofar as it fails to differentiate between various types and uses of totalizing models. Thus, we need to displace the poststructuralist critique from a categorical dismissal of totality to a contextualized adjudication of particular totalizing models.

V. Critical Remarks on Poststructuralism and Jameson

> The impossibility of the Hegelian system for us is not a proof of its intellectual limitations, its cumbersome methods and theological superstructure; on the contrary, it is a judgment on us and on the moment of history in which we live, and in which such a vision of the totality of things is no longer possible.
> —Jameson, *Marxism and Form*, 47

There can be no doubt that some articulations of totality are repressive and that there is a link between the violence of systematic thought and the violence of the state. I say "violence" here, because, in either case, difference is ignored and/or repressed, because particulars arc coerced into a centralized, universal scheme. Whether we are speaking of a bureaucratic hierarchy or a monolithic model, the goal is systematicity, regularity, and uniformity. The marginal, unknown, and unique cannot be tolerated and so must be silenced and violated, brought into conformity with the System.

But this is not the sole connotation or effect of totality. If totality can signify a dystopian nightmare of coercion, closure, and endorsed identity, it can also signify the utopian dream of personal development and social and ecological harmony, the end of crippling divisions such as between mental and manual labor, mind and body. Each view speaks a certain truth, articulates a definite aspect of the concept. "Totality" can lead *either* to

Walden Pond or Stalin's Gulag, *but only through specific theoretical and political appropriations.* Inherently, the concept has no telos, leads to no specific destination, for it is fundamentally polysemic and open to different articulations. And this is precisely why we must take so much care in clearly identifying its *dystopian* aspects so that we may positively specify its *utopian* aspects which can then guide our praxis and steer us safely between the Scylla of monopoly capitalism and the Charybdis of bureaucratic socialism. As Jameson has stated, "Without a conception of the social totality (and the possibility of transforming a whole system), no socialist politics is possible" ("CMP," 355). Lacking the category of totality, our struggles are doomed to either reformism (transforming only isolated aspects of the system) or reproduction of repressive dynamics (as sexism and bureaucracy lingers on in "existing socialist societies").

Poststructuralists, therefore, *essentialize* "totality" as having an inherent meaning and necessary destination when, in fact, the concept is nothing outside of its different uses. In the heterodox history of Marxism, it has a different meaning and function in Gramsci's work than it does in Korsch's, in Lukács' work than in Bloch's, in Habermas's work than in Adorno's, etc. (see Jay, *Marxism and Totality* 1984). Poststructuralists rarely speak of "theories of totality"; instead they vituperate against "totality" in the singular. Ironically, their critiques of totality are themselves totalizing; they initiate a general attack against all general theory. With some exceptions, poststructuralists tend to substitute buzz words for analysis, and their "war against totality" is merely a cold-war of hot rhetoric. When they do advance careful arguments, these tend to be strictly external in nature and they almost always fail to put forth any alternative program to a totalizing and utopian theory. This is perhaps because, as I noted earlier, they are unable to affirm anything and see affirmation as "ideological." It could also result from the current marketability of nihilism.

Rather than categorically dismissing the concept of totality, therefore, it must be critically confronted on an *ad hoc* basis. An adequate social theory must be rigorously contextualist with regards to the validity of a totalizing perspective. In some cases, a Derridean dissemination may be proper; in others, a unifying, systemic approach will be required. In either case, it is necessary to grasp the relational and historical context of "textuality," "play," or social practices, and while in some cases "totality" is wrongly theorized as a simple unity governed by an expressive center, the concept does not require, as Althusser's theorization of the decentered whole has shown, an immanent logic. It is, therefore, not the idea of totality itself which is under attack, but the more specific idea of system or systemic unity. But even the "differential network" in Derrida's "Living On Border Lines" is some kind of (decentered) system or totality, that is, some kind of relational and historical context.

Most importantly, however, while poststructuralists rightly deconstruct essentialist and repressive wholes, they fail to see how repressive and crippling the opposite approach of valorizing difference, plurality, fragmentation, and agonistics can be. The flip side of the tyranny of the whole is the dictatorship of the fragments. The unqualified rejection of holism, systemic analysis, and totality as a normative concept reproduces the alienation and fragmentation capitalism has already brought to social life. Without some positive and normative concept of totality to counter-balance the poststructuralist / postmodern emphasis on difference and discontinuity, we are abandoned to the seriality of pluralist individualism and the supremacy of competitive values over communal life. In Jameson's words, we can see poststructuralism itself as "a symptom and a reinforcement of the reification and privatization of contemporary life" (*PU*, 20). Like Anglo-American empiricism, poststructuralism can "serve as a check on social consciousness by suppressing any vision of the social whole" (*PU*, 367) and the celebration of heterogenity and difference coheres all too easily with consumerist ideology and practices ("HCC," 62).

It is a fundamental tenet of both dialectical and structuralist theory that there are no isolated bits of reality which can be understood in and of themselves. The belief in ontological self-sufficiency is a key ideological assumption of bourgeois ideology (such as expressed in British empiricism or logical positivism) and it was the decisive advance of structuralism (as well as dialectics and deconstruction) to understand the relational nature of social reality. Ironically, in some ways poststructuralism is really a pre-structuralism which *regresses* to a time before the structuralist breakthrough. The poststructuralist critique mystifies the fact that in capitalist society, there are not simply differences and autonomy, but also strong tendencies toward reified sameness, uniformity, and generality (mass production, propaganda, mass media, psychological uniformity, etc.). As with some Frankfurt School theorists, it has always been a key aspect of Jameson's defense of totality that he is simply mapping the totalization of capital itself, its growing saturation and homogenization of cultural, geographical, and psychic spaces. Any unqualified concentration on difference and heterogeneity, therefore, necessarily mystifies the most gruesome effects of the capitalist mode of production (what Wallerstein and Amin term a "world system").

While poststructuralists have made theoretical contributions by developing a theory of textuality, by refining our "sensitivity to differences," and by rigorously guiding our attention to dubious metaphysical assumptions, they have frequently adopted extreme and unsubstantiated positions (as are most obviously evident in Baudrillard's neo-Berkeleyian hyperreality or Kroker/Cook's obscure notions of "catastrophe" and "dead power"). The viewpoint of poststructuralism is valid as *a perspective* on the actual nature of an overdetermined, structured totality, and as a necessary corrective to reductive theories of totality, but it is only a perspective and it needs to be balanced by a complex totalizing viewpoint which grasps the ways in which relationality and systematicity are integral aspects of a decentered whole. While poststructuralism only offers a decentered perspective, a sophisticated Marxist theory such as Jameson's offers both systemic and decentering perspectives and therefore potentially provides a superior theory. The poststructuralist critique of totality, therefore, is valuable, not because it saves us from believing in wholes, but because it effectively calls into question reductive and illegitimate uses of totality.

Yet while I find that Jameson has developed Marxism in important ways, there are serious problems with his positions that stem from his eclecticism and totalizing methods. While eclecticism offers many advantages, enabling him to develop a sophisticated neo-Marxism which draws productively from other theories, the problem arises as to whether or not his project is a logically coherent one. In employing different aspects of diverse theories, Jameson may become ensnared in contradictory epistemological problematics. Specifically, one could point to the tensions created in his synthesis of the Lukácsian and Althusserian concepts of totality, such as we find in *The Political Unconscious* as well as his later work on cognitive mapping. While these two models may be complementary on some grounds (as discussed above), at another level they conflict in their adoption of completely opposed models of cognition—Lukács opting for a narrative and thus aestheticizing model of totality (see Sprinker 1984) and Althusser espousing a "scientific" model which privileges a "rigorous" mode of theoretical discourse. While one may claim that these are false oppositons, similar to the science-ideology distinction, or wish to privilege one model over another, such tensions require explicit acknowledgement and discussion. So far, Jameson's attempt to characterize his position in terms of "transcoding" rather than eclecticism (see his introduction to *IT*, vol. 2), brief and cryptic as it is, does nothing to resolve this problem (see Iffland 1984 for discussion of the issue).

Jameson's unsupported assumption that the Marxist theory of history and society is unproblematically correct in its most general claims raises some more problems. For Jameson this means a faithful utterance of orthodox Marxist litanies: the determination of the economic "in the last instance," history as the story of class struggle, and Marxism as master discourse. Such rhetoric provides the untheorized basis for his appeals to the legitimacy of historical continuity (diachronic totality), where he sees history—despite the discontinuity inaugurated by capitalism—as "one human adventure" where all the episodes have a "single fundamental theme" (*PU*, 19). The Ariadne thread, of course, is provided by the great abstractions "production" and "class struggle" as general categories applicable to all epochs of social history.

Jameson's rhetorical flourishes are surprising, given not only his critical acumen but his familiarity with the work of authors who have posed strong challenges to the Marxist theory of history.

Jean Baudrillard (1975), Marshall Sahlins (1976), and Anthony Giddens (1981) have all argued that labor, class, and production do not have the structural primacy in pre-capitalist social formations that they do in capitalism, that capitalism, therefore, is an even more radical rupture from preceding history than Jameson would allow. Indeed, Jameson seems to problematize his own position by analysing pre-capitalist societies in terms of "caste" rather than "class" ("Interview," 79). Other theorists have questioned the adequacy of seeing all human history as driven by the contradiction between forces and relations of production, as the progressive augmentation of social productive forces, or have challenged the validity of the concept of mode of production itself (see Foster-Carter 1978). The point here is not to substantiate such claims, but rather to suggest that Jameson's appeal to the "unbroken continuity" of history is a problematic and theoretically unsubstantiated claim, that he fails to address or specify key issues concerning the causal dynamics of history, and that no theorist today can rightfully assume key Marxist concepts as axiomatic.

While I earlier defended the general thrust of Jameson's account of postmodernity, I now want to suggest that it is here we can also see manifest some of Jameson's more reductive totalizing tendencies. This problem is perhaps most evident in his argument that the modernist psychological subject has been eclipsed by the new postmodernist subject in conditions where "concepts such as anxiety and alienation . . . are no longer appropriate" ("PCL," 63). Indeed, Jameson goes so far as to adopt the Baudrillardian view that we are in "a situation where subjects and objects have been dissolved" ("RPM," 47) and that a proper political position for today is to employ "fatal strategies." These unsupported claims are surely exaggerations which put Jameson in the peculiar position of attempting to radicalize non-existent subjects. He gives no indication that there might be a wide variety of subjects today—from the rural farmbelt to the urban ghettoes—who do not fit the postmodern categories. This is an instance where Jameson, unlike other places in the same essay, fails to put to use Williams' categories to articulate adequately the intersection between older and newer social conditions and the full complexity of the latter. Against many of Jameson's descriptions of postmodernism (such as the waning of affect), it could be plausibly objected that he has confused what are only "emergent" tendencies and characteristics with what strike him as "dominant."

In cases where Jameson's conception of postmodernism is too totalizing, it is, ironically, often because he abandons a properly Marxist perspective for an uncritical postmodernist one. It is perhaps for this reason that Jameson has not only been criticized for being too economistic in his theorization of postmodernism, but for not being "economistic" enough. This is the case when Mike Davis reinterprets postmodern architecture more in terms of "the rise of new international rentier circuits in the current phase of capitalism" and "the definitive abandonment of the ideal of urban reform as part of the new class polarization taking place in the United States" ("Urban Renaissance and the Spirit of Postmodernism," 108), rather than in more "culturalist" terms of a generalized depthlessness spreading throughout late-capitalist society. Here is an instance where a more traditional Marxist analysis seems far more illuminating than a "postmodern" theorization. In any case, Jameson has failed to convincingly defend his claim that postmodernism is the cultural dominant of late-capitalism and his attempted synthesis of Marxism and post-modernism frequently is no less strained than Benjamin's earlier attempt to incorporate messianic beliefs into a Marxist standpoint.

To conclude, I want to consider Jameson's argument—"his most scandalous claim" (Sprinker 1982, 62)—that Marxism is the master discourse. While there are times when this claim may be true, as stated by Jameson it is *a priori* and dogmatic; perhaps while what is needed is a more *a posteriori*, contextualist approach. In other words, whether or not Marxism assigns the ultimate place of other discourses is to be decided *only in specific cases*, with specific texts, on an *ad hoc* basis. It may result, for instance, that a feminist or psychoanalytic reading of a text is more appropriate and more powerful in some cases than a Marxist reading, that the mediations to class and economics are simply too abstract or remote. In such a case, Marxism would be decentered in favor of a different theoretical perspective.[8]

The *prima facie* validity of Jameson's position is gained through a key equivocation. At the most abstract level, Jameson is right to assert that history itself is the "ultimate ground as well as the untranscendable limit of our understanding in general and our textual interpretations in particular" (*PU*, 100). But he slips from the unobjectionable proposition that all understanding is historically mediated to the more questionable claim which reduces "History" to class and economics and so automatically privileges Marxism. To the extent that class and economics are dominant thematics within the text, or strong determinants of its form and content, then Marxism *is* the "master discourse" because, traditionally, it is *the* discourse of class and economics, or at least no adequate challenger has yet come to the fore. Still in Jameson's hands, "History" becomes an illegitimate abstraction which obscures the pluralities that comprise it, not only class, but race, kinship, culture, and sex—all of which need specific theorization, a theorization precluded by the illegitimate abstraction of "one humanity," an abstraction demystified by Barthes (1972).

Rather than an *a priori* monism, therefore, we require an *a posteriori* perspectivism. As Foucault has stated, "Discourse in general . . . is so complex a reality that we not only can, but should, approach it at different levels and with different methods" (*Order of Things*, xiv). It is reductionist to subsume all theoretical perspectives *a priori* to some discursive center. At this level then, the poststructuralist critique of Jameson is correct and a Nietzschean-Foucauldian perspectivism would constitute a legitimate decentering or deconstruction of Marxism. Against poststructuralism, however, and qualifying Foucault's claim above, we need to resist a too radical decentering, one which conflates hermeneutic *perspectivism* with hermeneutic anarchy, a relativism where all discourses—which would have to include bourgeois idealism or even fascism—are equally valid. This too is a false *a priori* strategy and one with obviously problematic political implications.

Thus, it may very well be the case that one sometimes employs a theoretical hierarchy by privileging one discourse over another. It is only that *the specific terms of the hierarchy* are to be decided *post factum* and not *a priori*, only after initial consideration of the thematics of the text. It is the immense merit of Jameson's work, particularly in our current post-Marxist climate, to provide so many detailed readings—texts from Balzac to Warhol—where Marxism does indeed seem to serve as an illuminating "interpretive horizon." While the contextualist approach I am suggesting is incompatible with Jameson's sometimes dogmatic apotheosis of Marxism, it does cohere with his critique of liberal pluralism, an ideology very much present in poststructuralist discourse—its valorization of particulars and inability to grasp systemic relations.

Notes

I would like to thank Bob Antonio, Belden Fields, Keith Hay-Roe, and Robert Resch for helpful critical remarks on earlier drafts of this paper. I owe a special thanks to Douglas Kellner who has worked with me closely on innumerable drafts of this paper and provided incisive criticisms at every point.

1. Cited in Martin Jay, *Marxism and Totality*, 21.

2. For Jameson, narrative is "the central function or *instance* of the human mind" (*PU*, 13). Whereas Ricoeur (1984) tries to substantiate this argument, Jameson never explicitly argues for this, although *The Political Unconscious* and its theory of allegory could be seen as a sustained attempt to support it.

3. Here one could point to some sort of teleological impulse in Jameson's work. While Althusser "has effectively discredited the Marxian versions of a properly teleological history," Jameson attempts "a provisional qualification of Althusser's antiteleological formula" (*PU*, 33, 36) in his theory of allegory and the political unconscious. While Jameson certainly rejects the continuist diachronic narrative of a single esssence unfolding throughout history (see Jameson, "Interview"), he has something of a quasi-teleology as represented in the Hegelian-Marxist story of struggling subjects and the historical emergence of human freedom. Where Althusser sought a history without a telos or a subject, Jameson attempts to retain both categories in modified form.

4. Of course, critics such as Laclau and Mouffe (1985) and Hindess and Hirst (1977) have argued that the theory of determination of the economic "in the last instance" is a vestigial essentialism and reductionism, a critique, of course, which would just as well apply to

Jameson. Compounding the difficulties, Althusser added that "the lonely hour of the 'last instance' never comes," risking conceptual incoherence in addition to covert reductionism.

5. While Jameson advances some bold claims to exonerate Lukács from the Althusserian critique, he does not convincingly defend the Lukácsian project. One interesting move is an attempt to relativize the meaning of Lukács' infamous remark that the proletariat is "the identical subject-object of history" by reinterpreting the remark within the quite local context of Lukács' polemics with German idealism: "The passing phrase marks the 'solution' to those specific traditional contradictions, in their own specific language or code, which is no longer our own" ("HCC," 66). The later parts of the essay are more concerned with the application of Lukács to feminism and "new social movements" in general. Jameson's (not surprising) move is to emphasize the specificity of each group's experience of domination, while asserting the ultimate commonality of their experiences within "late-capitalism."

6. "Homology" is meant to designate interconnections among social levels, but it is misleading insofar as it suggests a direct mirroring or reflection of the economic on the "superstructural" levels of society. While Jameson sometimes uses the term, he clearly does so in a highly qualified way and distinguishes his more complex use of mediations from those of Lucien Goldmann who sought to construct "rigorous homologies" between economics and culture.

7. In his "Introduction" to the second volume of *The Ideologies of Theory*, Jameson uses transcoding in a different sense, designating a hermeneutical method for negotiating among a welter of competing theoretical discourses in present-day intellectual life. Interestingly, Jameson here seems to relativize the truth-value of Marxism. In addition to allowing for a more inter-disciplinary outlook, transcoding "also implies that whatever its own (very considerable) truth claims, Marxism must also take its chances on this polemical level and . . . measure its range, by way of the transcoding operation, against its various methodological revivals or alternatives" (*IT*, ix).

8. And here I find a more satisfactory approach in a recent book by Douglas Kellner and Michael Ryan, *Camera Politica* (1988). Rather than simply favoring Marxism or deconstruction (the two dominant perspectives of the book), these authors combine different perspectives in different ways for the various films they interpret.

Afterword—
Marxism and Postmodernism

Fredric R. Jameson
Duke University

Marxism and postmodernism: people often seem to find this combination peculiar or paradoxical, and somehow intensely unstable, so that some of them are led to conclude that, in my own case, having "become" a postmodernist, I must have ceased to be a Marxist in any meaningful (or in other words stereotypical) sense. For the two terms (in full postmodernism) carry with them a whole freight of pop nostalgia images, "Marxism" perhaps distilling itself into yellowing period photographs of Lenin and the Soviet revolution, and "postmodernism" quickly yielding a vista of the gaudiest new hotels. The over-hasty unconscious then rapidly assembles the image of a small, painstakingly reproduced nostalgia restaurant—decorated with the old photographs, with Soviet waiters sluggishly serving bad Russian food—hidden away within some gleaming new pink and blue architectural extravaganza.

If I may indulge a personal note, it has happened to me before to have been oddly and comically identified with an object of study: a book I published years ago on structuralism elicited letters, some of which addressed me as a "foremost" spokesperson for structuralism, while the others appealed to me as an "eminent" critic and opponent of that movement. I was really neither of those things, but I have to conclude that I must have been "neither" in some relatively complicated and unusual way that it seemed hard for people to grasp. As far as postmodernism is concerned, and despite the trouble I took in my principal essay on the subject to explain how it was not possible intellectually or politically simply to celebrate postmodernism or to "disavow" it (to use a word to which I will return), avant-garde art critics quickly identified me as a vulgar-Marxist hatchet man, while some of the more simplehearted comrades concluded that, following the example of so many illustrious predecessors, I had finally gone off the deep end and become a "post-Marxist" (which is to say, a renegade and a turncoat).

I'm therefore particularly grateful to Doug Kellner for his thoughtful introductory demonstration of the ways in which this new topic is not alien to my earlier work but rather a logical consequence of it, something I want to rehearse again myself in terms of the notion of a "mode of production," to which my analysis of postmodernism claims to make a contribution. It is first worth observing, however, that my version of all this—which obviously (but perhaps I haven't said so often enough) owes a great debt to Baudrillard, as well as to the theorists to whom he is himself indebted (Marcuse, McLuhan, Henri Lefebvre, the situationists, Sahlins, etc., etc.)—took form in a relatively complicated conjuncture. It was not only the experience of new kinds of artistic production (particularly in the architectural area) that roused me from the canonical "dogmatic slumbers": I will want to make the point later on that as I use it, "postmodernism" is not an exclusively aesthetic or stylistic term. The conjuncture also offered the occasion for resolving a long-standing *malaise* with traditional economic schemas in the Marxist tradition, a discomfort felt by a certain number of us not in the area of social class, whose "disappearance" only true "free-floating intellectuals" could be capable of entertaining, but in the area of the media, whose shock-wave impact on Western Europe enabled the observer to take a little critical and perceptual distance from the gradual and seemingly natural mediatization of North American society in the 1960s.

Lenin on imperialism did not quite seem to equal Lenin and the media, and it gradually seemed possible to take his lesson in a different way. For he set the example of identifying a new stage of capitalism that was not explicitly foreseen in Marx: the so-called monopoly stage, of the moment of classical imperialism. That could lead you to believe, either that the new mutation had been named and formulated once and for all; or that one might be authorized to invent yet another one under certain circumstances. But Marxists were all the more unwilling to draw this second, antithetical conclusion, because in the meantime the new mediatic and informational social phenomena had been colonized (in our absence) by the Right, in a series of influential studies in which the first tentative Cold War notion of an "end of ideology" finally gave birth to the full-blown concept of a "post-industrial society" itself. Ernest Mandel's book *Late Capitalism* changed all that, and for the first time theorized a third stage of capitalism from a usably Marxian perspective. This is what made my own thoughts on "postmodernism" possible, which are therefore to be understood as an attempt to theorize the specific logic of the cultural production of that third stage, and not as yet another disembodied culture critique or diagnosis of the spirit of the age.

It has not escaped anyone's attention that my approach to postmodernism is a totalizing one. The interesting question today is then not why I adopt this perspective, but why so many people are scandalized (or have learned to be scandalized) by it. In the old days, abstraction was surely one of the strategic ways in which phenomena, particularly historical phenomena, could be estranged and defamiliarized; when one is immersed in the immediate—the year by year experience of cultural and informational messages, of successive events, of urgent priorities—the abrupt distance afforded by an abstract concept, a more global characterization of the secret affinities between those apparently autonomous and unrelated domains, and of the rhythms and hidden sequences of things we normally remember only in isolation and one by one, is a unique resource, particularly since the history of the preceding few years is always what is least accessible to us. Historical reconstruction, then, the positing of global characterizations and hypotheses, the abstraction from the "blooming, buzzing confusion" of immediacy, was always a radical intervention in the here-and-now and the promise of resistance to its blind fatalities.

But one must acknowledge the representational problem, if only to separate it out from the other motives at work in the "war on totality." If historical abstraction—the notions of a mode of production, or of capitalism, fully as much as of postmodernism—is something not given in immediate experience, then it is pertinent to worry about the potential confusion of this concept with the thing itself, and about the possibility of taking its abstract "representation" for reality, of "believing" in the substantive existence of abstract entities such as Society or class. Never mind that worrying about other people's errors generally turns out to mean worrying about the errors of other intellectuals. In the long run there is probably no way of marking a representation so securely *as* representation that such optical illusions are permanently forestalled, any more than there is any way to ensure the resistance of a materialistic thought to idealistic recuperations, or to ward off the reading of a deconstructive formulation in metaphysical terms. Permanent revolution in intellectual life and culture means that impossibility, and the necessity for a constant reinvention of precautions against what my tradition calls conceptual reification. The extraordinary fortunes of the concept of postmodernism are surely a case in point here, calculated to inspire those of us responsible for it with some misgivings: but what is needed is not the drawing of the line and the confession of excess ("dizzy with success," as Stalin once famously put it), but rather the renewal of historical analysis itself, and the tireless reexamination and diagnosis of the political and ideological functionality of the concept, the part it has suddenly come to play today in our imaginary resolutions of our real contradictions.

There is, however, a deeper paradox rehearsed by the periodizing or totalizing abstraction which for the moment bears the name of postmodernism. This lies in the seeming contradiction between the attempt to unify a field and to posit the hidden identities that course through it and the logic of the very impulses of this field, which postmodernist theory itself openly characterizes as a logic of difference or differentiation. If what is historically unique about the postmodern is thus acknowledged as sheer heteronomy and the emergence of random and unrelated subsystems of all kinds, then, or so the argument runs, there has to be something perverse about the effort to grasp it as a unified system in the first place: the effort is, to say the least, strikingly inconsistent with the spirit of postmodernism itself; perhaps, indeed, it can be unmasked as an attempt to "master" or to "dominate" the postmodern, to reduce and exclude its play of differences, and even to enforce some new conceptual conformity over its pluralistic subjects? Yet, leaving the gender of the verb out of it, we all do want to "master" history in whatever ways turn out to be possible: the escape from the nightmare of history, the conquest by human beings of control over the otherwise seemingly blind and natural "laws" of socio-economic fatality, remains the irreplaceable will of the Marxist heritage, whatever language it may be expressed in. It can therefore not be expected to hold much attraction for people uninterested in seizing control over their own destinies.

But the notion that there is something misguided and contradictory about a unified theory of differentiation also rests on a confusion between levels of abstraction: a system that constitutively produces differences remains a system, nor is the idea of such a system supposed to be in kind "like" the object it tries to theorize, any more than the concept of dog is supposed to bark or the concept of sugar to taste sweet. It is felt that something precious and existential, something fragile and unique about our own singularity, will be lost irretrievably when we find out that we are just like everybody else: in that case, so be it, and let's know the worst; the objection is the primal form of existentialism (and phenomenology), and it is the emergence of such things and such anxieties that needs to be explained. In any case, objections to the global concept of postmodernism in this sense seem to me to recapitulate, in other terms, the classical objections to the concept of capitalism: something scarcely surprising from the present perspective, which consistently affirms the identity of postmodernism with capitalism itself in its latest systemic mutation. Those objections turned essentially around one form or another of the following paradox: namely that although the various pre-capitalist modes of production achieved their capacity to reproduce themselves through various forms of solidarity or collective cohesion, the logic of capital is on the contrary a dispersive and atomistic, "individualistic" one, an anti-society rather than a society, whose systemic structure, let alone its reproduction of itself, remains a mystery and a contradiction in terms. Leaving aside the answer to the conundrum ("the market"), what may be said is that this paradox is the originality of capitalism and that the verbally contradictory formulas we necessarily encounter in defining it point beyond the words to the thing itself (and also give rise to that peculiar new invention, the dialectic). We will have occasion to return to problems of this kind in what follows: suffice it to say all this more crudely by pointing out that the very concept of differentiation itself (whose most elaborate development we owe to Niklas Luhmann) is itself a systemic one, or, if you prefer, turns the play of differences into a new kind of identity on a more abstract level (it being understood that one must also distinguish between dialectical oppositions and differentiations of this random, dispersive type).

The "war against totality" has finally its political motivation, which it is the merit of Horne's essay to reveal. Following Lyotard, he makes it clear that the fear of Utopia is in this case our old friend *1984*, and that a Utopian and revolutionary politics, correctly associated with totalization and a certain "concept" of totality, is to be eschewed because it leads fatally to Terror: a notion at least as old as Edmund Burke, but helpfully revived, after innumerable restatements during the Stalin period, by the Cambodian atrocities. Ideologically, this particular revival of Cold War rhetoric and stereotypes, launched in the demarxification of France in the 1970s, turns on a bizarre identification of Stalin's Gulag with Hitler's extermination camps (but see Arno Mayer's remarkable *Why Did the Heavens not Darken?* for a definitive demonstration of the constitutive relationship between the "final solution" and Hitler's anti-communism); what can be "post-modern" about these hoary nightmare images, except for the depolitization to which they invite us, is less clear. The history of the revolutionary convulsions in question can also be appealed to for a very different lesson, namely that violence springs from counterrevolution first and foremost, indeed, that the most effective form of counterrevolution lies precisely in this transmission of violence to the revolutionary process itself. I doubt if the current state of alliance or micro-politics in the advanced countries supports such anxieties and fantasies; they would not, for me at least, constitute grounds for withdrawing support and solidarity from a potential revolution in South Africa, say; finally, this general feeling that the revolutionary, Utopian or totalizing impulse is somehow tainted from the outset and doomed to blood by the very structure of its thoughts does strike one as idealistic, if not finally a replay of doctrines of original sin in their worst religious sense. At the end of this essay I will return to more concrete political issues and considerations.

Now, however, I want to return to the question of totalizing thought in a different way, interrogating it not for its truth content or validity but rather for its historical conditions of possibility. This is then no longer to philosophize exactly, or if you prefer to philosophize on a *symptomal* level, in which we step back and estrange our immediate judgments on a given concept ("the most advanced contemporary thinking no longer permits us to deploy concepts of totality or periodization") by way of asking the question about the social determinants that enable or shut down thought. Does the current taboo on totality simply result from philosophical progress and increased self-consciousness? Is it because we have today attained a state of theoretical enlightenment and conceptual sophistication, which permit us to avoid the grosser errors and blunders of the old-fashioned thinkers of the past (most notably Hegel)? That may be so, but it would also require some kind of historical explanation (in which the invention of "materialism" would surely have to intervene). This hybris of the present and of the living can be avoided by posing the issue in a somewhat different way: namely why it is that "concepts of totality" have seemed necessary and unavoidable at certain historical moments, and on the contrary noxious and unthinkable at others. This is an inquiry which, working its way back on the outside of our own thought and on the basis of what we can no longer (or not yet) think, cannot be philosophical in any positive sense (although Adorno attempted, in *Negative*

Dialectics, to turn it into a genuine philosophy of a new kind); it would certainly lead us to the intensified sense that ours is a time of nominalism in a variety of senses (from culture to philosophical thought). Such nominalism would probably turn out to have several pre-histories or overdeterminations: the moment of existentialism, for instance, in which some new social sense of the isolated individual (and of the horror of demography, or of sheer number or multiplicity, particularly in Sartre) causes the older traditional "universals" to pale and lose their conceptual force and persuasiveness; the age-old tradition of Anglo-American empiricism as well, which emerges from this death of the concept with renewed force in a paradoxically "theoretical" and hyper-intellectual age. There is of course a sense in which the slogan "postmodernism" means all this too; but then in that case it is not the explanation, but what remains to be explained.

Speculation and hypothetical analysis of this kind that bears on the weakening of general or universalizing concepts in the present is the correlative of an operation that can often look more reliable, namely the analysis of moments in the past when such conceptuality seemed possible; indeed, those moments in which the emergence of general concepts can be observed have often seemed to be historically privileged ones. As far as the concept of totality is concerned, I am tempted to say about it what I once said about Althusser's notion of structure, namely that the crucial point to be made is this: we can acknowledge the presence of such a concept, provided we understand that there is only one of them: something otherwise often known as a "mode of production." Althusserian "structure" is that, and so is "totality," at least as I use it. As for "totalizing" processes, that often means little more than the making of connections between various phenomena: thus, to take an influential contemporary example, although Gayatri Spivak offers her conception of a "continuous sign-chain" as an alternative to dialectical thought (*In Other Worlds*, 198), on my usage that conception would also stand as a specific (and non-dialectical) form of "totalizing."

We must be grateful to the work of Ronald L. Meek for the prehistory of the concept of a "mode of production" (as that will later be worked out in the writings of Morgan and Marx), which in the 18th century takes the form of what he calls the "four stages theory." This theory comes together in the mid-18th century, in France and in the Scottish Enlightenment, as the proposition that human cultures historically vary with their material or productive basis, which knows four essential transformations: hunting and gathering, pastoralism, agriculture, and commerce. What will then happen to this historical narrative, above all in the thought and work of Adam Smith, is that, having now produced that object of study which is the specifically contemporary mode of production, or capitalism, the historical scaffolding of the pre-capitalist stages tends to fall away and lend both Smith's and Marx's model of capitalism a synchronic appearance. But Meek wants to argue that the historical narrative was essential to the very possibility of thinking capitalism as a system, synchronic or not (*Social Science and the Ignoble Savage*, 219-221); and something like that will remain my own position with respect to that "stage" or moment of capitalism which projects the cultural logic of what some of us now seem to be calling "postmodernism."

I am here however essentially concerned with the conditions of possibility of the concept of a "mode of production," that is to say, the characteristics of the historical and social situation which make it possible to articulate and formulate such a concept in the first place. I will suggest, in a general way, that thinking this particular new thought (or combining older thoughts in this new way) presupposes a particular kind of "uneven" development, such that distinct and co-existing modes of production are registered together in the life world of the thinker in question. This is how Meek describes the preconditions for the production of this particular concept (in its original forms as a "four stages theory"):

> My own feeling is that thinking of the type we are considering which lays primary emphasis on the development of economic techniques and socio-economic relationships, is likely to be a function, first, of the rapidity of contemporary economic advance, and second, of the facility with which a contrast can be observed between areas which are economically advancing and areas which are still in

"lower" stages of development. In the 1750s and 60s, in cities like Glasgow and in areas such as the more advanced provinces in the north of France, the whole social life of the communities concerned was being rapidly and visibly transformed, and it was fairly obvious that this was happening as a result of profound changes taking place in economic techniques and basic socio-economic relationships. And the new forms of economic organization which were emerging could be fairly easily compared and contrasted with the older forms of organization which still existed, say, in the Scottish Highlands, or in the remainder of France—or among the Indian tribes in America. If changes in the mode of subsistence were playing such an important and 'progressive' role in the development of contemporary society, it seemed a fair bet that they must also have done so in that of past society. (*Social Science and the Ignoble Savage*, 127-128).

This possibility of thinking the new concept of a mode of production for the first time is sometimes loosely described as one of the newly emergent forms of historical consciousness, or historicity. It is not necessary, however, to have recourse to the philosophical discourse of consciousness as such, since what are being described might equally well be termed new discursive paradigms, and this more contemporary way of talking about conceptual emergence is reinforced, for literary people, by the presence alongside this one of yet another new historical paradigm in the novels of Sir Walter Scott (as Lukács interprets them in *The Historical Novel*). The unevenness that allowed French thinkers (Turgot, but also Rousseau himself!) to conceptualize a "mode of production" probably had as much as anything else to do with the pre-revolutionary situation in the France of that period, in which feudal forms stood out ever more starkly in their distinctive difference against a whole newly emergent bourgeois culture and class consciousness.

Scotland is in many ways a more complex and interesting case, for, as last of the emergent First World countries, or first of the Third World ones (to use Tom Nairn's provocative idea, in *The*

Break-up of Britain), Enlightenment Scotland is above all the space of a coexistence of radically distinct zones of production and culture: the archaic economy of the Highlanders and their clan system, the new agricultural exploitation of the Lowlands, the commercial vigor of the English "partner" over the border, on the eve of its industrial "take-off." The brilliance of Edinburgh is therefore not a matter of Gaelic genetic material, but rather owing to the strategic yet ec-centric position of the Scottish metropolis and intellectuals with respect to this virtually synchronic co-existence of distinct modes of production, which it is now uniquely the task of the Scottish Enlightenment to "think" or to conceptualize. Nor is this merely an economic matter: Scott, like Faulkner later on, inherits a social and historical raw material, a popular memory, in which the fiercest revolutions and civil and religious wars now inscribe the coexistence of modes of production in vivid narrative form. The condition of thinking a new reality and articulating a new paradigm for it therefore seem to demand a peculiar conjuncture and a certain strategic distance from that new reality, which tends to overwhelm those immersed in it (this would be something like an epistemological variant of the well-known "outsider" principle in scientific discovery).

All of which, however, has another secondary consequence of greater significance to us here and which bears on the gradual repression of such conceptuality. If the postmodern moment, as the cultural logic of an enlarged third stage of classical capitalism, is in many ways a purer and more homogeneous expression of this last, from which many of the hitherto surviving enclaves of socio-economic difference have been effaced (by way of their colonization and absorption by the commodity form), then it makes sense to suggest that the waning of our sense of history, and more particularly our resistance to globalizing or totalizing concepts like that of the mode of production itself, are a function of precisely that universalization of capitalism. Where everything is henceforth systemic the very notion of a system seems to lose its reason for being, returning only by way of a "return of the repressed" in the more nightmarish forms of the "total system" fantasized by Weber or Foucault or the *1984* people.

But a mode of production is not a "total system" in that forbidding sense, and includes a variety of counterforces and new tendencies within itself, of "residual" as well as "emergent" forces, which it must attempt to manage or control (Gramsci's conception of hegemony): were those heterogeneous forces not endowed with an effectivity of their own, the hegemonic project would be unnecessary. Thus, differences are presupposed by the model, something which should be sharply distinguished from another feature which complicates this one, namely that capitalism also produces differences or differentiation as a function of its own internal logic. Finally, to recall our initial discussion of representation, it is also clear that there is a *difference* between the concept and the thing, between this global and abstract model and our own individual social experience, from which it is meant to afford some explanatory difference but which it is scarcely designed to "replace."

A number of other reminders about the "proper use" of the mode of production model are probably also advisable: that what is called a "mode of production" is not a productionist model, it always seems worth saying. What also seems worth saying, in the present context, is that it involves a variety of levels (or orders of abstraction) which must be respected, if these discussions are not to degenerate into random shouting matches. I proposed a very general picture of such levels in *The Political Unconscious*, and in particular the distinctions that have to be respected between an examination of historical events, an evocation of larger class and ideological conflicts and traditions, and an attention to impersonal socio-economic patterning systems (of which the well-known thematics of reification and commodification are examples). The question of agency, which arises often in these pages, has to be mapped across these levels.

Featherstone, for example, thinks that "postmodernism" on my use is a specifically cultural category: it is not, and was rather for better and for worse designed to name a "mode of production" in which cultural production finds a specific functional place, and whose symptomatology is in my work mainly drawn from culture (this is no doubt the source of the confusion). He therefore advises me to pay closer attention to the artists themselves and to their publics, as well as to the institutions which mediate and govern this newer kind of production: nor can I see why any of those topics should be excluded, they are very interesting matters indeed. But it is hard to see how sociological inquiry at that level would become *explanatory*: rather, the phenomena he is concerned with tend at once to reform into their own semi-autonomous sociological level, one which then at once requires a diachronic narrative. To say what the art market is now, and the status of the artist or the consumer, means saying what it was before this transformation, and even at some outside limit leaving a space open for some alternate configuration of such activities (as is the case, for example, in Cuba, where the art market, galleries, investments in painting, etc., do not exist). Once you have written up that narrative, that series of local changes, then the whole thing gets added into the dossier as yet another space in which something like the postmodern "great transformation" can be read.

Indeed, although with Featherstone's proposals concrete social agents seem to make their appearance (postmodernists are then those artists or musicians, those gallery or museum officials or record company executives, those specific bourgeois or youth or working class consumers), here too the requirement of differentiating levels of abstraction must be maintained. For one can also plausibly assert that "postmodernism" as an ethos and a "life style" (truly a contemptible expression that one) is the expression of the "consciousness" of a whole new class fraction that largely transcends the limits of the groups enumerated above: this larger and more abstract category has variously been labeled as a new petty bourgeoisie, a professional-managerial class, or more succinctly as "the yuppies" (each of these expressions smuggling in a little surplus of concrete social representation along with itself).

This identification of the class content of postmodern culture does not at all imply that "yuppies" have become something like a new ruling class or "a subject of history," merely that their cultural practices and values, their local ideologies, have articulated a useful dominant ideological and cultural paradigm for this stage of capital. It is indeed often the case that cultural forms prevalent in a particular period are not furnished by the principal agents of the social formation in question (businessmen who no doubt have something better to do with their time, or are driven by psychological and ideological motive forces of a different type). What is essential is that the culture-ideology in question articulate the world in the most useful way functionally, or in ways that can be functionally reappropriated. Why a certain class fraction should provide these ideological articulations is a historical question as intriguing as the question of the sudden dominance of a particular writer or a particular style. There can surely be no model or formula given in advance for these historical transactions; just as surely, however, we have not yet worked this out for what is being called postmodernism. Meanwhile, another limitation of my own work on the subject (not mentioned by any of the contributors) now becomes clear, namely that the tactical decision to stage the account in cultural terms has made for a relative absence of any identification of properly postmodern "ideologies." Indeed, since I have been particularly interested in the formal matter of what I call some new "theoretical discourse," and also because the paradoxical combination of global decentralization and small group institutionalization has seemed to me an important feature of the postmodern tendential structure, I have seemed mainly to single out intellectual and social phenomena like "poststructuralism" and the "new social movements": thus, against my own deepest political convictions, all the "enemies" have still seemed to be on the Left, an impression I will try to rectify in what follows.

But what has been said about the class origins of post-modernism has as its consequence the requirement that we now specify another higher (or more abstract and global) kind of agency than any so far enumerated. This is of course multinational capital itself: it may as a process be described as some "non-human" logic of capital, and I would continue to defend the appropriateness of that language and that kind of description, in its own terms and on its own level. That that seemingly disembodied force is also an ensemble of human agents, trained in specific ways and inventing original local tactics and practices according to the creativities of the human freedom—this is also obvious, from a different perspective, to which one would only wish to add that for the agents of capital also the old dictum holds that "people make their history, but not in circumstances of their own choosing." It is within the possibilities of late capitalism that people glimpse "the main chance," "go for it," make money, and reorganize firms in new ways (just like artists or generals, ideologists or gallery owners).

What I have tried to show here is that although my account of the postmodern may seem in the eyes of some of its readers and critics to "lack agency," it can be translated or transcoded into a narrative account in which agents of all sizes and dimensions are at work. The choice between these alternate descriptions—focalizations on distinct levels of abstraction—is a practical rather than a theoretical one. It would however be desirable to link up this account of agency with that other very rich (psychoanalytic) tradition of psychic and ideological "subject positions." If it is now objected that the descriptions of agency described above are merely an alternative version of the base-superstructure model— an economic base for postmodernism on the one account, a social or class base on this other—then so be it, provided we understand that "base and superstructure" is not really a model, but a starting point and a problem, something as undogmatic as an imperative simultaneously to grasp culture in and for itself, but also in relationship to its outside, its content, its context, and its space of intervention and of effectivity. How one does that, however, is never given in advance. Gross' beautiful adaptation of Benjamin— postmodernism as the "afterimage" of late capitalism—reminds us not only how wonderfully supple Benjamin was in his formulations of this relationship (elsewhere he says that the "superstructure" is the *expression* of the "base," something that also radically modifies our stereotypes), but also how many new paths of exploration the new figure opens up and entails. Afterimages are objective phenomena which are also mirages and pathologies; they dictate attention to optical processes, to the psychology of perception, and also to the dazzling qualities of the object, and so on and so forth. I have proposed a "model" of postmodernism, which is worth what it's worth and must now take its chances independently; but it is the construction of such a model that is ultimately the fascinating matter, and I hope it will not be taken as a knee-jerk affirmation of "pluralism" if I say that alternate constructions are desirable and welcome, since the grasping of the present from within is the most problematical task the mind can face.

Most of my commentators and critics do not however propose alternate models of this kind (I have noted that whatever their positions they seem to take the modernism/postmodernism distinction as a given and as a meaningful category); but they do quite properly feel the need to judge my construction pragmatically, that is to say, in terms of its political consequences, which include consequences for the politics of culture. Thus Shumway's subtle and profound article turns on the positioning of poststructuralism within my scheme of things, although he has a remarkable lesson for me about Ricoeur (which I acknowledge with gratitude): he could not be aware how close I am to him on the significance of Gadamer (since my work on *Truth and Method* has not yet been published), any more than Huhn could be in a position to know how much more of his Adorno reading I would be prepared to endorse than he thinks (but here the slippage results from the term "ideology," which Adorno uses in a relatively restricted and old-fashioned sense, but which I wish to open up and generalize in ways consonant with a good deal of contemporary thought, whatever the language we decide to use for these matters). If I continue to assert that contemporary theory (that is to say essentially "poststructuralism," to be sure) is to be grasped as yet another postmodern phenomenon, bearing a family likeness to my other more cultural exhibits, this is because I am interested in the formal structure of the new "theoretical discourse," which seems to me radically different from the language and textual operations of what we may call "traditional philosophy": of course the content of "theoretical discourse" is determined and modified by the new form (as it could not but be), while the return to an older philosophical discourse today is no optional or simple matter. Nor would I dream of denying Shumway's assertion of the radical political uses of much of poststructuralism (but then the crucial tactical question would be: under what circumstances and to what ends, and for whom?).

I do tend to feel that something is lost when an emphasis on power and domination tends to obliterate the displacement, which made up the originality of Marxism as such, towards the economic system, the structure of the mode of production, and exploitation as such. Once again, matters of power and domination are articulated on a different level from those systemic ones, and no advances are gained by staging the complementary analyses as an irreconcilable opposition, unless the motive is to produce a new ideology (in the tradition, it bears the time-honored name of *anarchism*), in which case other kinds of lines are drawn and one argues the matter differently.

Indeed, I suspect that my most vigorous critics here are those who are in one way or another inspired by an anarchist and populist spirit. Thus Featherstone notes my "acknowledgment" of the emergence in postmodernism, of a more democratic and culturally literate public everywhere in the world today; but he wonders whether I celebrate this development with sufficient enthusiasm, and perhaps he is right to be suspicious. His own remarks about the new unemployment might have inspired different kinds of doubts as to the political role of some new mass culture among people thus radically disempowered. Goldstein meanwhile goes so far as to assert that I "disavow" "the 'merely' progressive feminist, Afro-American, working class, or third-world struggles to alter and to expand the traditional canon and literary study's limitation." Leaving aside the silliness of the verb (what would it mean to "avow" such things, and who am I to "disavow" them or to "avow" them either?), it is presumptuous of Goldstein to read my mind, and to attribute political attitudes to me which I "disavow" in any case; far from being opposed to the projects he enumerates, I strongly endorse all of them (he seems to have me confused with Lynne Cheney or William Bennett). He is however kind enough to spill the beans in his next sentence:

> As an engaged insider, a feminist, an Afro-American, a working class, or a third-world critic seeks to change and to improve literary institutions in a 'progressive' but not a utopian direction. In a reformist manner, such scholars ameliorate the 'ideological' present and do not map the

utopian future; they critique their institution's racist, chauvinist, or elitist discourses, not the irrationality of the whole modern era. (257, above)

Here Goldstein is putting words into other people's mouths, I hope as erroneously as he has done with me. This formulation of the old antithesis between reform and revolution does indeed strike me as disastrous; but there is no need to make it, and Mao Zedong used to talk about "walking on two legs." Local struggles and issues are not merely indispensable, they are unavoidable; but as I have tried to say elsewhere, they are effective only so long as they also remain figures or allegories for some larger systemic transformation. Politics has to operate on the micro- and the macro-levels simultaneously; a modest restriction to local reforms within the system seems reasonable, but often proves politically demoralizing.

Radhakrishnan offers me a different kind of lesson in alliance politics, but his example of the Rainbow coalition is singularly inappropriate, since Jackson's force and appeal has always consisted in a mediatory opposition which some might even think of as a kind of totalization: I have indeed never heard a Jackson speech which did not seek to unite its multiple "subject-positions" and constituencies by way of the common situation they share as working-class people. The concept of class thus seems alive and well in the very heart of the most promising recent Northamerican left political experiment.

Saul Landau has observed, about our current situation, that there has never been a moment in the history of capitalism when this last enjoyed greater elbow-room and space for maneuver: all the threatening forces it generated against itself in the past—labor movements and insurgencies, mass socialist parties, even socialist states themselves—seem today in full disarray when not in one way or another effectively neutralized; for the moment global capital seems able to follow its own nature and inclinations, without the traditional precautions. Here then we have yet another "definition" of postmodernism, and a useful one indeed, which only an ostrich will wish to accuse of "pessimism." This is a transitional period between two stages of capitalism, in which the earlier forms of the economic are in the process of being restructured on a global scale, including the older forms of labor and its traditional organizational institutions and concepts. That a new international proletariat (taking forms we cannot yet imagine) will reemerge from this convulsive upheaval it needs no prophet to predict: we ourselves are still in the trough, however, and no one can say how long we will stay there. This is the sense in which two seemingly rather different conclusions to my historical essays on the current situation (one on the Sixties and one on postmodernism) are in reality identical: in the first, I anticipate the process of proletarianization on a global scale which I have just evoked here; in the second I call for something mysteriously termed "cognitive mapping" of a new and global type.

But "cognitive mapping" was in reality nothing but a code word for "class consciousness" (as Steve Best notes in his shrewed and wide-ranging analysis): only it proposed the need for class consciousness of a new and hitherto undreamed of kind, while it also inflected the account in the direction of that new spatiality implicit in the postmodern (which Ed Soja's *Postmodern Geographies* now places on the agenda in so eloquent and timely a fashion). I occasionally get just as tired of the slogan of "postmodernism" as anyone else, but when I am tempted to regret my complicity with it, to deplore its misuses and its notoriety, and to conclude with some reluctance that it raised more problems than it solves, I find myself pausing to wonder whether any other concept can dramatize the issue in quite so effective and economical a fashion. "We have to name the system": this high point of the Sixties finds an unexpected revival in the postmodernism debate.

Fredric R. Jameson—
A Comprehensive Bibliography

Books

1961   *Sartre: The Origins of a Style.* New Haven: Yale University Press. Rpt. 1984, New York: Columbia University Press.

1971   *Marxism and Form: Twentieth Century Dialectical Theories of Literature.* Princeton: Princeton University Press.

1972   *The Prison-House of Language: A Critical Account of Structuralism and Russian Formalism.* Princeton: Princeton University Press.

1979   *Fables of Aggression: Wyndham Lewis, The Modernist as Fascist.* Berkeley: University of California Press.

1981   *The Political Unconscious: Narrative as a Socially Symbolic Act.* Ithaca, NY: Cornell University Press.

1987   *Postmodernism and Cultural Theories (Houxiandaizhuyi he Wenhualilun).* Lectures in China, Xi'an: Shanxi Teacher's University. Rpt. in journals in Taiwan and Hong Kong, 1988. Rpt. in Taiwan with new preface, 1989.

1988   *The Ideologies of Theory, Essays 1971-1986:* Vol. 1 *Situations of Theory.* Vol. 2 *The Syntax of History.* Minneapolis: University of Minnesota Press.

Forth- *Messages of the Visible: Film / Theory / Periodization.* New coming   York: Routledge & Chapman, Hall.
        The Concept of Postmodernism. Durham: Duke University Press.
        Dialectical Aesthetics. London: Verso Press.

Articles, Chapters, Essays

1967   "T. W. Adorno; or, Historical Tropes," *Salmagundi,* 5: 3-43.

1968   "On Politics and Literature," *Salmagundi,* 2-3: 17-26.

1969   "Walter Benjamin; or, Nostalgia," *Salmagundi,* 10-11: 52-68.

1969   "Introduction to T. W. Adorno," *Salmagundi,* 10-11: 140-143.

1970   "The Case for Georg Lukács," *Salmagundi,* 13: 3-35.

1970   "On Raymond Chandler," *Southern Review,* 6: 624-650.

1970   "Seriality in Modern Literature," *Bucknell Review,* 18: 63-80.

1971   "*La Cousine Bette* and Allegorical Realism," *PMLA,* 86: 241-254.

1971 "Metacommentary," *PMLA*, 86.1 (January): 9-18.

1972 "The Great American Hunter: Ideological Content in the Novel," *College English*, 34: 180-197.

1972 "Introduction" to and translation of W. Dilthey, "The Rise of Hermeneutics," *New Literary History*, 3: 229-244.

1972 "Three Methods in Sartre's Literary Criticism," *Modern French Criticism*. Ed. J. K. Simon. Chicago: University of Chicago Press. 193-227.

1973 "Generic Discontinuities in Science Fiction: Brian Aldiss' *Starship*," *Science Fiction Studies*, 2: 57-68.

1973 "Introduction" to Henri Avron, *Marxist Esthetics*. Ithaca, NY: Cornell University Press. vii-xxiv.

1973 "The Vanishing Mediator: Narrative Structure in Max Weber," *New German Critique*, 1 (Winter): 52-89. Rpt. 1974, *Working Papers in Cultural Studies*, 5 (Spring): 111-149.

1973 "Wyndham Lewis as Futurist," *Hudson Review*, 26: 295-329.

1974 "Benjamin as Historian, Or How to Write a Marxist Literary History," *Minnesota Review*, 3: 116-136.

1974 "Change, Science Fiction, and Marxism: Open or Closed Universes? In Retrospect," *Science Fiction Studies*, 1.4: 272-276.

1974 "Demystifying Literary History," *New Literary History*," 5: 605-612.

1974 "Review" of J. P. Stern, *On Realism*, *Clio*, 3: 346-352.

1974 "Review" of V. Voloshinov, *Marxism and the Philosophy of Language*, *Style*, 8: 535-543.

1975 "After Armageddon: Character Systems in P. K. Dick's *Dr. Bloodmoney*," *Science Fiction Studies*, 2.1: 31-42.

1975 "Beyond the Cave: Demystifying the Ideology of Modernism," *Bulletin of the Midwest Modern Language Association*, 8.1 (Spring): 1-20.

1975 "The Ideology of the Text," *Salmagundi*, 31-32 (Fall-Winter, 1976): 204-246.

1975 "L'Inconscient politique," *La lecture sociocritique du texte romanesque*. Eds. G. Falconer and H. Metterand. Hakkert. 39-48.

1975 "Magical Narratives: Romance as Genre," *New Literary History*, 7: 135-163.

1975 "Notes Toward A Marxist Cultural Politics," *Minnesota Review*, 5: 35-39.

1975 "The Re-invention of Marx," *Times Literary Supplement*, 22 August: 942-943.

1975 "World Reduction in Le Guin: The Emergence of Utopian Narrative," *Science Fiction Studies* 2.3: 221-230.

1975 "Authentic Ressentiment: The 'Experimental' Novels of

Gissing," *Nineteenth Century Fiction*, 31: 127-149.

1976 "Collective Art in the Age of Cultural Imperialism," *Alcheringa*, 2.2: 108-111.

1976 "Criticism in History," *Weapons of Criticism: Marxism in America and the Literary Tradition*. Ed. N. Rudich. Palo Alto, CA: Ramparts Press. 31-50.

1976 "Figural Relativism, or The Poetics of Historiography," *Diacritics*, 6.1 (Spring): 2-9.

1976 "The Ideology of Form: Partial Systems in *La Vieille Fille*," *sub stance*, 15: 29-49.

1976 "Introduction/Prospectus: To Reconsider the Relationship of Marxism to Utopian Thought," *Minnesota Review*, 6: 53-58.

1976 "Modernism and its Repressed: Robbe-Grillet as Anti-Colonialist," *Diacritics*, 6.2 (Summer): 7-14.

1976 "On Goffman's *Frame Analysis*," *Theory and Society*, 3: 119-133.

1976 "Political Painting: New Perspectives on the Realism Controversy," *Praxis*, 2: 225-230.

1977 "Class and Allegory in Contemporary Mass Culture: *Dog Day Afternoon* as a Political Film," *College English*, 38: 843-859. Rpt. *Screen Education*, 30 (1979): 75-92.

1977 "Ideology, Narrative Analysis, and Popular Culture," *Theory and Society*, 4: 543-559.

1977 "Imaginary and Symbolic in *La Rabouilleuse*," *Social Science Information*, 16.1: 59-81.

1977 "On Jargon," *Minnesota Review*, 9: 30-31.

1977 "Of Islands and Trenches: Neutralization and the Production of Utopian Discourse," *Diacritics*, 7.2 (Summer): 2-21.

1977 "Reflections in Conclusion," *Aesthetics and Politics*. Ernst Bloch, et al. London: New Left Books. 196-213.

1978 "Imaginary and Symbolic in Lacan: Marxism, Psychoanalytic Criticism, and the Problem of the Subject," *Yale French Studies*, 55-56: 338-395.

1978 "The Symbolic Inference: or, Kenneth Burke and Ideological Analysis," *Critical Inquiry*, 4.3 (Spring): 507-523.

1978 "Ideology and Symbolic Action: Reply to Kenneth Burke," *Critical Inquiry*, 5.2: 417-422.

1979 "But Their Cause is Just: Israel and the Palestinians," *Seven Days*, 3.9 (Sept. 28, 1979): 19-21. Rpt. *New Haven Advocate*, 31 October 1979: 6.

1979 "Marxism and Historicism," *New Literary History*, 11 (Autumn): 41-73.

1979 "Marxism and Teaching," *New Political Science*, 2-3: 31-35.

1979 "Reification and Utopia in Mass Culture," *Social Text*, 1: 130-148. French translation, Quebec.

1979   "Towards a Libidinal Economy of Three Modern Painters,"
       Social Text, 1: 189-199.
1980   "Balzac et le problème du sujet," *Le Roman de Balzac*. Eds. R. Le
       Huenen and P. Perron. Didier. 65-76.
1980   "SF Novel / SF Film," *Science Fiction Studies*, 22: 319-322.
1981   "From Criticism to History," *New Literary History*, 12.2: 367-
       376.
1981   "In the Destructive Element Immerse: Hans Jürgen Syberberg
       and Cultural Revolution," *October*, 17: 99-118.
1981   "Religion and Ideology: A Political Reading of *Paradise Lost*,"
       *1642: Proceedings of 1980 Essex Sociology of Literature
       Conference*. Ed. R. Barker. University of Essex. Rpt. 1986 in
       Literature Politics & Theory. Eds. F. Barker, et al. London:
       Methuen Press, 1981.
1981   "Sartre in Search of Flaubert," *New York Times Book Review*, 27
       December 1981: 5.
1981   "*The Shining*," *Social Text*, 4: 114-125.
1982   "Ulysses in History," *James Joyce and Modern Literature*. Eds.
       W. J. McCormack and Alistair Stead. London: Routledge &
       Kegan Paul. 126-141.
1982   "On Aronson's *Sartre*," *Minnesota Review*, 18: 116-127.
1982   "Futuristic Visions That Tell Us About Right Now" (on P. K.
       Dick), *In These Times*, 6.23 (May 17): 5-11.
1982   "On *Diva*," *Social Text*, 6: 114-119.
1982   "Progress versus Utopia; or, Can We Imagine the Future?"
       Science Fiction Studies, 27: 147-158.
1982   "Towards a New Awareness of Genre," *Science Fiction Studise*,
       28: 322-324.
1982   "Interview," *Diacritics*, 12.3 (Fall): 72-91.
1982   "Reading Hitchcock," *October*, 23: 15-42.
1982   "A Dialog with Fredric Jameson," by K. Ayyappa Paniker,
       Littcrit, 8.2 (December): 5-26.
1983   "Science Versus Ideology," *Humanities in Society*, 6: 2-3.
1983   "Euphorias of Substitution: Hubert Aquin and the Political
       Novel in Quebec," *Yale French Studies*, 65: 214-223.
1983   "L'éclatement du récit et la clôture californienne," *Littérature*,
       49 (February): 89-101.
1983   "Postmodernism and Consumer Society," *The Anti-Aesthetic*.
       Ed. Hal Foster. Port Townsend, WA: Bay Press. 111-125.
1983   "Pleasure: A Political Issue," *Formations of Pleasure*. Eds. T.
       Bennet, et al. London: Routledge & Kegan Paul.
1983   "Morality *versus* Ethical Substance; or Aristotelian Marxism in
       Alasdair MacIntyre," *Social Text*, 8 (Fall-Winter): 151-154.
1984   "Periodizing the Sixties," *The Sixties without Apologies*, Eds.

Sonya Sayres, et al. Minneapolis: University of Minnesota Press. 178-209.

1984 "Literary Innovation and Modes of Production," *Modern Chinese Literature*, 1.1: 67-68.

1984 "Postmodernism, or The Cultural Logic of Late Capitalism," *New Left Review*, 146: 52-92. Rpt. 1986 (Spanish) *Casa de las Americas*, 141-173. Rpt. 1989 (Italian) Garzanti Editore, 7-103.

1984 "The Politics of Theory—Ideological Positions in the Postmodernism Debate," *New German Critique*, 33 (Fall): 53-65.

1984 "Wallace Stevens," *New Orleans Review*, 11.1: 10-19.

1984 "Postmodernism and Consumer Society," *Amerikastudien-American Studies*, 29.1: 55-73.

1984 "Utopian and Fantasy Literature in East Germany—The Development of a Genre of Fiction, 1945-1979," (Review article of H. Heidtmann, *Science Fiction and the German Democratic Republic*), *Science Fiction Studies*, 11.33: 194-199.

1984 "Forword" to Jean-François Lyotard's *The Postmodern Condition*. Minneapolis: University of Minnesota Press.

1984 "Afterword" to Jameson's *Sartre: The Origins of a Style*. New York: Columbia University Press. 2nd Edition.

1984 "The Weakest Link: Marxism and Literary Studies," *The Left Academy: Marxist Scholarship on American Campuses*, vol. 11. New York: Pantheon. 1-24. With James H. Kavanagh.

1984 "Reification and Utopia in the Mass-Culture," *Études Françaises*, 19.3: 121-138.

1984 "Flaubert's Libidinal Historicism: Trois Contes," *Flaubert and Postmodernism*. Eds. N. Schor and H. F. Majewski. University of Nebraska Press. 76-83.

1984 "An Overview," *Rewriting Literary History*. Eds. Tak-wai Wong and M. A. Abbas. Hong Kong University Press. 338-347.

1985 "Introduction" to *Sartre after Sartre*, *Yale French Studies*, 68: iii-xi.

1985 "Baudelaire as Modernist and Postmodernist: The Dissolution of the Referent and the Artificial 'Sublime,'" *Lyric Poetry: Beyond New Criticism*. Eds. C. Hosek and Patricia Parker. Ithaca, NY: Cornell University Press. 247-263.

1985 "The Realist Floor Plan," *On Signs*. Ed. M. Blonsky. Baltimore: Johns Hopkins University Press. 373-383.

1985 "Architecture and the Critique of Ideology." *Architecture Criticism Ideology*. Princeton: Princeton Architectural Press. 51-87.

1985   "Forward" to Jacques Attali's *Noise: The Political Economy of Music*. Minneapolis: University of Minnesota Press.

1986   "An Introduction to *Essays on Theories of the Text*," *Texte-Revue de Critique et de Théorie Littéraire*, N5-6, A6-20.

1986   "Four Ways of Looking at a Fairy Tale," *The Fairy Tale: Politics, Desire, and Everyday Life*, October 30-November 26: 16-24. "Artist's Space."

1986   "Third World Literature in the Era of Multinational Capitalism," *Social Text*, 15 (Fall): 65-88.

1986   "On Magic Realism in Film," *Critical Inquiry*, 12.2: 301-325.

1986   "An Interview with F. R. Jameson by A. Stephanson on Post-modernism," *Flash Art* (Milano Press), 131: 69-73.

1987   "Science-Fiction as a Spatial Genre—Generic Discontinuities and the Problem of Figuration in Vonda McIntyre's *The Exile Waiting*," *Science Fiction Studies*, 14: 44-59. Rpt. in *Essays on the Culture of the Future*, 241-247.

1987   "Introduction to Borge" and "Interview with Thomas Borge" by F. R. Jameson, *New Left Review*, 164 (July-August): 51-64.

1987   "Post-Modernism and Video Text," *Poetics of Writing*. Eds. N. Fabb, et al. Manchester: University of Manchester Press.

1987   "On Habits of the Heart," *South Atlantic Quarterly*, 86.4 (Fall): 545-565. Rpt. in *Community in America*, eds. C. Reynolds and R. Norman. Berkeley: University of California Press.

1987   "Interview: Andrea Ward Speaks with Fredric Jameson," *Impulse*, (Winter): 8-9.

1987   "Some Difficulties Associated with the Description of War," (German) *Weimarer Beitrage*, 33.8: 1393-1398.

1987   "Postmodernism; Commodification and Cultural Expansion," Houxiandaizhuyi: Shangpinghua yu Wenhuakuouzhang (Interview in China, March) *Dushu*. Reprinted in Taiwan, 1988.

1987   "Discussion: Contemporary Chinese Writing," *Polygraph*, 1 (Fall): 3-9.

1987   "The State of the Subject (III)," *Critical Quarterly*, 29.4 (Winter): 16-25.

1987   "Regarding Postmodernism—A Conversation with Fredric Jameson," *Social Text*, 17: 29-54. Rpt. from *Flash Art*, 1986.

1987   "A Brief Response," *Social Text*, 17: 26-28.

1988   "Cognitive Mapping," *Marxism and the Interpretation of Culture*. Eds. Cary Nelson and Lawrence Grossberg. Urbana: University of Illinois Press. 347-360.

1988   "*History and Class Consciousness* as an 'Unfinished Project,'" *Rethinking MARXISM*, 1.1 (Spring): 49-72.

1988   "Postmodernism and Utopia," Boston: Institute of Contemporary Art. 11-32 (March).

1988   "Interview with Fredric Jameson," by Jay Murphy. *Left Curve*, 12: 4-11.

1988   "On Negt & Kluge," *October*, 46 (Fall): 151-177.

1988   "La Lecture sans l'interprétation le postmodernisme et le texte vidéo," *Extrait de Communications*, 48 (November): 105-120. Trans. V. Colonna, C. Liebow, and L. Allard.

1988   "Modernism and Imperialism," *Nationalism, Colonialism & Literature* (Field Day Pamphlet), #14. Derry, Ireland. 5-15.

1988   "Postmodernism and Consumer Society." *Postmodernism and Its Discontents*. Ed. E. Ann Kaplan. London: Verso Press. 13-29.

1989   "Nostalgia for the Present," *South Atlantic Quarterly*, 88.2 (Spring): 517-537.

1989   "The Space of Science Fiction: Narrative in A. E. Van Vogt," *Polygraph*, 2-3: 52-65.

Bibliography —
Theory: Marxism / Postmodernism

Abercrombie, N., S. Hill and B. S. Turner. (1980). *The Dominant Ideology Thesis*. London: Allen and Unwin.

Abercrombie, N. and J. Urry. (1983). *Capital, Labour, and the New Middle Classes*. London: Allen and Unwin.

Adorno, Theodor W. (1968). "Sociology and Psychology," *New Left Review*, 47 (Jan.-Feb.).

————. (1973). *Negative Dialectics*. Trans. E. B. Ashton. New York: Seabury Press.

————. (1974). *Minima Moralia: Reflections from Damaged Life*. Trans. E. F. N. Jephcott. London: New Left Books.

————. (1974). *Gesammelte Schriften*, Vol. 11. Frankfurt: Suhrkamp Verlag.

————. (1974). "Lyric Poetry and Society," trans. Bruce Mayo. *Telos*, 20 (Summer): 56-71.

————. (1977). "Commitment," *Aesthetics and Politics*. Ed. and trans. Ronald Taylor. London: New Left Books. 177-195.

————. (1977). "Reconciliation Under Duress," *Aesthetics and Politics*. Ed. and trans. Ronald Taylor. London: New Left Books. Originally published "Erpresste Versöhnung. Zu Georg Lukács: Wider den missverstandenen Realismus," *Der Monat*, 11 (November, 1938): 37-49.

————. (1978). "Culture and Administration," trans. Wes Blomster. *Telos*, 37 (Fall): 93-111.

————. (1981). *Prisms*. Trans. Samuel and Shierry Weber. Cambridge, MA: MIT Press.

————. (1984). "The Essay as Form," trans. Bob Hullot-Kentor and Fredric Will. *New German Critique*, 32 (Spring/Summer): 151-171.

————. (1984). *Aesthetic Theory*. Trans. L. Lenhardt. London: Routledge & Kegan Paul. *Ästhetische Theorie*, 2nd. ed. *Gesammelte Schriften*, Vol. 7 Frankfurt: Suhrkamp Verlag, 1974.

Althusser, Louis. (1970). *For Marx*. New York: Vintage Books. Rpt. London: Verso Press, 1977.

————. (1976). *Essays in Self-Criticism*. London: New Left Books.

Althusser, Louis and Etienne Balibar. (1970). *Reading Capital*. Trans. Ben Brewster. London: New Left Books. Also New York: Random House.

Anderson, Perry. (1984). *In the Tracks of Historical Materialism*. Chicago: University of Chicago Press. Rpt. from London: Verso, 1983.

————. (1987). "The Figures of Descent," *New Left Review*, 161 (January).

Arac, Jonathan. (1986). "Introduction," *Postmodernism and Politics*. Ed. Jonathan Arac. Minneapolis: University of Minnesota Press. ix-xliii.

Arato, Andrew and Eike Gebhardt, eds. (1978). *The Essential Frankfurt School Reader.* New York: Urizen Books.

Aronowitz, Stanley. (1981). *The Crisis in Historical Materialism: Class, Politics, and Culture in Marxist Theory.* New York: Praeger.

———. (1988). *Science as Power: Discourse and Ideology in Modern Society.* Minneapolis: University of Minnesota Press.

Bakhtin, Mikhail. (1981). *The Dialogic Imagination.* Trans. Caryl Emerson and Michael Holquist. Austin: University of Texas Press.

Barbalet, J. M. (1986). "Limitations of Class Theory and the Disappearance of Status: The Problem of the New Middle Class," *Sociology,* 20 (4): 557-575.

Barthes, Roland. (1972). *Mythologies.* Trans. Annette Lovers. New York: Hill and Wang.

———. (1974). *S/Z.* Trans. Richard Miller. New York: Hill and Wang.

Baudrillard, Jean. (1975). *The Mirror of Production.* Trans. Mark Poster. St. Louis: Telos Press.

———. (1981). *For a Critique of the Political Economy of the Sign.* Trans. Charles Levin. St. Louis: Telos Press.

———. (1983). *Simulations.* Trans. Paul Foss. New York: Semiotext(e).

———. (1983). "The Ecstasy of Communication," *The Anti-Aesthetic: Essays on Postmodern Culture.* Ed. Hal Foster. Port Townsend, WA: Bay Press. 126-134.

———. (1983). *Les strategies fatales.* Paris: Grasset.

———. (1989). *America.* Trans. Chris Turner. London: Verso Press.

Baudrillard, Jean and Paul Virilio. (1983). *In the Shadow of the Silent Majorities, or the End of the Social and Other Essays.* Trans. Paul Foss. New York: Semiotext(e).

Bauman, Zygmunt. (1985). "On the Origins of Civilization; A Historical Note," *Theory, Culture & Society,* 2 (3): 7-14.

———. (1988). "Is There a Post-Modern Sociology?" *Theory, Culture & Society,* 5 (2-3): 217-237.

Baynes, Kenneth, James Bohman and Thomas McCarthy, eds. (1987). *After Philosophy: End or Transformation.* Cambridge, MA: MIT Press.

Bell, Daniel. (1976). *The Cultural Contradictions of Capitalism.* New York: Basic Books.

———. (1980). *The Winding Passage: Essays and Sociological Journeys.* Cambridge, MA: ABT Books. Note "Liberalism in the Postindustrial Society"; "Beyond Modernism, Beyond Self"; "The Return of the Sacred: The Argument on the Future of Religion."

———. (1987). "Modernism Mummified," *American Quarterly,* 39 (1): 122-132.

Bendix, R. (1970). "Culture, Social Structure and Change." *Embattled Reason: Essays on Social Knowledge.* New York: Oxford University Press.

Benjamin, Walter. (1968). *Illuminations*. Trans. Harry Zohn. New York: Schocken Books. Note "On Some Motifs in Baudelaire" and "Theses on the Philosophy of History."

―――. (1983-84). "Theoretics of Knowledge; Theory of Progress," trans. Leigh Haffrey and Richard Sieburth. *The Philosophical Forum*, 15 (1-2).

Bennington, Geoff. (1982). "Not Yet, A Review of Fredric Jameson's *The Political Unconscious*," *Diacritics*, 12 (Fall): 23-32.

Berman, Marshall. (1982). *All that is Solid Melts into Air: The Experience of Modernity*. New York: Simon and Schuster.

Bernstein, Richard. (1985). *Philosophical Profiles: Essays in a Pragmatic Mode*. Cambridge: Polity Press.

Berthoud, J. A. (1985). "Narrative and Ideology: A Critique of Fredric Jameson's *The Political Unconscious*." *Narrative: From Malory to Motion Pictures*. Ed. Jeremy Hawthorn. London: Edward Arnold, Ltd.

Best, Steven. (1988). "The Commodification of Reality and the Reality of Commodification," *Current Perspectives in Social Theory*. Ed. Scott McNall. Greenwich, CT: JAI Press.

Best, Steven and Douglas Kellner. (1987). "(Re)Watching Television: Notes Toward a Political Criticism," *Diacritics*, 17 (Summer): 97-113.

Bloch, Ernst. (1986). *The Principle of Hope*. Trans. Neville Plaice, Stephen Plaice, and Paul Knight. Cambridge, MA: MIT Press.

Bourdieu, Pierre. (1984). *Distinction: A Social Critique of the Judgment of Taste*. Trans. Richard Nice. London: Routledge and Kegan Paul. Also Cambridge, MA: Harvard University Press.

―――. (1986). "Interview," by A. Honneth, H. Kocyba, and B. Schwibs. Trans. J. Bleicher. *Theory, Culture & Society*, 3 (3): 35-51.

Bradbury, M. (1983). "Modernism/Postmodernisms," *Innovation/Renovation*. Eds. Ihab Hassan and S. Hassan. Madison: University of Wisconsin Press.

Bürger, Peter. (1984). "Decline of the Modern Age," *Telos*, 62: 117-130.

Burris, Val. (1986). "The Discovery of the New Middle Class," *Theory and Society*, 15: 317-349.

Carter, Robert. (1985). *Capitalism, Class Conflict and the New Middle Class*. London and Boston: Routledge and Kegan Paul.

Cavell, Stanley. (1976). *Must We Mean What We Say?* Cambridge: Cambridge University Press.

Clark, Timothy. J. (1984). *The Painting of Modern Life: Paris in the Art of Monet and his Followers*. Princeton: Princeton University Press.

Cooke, Philip. (1988). "Modernity, Postmodernity, and the City," *Theory, Culture & Society*, 5 (2-3): 475-492.

Cornell, Drucilla and Selya Benhabib. (1987). *Feminism as Critique: Essays on the Politics of Gender in Late Capitalist Societies*. Cambridge: Polity Press.

Coward, Rosalind and John Ellis. (1977). *Language and Materialism*. London: Routledge and Kegan Paul.

Culler, Jonathan. (1975). *Structuralist Poetics: Structuralism, Linguistics, and the Study of Literature*. Ithaca, NY: Cornell University Press.

————. (1982). *On Deconstruction: Theory and Criticism after Structuralism*. Ithaca, NY: Cornell University Press.

Davis, Mike. (1985). "Urban Renaissance and the Spirit of Postmodernism," *New Left Review*, 151 (May-June): 106-124.

Debord, Guy. (1970). *The Society of the Spectacle*. Detroit: Red and Black.

Deleuze, Gilles and Felix Guattari. (1977). *The Anti-Oedipus: Capitalism and Schizophrenia*. Trans. Robert Hurley, Mark Seem, and Helen Lane. New York: Viking. Rpt.: Minneapolis: University of Minnesota Press, 1983.

de Man, Paul. "Kant and Schiller," unpublished typescript.

Derrida, Jacques. (1976). *Of Grammatology*. Trans. Gayatri Chakravorty Spivak. Baltimore: Johns Hopkins University Press.

————. (1977). *Criticism in Society: Interviews with Jacques Derrida and Others*. New York: Metheun.

————. (1978). "Structure, Sign and Play in the Discourses of the Human Sciences," *Writing and Difference*. Trans. Alan Bass. Chicago: University of Chicago Press. 278-293.

————. (1979). "Living On/Border Lines," *Deconstruction and Criticism*. Eds. Harold Bloom et al. New York: Seabury Press. 75-176.

————. (1981). *Dissemination*. Trans. Barbara Johnson. Chicago: University of Chicago Press.

————. (1981). *Positions*. Trans. Alan Bass. Chicago: University of Chicago Press.

————. (1982). *Margins of Philosophy*. Trans. Alan Bass. Chicago: University of Chicago Press.

————. (1983). "The University in the Eyes of Its Pupils," *Diacritics*, 13 (Fall): 3-20.

————. (1986). *Glas*. Trans. John P. Leavey and Richard Rand. Lincoln: University of Nebraska Press.

Dews, Peter. (1987). *Logics of Disintegration: Poststructuralist Thought and the Claims of Critical Theory*. London: Verso.

DiMaggio, P. (1987). "Classification in Art," *American Sociological Review*, 52 (4): 440-455.

Douglas, M. (1982). "The Effects of Modernization on Religious Change," *Daedalus*, 111 (1): 1-19.

Douglas, M. and B. Isherwood. (1978). *The World of Goods*. Harmondsworth: Penguin.

Dowling, William C. (1984). *Jameson, Althusser, Marx: An Introduction to The Political Unconscious*. Ithaca: Cornell University Press.

Dreyfus, Hubert. (1984). "Beyond Hermeneutics: Interpretation in Late Heidegger and Recent Foucault," *Hermeneutics: Questions and Prospects*. Eds. Gary Shapiro and Alan Sica. Amherst: University of Massachusettes Press. 66-83.

Dreyfus, Hubert and Paul Rabinow. (1983). *Beyond Structuralism and Herm-eneutics*, 2nd edition. Chicago: University of Chicago Press.

During, S. (1987). "Postmodernism or Post-Colonialism Today," *Textual Practice*, 1 (1): 32-67.

Eagleton, Terry. (1976). *Marxism and Literary Theory*. Berkeley: University of California Press.

————. (1981). *Walter Benjamin: Or Towards a Revolutionary Criticism*. London, Verso Press.

————. (1982). "Fredric Jameson: The Politics of Style," *Diacritics*, 12 (Fall): 14-22.

————. (1986). *Against the Grain*. London: Verso Press.

Easton, S., A. Hawkins, S. Laing and H. Walker. (1988). *Disorder and Discipline: Popular Culture from 1550 to the Present*. London: Temple Smith.

Elias, Norbert. (1978). *The Civilizing Process, Volume 1: The History of Manners*. Oxford: Basil Blackwell.

————. (1982). *The Civilizing Process, Volume II: State Formation and Civilization*. Oxford: Basil Blackwell.

————. (1984). "On the Sociogenesis of Sociology," *Sociologisch Tijdschrift*, 11 (1): 14-52.

Elwart, G. (1984). "Markets, Veniality and the Moral Economy," University of Bielefeld, mimeo.

Fabian, Johannes. (1983). *Time and the Other: How Anthropology Makes Its Object*. New York: Columbia University Press.

Featherstone, Mike. (1986). "French Social Theory: An Introduction," *Theory, Culture & Society*, 3 (3): 1-6.

————. (1987). "Lifestyle and Consumer Culture," *Theory, Culture & Society*, 4 (1): 66-70.

————. (1988). "In Pursuit of the Postmodern," *Theory, Culture & Society*, 5 (2-3): 195-215.

————. (1989). "Towards a Sociology of Postmodern Culture," *Culture and Social Structure*. Ed. H. Haferkamp. Berlin and New York: De Gruyter.

Fekete, John. (1978). *The Critical Twilight*. London and Boston: Routledge and Kegan Paul.

Flieger, Jerry Aline. (1982). "The Prison-House of Ideology: Critic as Inmate," *Diacritics*, 12 (Fall).

Foster, Hal. (1985). "(Post)Modern Polemics," *Recodings: Art, Spectacle, Cultural Politics*. Port Washington, WA: Bay Press.

Foster-Carter, Aidan. (1978). "The Modes of Production Controversy," *New Left Review*, 107 (Jan.-Feb.): 47-77.

Foucault, Michel. (1970). *The Order of Things: The Archaeology of the Human Sciences*. New York: Random House.

————. (1972). *The Archaeology of Knowledge*. Trans. A. M. Sheridan Smith. New York: Pantheon.

————. (1973). *The Birth of the Clinic*. Trans. A. M. Sheridan Smith. New York: Pantheon.

————. (1977). *Language, Counter-Memory, Practice*. Trans. Donald F. Bouchard and Sherry Simon. Ithaca, NY: Cornell University Press. Note "Theatrum Philosophicum" and "Intellectuals and Power."

————. (1977). *Discipline and Punish*. Trans. Alan Sheridan. New York: Pantheon.

————. (1980). *Power/Knowledge*. Trans. Colin Gordon, L. Marshall, J. Mepham, and K. Soper. New York: Pantheon.

Gadamer, Hans-Georg. (1975). *Truth and Method*. Trans. Garrett Darden and John Cumming. New York: Seabury.

————. (1976). *Philosophical Hermeneutics*. Ed. and trans. David E. Linge. Berkeley: University of California Press.

Gershuny, J. and I. D. Miles. (1983). *The New Service Economy*. London: F. Pinter.

Giddons, Anthony. (1981). *A Contemporary Critique of Historical Materialism*. Berkeley: University of California Press.

Gramsci, Antonio. (1971). *Selections from the Prison Notebooks of Antonio Gransci*. Ed. and trans. Quentin Hoare and Geoffrey Novell-Smith. London: Lawrence and Wishave.

Gross, David S. (1986). "Infinite Indignation: Teaching, Dialectical Vision, and Blake's *Marriage of Heaven and Hell*," *College English*, 48 (2): 175-186.

Habermas, Jürgen. (1968). *Knowlege and Human Interests*. Trans. Jeremy J. Shapiro. Boston: Beacon Press.

————. (1975). *Legitimation Crisis*. Trans. Thomas A. McCarthy. Boston: Beacon Press.

————. (1979). *Communication and the Evolution of Society*. Trans. Thomas A. McCarthy. Boston: Beacon Press. Note "What is Universal Pragmatics."

————. (1983). "Modernity—An Incomplete Project," trans. Selya Benhabib. *The Anti-Aesthetic: Essays on Postmodern Culture*. Ed. Hal Foster. Port Townsend, WA: Bay Press. 3-15.

————. (1984). *The Theory of Communicative Action*, 2 vols. Trans. Thomas A. McCarthy. London: Heinemann. Also Boston: Beacon Press.

————. (1987). *The Philosophical Discourses of Modernity: Twelve Lectures*. Trans. Frederick G. Lawrence. Cambridge, MA: MIT Press.

————. (1988). *On the Logic of the Social Sciences*. Trans. Shierry Weber Nicholsen and Jerry A. Stark. Cambridge, MA: MIT Press.

Hartz, Louis. (1955). *The Liberal Tradition in America*. New York: Harcourt, Brace.

Hassan, Ihab. (1971). *The Dismemberment of Orpheus: Toward a Postmodern Literature*. Madison: University of Wisconsin Press.

————. (1975). *Paracriticism*. Urbana: The University of Illinois Press.

————. (1985). "The Culture of Postmodernism," *Theory, Culture & Society*, 2 (3): 119-132.

Heidegger, Martin. (1962). *Being and Time*. Trans. John Macquarrie and Edward Robinson. London: SCM Press. Also New York: Harper and Row.

Hindness, Paul and Paul Q. Hirst. (1975). *Pre-Capitalist Modes of Production*. London: Routledge & Kegan Paul.

Hirsch, E. D. (1976). *The Aims of Interpretation*. Chicago: University of Chicago Press.

Horkheimer, Max and Theodor Adorno. (1972). *The Dialectic of Enlightenment*. Trans. John Cumming. New York: Herder and Herder.

Hutcheon, Linda. (1986-87). "The Politics of Postmodernism," *Cultural Critique*, 5: 174-207.

Huyssen, Andreas. (1984). "Mapping the Postmodern," *New German Critique*, 33: 5-52.

————. (1986). *After the Great Divide*. Bloomington: Indiana University Press.

Iffland, James. (1984). "The Political Unconscious of Jameson's *Political Unconscious*," *New Orleans Review*, 11 (1): 36-45.

Jacoby, Russell. (1987). *The Last Intellectuals: American Culture in the Age of Academe*. New York: Basic Books.

Jay, Martin. (1984). *Marxism and Totality: the Adventures of a Concept from Lukács to Habermas*. Berkeley: University of California Press.

Jay, Gregory S. (1987-88). "Values and Deconstruction," *Cultural Critique*, 6 (Winter): 153-196.

Jencks, Charles. (1972). *The Language of Post-Modern Architecture*. New York: Pantheon. Rpt. New York: Rizzoli, 1977.

Johnson, Richard. (1976). "Barrington More, Perry Anderson, and English Social Development," *Working Papers in Cultural Studies*, 9: 7-28.

————. (1981). "Histories of Culture / Theories of Ideology: Notes on an Impasse," *Ideology and Cultural Production*. Eds. M. Barrett et al. London: Croom Helm.

Karankas, Alexander. (1966). *Tillers of a Myth*. Chicago: University of Chicago Press.

Kavanagh, James H. (1984). "The Jameson Effect," *New Orleans Review*, 11 (1): 20-28.

Kellner, Douglas. (1984). *Herbert Marcuse and the Crisis of Marxism*. London: Macmillan. Also Berkeley: University of California Press.

————. (1988). *Camera Politica: The Politics and Ideology of Contemporary Hollywood Film*. Bloomington: Indiana University Press.

————. (1988). "Postmodernism as Social Theory: Some Challenges and Problems," *Theory, Culture & Society*, 5: 239-264.

————. (1989). *Critical Theory, Marxism, and Modernity: Development and Contemporary Relevance of the Frankfurt School*. Cambridge: Polity Press.

_____. (1989). *From Marxism to Postmodernism and Beyond: Critical Studies of Jean Baudrillard*. Cambridge: Polity Press.

Kroker, Arthur. (1985). "Baudrillard's Marx," *Theory, Culture & Society*, 2 (3): 69-84.

Kroker, Arthur and David Cook. (1986). *The Postmodern Scene: Excremental Culture and Hyper-Aesthetics*. New York: St. Martin's Press. Also Montréal: New World Perspectives.

LaCapra, Dominick. (1982). "Review of *The Political Unconscious*," *History and Theory*, 21: 83-106.

Laclau, Ernesto and Chantel Mouffe. (1985). *Hegemony and Socialist Strategy: Towards a Radical Democratic Politics*. Trans. Winston Moore and Paul Cammack. London: Verso.

Lash, Scott. (1988). "Discourse or Figure? Postmodernism as a Regime of Signification," *Theory, Culture & Society*, 5 (2-3): 311-336.

Lash, Scott and John. Urry. (1987). *The End of Organized Capitalism*. Cambridge: Polity Press.

Leal, O. F. and R. G. Oliven. (1988). "Class Interpretations of a Soap Opera Narrative," *Theory, Culture & Society*, 5(1): 81-99.

Lefebvre, Henri. (1976). *The Survival of Capitalism: Reproduction of the Relations of Production*. Trans. Frank Bryant. London: Allison and Bushby.

_____. (1986). *Dialectical Materialism*. Trans. John Sturrock. London: Jonathan Cape.

_____. (1970). *Le manifeste différentialiste*. Paris: Gallimard.

_____. (1971). *Everyday Life in the Modern World*. Trans. Sacha Rabinovitch. New York: Harper and Row.

Leiss, William. (1983). "The Icons of the Marketplace," *Theory, Culture & Society*, 1 (3): 10-21.

Lentricchia, Frank. (1980). *After New Criticism*. Chicago: University of Chicago Press.

_____. (1988). *Ariel and the Police: Michel Foucault, William James, Wallace Stevens*. Madison, WI: University of Wisconsin Press.

Lukács, Georg. (1964). *Realism in Our Time: Literature and Class Struggle*. Trans. John and Necke Mander. New York: Harper and Row. Originally published *Wider den missverstandenen Realismus*. Hamburg: Claassen Verlag, 1958.

_____. (1971). *The Theory of the Novel*. Trans. Anna Bostock. Cambridge, MA: MIT Press.

_____. (1971). *History and Class Consciousness: Studies in Marxist Dialectic*. Trans. Rodney Livingstone. Cambridge, MA: MIT Press.

_____. (1983). *The Historical Novel: A Historico-Philosophical Essay on the Forms of Great Epic Literature*. Trans. Hannah and Stanley Mitchell. Lincoln: University of Nebraska Press. Rpt. from London: Merlin Press, 1962.

Lyotard, Jean-François. (1971). *Discours, Figure*. Paris: Klincksieck.
_____. (1974). "Le désir nommé Marx," *Économie Libidinale*. Paris: Les Editions de Minuit. 117-188.
_____. (1983). *Le différend*. Paris: Les Editions de Minuit. English edition, *The Differend: Phrases in Dispute*. Trans. George Van Den Abbeele. Minneapolis: University of Minnesota Press.
_____. (1984). *The Postmodern Condition: A Report on Knowledge*. Trans. Geoff Bennington and Brian Massumi. Minneapolis: University of Minnesota Press.
_____. (1988). "Interview," *Theory, Culture & Society*, 5 (2-3): 277-309.
Lyotard, Jean-François and Jean-Loup Thebaud. (1985). *Just Gaming*. Trans. Brian Massumi. Minneapolis: University of Minnesota Press.
Mandel, Ernest. (1975). *Late Capitalism*. Trans. Joris De Bres. London: New Left Books. Revised edition, 1978.
Marcuse, Herbert. (1962). *Eros and Civilization: A Philosophical Inquiry into Freud*. New-York: Vintage Books.
_____. (1968). "The Affirmative Character of Culture," *Negations: Essays in Critical Theory*. Trans. Jeremy Shapiro. Boston: Beacon Press. 88-133. German original published in 1933.
Marx, Karl. (1971). "Economic and Philosophical Manuscripts," *Karl Marx: Early Texts*. Trans. and ed. David McLellan. Oxford: Basil Blackwell.
Marx, Karl and Fredrick Engles. (1848). *The Communist Manifesto*. New York: International.
_____. (1978). *The Marx-Engels Reader*. Ed. Robert Tucker. New York: Norton.
Mayer, Arno J. (1988). *Why the Heavens did not Darken: The "Final Solution" in History*. New York: Pantheon.
McCaffery, Larry. (1986). *Postmodern Fiction: A Bio-Bibliographical Guide*. New York: Greenwood Press.
McHale, Brian. (1987). *Postmodernist Fiction*. New York and London: Metheun.
Meek, Ronald L. (1976). *Social Science and the Ignoble Savage*. Cambridge: Cambridge University Press.
Merrill, Robert, ed. (1988). *Ethics/Aesthetics: Post-Modern Positions*. Washington, DC: Maisonneuve Press.
Meyrowitz, Joshua. (1985). *No Sense of Place: The Impact of Electronic Media on Social Behavior*. New York: Oxford University Press.
Mitchell, W. J. T. (1980). *On Narrative*. Chicago: University of Chicago Press.
_____. (1982). *The Politics of Interpretation*. Chicago: University of Chicago Press.
Mohanty, S. P. (1982). "History at the Edge of Discourse," *Diacritics*, 12 (3).
Nelson, Cary. (1986). *Theory in the Classroom*. Urbana: University of Illinois Press.

Nelson, Cary and Lawrence Grossberg. (1988). *Marxism and the Interpretation of Culture*. Urbana: University of Illinois Press.

Norris, Christopher. (1982) *Deconstruction: Theory and Practice*. New York: Metheun.

O'Neill, John. (1972). "Public and Private Space," *Sociology as a Skin Trade: Essays Towards a Reflexive Sociology*. New York: Harper and Row. 20-37.

_____. (1977). "Language and the Legitimation Problem," *Sociology*, 11 (2): 351-358.

_____. (1982). *For Marx Against Althusser, and Other Essays*. Washington, DC: University Press of America. Note "Marxism and Mythology" and "Naturalism in Vico and Marx: A Discourse Theory of the Body Politic."

_____. (1983). "Televideo Ergo Sum: Some Hypotheses on the Specular Functions of the Media," *Communication*, 7 (1): 221-240.

_____. (1985). *Five Bodies: The Human Shape of Modern Society*. Ithaca: Cornell University Press.

_____. (1986). "The Disciplinary Society: From Weber to Foucault," *British Journal of Sociology*, 37 (1): 42-60.

_____. (1987). "Marx's Humanist Theory of Alienation," *Georg Lukács and His World: A Reassessment*. Ed. Ernest Joós. New York: Peter Lang Publishing. 59-76.

_____. (1988). "Religion and Postmodernism: The Durkheimian Bond in Bell and Jameson," *Theory, Culture & Society*, 5 (2-3): 493-508.

Palmer, Richard. (1984). "On the Transcendability of Hermeneutics," *Hermeneutics: Questions and Prospects*. Eds. Gary Shapiro and Alan Sica. Amherst: University of Massachusettes Press. 84-95.

Parker, Andrew. (1985). "Futures for Marxism: An Appreciation of Althusser," *Diacritics*, 15 (Winter): 57-72.

Peckham, Morse. (1979). *Explanation and Power: The Control of Human Behavior*. New York: Seabury Press. Rpt. Minneapolis: University of Minnesota Press, 1988.

Pheby, Keith C. (1988). *Interventions: Displacing the Metaphysical Subject*. Washington, DC: Maisonneuve Press.

Poster, Mark. (1985). *Foucault, Marxism, and History: Mode of Production versus Mode of Information*. Cambridge: Polity Press.

Radhakrishnan, R. (1987). "Ethnic Identity and Post-Structuralist Différance," *Cultural Critique*, 6 (Spring): 199-220.

_____. (1989). "Towards an Effective Intellectual: Foucault or Gramsci?" *Intellectuals and Social Change*. Ed. Bruce Robbins. Minneapolis: University of Minnesota Press.

Reddy, William. M. (1984). *The Rise of Market Culture: The Textile Trade and French Society, 1750-1900*. Cambridge: Cambridge University Press.

Ricoeur, Paul. (1970). *Freud and Philosophy: An Essay on Interpretation*. Trans. Denis Savage. New Haven: Yale University Press.

_____. (1974). *Conflict of Interpretations: Essays in Hermeneutics*. Ed. Don Ihde. Evanston: Northwestern University Press.

_____. (1976). *Interpretation Theory: Discourse and the Surplus of Meaning*. Fort Worth: Texas Christian University Press.

_____. (1984). *Time and Narrative*. 3 vols. Trans. Kathleen McLaughlin and David Pelleur. Chicago: University of Chicago Press.

_____. (1984). *The Reality of the Historical Past*. Milwaukee: Marquette University Press.

Ross, Andrew. (1988). *Universal Abandon: The Politics of Postmodernism*. Minneapolis: University of Minnesota Press.

Rorty, Richard. (1979). *Philosophy and the Mirror of Nature*. Princeton: Princeton University Press.

_____. (1982). *Consequences of Pragmatism: Essays 1972-1980*. Minneapolis: University of Minnesota Press.

_____. (1984). *Philosophy in History: Essays on the Historiography of Philosophy*. Cambridge and New York: Cambridge University Press.

Ryan, Michael. (1982). *Marxism and Deconstruction: A Critical Articulation*. Baltimore: Johns Hopkins University Press.

_____. (1984). "Marxism-Deconstruction Debate in Literary Theory," *New Orleans Review*, 11 (1): 29-35.

Rybczynski, Witold. (1986). *Home: A Short History of an Idea*. New York: Viking.

Sahlins, Marshall. (1974). *Stone Age Economics*. London: Tavistock. Also Chicago: University of Chicago Press, 1972.

_____. (1976). *Culture and Practical Reason*. London: Tavistock. Also Chicago: University of Chicago Press.

Said, Edward. (1983). *The World, the Text, and the Critic*. Cambridge, MA: Harvard University Press.

Sartre, Jean-Paul. (1968). *Search for a Method*. Trans. Hazel E. Barnes. New York: Vintage.

Sayres, Sohnya et al. (1984). *The 60s Without Apologies*. Minneapolis: University of Minnesota Press.

Schlaffer, Heinz. (1981). *Faust Zwiter Teil: die Allegorie des 19. Jahrhunderts*. Stuttgart: J. B. Metzler Verlag.

Scholes, Robert. (1985). *Textual Power: Literary Theory and the Teaching of English*. New Haven: Yale University Press.

Sederberg, Peter. (1984). *The Politics of Meaning: Power and Explanation in the Construction of Social Reality*. Tucson: University of Arizona Press.

Smith, Dennis. (1988). "History, Geography and Sociology: Lessons from the Annales School," *Theory, Culture & Society*, 5 (1): 137-148.

Soja, Edward. (1989). *Postmodern Geographies: The Reassertion of Space in Critical Social Theory*. London: Verso.

Soltan, Margaret. (1988). "Architectural Follies," *Raritan*, 7 (3): 54-78.

Sontag, Susan. (1966). *Against Interpretation*. New York: Dell.

Spivak, Gayatri Chakravorty. (1976). "Translator's Preface," *Of Grammatology*. Baltimore: Johns Hopkins University Press. ix-lxxxvii.

————. (1987). *In Other Worlds: Essays in Cultural Politics*. London: Metheun.

Spivak, Gayatri and Ranagit Guha, eds. (1988). *Selected Subaltern Studies*. New York: Oxford University Press.

Sprinker, Michael. (1982). "The Part and the Whole," *Diacritics*, 12 (3): 14-22.

————. (1984). "Reinventing Historicism: An Introduction to the Work of Fredric Jameson," *American Critics at Work: Examinations of Contemporary Literary Theories*. Ed. Victor A. Kramer. Troy, NY: The Whitson Publishing Co.

————. (1987). *Imaginary Relations*. London: Verso. Also New York: Metheun.

Stallybrass, P. and A. White. (1987). *The Politics of Transgression*. London: Metheun.

Stauth, G. and B. S. Turner. (1988). "Nostalgia, Postmodernism and the Critique of Mass Culture," *Theory, Culture & Society*, 5 (2-3): 508-526.

Tafuri, Manfredo. (1980). *Theories and History of Architecture*. Trans. Giorgio Verrecchia. New York: Harper and Row. Note "Modern Architecture and the Eclipse of History."

Taylor, Laurie and Bob Mullan. (1986). *Uninvited Guests: The Intimate Secrets of Television and Radio*. London: Chatto and Windus.

Turner, B. S. (1987). "A Note on Nostalgia," *Theory, Culture & Society*, 4 (1): 147-156.

Urry, J. (1988). "Cultural Change and Contemporary Holiday-Making," *Theory, Culture & Society*, 5 (1): 35-55.

Venturi, Robert et al. (1972). *Learning From Las Vegas: The Forgotten Symbolism of Architectural Form*. Cambridge, MA: MIT Press. Rpt. 1977.

Vico, Giambatttista. (1968). *The New Science of Giambattista Vico*. Trans. Thomas G. Bergin and Max H. Fisch. Ithaca: Cornell University Press.

Wall, D. (1987). "Oppenheim Under the Sign of the Mirror," Paper presented at the International Association for Philosophy and Literature Conference, Lawrence, Kansas .

Wallis, Brian. (1984). *Art After Modernism: Rethinking Representation*. New York: The Museum of Contemporary Art.

Weber, Max. (1968). *Economy and Society: An Outline of Interpretative Sociology*. Trans. Ephraim Fischoff et al. New York: Bedminister.

Weber, Samuel. (1983). "Capitalizing History: Notes on *The Political Unconscious*," *Diacritics*, 13 (Summer): 14-28. Rpt. in *Institution and Interpretation*. University of Minnesota Press, 1987. 40-58.

Weinsheimer, Joel. (1985). *Gadamer's Hermeneutics: A Reading of Truth and Method*. New Haven: Yale University Press.

Wellmer, Albrecht. (1984). "Truth, Semblance, Reconciliation: Adorno's Aesthetic Redemption of Modernity," trans. Maeve Looke. *Telos*, 62 (Winter): 89-115.

_____. (1985). "On the Dialectic of Modernism and Postmodernism," *Praxis International*, 4 (4).

West, Cornel. (1986). "Ethics and Action in Fredric Jameson's Marxist Hermeneutics," *Postmodernism and Politics*. Ed. Jonathan Arac. Minneapolis: University of Minnesota Press.

White, Hayden. (1987). "Getting Out of History: Jameson's Redemption of Narrative," *The Content of Form: Narrative Discourse and Historical Representation*. Baltimore: Johns Hopkins University Press. 142-168.

Wiener, Martin J. (1981). *English Culture and the Decline of the Industrial Spirit, 1850-1900*. Cambridge and New York: Cambridge University Press.

Williams, Raymond. (1977). *Marxism and Literature*. Oxford: Oxford University Press.

Wolff, Janet. (1985). "The Invisible Flâneuse: Women and the Literature of Modernity," *Theory, Culture & Society*, 2 (3): 37-46.

Wolin, Richard. (1984). "Modernism vs. Postmodernism," *Telos*, 62: 117-130.

Wouters, C. (1986). "Formalization and Informalization: Changing Tension Balances in Civilizing Processes," *Theory, Culture & Society*, 5 (2-3): 1-18.

Zuidervaart, L. (1987). "Reconciliation Under Duress? *Realism in Our Time* Revisited," *Georg Lukács and His World: A Reassessment*. Ed. Ernest Joós. New York: Peter Lang Publishing. 117-148.

Zukin, Sharon. (1988). "The Postmodern Debate Over Urban Form," *Theory, Culture & Society*, 5 (2-3): 431-446.

_____. (1988). *Loft Living*. 2nd edition. London: Radius/Hutchinson.

Index

Thanks to Dennis Crow, Maria Hall, and Robert Merrill for preparing this index.

Notes on Contributors

Steven Best is a graduate student in Philosophy at the University of Chicago. He has published numerous articles on postmodernism and related topics in journals such as *Diacritics, Social Text,* and the *Canadian Journal of Social and Political Theory.* With Douglas Kellner, he is currently working on a book on postmodernism to be published by Macmillan.

Martin Donougho has published extensively on Hegel, Adorno, and on aesthetics (music, architecture, literature, and film). He holds degrees from the University of Sussex and the University of Toronto. He has taught at Northwestern and is currently Associate Professor of Philosophy at the University of South Carolina. During 1990-1991, he will undertake a year's study of Adorno's *Aesthetics* on an NEH Fellowship.

Mike Featherstone is a reader in Social Studies at Teesside Polytechnic, England. He is founding editor of *Theory, Culture and Society* and chairperson of the Centre for the Study of Adult Life. He is presently finishing a book on postmodernism for Sage Publications.

Philip Goldstein is Assistant Professor of English and Philosophy at the University of Delaware. He has published on Shakespeare and literary theory and is currently completing a book titled *The Politics of Literary Theory: An Introduction to Marxist Criticism* to be published by University of Florida Press.

David Gross is Associate Professor of English at the University of Oklahoma. He is the author of numerous articles in the areas of American, French, and British literature and critical theory. He is at work on two books, one on Flaubert and 1848 and a second one on Gramsci/hegemony in literature and modern theory.

Haynes Horne has studied Marx and Freud in both Vienna and Berlin. Currently, he is writing a dissertation at the University of Minnesota concerning a dialectic between the texts of enlightenment-modernist aestheticisms and the texts of de-ontologizing critiques of totality.

Thomas Huhn received his Ph.D. in Philosophy from Boston University in 1988. He is currently a postdoctoral Fellow at the Getty Center for the History of Art and the Humanities, where he is working on Theodor Adorno's aesthetic theory, ugliness, and the sublime. His publications include articles in *Telos, The Journal of Aesthetics and Art Criticism, CJPST,* and *Art & Text.*

Fredric Jameson is William A. Lane, Jr. Professor of Comparative Literature at Duke University and Director of the Graduate Program in Literature and the Duke Center for Critical Theory. He has taught at Harvard, Yale, and the University of California, San Diego and Santa Cruz campuses, as well as Peking University in the People's Republic of China. His publications are listed on pp. 389-395 above.

Douglas Kellner is Professor of Philosophy at the University of Texas at Austin and is author of books on Karl Korsch, Herbert Marcuse, and (with Michael Ryan), *Camera Politica: The Politics and Ideology of Contemporary Hollywood Film.* He has just completed *Critical Theory, Marxism, and Modernity,* and *Jean Baudrillard: From Marxism to Postmodernism and Beyond.*

John O'Neill is Distinguished Research Professor of Sociology at York University, Toronto, and an Affiliate of the Centre for Comparative Literature at the University of Toronto. He is the author of *Sociology as a Skin Trade* (1972), *Making Sense Together* (1974), *For Marx Against Althusser* (1982), *Essaying Montaigne* (1982), and *Five Bodies* (1985). He is Co-Editor of the international quarterly, *Philosophy of the Social Sciences.*

R. Radhakrishnan teaches cultural criticism and critical theory at the University of Massachusetts, Amherst. His book, *Theory in an Uneven World* is forthcoming from Basil Blackwell. He has published widely on poststructuralism, feminist theory, Marxism, and postcoloniality. Currently he is visiting Fellow at the Center for the Critical Analysis of Contemporary Culture at Rutgers University.

Christopher Sharrett is Associate Professor of Communications at Seton Hall University. He has published in the *Canadian Journal of Political and Social Theory, CineAction, Cineaste, Journal of Popular Film and TV, Film Quarterly, Persistence of Vision* and elsewhere. He is completing a book (with Arthur Kroker) on sacrifice and scapegoating in postmodernism culture.

Anders Stephanson is Co-Editor of *Social Text* and the anthology *The 60s Without Apology.* His research interests include aesthetics and foreign policy.

Lambert Zuidervaart is Professor of Philosophy at Calvin College in Grand Rapids, Michigan. He holds degrees from the Institute for Christian Studies in Toronto and the Free University in Amsterdam. Presently, he is completing a book on Adorno's aesthetic theory.